THE

ELEMENTS

OF

INTELLECTUAL PHILOSOPHY.

BY

FRANCIS WAYLAND,

LATE PRESIDENT OF BROWN UNIVERSITY, AUTHOR OF ELEMENTS
OF MORAL SCIENCE, ETC. ETC.

TWELFTH THOUSAND.

NEW YORK:
SHELDON & COMPANY, PUBLISHERS,
498 & 500 BROADWAY.

1868.

PREFACE TO THE PRESENT EDITION.

It was my design, soon after this volume was published, to subject it to a thorough revision, and make such corrections in the text as were evidently needed. I found myself, however, unable at the time to accomplish my intention, in consequence of several other unexpected and imperative obligations; and, subsequently, by reason of a long period of imperfect health. I have devoted to this work the first leisure that I have been able to command; and have corrected the text with all the attention in my power. I hope that I have improved it.

In this labor I have been greatly assisted by the aid of another. Some time since, I received from an anonymous friend a copious list of valuable corrections, of which I have freely availed myself. I take this method of expressing my sincere gratitude to my unknown benefactor; and I beg him to receive my thanks for his careful reading of the text, and for his many valuable suggestions. Most of these I have thankfully adopted.

F. WAYLAND.

Providence, R. I., *May*, 1865.

PREFACE.

The following pages contain the substance of the Lectures which, for several years, have been delivered to the classes in Intellectual Philosophy, in Brown University.

Having been intended for oral delivery, they were, in many respects, modified by the circumstances of their origin. Hence, illustrations have been introduced more freely than would otherwise have seemed necessary. In preparing them for the press, however, I was led to consider the class of persons for whose use they were principally designed. I remembered the difficulty of fixing definitely in the mind of the pupil the nature and limits of subjective truth; and therefore allowed my instructions to retain in general the form which they had previously assumed. Whether I have in this respect judged wisely, it is not for me to determine.

I have not entered upon the discussion of many of the topics which have called into exercise the acumen of the ablest metaphysicians. Intended to serve the purposes of a text-book, it was necessary that the volume should be compressed within a compass adapted to the time usually allotted to the study of this science in the colleges of our country. I have, therefore, attempted to present and illustrate the important truths in intellectual philosophy, rather than the inferences which may be drawn from them, or the doctrines which they may presuppose. These may be pursued to any length, at the option of the teacher. If I have not entered upon these discussions, I hope that I have prepared the way for their more ample and truthful development.

It has been my desire to render this work an aid to mental improvement. For this purpose, I have added practical suggestions on the cultivation of the several faculties. Earnest-minded young men frequently err in their attempts at self-improvement. It has seemed to me, therefore, that a work of this kind would be manifestly imperfect, did it not, directly as well as indirectly, aid the student in his efforts to discipline and strengthen his intellectual energies.

In order to encourage more extensive reading upon the subject than can be furnished in a text-book, I have added references to a number of works of easy access, specifying the places in which the topics treated of were discussed. In this labor, I have availed myself of the assistance of my former pupils, Mr. Samuel Brooks, now instructor in Greek, in this University, and Mr. Lucius W. Bancroft, of Worcester, Mass. To these gentlemen the student is indebted for whatever benefit he may derive from this feature of the work.

For the many imperfections of this volume, the author consoles himself with the reflection, that it has been written and prepared for the press under the pressure of other important and frequently distracting avocations. In the humble hope that it may, nevertheless, facilitate the study of this interesting department of human knowledge, it is, with diffidence, submitted to the judgment of the public.

Brown University, Sept 14, 1854.

CONTENTS.

CHAPTER IV.

CHAPTER V.

MEMORY.

CHAPTER VI.

REASONING.

CHAPTER VII.

IMAGINATION.

CHAPTER VIII.

TASTE.

APPENDIX.

INTRODUCTION.

DEFINITION OF THE INTELLECTUAL POWERS

INTELLECTUAL PHILOSOPHY treats of the faculties of the human mind, and of the laws by which they are governed.

The only forms of existence which, in our present state we are capable of knowing, are matter and mind. It is the mind alone that knows. When, therefore, we cognize matter, the object known, and the subject which knows, are numerically distinct. When, on the other hand, we cognize mind, the mind which knows and the mind which is known are numerically the same. The mind knows, and the mind is the object of knowledge.

1. The mind becomes cognizant of the existence and qualities of matter, that is, of the world external to itself, by means of the *Perceptive faculties*. It knows not what matter is, or what is the essence of matter, but only its qualities; that is, its power of affecting us in this or that manner. When we say, "This is gold," we do not pretend to know what the essence of gold is, but merely that there is something possessed of certain qualities, or powers of creating in us certain affections.

2. In a similar manner we become acquainted with the energies of our own mind. We are not cognizant of the mind itself, but only of the action of its faculties or sensibilities. When we think, remember, or reason; when we

are joyful or sad, when we deliberate or resolve, we know that these several states of the mind exist, and that they are predicated of the being whom I denominate I, or myself. The power by which we become cognizant to ourselves of these mental states is called *Consciousness*. When, by an act of volition, a particular mental state is made the object of distinct and continuous thought, the act is denominated ***Reflection***.

3. An idea of perception or of consciousness terminates as soon as another idea succeeds it. It is perfect and complete within itself, and is not necessarily connected with anything else. I see a ball either at rest or in motion; I turn my eyes in another direction and perceive a tree or a house; in a moment afterwards they are both violently thrown down. I am conscious of several separate perceptions, which follow each other in succession. Each one of these mental acts is complete within itself, and might have been connected with no other. We find, however, that these ideas of perception are not thus disconnected. They do not terminate in themselves, but give occasion to other ideas of great importance; ideas which, but for the acts of perception, could never have existed. Thus, we saw a house standing, we now see it fallen; there at once arises in the mind the idea of a cause, or of something which has occasioned this change. Several ideas following in succession, occasion the idea of duration. The existence of these secondary ideas under these circumstances is owing to the constitution of the human mind itself. It suggests to us these ideas, which, when once conceived, are original and independent. This power of the mind is termed *Original Suggestion.*

4. The knowledge acquired both by our perceptive faculties and by consciousness, as well as much that is given us by original suggestion, is the knowledge of things or acts as individuals. We perceive single objects; we are con

scious of single mental states. These pass away and become recollections. The recollections are like their originals, merely recollections of individuals. Had we no other power, our knowledge would consist of separate isolated ideas, without either cohesion or classification. Our knowledge would be all either of single individuals, or of single acts performed by particular agents. When, however, we reflect upon our knowledge, we find it to be of a totally different character. It is almost all of classes. With the exception of proper names, all the nouns of a language designate classes; that is, ideas of genera and species, and not ideas of individuals. There must, therefore, exist a power of the mind by which we transform these ideas of individuals into ideas of generals. We give to this complex power the name of *Abstraction*.

5. We have thus far considered the intellectual faculties without reference to the element of time. We, however, all know that the ideas obtained in the past remain with us at this present. The history of our lives from infancy is continually before us, or, at the command of the will, it may be spread out before our consciousness. We know that the ideas which we now acquire may be retained forever. Nay, more, we are conscious of a power of recalling at will the knowledge which we have once made our own. The faculty by which we do this is called *Memory*.

6. Possessed of these powers, we might obtain all the ideas arising from perception, consciousness and original suggestion; we might modify them into genera and species, we might treasure them up in our memory and recall them at will. But we could proceed no further. Our knowledge would consist wholly of facts, or the information which we have derived either from our own observation or the observation of others. But this manifestly is not our condition. We are able to make use of the knowl-

edge acquired by the powers of which I have spoken, in such a manner as to arrive at truth before unknown, truth which these powers could never have revealed to us. In this manner we make use of the facts in geology in order to determine the changes which have taken place in the history of our globe. Thus, from the axioms and definitions of geometry, we proceed to demonstrate the profoundest truths of that science. The faculty by which we thus proceed in the investigation of truth is termed *Reason.*

7. Thus far we have treated of those powers which give us knowledge of things and relations actually existing, or which modify and use this knowledge. Were we limited to these, we could consider no conception but as actually true. We could conceive of nothing except that which we had perceived, or which some one had perceived for us. But we find ourselves endowed with a power of taking the elements of our knowledge and combining them together at will. We thus form to ourselves pictures of things that never existed, and we give to them form and substance by the various processes of the fine arts. It was this power which conceived the group of Laocoon, or Milton's Garden of Eden. We give to this power the name of *Imagination.*

8. The exercise of all our faculties is generally agreeable, and sometimes is productive of exquisite pleasure. I look at a rainbow, I pursue a demonstration, I behold a successful effort in the fine arts, and in all these cases I am conscious of a peculiar emotion. The causes producing this emotion are unlike, but the mental feeling produced is essentially the same. Every one recognizes it under the name of the beautiful; and the sensibility by which we become capable of this emotion is called *Taste.*

The faculties which will be treated of in the present work may, then, be briefly defined as follows:

1. The *Perceptive* faculties are those by which we become

acquainted with the existence and qualities of the external world.

2. *Consciousness* is the faculty by which we become cognizant of the operations of our own minds.

3. *Original Suggestion* is the faculty which gives rise to original ideas, occasioned by the perceptive faculties or consciousness.

4. *Abstraction* is the faculty by which, from conceptions of individuals, we form conceptions of genera and species, or, in general, of classes.

5. *Memory* is the faculty by which we retain and recall our knowledge of the past.

6. *Reason* is that faculty by which, from the use of the knowledge obtained by the other faculties, we are enabled to proceed to other and original knowledge.

7. *Imagination* is that faculty by which, from materials already existing in the mind, we form complicated conceptions or mental images, according to our own will.

8. *Taste* is that sensibility by which we recognize the beauties and deformities of nature or art, deriving pleasure from the one, and suffering pain from the other.

It is by no means intended to assert that these are all the powers of a human soul. Besides these, it is endowed with conscience, or that faculty by which we are capable of moral obligation; with will, or that motive force by which we are impelled to action; with the various emotions, instincts and biases, which, as observation teaches us, are parts of a human soul. These are, however, the most important of those that are purely intellectual. In the following pages we shall consider them in the order in which they have been named.

REFERENCES

TO PASSAGES IN WHICH ANALOGOUS SUBJECTS ARE TREATED.

Importance of Intellectual Philosophy — Reid's Inquiry, chap. 1, sec. 1

Difficulty of the study — Reid's Inquiry, chap. 1, sec. 2.

Cultivation of mind distinguishes us from brutes — Inquiry, chap. 1, sec. 2.

What are matter and mind — Reid's Introduction to Essays on the Intellectual Powers.

Matter and mind relative — Stewart's Introduction to vol. I.; Reid's Essays on certain powers, Essay 1, chap. 1.

Origin of our knowledge — Locke, Book 2d, chap. 1, sec. 2—5 and 24.

CHAPTER I.

THE PERCEPTIVE FACULTIES

SECTION I. — OF OUR KNOWLEDGE OF MATTER AND MIND. THERE IS NO REASON FOR SUPPOSING THE ESSENCE OF MATTER AND MIND THE SAME. THE RELATION OF MIND TO MATTER IN OUR PRESENT STATE.

OF the essence of mind, as I have remarked, we know nothing. All that we are able to affirm of it is, that it is *something* which perceives, reflects, remembers, believes, imagines, and wills; but what that something *is*, which exerts these energies, we know not. It is only as we are conscious of the action of these energies that we are conscious of the existence of mind. It is only by the exertion of its own powers that the mind becomes cognizant of their existence. The cognizance of its powers, however, gives us no knowledge of that essence of which they are predicated.

In these respects, our knowledge of mind is precisely analogous to our knowledge of matter. When we attempt to define matter, we affirm that it is something extended, divisible, solid, colored, etc.; that is, we mention those of its qualities which are cognizable by our senses. In other words, we affirm that it is something which has the power of affecting us in this or that manner. When, however, the question is asked, what is this something of which these qualities are predicated, we are silent. The knowledge of the qualities gives no knowledge of the essence to which they belong. We cognize the qualities by means of our perceptive powers; but we have no power by which we are able to cognize essence, or absolute substance.

This does not seem to be the fact by accident, but from necessity. If we reflect upon the nature of our faculties, we shall readily be convinced that, by our perceptive powers, we learn that a particular object affects us in a particular manner, creates in us a certain state of mind, or, in other words, gives us a certain form of knowledge. I look upon snow, and there is created in my mind the idea of white. I look upon gold, I have at once the idea of yellow. Besides this, there is another idea created, which is, that this quality, or power of creating in me this notion, belongs to the object which I contemplate. I thus not only gain the idea of white or yellow, but the additional conviction that snow is white and gold is yellow.

The same remarks apply to our knowledge of mind. I am conscious of perception, of recollection, of pleasure, or pain. I thus acquire a notion of these several mental acts, and thus a certain form of knowledge is given to me. Besides this, I have an instinctive belief that the mental energy which gives rise to this particular form of knowledge is predicated of the thinking being whom I call I, or myself. If the knowledge which we derive from perception and consciousness be analyzed, I think it will be found to go thus far, but that, from the constitution of our nature, it can go no farther.

But, while our knowledge of mind and our knowledge of matter agree in this respect, that neither of them gives us any information concerning essences, these two forms of knowledge are in other respects quite dissimilar.

1. In the first place, it is obvious that the energies of the one and the qualities of the other are made known to us by different powers of the mind. The qualities of matter are

revealed to us by our perceptive faculties, in which our spiritual and material natures are intimately united. The energies of mind are revealed to us by consciousness, one of the elements exclusively of our spiritual nature. It is almost needless to remark, here, that this difference in the mode in which these forms of knowledge are revealed to us does not affect the evidence of the truth of either. Perception and consciousness are both original and legitimate sources of belief. We cannot philosophically deny the existence of either. The world without us and the world within us, the *me* and the *not me*, are both given to us by the principles of our constitution as ultimate facts, which, whatever may be his theory, every man, from the necessity of his constitution, practically admits.

2. We always express the attributes of matter and the energies of mind by terms generically dissimilar. The qualities of matter we designate by adjectives, or terms meaning something added to a substance, and wholly incapable of an active signification. Thus, we say of a material object, it is hard, soft, white, black, warm or cold. On the other hand, we designate the energies of mind by active verbs or participles, terms which indicate a power residing in the substance itself. We say of mind, it thinks remembers, wills, imagines; or, that it is a thinking, willing, remembering, imagining substance. This difference in our mode of speech is not accidental, but of necessity. If any one will make the experiment, he will find it impossible to express his conceptions on these subjects in any other manner. We are unable to conceive of thinking, reasoning, remembering, as qualities, or of white, black, or color, as energies. We are so made that we are obliged to think of these different attributes as at the farthest remove from each other.

From these remarks we discover the limit which has been

fixed by our Creator to our investigations on these subjects. We perceive in the objects around us various qualities, and we know that these qualities must be predicated of something, — for nothing, or that which does not exist, can have no qualities, — but what that something is we know not. So again, we are conscious of the energies of mind, and we know that these energies must be energies of something, while of the essence of that something we are equally ignorant. Hence, in all our investigations respecting either matter or mind, we must abandon at the outset all inquiries respecting essences or absolute substance, and confine ourselves to the observation of phenomena, their relations to each other, and the laws to which they are subjected. The progress of physical science within the last two centuries has been greatly accelerated by the practical acknowledgment of this law of investigation. Intellectual science can advance in no other direction.

If, then, it be affirmed that the soul or the thinking principle in man is material, or that its essence is the same as the essence of matter, we answer:

First, that the assertion is unphilosophical, inasmuch as it transgresses the limits which the Creator has fixed to human inquiry. We have been endowed with no powers for cognizing the essence of anything, and therefore we pass beyond our legitimate province in affirming anything on the subject. We can neither prove nor disprove it. We may show that no evidence can be adduced in favor of it; that all the analogies bearing on the subject would lead to a different conclusion; and thus we may form the basis of an opinion merely, but we can go no further. The nature of the case excludes all positive knowledge.

Secondly, we reply that the assertion is nugatory. It is affirmed that the essence of the soul is the same as the essence of matter. But what is the essence of matter? We are obliged to confess that we do not know. When, therefore, we assert that the essence of the soul is the same as the essence of matter, we merely assert that it is the same as something of which, by confession, we know absolutely nothing. Were this assertion granted, it would then add nothing whatever to the sum of human knowledge. Would it not be better frankly to confess our ignorance on the subject?

Thirdly, so far as the grounds for an opinion exist, they favor precisely the opposite opinion.

The qualities of matter and the energies of mind are as widely as possible different from each other. In all languages they are designated by different classes of words We recognize them by different powers of the mind, powers which cannot be used interchangeably. Our senses cannot recognize the thoughts of the mind, nor can consciousness recognize the qualities of matter. To assert, then, that the essence of mind and of matter is the same, is to assert, without the possibility of proof, that two things are the same, which not only have no attribute in common, but of which the attributes are as unlike as we are able to conceive.

It may not be out of place to enumerate the several mental states consequent upon the enunciation of any given proposition. In the first place, the assertion is made without any evidence either in favor of or against it. In this case (supposing the veracity of the assertor not to be taken into view) my mind remains precisely as it was before. The assertion goes for nothing. I have no opinion either the one way or the other. I neither believe nor disbelieve, nor have any tendency in either direction. In the second case the assertion is made, and though sufficient proof is not presented to create belief, yet considerations, as, for instance, analogies, are shown to exist, which create a probability either in favor of or against the thing asserted. Here, then, is ground for an opinion, and the state of mind is changed. We neither believe nor disbelieve, but we hold an opinion either in favor of, or contrary to the assertion. In the third case, the assertion is sustained either by syllogistic reasoning, or by testimony conformed to the laws of evidence. Here a different state of mind is produced. I believe it. I rely upon it as I would upon a matter which came within the cognizance of my own perception or consciousness. To illustrate these cases. A man asserts that the moon is a mass of silver. His assertion leaves my mind where it was before. I know nothing about it. Another man asserts that the planet Jupiter is or is not inhabited. He cannot prove it, but he presents various analogical facts in harmony with this assertion. I form an opinion on the subject. In the third case, a man asserts that the sun is so many millions of miles from the earth, and he proves, by testimony, that the observations forming the data were made, and he explains the mathematical reasoning by which this result is obtained. I believe it, and in my mind it takes its place with other established facts. Any one, who will reflect upon the evidence presented in favor of the materiality of the mind, can easily determine which of these mental states it is entitled to produce.

But it has been sometimes said that the brain itself is the mind, and that thought is one of its functions. The reason given for this belief is, that diseases of the brain and nerves affect the condition of the mind; that the mind declines as they become debilitated by age, and that the mind becomes deranged when the brain suffers from disease.

To this I would reply, that, so far as I have observed, the facts are hardly stated with accuracy when this course of argument is adopted, and a large class of facts bearing in an opposite direction is too frequently left out of view.

But, granting the facts, they do not justify the conclusion that is drawn from them. Suppose the brain to be the instrument which the mind uses in its intercourse with the external world,— as, for instance, suppose the brain to secrete the medium by which the mind derives impressions from without, and sends forth volitions from within,— any derangement of this organ would, by necessity, create derangement in the forms of mental manifestation connected with that derangement. Disease of the nerves may create false impressions, or may lead to acts at variance with the spiritual volitions. As the facts may be thus accounted for on the supposition that the brain is an organ used by the mind, as well as on the supposition that the brain is itself the organ of thought, they leave the question precisely where they found it.

If, then, it be asked, what is the relation which the mind holds to the material body? our answer would be as follows: The mind seems to be a spiritual essence, endowed with a variety of capacities, and connected with the body by the principle of life. These capacities are first called into exercise by the organs of sense. So far as I can discover, if a mind existed in a body incapable of receiving any impression from without, it would never think, and would, of course, be unconscious of its own existence. As soon, however, as it has been once awakened to action by impressions from without, all its various faculties in succession are called into exercise. Consciousness, original suggestion, memory, abstraction, and reason, begin at once to act. These various powers are developed and cultivated by subsequent exercise, until this congeries of capacities, once so blank and negative, may at last be endowed with all the energies of a Newton or a Milton.

Locke compares the mind to a sheet of blank paper; Professor Upham, to a stringed instrument, which is silent until the hand of the artist sweeps over its chords. Both of these illustrations convey to us truth in respect to the relation existing between the mind and the material system which it inhabits. The mind is possessed of no innate ideas, its first ideas must come from without. In this respect it resembles a sheet of blank paper. In its present state it can originate no knowledge until called into action by impressions made upon the senses. In this respect it resembles a stringed instrument. Here, however, the resemblance ceases. Were the paper capable not only of receiving the form of the letters written upon it, but also of combining them at will into a drama of Shakspeare or the epic of Milton; or, were the instrument capable not only of giving forth a scale of notes when it was struck, but also of combining them by its own power into the Messiah of Handel, then would they both more nearly resemble the spiritual essence which we call mind. It is in the power of combining, generalizing, and reasoning, that the great differences of intellectual character consist. All men open their eyes upon the same world, but all men do not look upon the world to the same purpose.

REFERENCES.

Mind first called into action by the perceptive powers — Locke, Book 2, chap. 1, sec. 9; chap. 9, sections 2—4, and sec. 15.

On the proper means of knowing the operations of our own minds — Reid, Essay 1, chap. 5.

No idea of substance or essence, material or spiritual — Locke, Book 2 chap. 23, sections 4, 5, 16, 30.

Energies of mind expressed by active verbs — Reid, Essay 1, chap. 1.

Explanation of terms — Ibid.

Affirmation concerning the essence of mind unphilosophical — Stewart, Introduction.

As much reason to believe in the existence of spirit as of body — Locke. Book 2, chap. 23, sections 5, 15, 22, 30, 31.

SECTION II. — OF THE PERCEPTIVE POWERS IN GENERAL.

BEFORE entering upon the consideration of the individual senses, it may be of use to offer a few suggestions respecting the perceptive powers in general. I propose to do this in the present section.

1. I find myself, in my present state, in intimate connection with, what seems to me to be, an external world. I cannot help believing that I am in my study; that, looking out of the window, I behold in one direction a thronged city, in another green fields, and in the distance beyond a range of hills. I hear the sound of bells. I walk abroad and am regaled with the odor of flowers. I see before me fruit. I taste it and am refreshed. I am warmed by the sun and cooled by the breeze. I find that all other men in a normal state are affected in the same manner. I conclude that to be capable of being thus affected is an attribute of human nature, and that the objects which thus affect me are, like myself, positive realities.

I cannot, then, escape the conviction that I am a conscious existence, numerically distinct from every other created being, and that I am surrounded by material objects possessed of the qualities which I recognize. The earth and the trees seem to me to exist, and I believe that they do exist. The grass seems to me to be green, and I believe that it is green. I cannot divest myself of the belief that the world around me actually is what I perceive it to be. I know that it is something absolutely distinct from the being whom I call myself. I am conscious that there is a *me*, an *ego*. I perceive that there is a *not me*, a *non ego*. I observe that all men have the same convictions, and that in all their conversation and reasonings they take these things for granted.

2. I, however, observe that my power of cognizing the existence and qualities of the objects around me is limited. There are but five classes of external qualities which I am able to discover; these are odors, tastes, sounds, tactual, and visible qualities. For the special purpose of cognizing each of these qualities I find myself endowed with a particular organization, which is called a sense. These are the senses of smell, taste, hearing, touch, and sight. Each sense is limited to its own department of knowledge, and has no connection with any other. We cannot see with our ears, or hear with our fingers. Each sense performs its own function, irrespective of any other. That matter has no other qualities than those which we perceive, it is not necessary to assert; but if it have other qualities, inasmuch as we have no means of knowing them, we must be forever, in our present state, ignorant of their existence.

This limitation, however, exists, not by necessity, but by the ordinance of the Creator. He might, if he had so pleased, have diminished the number of our senses. The deaf and the blind are deprived of means of knowledge which other men enjoy. The number of the senses in many of the lower animals is exceedingly restricted. We might possibly have been so constituted as to hold intercourse with the world around us without the intervention of the senses. We suppose superior beings to possess more perfect means of intelligence than ourselves; but no one imagines them to be endowed with material senses. Our Creator might, probably, have increased the number of our senses, if he had seen fit, and we should then have enjoyed other inlets to knowledge than those which we now possess. It is not improbable that some of the inferior animals possess senses of which we are destitute. Migratory birds and fishes are endowed with a faculty by which, either by day or by night, they pursue their way, with inevitable certainty, through the air or the ocean. May not this power be given them by means of an additional sense?

3. When our senses are brought into relation to their appropriate objects, under normal conditions, a state of mind is created which we call by the general name of thought, or knowledge. If a harp is struck within a few feet of me, a state of mind is produced which we call hearing. So, if I open my eyes upon the external world, a state of mind is produced which we call seeing. This mental state is of two kinds. It is sometimes nothing more than a simple knowledge, as when my sense of smelling is excited by the perfume of a rose. At other times it goes further than this, and we not only have a knowledge or a new consciousness, but also the belief that there exists some external object by which this knowledge is produced.

The external conditions on which these changes depend are as numerous as the senses themselves. Each sense has probably its own media, or conditions, through which alone its impressions are received. We see by means of the medium of light. We hear by means of the vibrations of air. None of these media can be used interchangeably Each medium is appropriated to its peculiar organ.

4. Physiologists have enabled us to trace with considerable accuracy several steps of the process by which the intercourse between the spiritual intellect and the material world is maintained; by which impressions on our material organization result in knowledge, and the volitions of the soul manifest themselves in action. A brief reference to our organization in this respect is here indispensable.

The nervous system in general is that part of our physical organization by which the mind holds intercourse with the external world, and through which it obtains the elements of knowledge. The nervous system is, however, of a two-fold character. A part of it is employed in giving energy to those processes by which life is sustained. These have their appropriate centres either in the spinal marrow, or in the different ganglia. Thus the heart, arteries and lungs, have their appropriate system of nerves, with their proper centre. The digestive apparatus has its own nervous system. These are all parts of the general arrangement of brain, spinal marrow and nerves, but their functions are performed without volition or thought. Hence many of the lower animals, which have no need of thought, have no other nervous apparatus. The brain may be removed from some of the cold-blooded animals without, for a considerable period, producing death. In such cases sensation will produce motion, the arterial and digestive processes will continue for a while uninterrupted. Thus a common tortoise will live for several days after its head has been cut off. Thus we also perform these various functions without any intervention of the will. We digest our food, we breathe, our hearts pulsate, without any care of our own; and these functions are performed as well when we sleep as when we wake,— nay, they proceed frequently for a while with entire regularity, when consciousness has been suspended by injury of the brain.

As this part of the nervous system has nothing to do with thought and volition, we may dismiss it from our consideration, and proceed to consider that other portion of it which stands in so intimate connection with the thinking principle.

The organism which we use for this purpose consists of the brain and nerves. The part of the brain specially concerned in thought is the outer portion, called the cerebrum. From the brain proceed two classes of nerves, which have been appropriately termed afferent and efferent. The afferent nerves connect the various organs of sense with the brain, and thus convey to it impressions* from without. When an image from an external object is formed on the retina of the eye, a change is produced along the course of the optic nerve, which terminates in the brain, and the result is a change in the state of the mind which we call seeing. When the vibrations of the air fall upon the ear, another change is produced on the auditory nerve which is continued until it reaches the brain, and the result is a change in the state of the mind which we call hearing. The other, or the efferent class of nerves, proceed from the brain outwardly, and terminate in the muscles. By these the volitions of the mind are conveyed to our material organs, and the will of the mind is accomplished in action. The process just now mentioned is here reversed. The volition of the mind acts upon the brain, the change is communicated through the nerves to the muscles, and terminates in external action. Thus the brain is the physical centre to which all impressions producing knowledge tend, and from which all volitions tending to action proceed.

The proof of these truths is very simple. If the connection betwen the organ of sense and the brain be interrupted by cutting, tying or injuring the nerve, perception immediately ceases. If, in the same manner, the connection between the brain and the voluntary muscles be interrupted, the limbs do not obey the will. Sometimes, by disease, the nerves of feeling alone are paralyzed, and then, while the power of voluntary motion remains, the patient loses entirely the sense of touch, and will burn or scald himself without consciousness of injury. At other times, while the

* I of course use the word impression here, in a general sense, to convey the idea of a change produced, and not of literal impression or change of material form

nerves of sensation are unaffected, the nerves of volition are paralyzed. In this case, feeling and the other senses are unimpaired, but the patient loses the power of locomotion. Sometimes an effect of this kind is produced by the mere pressure upon a nerve. Sometimes, after sitting for a long time in one position, on attempting to rise we have found one of our feet "asleep." We had lost the power of moving it, and all sensation for the time had ceased. It seemed more like a foreign body than a part of ourselves. Long-continued pressure on the nerve had interrupted the communication between the brain and the extremities of the nerves. As soon as this communication was reëstablished, the limb resumed its ordinary functions.*

These remarks respecting the nerves apply with somewhat increased emphasis to the brain. If by injury to the skull the brain becomes compressed, all intelligent connection between us and the external world ceases. So long as the cause remains unremoved, the patient in such a case continues in a state of entire unconsciousness. The powers of volition and sensation are suspended. If the brain becomes inflamed, all mental action becomes intensely painful, the

* Sometimes this communication is so entirely suspended that a limb in this state, when touched by the other parts of the body, appears like a foreign substance. An instance of this kind, which many years since occurred to the author himself, may serve to illustrate this subject. He awoke one night after a sound sleep, and was not agreeably surprised to find a cold hand lying heavily on his breast. He was the sole occupant of the room, and he knew not how any one could have entered it. It was so dark that he could perceive nothing. He, however, kept hold of the hand, and, as it did not move, was somewhat relieved by tracing it up to his own shoulder. He had lain in an awkward position, so that he had pressed upon the nerve until all sensation had ceased. Probably many stories of apparitions and nightly visitations may be accounted for by supposing a similar cause.

perceptions are false or exaggerated, and the volitions assume the violence of frenzy.*

It may illustrate the relation which the nervous system sustains to the other parts of our material structure, to suppose the brain, nerves and organs of sense separated from the rest of the body, and to exist by themselves, without loss of life. In such a case, all our intellectual connections with the external world could be maintained. We could see, and hear, and feel, and taste, and smell, and remember, and imagine, and reason. All that we should lose would be the power of voluntary motion, and the conveniences which result from it. If, then, we should put this nervous system into connection with the bones, muscles, and those viscera which are necessary for their sustentation, we should have our present organization just as we actually find it. We see, then, that the other parts of our system are not necessary to our power of knowing, but mainly to our power of acting.

5. Of sensation and perception.

I have said that when our senses, under normal conditions, are brought into relation to the objects around us, the result is a state or act of the mind which we call knowing. A new idea or a new knowledge is given to the mind. This knowledge is of two kinds. In one case it is a simple

* Sometimes, however, astonishing lesions of the brain occur without either causing destruction of life or even any permanent injury. A case was a few years since published in the daily papers, under the authority of several eminent physicians, more remarkable than any with which I had been previously acquainted. A man was engaged in blasting rocks and as he stood over his work, and was, I think, drawing the priming-wire, the charge exploded, and drove through his head an iron rod of some two or three feet in length. The rod came out through the top of his head, and was found covered with blood and brain. He nevertheless walked home without assistance, and under ordinary medical care recovered in a few weeks.

knowledge, connected with no external thing. Thus, suppose that I had never yet received any impression from the external world. In profound darkness a rose is brought near to me. I am at once conscious of a new state of mind. I have a knowledge, something which I can reflect upon, which we call smell. This knowledge, however, exists solely in my mind. I refer it to nothing, for I know nothing to which I can refer it. This simplest form of knowledge is called *sensation.*

But there is another form of knowledge given us through the medium of our senses. In some cases we not only obtain a new idea, or a knowledge of a quality, but we know, also, that this quality is predicated of some object existing without us. We know that there is a *not me*, and that this is one of its attributes. Suppose, as in the other case, I am endowed with the sense of sight, and in daylight the rose is placed before me. I know that there is an external object numerically distinct from myself, and that it is endowed with a particular form and color. This act is called *perception.*

These two forms of knowledge are united in the sense of touch, and may be clearly distinguished by a little reflection. The illustration of Dr. Reid is as follows: "If a man runs his head with violence against a pillar, the attention of the mind is turned entirely to the painful feeling, and, to speak in common language, he feels nothing in the stone, but he feels a violent pain in his head." "When he leans his head gently against the pillar, he will tell you he feels nothing in his head, but feels hardness in the stone." — Reid's Inquiry, chap. 5, sec. 2. So I prick a person with the point of a needle; a new knowledge is created in his mind, which he denominates pain. I draw the needle lightly over his finger, and I ask him what it is; he replies, the point of a needle. So, if I place my fingers lightly on a table with my attention strongly directed to the feeling, I am conscious of a sensation. If I move my hand slowly over the table in order to ascertain its qualities, I am conscious of a perception; that is, of a knowledge that the table is smooth, hard, cold, etc. The smell of a rose, the feeling of cold, the pain of the toothache, are sensations. The knowledge of hardness, of form, of a tree, or a house, are perceptions.

It has been commonly supposed that every perception was preceded by and consequent upon a sensation. Hence the question has frequently arisen, since the perception is predicated upon the sensation, and the sensation conveys to us no knowledge of an external world, whence is our knowledge of an external world derived? From these data it has seemed difficult to answer the question satisfactorily. Dr. Brown has attempted to solve the difficulty by supposing the existence of a sixth sense, which he calls the sense of muscular resistance. He suggests that the pressure of the hand against a solid body produces a peculiar sensation in the muscles by which we become cognizant of the existence of an external world. To me this explanation is unsatisfactory. The question is, how does sensation, which is a mere feeling, and gives us no knowledge of the external, or the not me, become the cause of perception, which is a knowledge of the external? Dr. Brown attempts to remove the difficulty by suggesting another sensation, which, being a mere sensation also, has no more necessary connection with the knowledge of the external than any other.

It is my belief that the idea of externality, that is, of objects numerically distinct from ourselves, is given to us spontaneously by the senses of touch and sight. When we feel a hard substance, the notion that it is something external to us is a part of the knowledge which at once arises in the mind. When I look upon a tree I cannot divest myself of the instantaneous belief that the tree and myself are distinct existences, and that it is such as I perceive it to be. Unless this knowledge were thus given to us by the constitution of our minds, I know not how we should ever arrive at it. That this view of the subject is correct, is, I think, evident from what we observe of the conduct of the young of all animals. The lamb, or the calf, of a few hours old, seems by sight to have formed as distinct conceptions of externality, of qualities, of position, and of distance, as it ever obtains. We cannot suppose that its knowledge arises from any sense of muscular resistance, but must believe that it is given to it originally with the sense of sight. So an infant turns to the light, grasps after a candle, just as it does after any visible object in later life. I therefore believe that this complex knowledge is given to us by the senses of sight and touch, just as the simpler knowledge is given to us by the senses of smell and taste.

REFERENCES.

Perception in general — Reid's Inquiry, chap. 6, sec. 20.
Process of nature in perception — Reid's Inquiry, chap. 6, sec. 21.
Mode of perception — Essays on Intellectual Powers, Essay 2, chap. 1.
Perception limited by the senses — Essay 2, chap. 2.
The evidence of perception to be relied on — Essay 2, chap. 5.
Sensation and perception — Abercrombie's Intellectual Powers, Part 2, sec. 1.

SECTION III. — OF THE MODE OF OUR INTERCOURSE WITH THE EXTERNAL WORLD.

In the preceding sections we have treated of both the physical and spiritual facts concerned in the act of perception. We have seen that in order to the existence of perception, some change must be produced in the organ of sense; this must give rise to a change transmitted by the nerves to the brain, and the brain must be in a normal state in order to be affected by the change communicated by the nerves. If either of these conditions be violated, neither sensation nor perception can exist. When, however, these organs are all in a normal state, and its appropriate object is presented to an organ of sense, the result is a knowledge or an affection of the spiritual soul. The first part of the process is material—it consists of changes in matter; the last part is thought, an affection of the immaterial spirit. The question is, how can any change in matter produce thought, or knowledge, an affection of the spirit? Or, still more, how can this modification of the matter of the brain produce in us a knowledge of the external world, its qualities and relations? The lighting of effluvia on my olfactory nerve is in no respect like the state of my mind which I call the sensation of smell. The vibrations of the tympanum, or the undulations of the auditory nerve, are in no respect similar to the state of my mind when I hear an oratorio of Handel. The two events are as unlike to each other as any that can be conceived. In what manner, then, does the one event become the cause of the other?

A variety of answers has been given to these questions The manner in which the subject has been formerly treated is substantially as follows: It was taken for granted that the mind was a spiritual essence, whose seat was the brain; that the mind could only act or be acted upon in the place where it actually resided, and that, as external objects were at a distance from the mind, it was necessary for images of external objects to be present to it, in order that it might obtain a knowledge of their existence.

Hence arose the doctrine of what has been called representative images. By some of the ancient philosophers it was supposed that forms or species of external objects entered the organs of sense, and through them became present to the mind. It was the opinion of Locke, so far as I can understand him, that, in every act of perception, there is an intermediate image of the external object present to the mind, which the mind cognizes immediately, instead of the object itself. I am aware that the language of Locke is, on this subject, exceedingly uncertain and ambiguous. Sometimes he seems to use the word *idea* to express merely an act of the mind, and, at other times, something present to the mind, but numerically distinct from it, which is the immediate object of knowledge. That, however, he really believed that in perception there must exist something, a positive entity, different both from the mind and its perceptive act, is evident from such passages as the following: "There are some *ideas* which *have admittance* only through one sense which is peculiarly adapted to receive them."—"And if these organs, or the nerves which are the *conduits to convey them* from without to their audience in the brain, the mind's presence-room (as I may so call it), are any of them so disordered as not to perform their functions, they have no postern to be admitted by, no other way to bring themselves into view and be perceived by the understanding."—Book II., chap. 3, sec. 1.

Again: "If these external objects be not united to our minds when they produce ideas therein, and yet we perceive their original qualities in such of them as singly fall under our senses, it is evident that some motion must be thence continued by our nerves or animal spirits, by some parts of our bodies, to the brain or seat of sensation, there to produce the particular ideas we have of them. And since the extension, figure, number and motion, of bodies of an observable bigness, may be perceived at a distance by sight, it is evident *some singly imperceptible bodies must come* from them to the eyes, and thereby convey to the brain some motion which produces these ideas which we have of them." — Book II., chap. 8, sec. 12.

Again: "I pretend not to teach, but to inquire, and therefore cannot but confess here, again, that external and internal sensation are the only passages that I can find of knowledge to the understanding. These alone, as far as I can discover, are the windows by which light is let into this dark room; for, methinks, the understanding is not much unlike a closet wholly shut from the light, with some little opening left to let in *external visible resemblances or ideas of things without.* Would the pictures *coming into* such a dark room but stay there and lie orderly, so as to be found upon occasion, it would very much resemble the understanding of a man in reference to all objects of sight and the ideas of them."— Book II., chap. 2, sec. 17.

From these quotations, — and many of the same kind might be added, — two things are evident: first, that Locke used the word idea to designate both the act of the mind in perception, a mere spiritual affection; and also something proceeding from the external object which was the cause of this state. Secondly, that he did really recognize this intermediate something as a positive entity which the soul cognizes instead of the outward object. He speaks of the nerves as the *conduits to convey these ideas to their presence-chamber, the brain; of imperceptible bodies* which must *come from them* (external objects) to the eyes, and be conveyed to the brain. These expressions are too definite to be used figuratively, and we must, therefore, accept this explanation of the phenomena as a statement of the belief of our illustrious author. This belief, however, was by no means peculiar to him. It was a common belief at the time, and he always refers to it as a matter well understood, and received without question, by his cotemporaries. The student who wishes to pursue this subject farther, will read with pleasure the passages referred to at the close of the chapter.

The belief, then, prevalent at the time of Locke, may be stated briefly thus: The soul is located in the brain. It can cognize nothing except where it exists in space. External objects, being separated from it, can never be the immediate objects of its perception. There must, therefore, proceed from the external object to the mind some images or forms, which, entering by the senses, become present to the mind, and are there the objects of perception. Hence the mind never cognizes external objects; this is, from the nature of the case, impossible. It only cognizes these images in the brain, and, from their resemblance to external objects, it learns the existence and qualities of the external world.

Dr. Reid for a while believed this doctrine, but, startled at the conclusions to which it led, was induced to examine the foundations on which it rested. Upon reflection, he soon arrived at the following conclusions:

1st. The existence of these images is inconceivable. We can conceive of the image of a form, but how can we conceive of the image of a color as existing in absolute darkness; and still more of the image of a smell, a sound, or a taste? Or how can we conceive of distinct images of all of these various qualities forming the conception of a single object?

2d. Were this theory conceivable, it is wholly destitute of proof. It is merely the conception of a philosopher's brain. Who ever saw such images? Who, by his own consciousness, was ever aware of their existence? What shadow of proof of their existence was ever given to the world? Are we, then, called upon to believe an inconceivable hypothesis on no other evidence than merely the assertion of philosophers?

3d. Were the existence of intermediate images proved, it

would relieve the subject of no essential difficulty. It might reasonably be demanded, is it easier to cognize a small object than a large one? If the image be matter, then the question still remains unanswered, how does a change of matter create thought, an affection of the soul? Is the image spirit? Then it cannot resemble the external object, and can give us no notion of its qualities. And, more than all, if we never cognize the object, but only the image, how can we have any knowledge whatever either of the external object or of its qualities?

The suggestion of these considerations abolished at once the doctrine of a representative image. Since the time of Dr. Reid, it has, I think, been conceded, by the most judicious writers on this subject, that we know nothing concerning the mode of perception beyond a statement of the facts. There is a series of physical facts which can be proved by experiment to exist. When these terminate there arise knowledges of two kinds: the one a simple knowledge, as when I am conscious of a smell or a sound; the other a compound knowledge, embracing a simple idea, as of color or form, and also an idea of an external object of which these qualities are predicated. Both of these are pure and ultimate cognitions. We are as perfectly convinced of the truth of the one as of the other. I as fully believe that I see a rose, that its leaves are green and its petals red, as that I smell an odor which I have learned to call the smell of a rose. I cognize no image, I cognize the rose itself; and I am as sure of its existence as I am of my own. Such seems to be the law of perception under which I have been created. I can neither change these perceptions, nor help relying with perfect confidence on the truths which they reveal to me. If I am asked to explain it any farther, I confess myself unable to do so. If investigation shall enable us to establish any additional facts in the series by which the material change terminates in thought, we will accept its discoveries with thankfulness. Until this is done, it is far better, when we have reached the utmost limit of our knowledge, humbly to confess our ignorance of all that is beyond.

The doctrine of a representative image would not, at the present day, deserve even a passing notice, were it not for the consequences which were deduced from it. Some of these are worthy of remark.

In the first place, it was difficult to conceive how the soul could be affected and thought produced by any change in matter. It was supposed that this difficulty could be relieved by the hypothesis of representative images. But then it was demanded, are these images matter or spirit? If they are matter, and matter cannot act but upon matter, since they act on the mind, the mind must be matter. Hence was deduced the doctrine of materialism. Or, on the other hand, are these images spirit? In this case, spirit might act upon spirit; but then how could spiritual images proceed from matter, and, more still, how could they resemble matter? If, then, we cognize nothing but these, whence is the evidence of any material world? Hence the doctrine of idealism.

But again. It is granted in this hypothesis that we can cognize in itself nothing external. We cognize nothing but images, and it is impossible for us to cognize anything else. But it was apparent that no images, which could by possibility pass through the nerves, could resemble external qualities; what reason, then, have we to believe that the external quality is, in any respect, like the image which alone we are able to contemplate? Again: in order to know that the images are similar to the objects which they represent, we must know both the object and its representative. But by necessity we can know only the one; how can we affirm that it resembles the other? If I enter a gallery of paintings, how can I determine whether the pictures are likenesses or are mere productions of the fancy; if neither I nor any other man had ever seen any originals of which they could be the resemblances? Hence it is manifest that the evidence of the existence of a material world, or of anything existing out of the mind, is at once swept away. Reasoning in this manner, Bishop Berkeley arrived at idealism. He denied the existence of an external world, and concluded that nothing existed but spirit and the affections of spirit.

But this idea was generalized. It was admitted that we could not cognize external objects directly, but only through the medium of representative images. If this is true of material, why is it not true of spiritual objects,— of the cognitions of consciousness? Why do we not cognize them by means of representations? But if we cognize them thus, and have no cognition of the objects themselves, how do we know that there is any such existence as mind or its faculties? In short, how do we know that anything exists but ideas and impressions? How do we know that any such realities exist as time, space, eternity, Deity? All is resolved into a succession of ideas, which follow each other by the laws of association, and besides these there is nothing in the universe. This is nihilism, and such consequences were actually deduced by some philosophers from this doctrine. It was surely important to examine the evidences of an hypothesis which led to such results.

This imperfect fragment of the history of intellectual philosophy is not without its value. It teaches us the vast superiority of the acknowledgment of ignorance, to the gratuitous assumption of knowledge. When we have reached the limits of our knowledge, there is no harm in confessing that beyond this we do not know. But to look out into the darkness, and dogmatically to affirm what exists beyond the reach of our vision, may exclude invaluable truth, and introduce the most alarming error. Thus, in the present in stance, a hypothetical explanation of a fact, which in our present state does not seem to admit of explanation, when carried out to its legitimate results was found to terminate in universal scepticism, and furnish a foundation for consistent atheism. Philosophy will certainly have made important progress when it shall have been able accurately to determine the limits of human inquiry.

REFERENCES.

Representative images — Locke, Book 2, chap. 3, sec. 1 ; chap. 8, sec. 12 ; chap. 11, sec. 17. Reid's Inquiry, chap. 1, secs. 3—7 ; 2d Essay, chaps. 4, 7, 9, 14. Stewart, vol. 1, chap. 1, sec. 3. Introduction, Part 1, vol. 2, chap. 4, sec. 1 ; chap. 1, sec. 3. Cousin, Psychology, chaps. 6 and 7.

Knowledge an agreement between the idea and object — Locke, Book 4, chap. 1, sec. 2 ; chap. 4, sec. 3., Cousin, chap. 6.

Consciousness an authority — Chapter 1.

Three things existent in perception — Reid, 2d Essay, chap. 5.

Idealism and Nihilism — Cousin, chap. 6, last part, and chap 7 Reid 2d Essay, chaps. 10—12.

THE INDIVIDUAL SENSES SEPARATELY CONSIDERED

SECTION IV. — OF THE SENSE OF SMELL.

HAVING, in the preceding chapter, treated of our perceptive powers in general, I proceed to describe the particular senses with which we have been endowed. Proceeding from the simpler to the more complex, I shall examine, in order, smell, taste, hearing, touch and sight.

The organ of smell is situated in the back part of the nostrils. It is composed of thin laminæ of bone, folded together like a slip of parchment, over which the olfactory nerve is spread, covered by the ordinary mucous membrane which lines the mouth and posterior fauces. It is so situated that the whole surface of the organ is exposed to the current of air in the act of inspiration.

In those animals which seek their prey by scent, this organ is found larger, exposing a greater amount of surface to the air, than in those which pursue their prey by sight The perfection in which this sense is enjoyed by some of the lower animals has always been a subject of remark. A dog will track the footsteps of his master through the streets of a crowded city, and, after a long absence, will recognize him by smell as readily as by sight or hearing.

When we are brought near to an odoriferous body, we immediately become sensible of a knowledge, a feeling, or a particular state of mind. If a tuberose is brought near a person who has never smelled it, he is at once conscious of a form of knowledge entirely new to him. If we do not by our other senses, know the cause of the sensation, we have no name for it, but are obliged to designate it by referring to the place where we experienced it. If, by our other senses, we have learned the cause of the sensation, we designate it by the name of the object which produces it. Were the perfume of a rose present to me for the first time, and did I not see the flower, I could give to it no name As soon as I have ascertained that the perfume proceeds from the rose, I call it the smell of a rose. We thus see clearly that from this sense we derive nothing but a sensation, a simple knowledge, which neither gives us a cognition of anything external, nor teaches us that anything exists out of ourselves.

The exercise of this sensation is either agreeable, indifferent or disagreeable. The perfume of flowers, fruit, aromatic herbs, &c., is commonly pleasant. The odor of objects in common use is generally indifferent. The odor of putrid matter, either animal or vegetable, is excessively disagreeable. In general, it may be remarked that substances which are healthful for food are agreeable to the smell; while those which are deleterious are unpleasant. The final cause of this general law is evident, and the reason why the organ of smell in all animals is placed directly over the mouth. Odors of all kinds, however, if they be long continued, lose their power of affecting us. We soon become insensible to the perfume of the flowers of a garden; and men, whose vocation requires them to labor in the midst of carrion, after a short time become insensible to the offensive effluvia by which they are surrounded.

Pleasant odors are refreshing and invigorating, and restore, for the time, the exhausted nervous energy. Offensive odors, on the other hand, are depressing to the spirits, and tend to gloom and despondency. The former of these effects is alluded to with great beauty in the well-known lines of Milton

> "As when to them who sail
> Beyond the Cape of Hope, and now are past
> Mozambique; off at sea, north-east winds blow
> Sabean odors from the spicy shore
> Of Araby the blest; with such delay
> Well pleased, they slack their course, and many a league,
> Cheered with the grateful smell, old Ocean smiles."
>
> *Paradise Lost, Book* 4, *lines* 159—165.

Concerning the manner in which this sensation is produced, I believe that but one hypothesis has been suggested. The received opinion is that what is called effluvia, or extremely minute particles, are given off by the odorous body, that these are dissolved in the air, and brought in contact with the organ of this sense in the act of breathing. That this may be so is quite probable. It is, however, destitute of direct proof, and is liable to many objections. It is difficult to conceive how a single grain of musk can, for a long time, fill the area of a large room with ever so minute particles, without visible diminution of either volume or weight. Until, however, some better theory shall be presented, we seem justified in receiving that which even imperfectly accounts for the facts in the case. Still, we are to remember that it is merely a hypothesis, to be abandoned as soon as any better explanation is established by observation.

From what has been already remarked, it must be, I think, evident that the sense of smell gives us no perception. It is the source of a simple knowledge which alone would never lead us out of ourselves. This sensation clearly gives us no notion whatever of the quality which produces it, nor have philosophers ever been able to determine what that quality is. It is possible that the suggestion of cause and effect might indicate to us the probability of a cause but the sense itself would neither awaken this inquiry nor furnish us with the means of answering it.

Does the sense of smell furnish us with any conception? By conception, I mean a notion of a thing, such as will enable us, when the object itself is absent, to make it a distinct object of thought. Thus I have seen a lily; I can form a distinct notion of its form and color, and I can compare it with a rose, and from my conceptions point out the difference between them. I could describe this lily, from my conception of it, so that another person could have the same notion of it as myself. Were I a painter, I could express my conception on canvas. Now, is there a similar power of forming a conception of a smell? Can I form a distinct notion of the smell of an apple or a peach, and can I compare them together, or describe them by language, or in any other manner transfer my conception to another? So far as I can discover, from observing the operation of my own mind, all this is impossible. After having smelled an odorous body, I know that I should be able to recognize that particular odor again. I cannot form a conception of the smell of a rose, but I know that I could, if it were present, immediately recognize it and distinguish it from all other odors. Beyond this I am conscious of no power whatever.

This, however, I am aware, is but the experience of a single individual. Other persons may be more richly endowed than myself. I have frequently put this question to the classes which I have instructed, and I find the testimony not altogether uniform. Some few young gentlemen in every class have assured me that they had as definite a conception of a smell as they had of a color or a form. The greater part, however, have agreed with me that they had no power to form the conception in question.

It has, very probably, occurred to the reader that the words, "the smell of a rose," convey two entirely different meanings; the one objective, the other subjective. The "smell of a rose" may designate a peculiar feeling or knowledge existing in my mind, or it may designate the unknown cause of that feeling. Thus, when I say the smell of a rose is sometimes followed by fainting, I mean the sensation produced in the mind. I say the apartment is filled with the smell of a rose. I here mean the unknown quality existing in the rose. Both of these expressions I suppose to be correct, and in harmony with the idiom of the English language. The same ambiguity exists in all the terms commonly used to designate sensations. Thus, the taste of an apple, heat, cold, sweet, sour, and many others, admit of a similar twofold signification.

Chemical philosophers, aware of this ambiguity in language, have wisely introduced a new term, by which, in a particular case, this difficulty may be obviated. Observing that the term "heat" may signify a certain feeling in my mind, as well as the unknown cause of that feeling existing in a burning body, and as they were continually treating of the one, and almost never of the other, they have designated the two ideas by different words. Retaining the term heat to signify the sensation of a sentient being, they use the word "caloric" to designate the unknown cause of the sensation. Every one must perceive how much definiteness the use of this term has added to this branch of philosophical inquiry.

REFERENCE.

Reid's Inquiry, chapter 2, the whole chapter.

SECTION V.—THE SENSE OF TASTE.

THE nerves of taste are spread over the tongue and the back part of the fauces. They terminate in numerous papillæ, or small excrescences, which form together the organ of taste. It is almost needless to observe that the nerves are everywhere covered with the membrane lining the mouth, and never come in immediate contact with the sapid substance. These papillæ are most numerous on the tip, the edges, and the root of the tongue, leaving many portions of the intermediate surface almost destitute of this sensation.

The sense of taste is never excited except by solutions. The saliva, which is copiously furnished by the glands of the mouth, is an active solvent. By mastication, the solid food becomes intimately mixed with this animal fluid, is partially dissolved by it, and, in this condition, is brought into relation to the papillæ which constitute the organ of taste. Insoluble substances are, therefore, tasteless. When the papillæ of the tongue either become dry, or are covered with the thick coating produced by fever, taste becomes imperfect or is wholly suspended.

When a sapid body, under normal circumstances, is brought into relation with the organ of taste, a sensation either pleasing or displeasing immediately ensues. When the sensation is pleasant, we are instinctively impelled to swallow, and with the act of swallowing the sensation is perfected and ceases. When the sensation is unpleasant, we are, on the other hand, impelled to reject whatever may be the cause of it, and frequently it requires a strong effort of the will to control this impulse. The sensation of taste is not consummated without the act of swallowing. It would seem probable that the anterior and posterior nerves of the tongue were designed to perform different offices, the former giving us an imperfect sensation, which creates the disposition either to swallow or to reject the sapid substance; the latter awakening the perfected sensation as the substance passes over it.

As in the case of smell, so in that of taste, I think that with the sensation no perception is connected. A particular sensibility is excited; a feeling either pleasant or unpleasant is created; a simple knowledge is given us; — but no cognition of anything external can be observed. Whatever notions of externality come to us, by means of this sense, are derived from other sources than the sense itself. Thus, we can receive nothing into the mouth except by bringing it into contact with the lips. The sense of touch then cognizes it as something external to ourselves. The suggestion of cause and effect might lead us possibly to the same conclusion. These, however, are no parts of the sense of taste. The taste in the mouth which frequently accompanies disease, awakens no idea of anything external. When, however, by means of our other senses, we have learned that a particular flavor is produced by any substance, we associate the flavor with the substance, and give it a name accordingly. We thus speak of the taste of an apple, a pear, or a peach.

So far as I am able to discover, the remarks made in the last section, respecting conception as derived from smell, apply with equal truth to the sense of taste. I think that men generally have no distinct conception of an absent taste, but only a conviction that they should easily recognize it if it were again presented to them. This form of recollection may be so strong as to create a longing for a particular flavor, but still there is no conception like that produced by either sight or touch.

The same ambiguity may be observed here as in the analogous sense. The taste of an apple, means both the quality in the fruit which produces the sensation and the affection of the sentient being produced by it. The one is objective, belonging exclusively to the *non ego;* the other is subjective, belonging wholly to the *ego.* Of the sensation we have a very definite knowledge; it can be nothing but what we feel it to be. Of the cause we are, as in the sense of smell, wholly ignorant.

The number of sensations derived from taste is, I think, much greater than that derived from smell. An epicure becomes capable of multiplying them, and distinguishing them from each other to a very great extent. We are able, also, to classify our sensations of taste much more definitely than those of smell. Thus, we speak of acid, subacid, sweet, bitter, astringent, and many other classes of tastes, to which we refer a large number of individuals. In this manner we designate various kinds of fruit, medicines, &c. While, therefore, these two senses seem to be governed by the same general laws, I think that in man the knowledge derived from taste is more definite and more varied than the other. By means of the sense of touch, which so completely surrounds the sense of taste, we should, in the use of it, also arrive at the idea of externality. In this respect it is indirectly the source of knowledge which is not given us by the sense of smell. In blind mutes, however, to whom the sense of smell becomes much more important, in all probability the case is reversed, and smell furnishes more numerous and definite cognitions than taste.

I have said above that the sensation of taste is not perfectly experienced unless the sapid substance is swallowed. Whatever is swallowed enters the stomach, undergoes the process of digestion, and, whether nutritious or deleterious, enters the circulation and becomes assimilated with our material system. It is manifest, therefore, that if a substance be pleasing to the taste, we may, by gratifying this sense, swallow either what is in itself deleterious, or that which becomes deleterious by being partaken of in excess. It is, hence, evidently important that the gratification of the sense be made subordinate to the higher design: that of promoting the health and vigor, physical and intellectual, of the whole man.

In brutes, for the most part, the gratification of the appetite is controlled by instinct. The instances are very rare in which one of the lower animals has any desire for food which is not nutritious, or desires it in larger quantity than the health of the system demands. Man, however, is endowed with no such instinct. The regulation of his appetite is submitted to his will, directed by reason and conscience. Guided by these, a perfect harmony will exist between his gustatory desire and the wants of his material and intellectual organization.

But suppose it to be otherwise. Suppose the human being to swallow neither what nor as much as his health requires, but what and as much as will furnish gratification to his palate. He will eat or drink much that is deleterious, and much which, by excess, becomes destructive to health. When, by frequent indulgence, this subjection to appetite has grown into a habit, the control of the spiritual over the sensual is lost, and the man becomes either a glutton or a drunkard, and very commonly both.

The effects of these forms of indulgence are too well known to require specification. Gluttony, or the excessive love of food, renders the intellect sluggish, torpid and inefficient, cultivates the most degrading forms of selfishness, exposes the body to painful and lingering disease, and frequently terminates in sudden death.

"The full-fed glutton apoplexy knocks
Down to the ground at once, as butcher felleth ox."
Thompson's Castle of Indolence.

The appetite for deleterious drinks leads to consequences still more appalling. In a very short time it ruins the health, enfeebles the intellect, maddens the passions, destroys all self-respect, and, in the most disgusting manner, brutalizes the whole being. It speedily and insensibly grows into a habit which enslaves the nervous organism, sets at defiance the power of the will, and thus renders the ruin of the being, both for time and eternity, inevitable. We hence perceive the importance of holding our appetites in strict subjection to the dictates of reason and conscience, and especially of excluding the possibility of our ever becoming the victims of intemperance.

REFERENCE.

Reid's Inquiry, chapter 3

SECTION VI.—THE SENSE OF HEARING.

THE organ of this sense is the ear. It is composed of two parts, the external and internal ear. The external ear is intended merely to collect and concentrate the vibrations of the air, and conduct them to the *membrana tympani*, which separates the two portions of this organ. The external ear thus performs the functions of an ear-trumpet. The *membrana tympani* is a thin membrane stretched across the lower extremity of the tube in which the outward ear terminates. The vibrations of the air, thus produced upon the tympanum, are, by a series of small bones occupying its inner chamber, transmitted to certain cells filled with fluid, in which the extremity of the auditory nerve terminates. From these cells the nerve proceeds directly to the brain.

The medium by which the auditory nerve is affected, is the atmospheric air. Sonorous bodies of all kinds produce vibrations or undulations in the air, which strike upon the tympanum, and are, by the apparatus above alluded to, conveyed to the auditory nerve. The effect produced upon the nerve is simply that of mechanical vibration, and this vibration, so far as we can discover, is the cause of the sensation of sound. A mere fluctuation in the extremities of the nerve is the occasion of all the delight which we experience in listening to the sublimest compositions of a Handel or a Mozart. No more convincing proof can be afforded that there is no conceivable resemblance between the change in the organ of sense, and the delightful cognition of the soul, which it occasions.

The number of sounds which the human ear is able to distinguish is very great. Dr. Reid remarks that there are five hundred tones which may be distinctly recognized by a good ear; and that each tone may be produced with five hundred degrees of loudness. This would give us two hundred and fifty thousand different sounds which could be perceived by an ear of ordinary accuracy. This I presume is true; but a little reflection will convince us that the number of sounds which we are able to distinguish far transcends all human computation. The voice of every human being may easily be distinguished from that of every other, while the number of separate sounds which every individual is able to produce, including tones, loudness, stress and emphasis, is absolutely incalculable. If the same note be struck by ever so many different instruments, the sound of each instrument can be readily recognized. If ten thousand instruments of the same kind were collected, it is probable that no two could be found whose sounds would be identical. Numbers which accumulate by such masses set all computation at defiance.

Although our power of distinguishing the smallest variation of sound is so remarkable, it has been observed that there are some sounds which are inaudible to particular persons. It seems probable that each ear is endowed with the power of cognizing sounds within a particular range, but that this range is not the same in every individual. This difference is, I think, most observable in the shrillest sounds, or those pitched on the highest key, and produced by the most rapid vibrations. I have known some persons who were unable to hear the sound produced by a species of cricket, while to other persons the sound was so loud as to be unpleasant. I think that Dr. Reid remarks the same peculiarity respecting himself.

We all possess, to a considerable degree, the power of determining the direction from which sounds proceed. We derive this power, probably, in part, from the fact that our ears are separated at some distance from each other, on opposite sides of the head, and hence a sound must, in many cases, affect the one differently from the other. Persons who have lost the use of one ear much less easily determine the direction of sounds. This power, moreover, is greatly improved by practice. We learn, in this manner, to form a judgment of the distance of sounds, and to associate with them much other knowledge which properly belongs to the other senses. Thus, it is said that Napoleon was never deceived as to the direction or distance of a cannonade, and the remarkable precision of his judgment always excited the wonder of his friends.

It is in this manner, I presume, that ventriloquism, as it is termed, is to be explained. We have learned by experience to determine the distance and direction of sounds. For instance, I hear a person speaking. The quality of the sound, its degree of loudness and distinctness, teach me that it is produced by some one on my left hand, and in the street which passes by my window. If a person in the room with me were able to produce a sound which should strike upon my ear precisely like that which I just now heard, I should suppose that it proceeded from the same place as before. The effect would be more remarkable, if he should, by some ingenious device, direct my attention to the window, and create in me the impression that some one was outside of it. In order to accomplish this result, it is necessary that the performer be endowed with an ear capable of detecting every possible variety in the quality of sound, and vocal organs of such extreme delicacy that they are able perfectly to obey the slightest intimation of the will. I have never witnessed any performance of this kind, but I have known one or two persons who possessed this power in a modified degree, and this is the account which they have given me concerning it. I am told that those who perform these feats publicly are also able to create the sounds which we hear, without moving, in the least, the visible organs of speech. How they are able, in this manner, to produce articulate sounds, I am unable to explain.

Is hearing a sensation or a perception? That is, does it furnish us with a simple knowledge, without giving us any cognition of an external world; or does it furnish us with a complex knowledge, that is, a knowledge of a quality and of the object in which it resides?

The knowledge furnished by this sense seems to me to be of the following character: it is purely a sensation, a simple knowledge, giving us no intimation of anything external. The knowledge, however, derived from this sense, differs from those which we have already considered, in many particulars. Some of these are worthy of attention.

The sensation of hearing is much more definite, varied,

and intensely pleasing, than that derived from either of the preceding senses. It has, moreover, a power of strongly affecting the tone of mind of the hearer. These impressions being made upon a being endowed with original suggestion, would naturally occasion an inquiry for a cause. While hearing a strain of music, it would at once occur to us that we did not produce it, that we could not prolong it, and, hence, that it must originate from something external to ourselves. We should thus learn that there existed something out of ourselves; but what that something was, the sense of hearing would furnish us with no means of determining. Let a man hear a violin, a bugle, or a piano, and, though he would readily observe a difference between them, he could by this sense alone form no conception of the nature of either instrument, or of the medium through which an impression was made upon his auditory nerve. When did a peal of thunder ever suggest to man the nature of the cause which produced it? In this respect, therefore, the sense of hearing differs from those already considered. It suggests to us the idea of a cause, but gives us no knowledge of the nature of that cause.

In another respect, however, the sensation of hearing is peculiar. It enables us to form very definite conceptions. Smell and taste possess this power, if at all, in a very limited degree. By no power of language can we convey to another the knowledge which they give us. The sense of hearing enables us to proceed much further. We hear a sound; we can repeat it. We hear a tune; we can mentally recall it without producing any sound whatever, and we can derive pleasure from this silent conception of it. Still more, we are able to designate a great variety of articulate sounds by the alphabet. By means of this notation, the sounds of a speaker's voice can be so recorded, that another person who has not heard him, and who may not even understand the language in which he has spoken, may be able accurately to repeat all that he has said. The case is still stronger when the words uttered are set to music. Here it is not only possible to note down the words, but also the precise musical notes in which they were expressed, so that the song, and the tune in which it was sung, may be accurately repeated by a person on the other side of the globe.

I have remarked that our conception of musical sounds may give us pleasure in perfect silence; as when we remember a strain which we have heard on a former occasion. This is yet more observable when sounds are described by their appropriate notation. A skilful musician will read the notes of an opera or oratorio, form the conception as he proceeds, and derive from them as definite a pleasure as he who reads the pages of a romance or a tragedy. It has frequently happened that the most eminent musicians have been afflicted with deafness. It is delightful to observe that this infirmity in only a modified degree deprives them of their accustomed pleasure. They sit at an instrument, touching the notes as usual, and become as much excited with their own conceptions as they were formerly by sounds. Under these circumstances, some of them have composed their most elaborate and successful productions. These facts establish a wide difference between the sense of hearing and the senses of taste and smell. The latter produce in us no definite conceptions, and are susceptible of being formed into no such language. Hearing is evidently a much more intellectual sense than either of those which we have thus far considered.

Besides, musical sounds have an acknowledged power over the tone of the human mind. By the tone of mind, I mean that condition of our emotional nature which inclines us to be grave or gay, lively or sad, kind or austere, apprehensive or reckless. Now, it is well known that music has the power not only to harmonize with any of these tones of mind, and thus increase it, but in many cases to alter and control it. Every one knows the difference between a sportive and a melancholy air, between a dirge and a quickstep; and every one also knows how readily his tone of mind assimilates with the character of the music which he chances to hear. Sacred music, well performed, renders deeper the spirit of devotion. The hilarity of a ball-room would instantly cease if the music were withdrawn. I question if the martial spirit of a nation could be sustained for a single year, if music were banished from its armies; and military evolutions, whether on parade or in combat, were performed under no other excitement than the mere word of command.

From these well-known facts, an æsthetical principle may be deduced of some practical importance. The design of music is to affect the tone of mind. To do this, it must be in harmony with it. No one would think a psalm tune adapted to a charge of cavalry; and every one would be shocked to hear a devotional hymn sung to the tune of a martial quickstep. It hence follows, that what may be good music for one occasion, may be very bad music for another. If we are called upon to judge of the excellence of any piece of music, it is not enough that the music be good,—the question yet remains to be decided, is it good for this particular occasion; that is, does it harmonize with the particular tone of mind which the words employed would naturally awaken? If it do not, though it may be very good music for some occasions, it is bad music in this particular case. The Il Penseroso and the L'Allegro of Milton have, I believe, been set to music, and, if the music were adapted to the thought, the effect of these beautiful poems would be increased by it. But every one sees that the music adapted to the one must be very unlike that adapted to the other. Let the music be transferred from the one to the other, and the incongruity would be painful; and what was just now good music would become at once intolerable. Much of the church music at present in vogue seems to me to partake of the incongruity of such a transposition.

Here, also, the question may be asked, whether all poetry is adapted to music. From the preceding remarks it would seem that it is not, unless it awaken some emotion. And again, the emotion in some cases may not be adapted to music. Terror, horror, the deepest impressions of awe, are probably not adapted to musical expression. The attempts which have been made to convey such emotions by music have, I apprehend, generally failed. They may, like much other music, display the skill of the composer or the performer, but they leave the audience unmoved.

Another peculiarity of this sense deserves to be mentioned By it we are capable of forming a natural language understood by all men. Our emotions instinctively express themselves by the tones of the voice, and these are easily recognized by those to whom they are addressed. Every one understands the tones indicative of kindness, of authority, of pity, of rage, of sarcasm, of encouragement and contempt. Should a man address us in an unknown tongue, we should immediately learn his temper towards us by the tones of his voice. The knowledge of these tones is common to all men, under all circumstances. Children of a very tender age learn to interpret them; nay, even brutes seem to understand their meaning very distinctly. It would seem, then, that the tones of the voice form a medium of communication, not only between man and man, but even between man and some of the inferior animals.

I have said that these tones of the voice are universally understood. It is also true that they have the power of awakening an emotion, similar to that which produced them, in the mind of the hearer. A shriek of terror will convulse a whole assembly. It is said that Garrick once went to hear Whitefield preach, and was much impressed with the power of that remarkable pulpit orator. Speaking afterwards of the preacher's eloquence, he is reported to have said, "I would give a hundred pounds to utter the word Oh! as Whitefield utters it." It is probable that it is in the power of expressing our emotions by the tones of the voice, more than in anything else, that the gift of eloquence consists. This was, I presume, the meaning of Demosthenes, who, when asked what was the first, and the second, and the third element of eloquence, replied, successively, "Delivery, delivery, delivery!" This is, I think, illustrated in the case to which I have alluded. Whitefield's printed sermons do not place him high on the list of English preachers; while, as they were delivered by Whitefield himself, they produced effects which can only be ascribed to the very highest efforts of eloquence.

The relation of these remarks to the cultivation of eloquence is obvious. Suppose a public speaker to be able to construct a train of thought which shall lead the minds of men, by logical induction, to a given result. Suppose, moreover, that this train of reasoning is clothed in appropriate diction, so that it is adapted not only to convince, but to please an audience. It is now to be delivered in the hearing of men. It may be delivered in so monotonous tones as to put an assembly to sleep, or in tones so inappropriate and grotesque as to provoke them to laughter. It is now necessary that the orator be deeply moved by his own conceptions, and that he be able to give utterance to his own emotions in the tones of his voice. His organs of speech must be capable of every variety of expression, and they must so instinctively respond to every emotion, that the thought which the speaker enunciates is lodged in the mind of the hearer, animated by the precise feeling of him who utters it. He who is thus endowed can hardly fail of becoming an orator. Hence, if we would improve in eloquence, we must studiously cultivate the natural tones of emotion; in the first place by feeling truly ourselves, and, in the second, by learning to express our emotions in this language which all men understand.

REFERENCE.

Reid's Inquiry, chap. 4, sections 1, 2

SECTION VII.—THE SENSE OF TOUCH.

THE nerves of feeling are situated under the skin, and are plentifully distributed over the whole external surface So completely does the network which they form cover the whole body, that the point of the finest needle cannot puncture us in any part without wounding a nerve, and giving us acute pain. It is in this manner that we are guarded from injury. Were any portion of our body insensible, we might there suffer the most appalling laceration without being aware of our danger.

The chief seat of the nerves of touch is, however, in the palm of the hand, and in the ends of the fingers. The other parts of the body render us sensible of injury from external sources, but they are incapable of furnishing us with any definite perceptions. The hand, on the contrary, conveys to us very exact knowledge of the tactual qualities of bodies. For this purpose it is admirably adapted. The separation of the fingers from each other, their complicated flexions, the extreme delicacy of their muscular power, all combine to render this organ susceptible of an infinite variety of definite impressions.

Though the fingers are separated, yet in using them together, when a single object is presented, but one perception is conveyed to the mind. It would seem, however, that, in order to produce this result, corresponding points of the fingers must be applied to the object. If we change them from their normal position, by crossing the second over the fore-finger, two perceptions will be produced, and a small object, as a pea, will seem to us double.

The sensation of touch is of two kinds, as it is caused, first, by *temperature*, and secondly by *contact*.

The sensation produced by temperature is that of cold or heat. It is awakened by any body whose temperature differs from that of our external surface. When we place our hands in water only blood warm, we are not conscious of this sensation. If we place one hand in hot, and the other in cold water, for a few minutes, and then remove them both to tepid water, we experience the sensation of heat in the one and of cold in the other.

The effect produced upon us by temperature is a simple knowledge, a pure sensation. It gives us no knowledge of anything external. During the first chill of a fever we are unable to determine whether the weather is cold, or our system diseased; that is, whether the sensation proceeds from without or from within. And when the sensation proceeds from without, it gives no information respecting its cause, or the manner in which it affects us.

Heat and cold are merely affections of a sensitive organism. That which causes them is called by chemists caloric. This quality in bodies has opened a wide field for philosophical investigation, which, by developing the laws of steam, has modified the aspects of modern civilization.

Secondly, the sense of touch is excited by contact. I use the term contact here in its common, and not in its strict meaning. The nerves are always covered with the skin, and when by accident the skin is abraded, we feel pain, but we are conscious of no perception. Nor, in fact, is the skin itself ever in absolute contact with the external object. A layer of air always interposes between them.

When the hand is thus brought into proximity to an external body, we are immediately made conscious of its existence. In this act there may, I think, be discovered both a sensation and a perception. I have referred to this fact in a previous section. Nothing further will here be necessary than to appeal to the experience of every individual. Let any one place his hand lightly upon a piece of marble, or any external object, fixing his attention as much as possible upon his sensation, and he will, I think, find himself conscious of a feeling into which the idea of externality does not enter, and which gives him no knowledge of the qualities of body. Let him now take up the marble, and attempt to cognize its several qualities, and I think he will be conscious of a very different knowledge, involving the notions of externality, hardness, smoothness, form, and, it may be, some others. In this case he pays no attention to his sensations. It does not occur to him that they exist. All he is conscious of is the various qualities of the external object, and of these he obtains a very distinct cognition. It may require a small effort at first to distinguish these two forms of knowledge from each other, but I am persuaded that any one may do it who will be at the pains for a few times to make the experiment.

The perceptions given us by this sense are exceedingly definite and perfect. By it we not only know that a quality exists, but also what it is. We have the knowledge, and we know what it is that produces it. In this manner the

6

perceptions by touch lie at the foundation of all our knowledge of an external world. We rely upon them with more certainty than any other. Many of the qualities revealed to us by touch are also revealed to us by sight. If, however, in any case, we have reason to doubt the evidence of sight, we instinctively apply to the sense of touch in order to verify our visual judgment.

The principal qualities cognized by touch, besides externality, are extension, hardness, softness, form, size, motion, situation, and roughness or smoothness. Besides these, however, there are various sensations of pain and pleasure given by this sense, the specific effect of particular agents, as of electricity and galvanism, the sensation of tickling, and many others of the same kind. To this sense have also been ascribed the sensation of hunger and thirst, and the various affections belonging to our sensitive organism.

Confining ourselves, however, to the *perceptions* of touch, we find that they are almost exclusively given us by the hand. In this manner we obtain a distinct knowledge of extension, of size, of hardness, softness and form. When the body is small, or the discrimination delicate, we rely almost wholly on the perceptive power of the fingers. In this manner we obtain, experimentally, nearly all our knowledge of the primary qualities of body.

We may here remark the difference between the knowledge obtained by this sense, and that obtained by the senses previously considered. The others give us each a particular class of sensations, and only one kind of knowledge. By touch we are conscious of heat and cold, together with a great variety of other sensations, and also of the various perceptions of primary qualities mentioned above. The others give us no direct knowledge of an external world. This gives us that knowledge directly and immediately. The others, when the existence of an external world is suggested, give us no knowledge of its qualities. This gives us a positive knowledge of several of the most essential of them. We know, for instance, that form is precisely what it appears to be, and that our knowledge of it exactly conforms to the reality. We know that it must, under all circumstances, be exactly what we perceive it to be. We thus derive from it a distinct conception; we can make it an object of thought, and can form concerning it the most complicated processes of reasoning. When we see a blind person read with his fingers, we must be convinced that he has as definite a conception of the forms of letters as we ourselves have by sight. We thus learn that not only does this sense enable us to make large additions to our knowledge, but that it is really the original source of a great part of our knowledge of the world around us. Of its intrinsic importance we may form an opinion from the fact that there is no case on record in which a human being has been born without it. By it alone, as in the case of Laura Bridgman, we may learn our relations to the world around us; may be taught the use of language, and may even acquire the power of writing it with considerable accuracy. This sense is lost only in paralysis, and in those cases in which the individual, drawing near to dissolution, has no farther need of any of the organs of sense.

REFERENCE.

Reid's Inquiry, chap. 5, sections 1, 2.

SECTION VIII.— THE SENSE OF SIGHT.

THE organ of vision is the eye. It is an optical instrument, of exquisite construction, adapted in the most perfect manner to accomplish the purposes of its formation. At will, we can admit the light or surround ourselves with total darkness. As we frequently pass from darkness to light, the eye is provided with a curtain, by means of which the pupil is either expanded or contracted, so that no more light than is required falls upon the retina. We can turn the eyes in every direction. By them we can discern objects either gigantic or microscopic, within a few inches of us, or at the distance of several miles. It gives us instantaneously a knowledge of the qualities of bodies, which could be discovered by the other senses only after a long and patient investigation, and of many qualities which, without this sense, could never be discovered at all. Although capable of such complicated action, and always in use except when we sleep, the eye is comparatively seldom liable to accident or disease. It is protected from ordinary violence by the overhanging brows. The fine particles of dust which fall upon it are perpetually washed away by the combined action of the eyelids and the lachrymal gland. Its rapid and incessant change of position, by calling into action different portions of the optic nerve, preserves it from severe exhaustion. Thus it happens that a large portion of mankind pass through life without ever knowing that their eyes are even liable to disease.

The manner in which the impression is produced upon the organ of vision has been fully explained by physiologists. The human eye is a small globe, so constructed that the rays of light coming from a visible body which fall upon it, are formed into a small image upon its inner posterior surface. This image is inverted. The rays of light first fall upon the visible object, and are from it reflected upon the eye. Of course, where there is no light, that is, when no rays can be either received or reflected, there can be no vision.

Over the back part of the eye is spread out an expansion of the optic nerve, called the retina. Immediately behind this, is a thin membrane, on which is laid a black pigment for the absorption of the light producing the image. In order to produce distinct vision, this image must be accurately defined. Hence, in twilight, when the light is insufficient, an object is but imperfectly seen. When, owing to slight malformation of the eye, as in near-sighted or in aged persons, the image is not accurately delineated on the retina, vision is also indistinct; nor can the infirmity be relieved until by artificial means we cause the rays of light to form a true image on the expansion of the optic nerve. If the nerve become paralyzed, vision ceases. If it be inflamed, vision is so intensely painful that the patient cannot, without severe suffering, bear the least glimmer of light. The nerves of vision do not proceed from each eye directly to the brain, but first meet at what is called the decussation of the optic nerve, where their fibres intermingle, after which they separate and enter the substance of the brain. What purpose is answered by an arrangement so different from that observed in the other nerves of sense, has not yet been discovered.

When, under normal circumstances, the visual image is formed on the retina, a mental state succeeds which we call vision. What this is we all know by experience. The question, however, remains, Is sight a sensation or a perception? and, if a perception, is it like the sense of touch preceded by a sensation? Before proceeding further, let us attempt to answer these questions.

Is sight a sensation or a perception? A sensation is a simple knowledge, a state of mind terminating in itself, and, so far as our consciousness is concerned, having no original connection with anything external. Now, if merely the cognition of color is considered, we must admit that it resembles in many respects, the cognition of hearing. The notion or knowledge of red, for instance, is an affection of the mind, and wholly unlike the cause from which it proceeds. No one supposes that the rose has the simple knowledge which we designate by the word red. And, moreover, this simple knowledge gives us not the most distant idea of its cause. Sight gives us no more knowledge of that quality in bodies which produces in us the notion of color, than hearing designates the size and form of the instrument which produces the sound to which we are listening, or the atmospheric change which precedes the clap of thunder at which we tremble. In this respect the act of seeing resembles a mere sensation.

On the other hand, it is to be remarked, that, although the knowledge of color is a sensation, a subjective affection, yet we are so made as to refer this knowledge directly and immediately to the external object. When we reflect upon the subject we know that the notion of red is a spiritual affection, and yet that affection seems to be a part of the rose. When we are conscious of an odor, we do not, so far as the sense of smelling is concerned, assign it to any external location. When we hear a sound, so far as this sense is concerned, we do not determine the place of its origin. The music seems to float around and envelop us, like the atmosphere. But when we are sensible of a color, we see it in a determined locality, we see it now and there, and at once fix the limit of its existence.

Here, however, it may be said, that in this respect the perception by sight is similar to that of touch; that in touch we equally transfer our notion of form to the object which we perceive. The cases, I admit, are similar, but I think by no means identical. When I feel of a cube, and obtain a knowledge of its form, it is obvious that the thought of my mind is not like the cube—that is, it is not solid, equiangular and equilateral. It is, nevertheless, a positive knowledge that such are the qualities of the cube. I know that the thought of my mind represents to me these qualities just as they are. They are the sufficient cause of that particular idea, and nothing else could have been the cause of it. It is a definite knowledge of a mode of the not me admitting of no intermediate question. When, however, I see a color, the case is quite dissimilar. My notion of color gives me no knowledge of its cause. I have by it no knowledge of a particular mode of the not me, which, of necessity, if it produce in me any knowledge, must produce precisely that of which I am conscious. My sense of sight does not inform me at all what color (objective) is. That the existence of light is necessary to it, all men know; but what light is, in what manner it produces color, whether by rectilinear rays reflected from the object, or by a succession of waves of a universal medium, is yet a matter of dispute among philosophers. In the case of sight, then, if the question be asked, what produces this knowledge, we can give no answer. In the case of touch, we answer at once, the form of a cube,— we all know what that form is,— and the subject admits of no farther discussion.

I do not know whether I have made this distinctly obvious to others, or whether I have analyzed the act of vision accurately. I have, however, endeavored as well as I am able to state the facts in the case as they appear to my own consciousness.

Is there in sight, as in touch, a sensation antecedent to perception, or a sensation which it is in our power to distinguish from perception? For myself, I have never been able to discover it. I place my hand, under different conditions, on a cube, and I am able to distinguish the sensation from the perception, and can make either of them, separately, a matter of thought. I can discover no such distinct states of mind in the act of vision. I open my eyes I see a book. The first thing of which I am conscious is the cognition of an external object. I am conscious of no intermediate or different mental state. I must, therefore, believe that none exists. It may be said that one has existed, but that, from long neglect, we have lost the power of observing it. To this I reply, that we habitually neglect the sensation in the perception of touch, but, when it is pointed out to us, we easily recognize it. If it existed in the sense of seeing, I see no reason why we should not as easily observe it. The simple fact seems to be, that, as soon as we are conscious of the knowledge of color, we are, at the same instant, conscious of the knowledge of the object in which the color seems to reside. We cannot separate the one from the other.

The perception of an object as endowed with color is, however, in some respects, unlike the perception of an object as endowed with form.

The perception by touch is fixed and definite, in all positions remaining precisely the same. The perception by sight varies by every change of position. For instance, if a small cube is placed in my hands, I turn it over and feel of it on all sides, and it ever presents itself to me as the same figure. On the other hand, I look upon it with one of its faces directly before me, and it presents one appearance. I turn one of the angles towards me, and it presents another. I change its position a hundred times, and at every time it presents a different appearance.

Again, the perception by touch is unaffected by distance. I feel of a cube, and I derive a clear knowledge of its form. I extend my arms to their utmost length, and the perception is the same. I think of it a mile off, and my notion of it does not vary. But it is not so with the perception of sight. I look at a cube at a distance of twelve inches from my eyes, it has one magnitude. I remove it ten feet off, and its apparent magnitude is ten times less. Its color is less vivid, and its outline less distinct. I remove it to the distance of an hundred feet, and it is diminished to an indistinct speck. If I would represent it to another person, I must represent it thus indistinctly. Hence the distinction made between tactual and visual form and magnitude.

We have the means of associating these two ideas together in a manner hereafter to be considered. We are able to translate the language of sight into the language of touch. This, however, would be unnecessary, were there not this difference in the two perceptions to which I have here referred.

If we observe the relation in which the senses stand to each other, we shall at once perceive the importance of sight. Smell and taste give us simple knowledges, without any cognition of the not me, and, also, I think, without the power of forming conceptions. Hearing *suggests* the not me, and gives us the power of forming conceptions; but it gives us no knowledge of any of the attributes of the sonorous body, save its power of awakening this sensation. Touch gives us an immediate and positive knowledge of the not me, and of all its primary attributes, and leaves upon the mind a most definite conception. Sight enables us to determine most of the qualities revealed to us by touch, not only near at hand, but at great distances; by the delicacy of its language, it enables us to discover many of the qualities revealed by the other senses; and, while performing all these functions, it is a source of most exquisite pleasure.

That the conceptions of sight are more definite than those received by our sense of touch, I will not affirm. It is, however, certain that they are much more easily retained in the memory. When we recollect an external object, I think we much more readily recall the visual conception than any other. I may feel of a sphere, and obtain a knowledge of its form and magnitude; but when I think of it, the visual appearance presents itself most readily to my mind. Almost all the conceptions of figurative language are derived from sight. The power of originating such conceptions is called imagination, or the power of forming images. The fine arts, with the exception of music, address themselves wholly to this mode of perception. Almost all the other senses are, in some manner, tributary to it, and thus enable us to employ it in order to arrive at the most varied and distant forms of knowledge.

Let us now proceed to inquire, what are the qualities of the external world which are cognized by means of this sense?

1. If the above remark be true, that we are so made as to refer our visual conception to the external object, it will follow that we derive our cognition of externality as truly from this sense as from touch. Touch gives us a distinct and immediate notion of the existence and qualities of an external object. Sight gives us a conception of an unknown cause of a known effect; it also teaches us that this cause is numerically distinct from ourselves, and assigns to it its position in space.

The existence of this function of vision has frequently been denied, and it has been affirmed that, until aided by touch, sight gives us no idea of externality, any more than smell or hearing. The principal ground for this opinion is the authority of Cheselden,* who, long since, published an account of a young man whom he couched for cataract, and who, on restoration to sight, thought, at first, that every object touched his eyes. On this statement I would observe, that, on the first admission of light to the unnaturally sensi-

* Philosophical Transactions, 1778, No. 402.

tive retina, a sensation unlike to sight would be likely to arise, which the patient might very probably designate by saying that the object touched his eyes. Every one, in passing from darkness into a strong light, has felt a sensation of this kind, and he may remember that it is more nearly akin to touch than to sight. If we had before known everything by touch, we should naturally use this language in describing it. On this account, I think the case does not warrant the stress that has been laid upon it. But, secondly, if it were so, if he thought that the objects touched his eye, then, as Sir W. Hamilton has happily remarked, "still they appeared external to the eye," for it is evident that two things cannot seem to touch each other, unless, at the same time, also, they appear numerically distinct. That which is numerically distinct from the eye must be the non ego. Besides, the young of all animals, as soon as they open their eyes, recognize external objects as external, and, with evident design, move either towards or away from them. In fact, they use their eyes at first just as they use them afterwards. A new-born infant teaches us the same truth. Who ever saw a young child place its hand on its eyes when an object was placed before it? It reaches out its hand towards the object, without, it is true, any correct idea of distance, but with a correct conception of externality and direction. I think that all our observation upon our own use of this faculty must lead us to the same conclusion.

2. From this sense, exclusively, we obtain our knowledge of color. Of the nature of this cognition I have already had occasion to express my opinion. It is a simple knowledge in itself, an affection of the sentient being, which, however, we naturally and immediately refer to the external object. Of this quality, thus recognized, the varieties are numerous, and they are indefinitely multiplied by the cir

cumstances of light and shade, distance and proximity, degree of illumination, and many others. Hence it is that external nature presents to us an exhaustless and ever-varied scene of beauty and sublimity. Every object in the world around us, which the hand of God has formed, is made to minister to our happiness. But this is only a small part of the benefit which we derive from this function of sight. Every change of color, and every variation in the degree of color, is indicative of some change which is originally cognized by some other sense. Hence it is that sight, which acts instantaneously, and cognizes its objects at large distances, is enabled, by changes of visual appearance, to detect an immense number of qualities which vision alone could never have discovered. All the senses become tributary to it, and it does the work of all. Of the manner in which this is done, we shall treat more particularly in the following section.

3. To the qualities of external bodies, rendered cognizable by sight, we must undoubtedly add extension. If we refer our notion of color to an external object, I do not see how it is possible to exclude from our minds the knowledge that the colored object is extended. If we look upon anything colored, that color covers a definite portion of space. Let any one look upon a surface marked alternately by different colors, and the limitations of each are distinctly defined. Hence, also, arises the idea of form in one dimension. We can as well cognize a circle or square by sight as we can do it by touch. We read as rapidly by the eye as the blind by their fingers.

4. Lastly, we must now add solidity, or extension in three dimensions, to the perceptions given us by sight. Until quite lately, this power has been denied to the faculty of vision. It has been the generally received opinion that sight gives us nothing but the different shades of color,

represented on a plane surface, as we perceive them in a painting; but that by touch we learn to associate the shading with the form, and thus indirectly learn to cognize solidity by the eye. This view was universally received, until the researches of Professor Wheatstone, of King's College, London, threw new light upon the whole subject. The brilliant discoveries of this philosopher have added a new function to the organ of vision, and demonstrated that, by the eye alone, we are enabled to cognize solidity as well as simple extension. He has shown that, in consequence of binocular vision, we are able to determine the form of bodies within a certain distance. The manner in which this is accomplished is as follows: It must be obvious to every one, that, inasmuch as the right and left eye occupy different positions in space, the images which an external object forms on the two eyes must be slightly dissimilar. I look upon an inkstand on the table before me, closing first my right eye and then the left. I can clearly discover a difference between the right and left image. Now, it is this difference of figure in the two images that gives us the notion of solidity. This is proved by the stereoscope, an invention of Professor Wheatstone. This instrument is so constructed that we can see separately the image of an object formed on the right eye, and then that formed on the left.

When seen in this manner, each figure appears to us as a mere drawing on a plane surface. When now we look at them with both eyes, we do not perceive two plane drawings, but a distinct, and, I had almost said, palpable solid. It is however evident that this effect can be produced only when the body is at so small a distance, and of such a magnitude, that two images can be formed. If it be far off, so that the rays become parallel, and thus form the same image on both eyes, no effect from binocular vision is produced. We

7

observe the truth of this law in our daily experience. When we look upon a well-executed painting, every figure, when viewed from a proper position, appears to stand out from the canvas. It seems to us impossible that it should be a plane surface. But if we draw near, the illusion vanishes. When we arrive at the position at which the figures, if solid, would form different images on the two eyes, and no such difference exists, we know at once that the surface is a plane. If it be objected that persons with one eye are able to distinguish solidity, it is replied that they do it less perfectly than others; that they are obliged to do it by observing the shading of the surface, and that they are frequently seen to move the head in a horizontal direction rapidly, in order to form the different images on the same eye.*

In consequence of this discovery, a very beautiful optical instrument has been invented, by which the effect of daguerreotype pictures has been much improved. A picture is taken separately for each eye. When these are looked at together, through glasses adapted to the purpose, we perceive only one figure; but it has all the appearance of solidity. Daguerreotypes of statuary have thus all the effect of the original marble.

The question has frequently been asked, How do we see objects single with two eyes? To this question I do not know that any more satisfactory answer has been given than the plain statement of the fact that so we were created. It seems to me not half so strange as the fact that we see at all. But I would inquire, is it more remarkable that we receive a single impression from two organs of sight, than from any of our other senses? All our nerves of sense are double. Every other sense has a right and a left nerve; yet all the impressions made upon us from a single object are

* Transactions of the Roya Society, vol. 56, p. 871. June 21, 1838.

single. Each ear receives an auditory impulse, yet we hear but one sound. When we feel of an object, each hand receives a distinct impression, yet we perceive but one object. It does not seem strange to us that we do not hear two sounds with two ears, or that we do not feel two cubes when we hold one with our two hands. The case, however, seems to me precisely similar to that in which we look upon one object with our two eyes. The sense of sight, then, merely conforms to the general law by which all our senses are governed. It would seem, then, unnecessary to proceed farther than to refer the case of sight to the general law of the senses. The question thus resolves itself into the general one, How are single impressions made with double organs? To this I do not know that any answer has been either given or attempted.

Again, it has been asked, How do we see objects erect, when the image on the retina is inverted? Dr. Reid answers this question by stating it as a general law that we see every object in the direction of the right line that passes from the picture of the object on the retina to the centre of the eye, "as the rays from the upper part of the object form the lower part of the image, and, *vice versa*, we see the upper part of the object with the lower part of the retina, and the contrary; and thus we see the object as it is, that is, we see it erect." In how far this relieves the difficulty, or carries us back to a more general law, I will not pretend to determine. To me it does not seem to throw that light on the subject which seems obvious to others. I have thought that, possibly, this effect was in some way connected with the decussation of the optic nerve. No nerves, except those of sight, unite before entering the brain, and in no other case is this peculiarity observed. May there not be some connection between the facts?

Persons who have been couched for cataract see objects

erect as soon as their power of vision is restored. At least, Cheselden and other observers have never stated anything to the contrary. This could hardly have been the case if so striking a phenomenon had passed under their notice. To this there seems but one exception. Sir W. Hamilton quotes a case from Professor Leidenfrost, of Duisburg, 1793, in which the fact was otherwise. A young man, blind from birth, had reached his seventeenth year, when his sight was restored after an attack of ophthalmia. When he first saw men, they seemed to him inverted; that is, their heads were towards his feet; and trees and other objects seemed to hold the same position. I am unable to account for this difference from ordinary experience. I would only remark, that we are always liable to err in reasoning from instances of this kind, because, when the condition of an organ is decidedly abnormal, it is impossible to say to what extent and in what direction the abnormal cause has been exerted.

REFERENCES.

Sense of sight — Reid's Inquiry, chap. 6.
Sight the noblest of our senses, " " section 1.
No sensation in sight, " " section 8.
Relation of visual to real figure, " " sections 23 and 7.
Color a quality of body, " " sections 4 and 5.
Parallel motion of the eyes, " " section 10.
How we see objects erect, " " sections 11 and 12.
How we see objects single, " " section 13.
We know not how the image on the retina causes vision, section 12.
Carpenter's Physiology, article sight.
Cheselden's case — Phil. Transactions, 1728, No. 402.
Wheatstone's paper, Phil. Trans., vol. 56, p. 371.
Prof. Liedenfrost's case, Sir W. Hamilton — Reid, p. 158.

SECTION IX. — OF ACQUIRED PERCEPTIONS, OR THE INTERCHANGEABLE USE OF THE SENSES.

It has been already remarked that each of our senses furnishes us with a distinct species of knowledge. We cognize odors by smell, sounds by the ear, colors by the eye, and so of all the rest. Neither of the senses can be used in the place of the other. We can neither see with our ears, hear with our fingers, nor smell with our tongue. Such is manifestly the fact, if our senses be considered separately.

But when the senses are considered collectively, we find that the above statement does not convey the whole truth. One sense seems to convey to us knowledge which could have been gained only by another. A single perception will frequently furnish us with knowledge, which we find, upon reflection, to have been originally given us by the action of another sense, or by the combined action of several of the senses. Considered in this light, our whole sensual organism seems to be one complicated system, designed in the most rapid and convenient manner to make us acquainted with the external world. We find ourselves, in a thousand cases, using one sense for another, whenever we can do it with advantage; and if by misfortune we are deprived of any particular sense, it is surprising to observe how readily the remaining senses come to our aid, and enable us to cognize objects in a manner which, at first view, would seem utterly impossible.

The process by which this effect is produced is the following: We have already observed that the variety of impressions which may be received by several of our senses is beyond the power of computation. Who can estimate the infinite number of sounds which we are capable of hearing;

or of color and shading which we are capable of seeing, and of distinguishing from each other? Now, we find that a quality cognized by one sense is, by the kind provision of our Creator, connected with some modification of a quality perceived by another sense. Observing this connection, we learn to associate the original with the secondary quality, and, from the observation of the one, to infer the existence of the other. For example, if I wish to learn whether a body is hard or soft, I employ the sense of touch. This is the sense originally given to me for the purpose of gaining this knowledge. I see before me a piece of polished marble, and a piece of velvet, of the same color. I feel of them both, and ascertain that the one is hard, and the other soft. But I also observe that the visual appearance of these two substances is dissimilar. I carefully note this difference. When I see the same objects again, I shall not be obliged to feel them; I know, at a glance, not only the visual but the tactual character of each. I go farther; I generalize this difference. I know that one visual appearance, wherever it is seen, indicates hardness, and another softness. Hence, when we, for the first time, look upon a substance, we commonly form an opinion of its hardness or softness from its peculiarity of color. Hence, also, we frequently use the language of one sense for that of another. We say of a surface that it *looks* hard or it *looks* soft. So painters, having observed that warm weather in summer is accompanied by a particular appearance of the sky, associate the language of feeling with that of sight, and speak of a warm sky, of warm or of cold coloring, and of other distinctions of a similar character.

Illustrations of acquired perceptions are presenting themselves to us every day, in the ordinary experience of life. The apothecary learns how to distinguish medicines by their smell as accurately as by their taste. The mineralogist by breathing upon a mineral, and observing its smell, will know in an instant whether it is or is not argillaceous. Or again, he will distinguish a calcareous from a magnesian mineral by the touch; or he will determine the character of another by its fracture. If a grocer wishes to know whether a cask is full or empty, he does not look into it, but merely strikes upon it, and ascertains the fact in an instant by sound. A mason who wishes to know if a wall in a particular spot is solid, does not pull it down, but strikes it with his hammer. In the same way we determine whether an object before us is made of wood, or metal, or stone. When these indications are closely observed, the accuracy of the judgments to which they lead is frequently very remarkable. It is said that an Indian hunter, on the prairies, by placing his ear on the ground, will discover the approach of an enemy long before he can be recognized by the eye, and will distinguish a herd of buffaloes from a troop of dragoons with unerring certainty. We are told that the Arabs will tell the tribe to which a passer-by belongs, by the print of his foot in the sand, and by the track of a hare will know whether it be a male or a female.

Inasmuch, however, as our visual perceptions are more varied and more rapid than those of our other senses, and as we, by the eye, cognize objects at great distances, the greater part of our acquired perceptions are referred to this sense. We judge of the qualities of almost all the substances in daily use by the eye alone. We continually determine distance and magnitude by the eye. The manner in which this is done is worthy of special notice. It is well known that, as an object recedes from us, its visual appearance presents several observable changes. First, its magnitude diminishes. Secondly, its color becomes dim and misty. Thirdly, its outline becomes indistinct; and, fourthly as its distance increases, the number of intervening objects becomes greater. It is by the observation of these changes that we determine whether objects are receding from, or advancing towards us. In the same manner, by comparing these indications, we judge of the distance and magnitude of any object. In every case of this kind we go through a complicated act of judgment; yet, from habit, we do it so rapidly, that we should hardly be aware of it but from the mistakes which we occasionally commit. For instance; I see an object presenting a certain dimness of color, of a certain indistinctness of outline, and of a given visual magnitude, and observe various objects intervening between it and me. This is all that the sense of sight gives me. I immediately judge it to be a man of ordinary size, half a mile off; and my judgments are so generally accurate, that I am surprised if I find myself in error.

When, however, any one of these conditions is changed, we are liable to be deceived. This is commonly the case when objects are seen through a mist. The deception here is not occasioned, as is generally supposed, by refraction of the rays of light, causing the object to seem larger. The object really seems to us of the proper size. The mist, however, renders the color and the outline indistinct, and we suppose the object to be at a much greater distance than it is. The body has the magnitude belonging to a quarter of a mile in distance, with the indistinctness of half a mile. With this magnitude, at the latter distance, it would, of course, seem to us much larger than it actually is An incident, illustrative of this fact, once occurred to the author. He was, early in the morning, in a dense fog, sailing through the harbor of Newport, and passed near the wharf of Fort Adams. He observed on the wharf some very tall men, and mentioned their remarkable size to the friends who accompanied him. Presently he was struck with their behavior. They were jumping and playing like children, in a manner that seemed to him wholly unaccountable Presently, as the sun dispersed the fog, he found himself close to the wharf, and these gigantic men dwindled down to a company of playful little boys, who were amusing themselves in childish gambols.

In the same manner we mistake if the atmosphere is more transparent than that to which we are accustomed. Bishop Berkeley, I think, remarks that English travellers in Italy, unaccustomed to the clear sky of southern Europe, were liable to continual misjudgment respecting the distance of objects seen in the horizon. The clearness of the color, and the distinctness of the outline, led them to suppose castles, mountains, &c., much nearer than they really were. In the same manner, when there are no intervening objects, we frequently find our judgments at fault. Thus, in looking over a sheet of water, we always underrate the distance. When we throw a stone at an object in the water, we always find that our eye has deceived us, and the stone falls far short of the mark. For the same reason, objects seen on the shore from the water seem much less than their natural size. The fact is, they appear of the magnitude which belongs to the distance, but we suppose the distance less than it is; and, associating this magnitude with diminished distance, they appear to us less than they really are.

In order to form these judgments correctly, one of these elements must be fixed. From this we learn to institute a comparison, and then an accurate opinion is formed. If we have the magnitude of the object, the change in its color and outline teaches us its distance. If we know its distance, we can judge of its magnitude. Hence, painters, in order to give us a correct notion of an object which they represent, always place in its vicinity something with whose real magnitude we are familiar. Thus, if I drew a pyramid, it might be difficult to determine whether I intended to represent it as large or small. If, however, I drew an Arab standing by his camel at the foot of it, my intention would at once become apparent. Every one knows the size of a camel, and from this he would judge of the magnitude of the pyramid.

The benefits which we derive from this interchangeable use of the senses are innumerable. We are thus enabled to transfer to one sense the cognitions which belong to another, always using that which we can employ with the greatest rapidity and convenience. Our whole sensitive organism is thus capable of being used for almost every form of cognition. Very much of our early education, especially the education which enables us to perform any art, consists in the acquisition of these secondary perceptions. It is thus that the physician, from symptoms, or external indications which another person would not observe, is enabled to discover the locality, the nature, and the progress of disease, and frequently to foretell the result with unerring accuracy.

The benefit of this arrangement is specially evident when we are unfortunately deprived of any one of our senses. Our acquired perceptions are then almost indefinitely multiplied, and the knowledge which we derive from our remaining senses is sometimes so great as to appear almost incredible. Thus, the blind, by paying strict attention to the indications derived from touch and hearing, acquire an accuracy of judgment, respecting things known to others by sight alone, which greatly surprises us. It is said that they can learn to determine, with great accuracy, the number of persons in a room by observing the sound of a speaker's voice, and that, by striking on the floor, they will form a very correct opinion as to the size of an apartment. Dr. Abercrombie mentions two blind men who were remarkably good judges of horses. One of them discovered, on a particular occasion, that a horse was blind by observing the manner in which he placed his feet upon the ground when in motion, although the fact had not been noticed by any other person of the company. Another discovered that a horse was blind of one eye, by observing that the temperature of the eyes was different. On the other hand, the deaf acquire great skill in judging of the qualities of bodies by touch and sight. They will learn to understand a speaker by the motion of his lips, and to interpret the minutest shades of emotion by the changes in the countenance. When both sight and hearing are denied, a large amount of knowledge may be acquired by smell and feeling. Persons in this unfortunate condition have been known to select their own clothes, out of a pile of clean linen, by smell. The most remarkable instance on record of the education of a person under these circumstances, is found in the case of Laura Bridgman, who has been for several years under the care of Dr. Samuel G. Howe, of the Massachusetts Asylum for the Blind. She has from infancy been deprived both of hearing and sight. She has, nevertheless, been taught the alphabet for the blind; she converses rapidly with her fingers, writes very intelligibly, and uses the language which designates the qualities of color and sound with considerable accuracy, knows her friends and instructors, and feels for them every sentiment of gratitude and affection.

It will readily occur to every one that great use may be made of acquired perceptions in the practice of the various arts and professions. We thus are enabled to determine facts and form judgments which would otherwise be impossible. An illustration of this kind presents itself in the use of the stethoscope, a small ear-trumpet, by means of which physicians listen to the sound made by the lungs in breathing, and by the heart in pulsation. A few years since. it was observed that these sounds varied with the con dition of these organs in health and in disease. This observation led to a very important result. First, the sound made by the lungs in health was distinctly ascertained. Then the variations from it were noticed. If the disease terminated in death, the condition of the lungs was ascertained by inspection. The sound was thus associated with the particular disease which occasioned it. This mode of observation was continued until almost every form of disease in the chest was recognized and made to speak an audible language. When this language has been learned by one man, it can be taught to another; and thus this important means of acquiring knowledge has become common to physicians. Practitioners, who have paid sufficient attention to this subject, and who are endowed with great delicacy of hearing, have been able to discover with remarkable accuracy the condition of the organs of the chest, the form of disease under which the patient has been laboring, and even to mark out on the surface the precise portion of the lungs which was suffering from inflammation.

The manner in which our acquired perceptions may be improved is manifestly as follows. In the first place, we learn to observe with the greatest accuracy the minutest differences in the impressions made upon our organs of sense. We are thus enabled to discover the slightest change of color or of outline, the minutest differences in hardness, smoothness or temperature, and the almost imperceptible variations in sound and interval. The nicer our discrimination in these respects becomes, the wider is the field of observation open to discovery. In this respect, much must depend upon the original perfection of the organs themselves: but that more depends upon careful cultivation, is evident from the fact that whole tribes of savages, of by no means delicate organization, attain to remarkable accuracy in the use of their organs of sense.

Secondly, we must learn to associate with each variation observed by one sense, the quality or condition discovered by another sense. In this manner we acquire the language of nature, and are enabled to interpret it for our own benefit and the benefit of others. We are thus able to form judgments which, to the uninitiated, seem like the result of magic. Thus, distinctness and indistinctness of color and outline teach us the magnitude and distance of objects many miles off. Thus the Indian, by observing minute differences of sound, will form an accurate judgment under circumstances which would leave other men wholly in darkness.

The physician, by placing his ear on the chest of his patient, can tell whether the organs within are healthy or diseased, and can thus the better employ such means of cure as will accomplish the result which he proposes.

It is hardly necessary to remark that the progress of the arts enables us to cultivate our acquired perceptions with greater success. The microscope and the telescope have greatly increased our power in this respect. Instruments for observing infinitesimal changes in temperature will probably lead to similar results. The tendency of science is in this direction, and it will, without doubt, lead to a rich harvest of discovery.

Before closing this section, it is proper to remark, that in the use of acquired perceptions we are liable to form false judgments, and then to complain that our senses have deceived us. I once saw, on a door-post, the painting of a key hanging on a nail, and it was so well executed that I was not aware of the deception until I attempted to take it down. Here it might be said that my senses deceived me, but such was not the fact. My eyes testified truly to all that they promised to make known. They testified to a certain color and shading. This evidence was in its nature ambiguous, for the effect might be produced either by a painting or by a real key. Without sufficient attention, I inferred that it was a key, when I ought to have examined it more carefully. But my senses did not deceive me, for the eye testified truly, and when I applied to another sense, it enabled me to form a true judgment. I was misled by my own negligence, and not by any defect in my senses. I ought, perhaps, to add that the deception in this case was aided by my companion, who directed my attention to the door, and asked me to hand him the key that he might open it. Had it not been for this circumstance, I should probably have discovered the truth from the effect of binocular vision. It will be found that all the cases which are commonly ascribed to deception of the senses are of the same character as that to which I have here referred. Our senses always testify truly, but we sometimes deceive ourselves by the inference which we draw from their evidence. The defect resides in our inference, and not in our senses, for it is by the use of our senses, alone, that we are enabled to correct the error into which we have fallen by our own inadvertence.

REFERENCES.

Original and acquired perceptions — Reid's Inquiry, chap. 6, sec. 20–23. Abercrombie, Part II., sec. 1.

Improvement of the senses — Reid, Essays on the Intellectual Powers Essay 2, sec. 21.

SECTION X. — OF THE NATURE OF THE KNOWLEDGE WHICH WE ACQUIRE BY THE PERCEPTIVE POWERS.

Having, in the preceding sections, treated of the manner in which our knowledge of the external world is acquired,

I propose, in the present section, to offer some suggestions on the nature of this knowledge.

1. The knowledge which we acquire by perception is always of individuals. If we see several trees, we see them not as a class, but as separate and distinct objects of perception. If we see several men, as John, James, Edward, we see each one as a distinct individual. The same remark applies to the acts which we observe. We see John strike James; that is, we see a particular individual perform a particular act. We thus see, that while, from the knowledge gained by the perceptive faculties, we subsequently form genera and species, yet, without the aid of some other powers of the mind, to form genera and species would be impossible. Our several items of knowledge would be like separate grains of sand, without cohesion and without affinity.

2. The knowledge derived from the perceptive powers is always knowledge of the concrete. When we perceive a body, we do not cognize the color, figure, temperature, etc., each as an abstract quality, and then afterwards unite them in one conception; but we perceive a body, colored, of such a figure and temperature; that is, a body in which all these qualities are united. The first impression made upon us is the cognition of an external object possessing all these qualities; or, at least, so many as are cognizable by the senses which are at the time directed towards them. We have the power of separating these qualities, in thought, the one from the other, and of making each of them a distinct object of attention. This, however, is the function of a faculty of the mind to be treated of hereafter.

3. Of primary and secondary qualities.

It has been already stated that our knowledge is of qualities, not of essences. We do not cognize the objects around us absolutely, we cognize them as possessed of certain means of affecting us, and thus giving us notice of the modes of their existence.

The qualities of matter have, of old, been divided into two classes, which, at a later period, have been denominated primary and secondary. The primary qualities are those which, by necessity, enter into our notion of matter; which we must conceive of as belonging to body, as soon as we conceive of body at all. Such are extension, divisibility, magnitude, figure, solidity, and mobility. We cannot think of matter, without involving these qualities in our very notion of it. If we conceive of matter as the only thing created, before any sentient being was created to cognize it, we think of it as possessing all these qualities in as perfect a manner as at present.

The secondary qualities are those which are not necessary to our conception of matter as matter, yet which give it the power of variously affecting us as sentient beings possessed of such or such an organism. Such are smell, taste, sound, color, hardness, softness, and many others. These might all be absent, or wholly unrecognized, and yet our idea of matter as matter would be definite and precise. They are only cognized by means of their appropriate media. If the media had not been created, no conception of them could ever have been formed. We cognize them only by means of our peculiar organism. Had this organism been created of a different character, these qualities could never have been known. Of the primary qualities themselves we form a definite idea; we know that they are what they seem to us to be. Of the secondary qualities, in themselves, we know nothing more than this, that some occult cause possesses the power of affecting us by means of our senses in this or that manner, or of creating in us such or such cognitions.

These secondary qualities have been, more lately, very

properly divided into two classes. First, those which we cognize by their relation to our own organism: and, secondly, those which we cognize by their relations to other bodies. Thus, malleability, ductility, and various other qualities, are cognized by the action of various metals on each other. Gold and steel are, to our organism, equally unmalleable; that is, we can make no impression upon either by voluntary effort. But when gold is brought into forcible contact with steel, its quality becomes manifest. The same is true of brittleness, and various other qualities.

Sir William Hamilton, after examining this subject with unsurpassed acuteness, has suggested another classification of the qualities of matter. It will be found, treated of in full in note D to his edition of the works of Dr. Reid. To pursue the subject at length, would be impossible within the limits that must be assigned to the present work. I shall attempt no more than to present a condensed view of some of the most important elements of his classification.

Sir William Hamilton divides the qualities of matter into three classes. First, primary or objective; second, secundo-primary or subjecto-objective; and third, secondary or subjective qualities. The primary are objective, not subjective, percepts proper, not sensations proper; the secundo-primary are both objective and subjective, percepts proper and sensations proper; the secondary are subjective, not objective, sensations proper, not percepts proper.

1. Of the primary qualities.

These are all deducible from two elementary ideas. We are unable to conceive of a body except, first, as occupying space, and second, as contained in space. From the first of these follow, by necessary explication, extension divisibility, size, density or rarity, and figure; from the second are explicated incompressibility absolute, mobility, situation.

2. The secundo-primary.

These have two phases, both immediately apprehended. "On their primary or objective phasis, they manifest themselves as *degrees* of resistance opposed to our locomotive energy; on their secondary or subjective phasis, as *modes* of resistance, a presence affecting our sentient organism." "Considered physically, or in an objective relation, they are to be reduced to classes corresponding to the different sources, in external nature, from which resistance or pressure springs. These sources are three.

I. Co-attraction. II. Repulsion. III. Inertia.

From co-attraction result gravity and cohesion.

From gravity result heavy and light.

From cohesion follow, 1. Hard and soft; 2. Firm and fluid; 3. Viscid and friable; 4. Tough and brittle; 5. Rigid and flexible; 6. Fissile and infissile; 7. Ductile and inductile; 8. Retractile and irretractile; 9. Rough and smooth; 10. Slippery and tenacious.

From repulsion are evolved, 1. Compressible and incompressible; 2. Resilient and irresilient.

From inertia are evolved, Movable and Immovable.

3. The secondary qualities.

"These are not, in propriety, qualities of bodies at all. As apprehended, they are only subjective affections, and belong only to bodies in so far as these are supposed furnished with the powers capable of specifically determining the various parts of our nervous apparatus to the particular action, or rather passion, of which they are susceptible; which determined action or passion is the quality of which we are immediately cognizant; the external concause of that internal effect remaining to the perception altogether unknown."

"Of the secondary qualities," that is, those phenomenal affections determined in our sentient organism by the agency of external bodies, "there are various kinds; the variety principally depending on the differences of the different parts of our nervous apparatus. Such are the proper sensibles, the idiopathic affections of our several organs of sense, as color, sound, flavor, savor, and tactual sensation; such are the feelings from heat, electricity, galvanism, etc., and the muscular and cutaneous sensations which accompany the perception of the secundo-primary qualities. Such, though less directly the result of foreign causes, are titillation, sneezing, horripilation, shuddering, the feeling of what is called setting the teeth on edge, etc. etc. Such, in fine, are all the various sensations of bodily pleasure and pain, determined by the action of external stimuli."

Concerning these in general, it may be remarked,

1. "The primary are qualities, only as we conceive them to distinguish body from not-body; they are the attributes of body as body, *corporis ut corpus*. The secondary and secundo-primary are more properly denominated qualities, for they discriminate body from body. They are the attributes of body, as this or that kind of body, *corporis ut tale corpus*."

2. "The primary arise from the universal relations of body to itself; the secundo-primary, from the general relations of this body to that; the secondary, from the special relations of this kind of body to this or that kind of sentient organism.

3. "Under the primary we apprehend the modes of the non ego; under the secundo-primary we apprehend the modes both of the ego and the non ego; under the secondary we apprehend modes of the ego, and infer modes of the non ego.

4. "The primary are apprehended as they are in bodies; the secondary, as they are in us; the secundo-primary, as they are in bodies and as they are in us.

5. "The terms designating primary qualities are univocal,

marking out one quality; those designating the secundo-primary and secondary are equivocal, denoting both a mode of existence in bodies and a mode of affection in our organism."

Of these qualities, in particular, considered as in bodies,

1. "The primary are the qualities of a body in relation to our organism as a body simply; the secundo-primary are the qualities of a body in relation to our organism as a propelling, resisting, cohesive body; the secondary are the qualities of body in relation to our organism as an idiopathically excitable and sentient body.

2. "The primary are known immediately in themselves; the secundo-primary, both immediately in themselves and mediately in their effects on us; the secondary, only mediately in their effects on us.

3. "The primary are apprehended objects; the secondary, inferred powers; the secundo-primary, both apprehended objects and inferred powers.

4. "The primary are conceived as necessary and perceived as actual; the secundo-primary are perceived and conceived as actual; the secondary are inferred and conceived as possible.

5. "The primary may be roundly characterized as mathematical; the secundo-primary, as mechanical; the secondary, as physiological."

Of these qualities, considered as cognitions,

1. "We are conscious as objects, in the primary qualities, of the modes of the not-self; in the secondary, of the modes of a self; in the secundo-primary, of the modes of a self and a not-self, at once.

2. "Using the terms strictly, the apprehensions of the primary are perceptions, not sensations; of the secondary, sensations, not perceptions; of secundo-primary, sensations and perceptions together.

3. "In the primary there is thus no concomitant second-

ary quality; in the secondary, no concomitant primary quality; in the secundo-primary, a secondary and quasi-primary quality accompany each other.

4. "In the apprehension of the primary, there is no subject-object determined by the object-object; in the secundo-primary, there is a subject-object determined by the object-object; in the secondary, the subject-object is the only object of immediate cognition."

I have not, in the above quotations, inserted all the acute and valuable distinctions of our author. I have selected those only which seemed to me the most important, and which discriminate most clearly the characteristic elements of these modes of cognition. For a more extended view of the subject I must refer the reader to the work itself, where he will find every distinction wrought out with a power of metaphysical analysis which has never been surpassed.

In regard to Sir William's classification, if I may hazard an opinion, I think that his distinctions are rendered obvious and beyond dispute. Whether his classification includes all the secundo-primary qualities, I am by no means certain. In so far as these qualities are apprehended by their effects on our organism, his classification appears exhaustive. But what shall we say of that class of qualities which arise from the relations of insentient bodies to each other, as malleability, chemical affinity, and various others? These are not known by any impression on our organism, as a propelling, resisting, cohesive body. They are not primary qualities. They are not cognized by our idiopathic sentient organism. They must be secundo-primary, but I think are not included in our author's classification.

4. Leaving now the subject of primary and secondary qualities, I proceed to remark, that the knowledge derived from

perception is truly knowledge; that is, the evidence of our senses is worthy of belief.

Thus, I open my eyes, and I perceive before me a book I put forth my hands, and feel of it. My perceptions perfectly coincide. They both testify to the existence of an external object, numerically distinct from myself, of such a magnitude, form, situation. I am conscious of a state of mind which I call perception; and of that state of mind one of the elements is an unalterable conviction that the object exists now and here, just as I perceive it. This conviction is a necessary part of my state of mind, if, indeed, it be not the state of mind itself. This conscious perception is to me the knowledge that this book exists. If I am asked why I believe thus, or have this conviction, I can give no other account of it than that I am so made It is a cognition given me in virtue of my creation. If I am asked to prove it, I must plead my inability to do so. I can prove no proposition except by some other proposition of higher authority. But there is no proposition of higher authority than this cognition given me by my Creator, who made me so that, under certain conditions, I cannot choose but have it. If I am asked to prove that I exist, I am unable to do it for the same reason, namely, that I have no more evident proposition which can be used as a medium of proof. I am so made that the existence of an external world is revealed to me at the same time and just as obtrusively as my own existence. By the constitution of my mind, the one fact is as clearly revealed to me as the other.

But this subject is capable of more extended illustration and explication.

1. "Our cognitions, it is evident, are not all at second hand." Demonstration must at last rest upon propositions which carry their own evidence, and necessitate their own admission. Were it otherwise, were there no truths *which*

revealed themselves to the human mind, all proof would be nugatory; it would be a succession of arguments, each one resting on something yet to be proved. Some truth must then be given to us in our creation as intelligent beings, on which we may found our reasoning, and from which all demonstration must proceed.

If it be asked, how do these primary cognitions assure us of their truth and certify us of their verity, the only answer is that they are results of our mental constitution. As soon as a human mind apprehends them, without argument or proof, it immediately knows them to be true. The only answer we can give to him who asks us a reason of these beliefs is, that we are so made, we are created to believe them. To suppose their falsehood, is to suppose that we are created thus simply in order that we may be deceived. And as, besides this, it is upon these beliefs that all subsequent knowledge is founded, if we deny them, all knowledge is a delusion, and truth and falsehood are unmeaning terms. This, surely, without any proof, cannot be asserted; and, hence, I think it must be conceded that we must in the first instance receive these beliefs as true, until they are shown to be false, and just in so far as they are shown to be false. That we do thus by the constitution of our nature believe in the testimony of our senses, that we do thus universally admit it, is, I think, beyond controversy. It is, therefore, to be believed until it is shown to be unfounded.

But it may possibly be denied that this belief is one of those given us by our creation, or one of the first truths revealed to the common sense of man by virtue of his intellectual constitution. What, then, are the characteristics by which these truths may be known?

Sir W. Hamilton reduces these characteristics to the four following:

1. *They are incomprehensible.* "A conviction is in

comprehensible when there is merely given us in consciousness *that its object is*, and when we are unable to comprehend, through a higher notion or belief, *why or how it is*.

"When we are able to comprehend why or how a thing is, the belief of the existence of that thing is not a primary datum of consciousness, but a subsumption under the condition or belief which affords its reason."

2. *They are simple.* "It is manifest that if a cognition or belief be made up of, and can be explicated into, a plurality of cognitions or beliefs, that, as compound, it cannot be original."

3. *They are necessary and universal* "If necessary, they must, of course, be universal. The necessity here spoken of is of two kinds. The first kind is when we cannot construe it to our minds that the deliverance of consciousness is not true, or when the opposite of the assertion is unthinkable. Thus the proposition that a part is greater than the whole, or that two straight lines can at the same time be parallel and at right angles in the same plane, is unthinkable. There is another necessity, however, which is not unthinkable, when the deliverance of consciousness may be false, but when, at the same time, we cannot but admit that it is of such or such an import. This is the case in contingent truths, or what may be called matters of fact. In this case, the thing is not conceived as absolutely impossible, but impossible under the present constitution of things, or we being as we are. Thus, I can theoretically suppose that the external object of which I am conscious in perception may be in reality nothing but a mode of mind, or self. I am unable, however, to think that consciousness does not compel me to regard it *as* external, as a mode of matter or not self. Such being the case, I cannot practically believe the supposition which I am able speculatively to maintain; for I cannot believe this supposition without believing that

the last ground of all belief is not to be believed, which is self-contradictory.

4. *Their comparative evidence and certainty.* "These truths are so clear and obvious that nothing more clear or obvious can be conceived by which to prove them." According to Buffier, they "are so clear, that if we attempt to prove or disprove them, this can be done only by propositions which are manifestly neither more evident nor more certain."

Now, so far as I can perceive, all these characteristics belong to the deliverance of consciousness in perception. They are incomprehensible, simple, practically necessary, and of such clearness of manifestation that they can neither be proved nor disproved by anything more evident. We are then entitled to consider them first truths, or truths revealed to man in the constitution of his nature. If such deliverances are not to be believed, then nothing is to be believed, and all knowledge is essentially impossible.

But the subject may be finally considered from another point of view.

The data of consciousness may be considered as two-fold.

1. "As apprehended facts or actual manifestations." As when I say, I see a tree, or I feel a cube, there is an actual manifestation to me that I am in that particular state of mind described by these words. Consciousness reveals to me that fact as the present state of my mind.

2. "These deliverances of consciousness may be considered as testimonies to the truth of facts beyond their own phenomenal reality." These acts of consciousness are the testimonies to the fact that that tree and that cube are now existing. It is, however, to be observed that the testimony to the existence of this state of mind, and to the existence of the tree which this state of mind cognizes, is given us in the same act.

The truth of this first testimony of consciousness is admitted by all. When consciousness testifies that I am now in a mental state which I call perception, it cannot be doubted that such is the fact. The doubt, in this case, is clearly suicidal. The state of mind called perception is attested by consciousness. The state which I call doubting is attested by the same consciousness. If, then, consciousness is not to be believed when it testifies to perception, neither is it to be believed when it testifies to doubting. So that, if a man doubts whether he is really in the state of mind called perception, he must equally doubt whether he is in the state of mind which he calls doubting. He must doubt whether he doubts, just as much as he doubts whether he perceives, meaning, by this term, a mere subjective act, a state of the thinking subject.

There may, however, be without absurdity a doubt as to the other part of the act; that is, to the truth of this testimony as to something numerically different from the subject. It may be said that this is merely a subjective state of the mind itself; that it is merely a form of the *ego* produced by the action of some subjective cause, and that it gives us no knowledge of anything external.

To this objection it may be answered,

1. "It cannot but be acknowledged that the veracity of consciousness must, at least in the first instance, be conceded. *Neganti incumbit probatio.* Nature is not gratuitously to be assumed to work, not only in vain, but in counteraction of herself. Our faculty of knowledge is not, without a ground, to be supposed an instrument of illusion. Man, unless the melancholy fact be proved, is not to be held organized for the attainment and actuated by the love of truth, only to become the dupe and victim of a perfidious Creator."

2. "But, granting that these convictions are at the be-

ginning to be received as true, it is yet competent to attempt to prove them false, and thus correct an error into which we have been led by our constitution. But how shall this be done? As the ultimate grounds of knowledge, these convictions cannot be redargued from any higher knowledge; and as derivative beliefs they are paramount in certainty to every derivative knowledge. They cannot, therefore, be disproved by knowledge derived from any other source, for the most certain knowledge which we possess must rest upon the same foundation as the testimony of our own consciousness."

3. "If, then, these convictions be disproved, they must be disproved by themselves. This can be done only by one of two methods. First, it must be shown that these primary data are directly and immediately contradictory of themselves." "They are many, they are in authority co-ordinate, and their testimony is clear and precise." Now, if this testimony is intellectually or in fact, at variance, then we must conclude either that one or the other, or both, testimonies are false. Or, secondly, it must be proved "that they are mediately or indirectly contradictory, inasmuch as the consequences to which they necessarily lead, and for the truth or falsehood of which they are therefore responsible, are repugnant. In no other way can the veracity of consciousness be assailed. It will argue nothing to show that they are incomprehensible, for nothing can be more absurd than to make the comprehensibility of a datum of consciousness, the criterion of its truth. To ask how an immediate fact of consciousness is possible, is to ask how consciousness is possible; and to ask how consciousness is possible, is to suppose we have another consciousness above and before that human consciousness concerning whose mode of operation we inquire. Could we answer this, verily we should be as gods." Neither of these attempts has ever been

made. We may, therefore, receive the testimony of consciousness as true beyond the reach of argument or contradiction.

4. And, lastly, consciousness testifies to two things: first that there is now existing a state of mind; and, secondly that that state of mind is an actual cognition of an external world possessing such or such qualities. Suppose we admit the first testimony; how, then, admitting this, can we reject the other testimony of which it forms a part? What distinction can we take between the two items of the same testimony, by which we can receive the one and reject the other. Or, on the other hand, suppose we deny the testimony of consciousness to the truth of the perception, how can we admit it when it attests to an existing state of mind? If the one is false, the other may be true, but it is surely not to be credited. Thus the very facts of our subjective existence would be shown to be unworthy of belief, and the evidence of the existence of the ego and the non ego would be swept away together.

In this and the preceding article I have used the thoughts, and, for the most part, the language of Sir W. Hamilton. It gives me pleasure to acknowledge my obligations to a gentleman, whose boundless learning in every department of human knowledge, united with unrivalled acuteness and rare power of examining with perfect distinctness the minutest shades of thought, have long since given him a position among the profoundest philosophers of this or any other age.

5. I close this section with a few remarks upon the law of perception in its relation to evidence. This law may be stated in few words.

1. When all our faculties are in a normal state, and an appropriate object is presented to an organ of sense, a sensation or a perception immediately ensues. We cannot by

our will prevent it. If I open my eyes, I cannot escape the sight of the object before me. If a sound is made, near to me, I cannot by my will prevent hearing it; and the same is true of all other senses.

2. On the other hand, my faculties being in their normal condition, if no object is presented to my organs of sense, I can perceive none. I cannot perceive what I will, but only what is presented to me. I cannot see a tree, unless a tree is before me. I cannot hear a sound, unless a sound is produced within hearing; and so of the rest.

3. Hence it follows that if, under normal conditions, I am conscious of perceiving an external object, then that object exists when and where I perceive it. The conscious perception could exist under no other conditions. It is a fact which admits of being accounted for in no other manner. And, on the other hand, if, under normal circumstances, I perceive no object, then no object exists to be perceived.

These simple laws lie at the foundation of the evidence of testimony. If we perceive an event, we know that that event is transpiring. If we remember that we perceived it, we know that it has transpired. So, if we are satisfied that credible witnesses were conscious of perceiving an object, we know that the object existed as perceived. If under circumstances, such that if it were present they must have perceived it, and they were conscious of no perception, then we know that the object was not present. The further consideration of the conditions by which these laws are limited belongs to the science of evidence. The statement of the law itself is all that concerns to our present inquiry.

Within a few years past various statements have been made which seem to modify the above laws. It has been asserted that persons, under the influence of what is called mesmerism, can be rendered perfectly unconscious of what is passing around them; that they are able to cognize persons and events without the intervention of the appropriate media, and under circumstances which render it certain that such cognitions could not have originated in the ordinary use of the organs of sense. This subject has attracted considerable attention, both in this country and in Europe. Sir W. Hamilton remarks: "However astonishing, it is now proved, beyond all rational doubt, that, in certain abnormal states of the nervous organism, perceptions are possible through other than the ordinary channels of the senses."—Hamilton's Reid, page 246, note 2, Edinburgh edition.

It has been, I believe, proved beyond dispute, that patients under this influence have submitted to the most distressing operations without consciousness of pain; that other persons have cognized events at a great distance, and have related them correctly at the time; and that persons totally blind, when in the state of mesmeric consciousness have enjoyed for the time the power of perceiving external objects. So far as I have been informed, while these distant cognitions are sometimes correct, they are as frequently wholly erroneous, and the person is totally unable to distinguish the true from the false. The subject seems to me well worthy of the most searching and candid examination. The facts seem to indicate some more general laws of external cognition than have yet been discovered. The matter is by no means deserving of ridicule, but demands the attention of the most philosophical inquirers.

REFERENCES.

Knowledge acquired by perception is of individuals — Locke, Book 4, chap. 7, sec. 9; Reid, Essay 5, chap. 1.

The knowledge acquired by perception is real — Reid, Essay 2, chaps. 5 and 20

Primary and secondary qualities — Locke, book 2d, chap. 8, sec. 9, 10, 23, 24 ; Reid, Essay 2d, ch. 17 ; Cousin, ch. 6.

Sir W. Hamilton, Dissertation supplementary to Reid ; note D.

Laws of Perception — Reid, Essay 2d, ch. 1, 2.

The credibility of the evidence of perception demonstrated — Sir W Hamilton's Dissertation on Common Sense. Note A, as above.

SECTION XI. — OF CONCEPTION.

THE subject of conception is, in its origin, so intimately allied to perception, that, although it enters as a constituent element into almost every act of the mind, there seems a propriety in treating of it here.

The word conception has already frequently occurred in the preceding pages. It is proper that it should be more definitely explained.

Conception has been defined as that act of the mind in which we form a notion or thought of a thing. To this, however, it has been objected, that the word notion or thought in this place means the same as conception, and that we might with the same propriety reverse the definition, and say that the having a notion of a thing was the forming a conception of it. There seems to be force in this objection. The fact is, that a simple act of the mind is incapable of definition. We can do no more than present the circumstances under which it arises, and our own consciousness at once teaches us what is meant.

1. To proceed in this manner, then, I would observe that when I look upon a book, or any external object, I instantly form a notion of it, of a particular kind. I know it as an external body, numerically distinct from myself, of a certain form color and magnitude, at this moment and in this place existing before me. When I handle a book, I have the

same notion, the quality of color only excepted. This knowledge is called perception.

2. Secondly, I find that when the object of perception is removed, and the act of perception ceases, a knowledge of the object is still present to my mind. This is called a conception. Thus, the book which I just now perceived is removed, but the conception of it is still an object of consciousness. A cube which I saw is burned to ashes, but I have a distinct conception of its form and dimensions. I can recall to my mind the cataract which I saw last summer, the house in which I slept, or particular portions of the road over which I passed. In these cases, however, the conception is not simple; it is combined with the act of memory. I have not only the conception, but the assurance or belief, that at a certain time these objects actually existed as I now conceive of them.

3. But let us now separate this act of conception from the act of memory. We can conceive of a tree or a cataract without connecting it with the idea either of present or past existence. We are doing this continually in the course of our own thoughts. We do it when we read a romance. We are here continually forming images of things, places, and persons, which we know never existed. So, in a geometrical demonstration, we form for ourselves the conception of a figure, and proceed to reason upon it, though we have never seen it represented to the eye.* A concept or concep-

* The word conception is commonly used in two or three significations. It is employed to designate the power or faculty, the individual act of that faculty, and that act considered as an object of thought. On this subject Sir W. Hamilton remarks, "We ought to distinguish *imagination* and *image*, *conception* and *concept*. Imagination and conception ought to be employed in speaking of the mental modification, one and indivisible, considered as an act; image and concept, in speaking of it, considered as product or immediate object." — Note to page 263.

tion is, therefore, that representation or cognition of a thing which we form in the mind when we are thinking of it.

4. Again, when we think of an act of the mind as thinking, willing, believing, or of any emotion, as joy or sorrow, we form a conception of it. We cannot think it unless we can do this. Hence, when a state of mind is spoken of which we cannot represent to ourselves in thought, we say we cannot conceive of it; that is, the words spoken do not awaken in us any corresponding conception.

5. Again, by the faculty of abstraction we may analyze the elements of these concrete conceptions, and combine them into general or abstract ideas. Thus, from several individual horses we form the general notion of a horse, meaning the genus, and having respect to no individual horse existing. These are general conceptions, or conceptions of genera or species.

6. We have also conceptions of general intuitive truths, such as the axioms of mathematics. We conceive of the truth that the whole is greater than its part, or that if equals be added to equals the wholes are equal. So we form conceptions of general relations, as of cause and effect, power, and many others.

7. Lastly, we are able to form images by combining into one whole, elements previously existing in the mind, as when a painter conceives of a landscape, or of a historical group. This form of conception is more properly styled imagination.

In all cases of conception where the act is completed, if I do not mistake, we form something of the nature of a picture, which the mind contemplates as the object of thought. I am aware that, in speaking and writing, when the terms are perfectly familiar, we do not pause and form the conception. Thus, we use the axioms, in demonstration, without pausing to reflect upon the words we employ, and yet we use them with entire accuracy. Thus we speak of cause and effect, number, and various other ideas. When, however, we attempt to dwell upon any one of these ideas, so far as I can observe, we form a concept of it in the mind. Thus, when I think of the term horse as a genus, and dwell upon it in thought, there is before me, as an object, a concept of such an animal. So, if I think the axiom the whole is greater than its part, two magnitudes corresponding to these terms present themselves before me. From this remark, however, must be excepted those cases in which we recognize a truth as a necessary condition of thought, as duration, space, and ideas of a similar character. Even here, however, we find the mind from its natural impulse striving to realize something which shall correspond to a concept.

Of conceptions thus explained it may be remarked in general:

1. In conception there is nothing numerically distinct from the act of the mind itself. From the analogies of language we are liable to be misled in thinking of this subject. We speak of forming a conception, and of forming a machine; of separating the elements of a conception, and of separating the parts of an object from one another. As in the one case there is some object distinct from the *ego*, we are prone to suppose that there must be also in the other. There is, however, in conception nothing but the act of the mind itself. We may, nevertheless, contemplate this act from different points of view; first, as an act of the mind, or as the mind in this particular act, and, secondly, as a product of that act which we use in thinking. There is, however, numerically nothing but the act of the mind itself.

2. Conception enters into all the other acts of the mind. In the simplest sensation there is, for the time being, a knowledge or a notion, though it may remain with us not a

moment after the object producing it is withdrawn. We can have a knowledge of our own powers only as we have conceptions of them. We can remember, or judge, or reason, only as we have conceptions. In fact, all our mental processes are about conceptions. Of them, all our knowledge consists.

3. Our conceptions are to us the measure of possibility. When any proposition cannot be conceived, that is, is unthinkable, we declare it impossible or absurd. Thus, if it be said that a part is greater than the whole, that two straight lines can enclose space, or that a change can take place in a body while all the conditions of its existence remain absolutely the same, I understand the assertion; but when I attempt to form a conception of it, that is, to think it, I find myself unable to do so. I affirm it to be impossible. On the other hand, I may think of a communication between the earth and the moon. In the present state of science it is impracticable, but it is within the limits of thought, and my mind is not so organized that I feel it to be impossible. This case, is, however, to be distinguished from the unconditional, the incomprehensible. This, from the nature of our intellect, we know to be necessary; it is not contradictory to thought, though to grasp the conception is impossible. In the other case we are able to comprehend the terms, but we are unable to construe them in thought; in other words, the relation which is affirmed is unthinkable.

4. In simple conception, or where it is unattended by any other act of the mind, there is neither truth nor false hood. I may conceive of a red mountain, of a blue rose, of a winged horse, but the conception has nothing to do with my belief in the existence of either of these objects. If the conception is united with an act of judgment or memory, then it at once becomes either true r false. In the concep-

tion itself, however, I can discover neither. Stewart, I know, advances a contrary opinion ; but I must confess myself wholly unconvinced by his reasoning.

5. Conceptions may be either clear and distinct, or obscure and indistinct. We easily observe the difference here spoken of in the effects produced on us by different descriptions. Some authors describe a scene with so graphic a power that we at once form a conception as definite as though we had ourselves beheld it. Others use emphatic and imposing language, but they leave on us no distinct impression. We are deluged by a shower of words, but no conception is imprinted on the memory.

6. Conceptions may be strong and vivid, or faint and languid. The same scene may with equal faithfulness be described to us by two persons. The one deeply affects us, while the other hardly interests us sufficiently to command our continued attention. We observe the same effect in ourselves, resulting from the accidental tone of our own minds. At some times we find our conceptions much stronger than at others, under precisely the same external circumstances.

From what has been observed, it will readily appear that the power of forming conceptions differs greatly in different individuals. Every teacher must have remarked this fact, in his attempts to communicate instruction. Some persons will at once seize upon the salient points of a conception, discover its bearing and relations, and hold it steadily before the mind, until it becomes incorporated with their knowledge. They never can be satisfied until they have attained to this result. Others require repeated explanations, and, when they suppose themselves to have mastered a conception, we are surprised to observe that no important point seems to have arrested their attention, but that there rest on their minds only considerations of inferior importance blended together in dim and uncertain confusion.

The difference, in this respect, is still more remarkable in the connection of conception with the fine arts, though perhaps this exercise of the power belongs rather to the imagination. A portrait-painter will form so distinct a conception of a countenance that, years afterward, he will represent it correctly on canvas. The same power of forming distinct conceptions is essential to the poet or novelist. No one can read the descriptions of Sir Walter Scott without being sensible of his high endowment in this respect. Nor was this power limited to the scenes which he himself had witnessed. His description of a summer day in the deserts of Syria could not have been surpassed by the most gifted Bedouin Arab. It was to this power that he owed much of that brilliant conversational eminence, which rendered him the centre of attraction in every circle in which he chose to unbend himself.

REFERENCES.

Conception — Reid, Essay 1, chap. 1
- Formed at will — Reid, Essay 4, chap. 1.
- Enter into every other act of the mind — Reid, Essay 4, chap. 1.
- Neither true nor false — Reid, Essay 4, chap. 1.
- Ingredients derived from other powers — Reid, Essay 4, chap. 1.
- Analogy between painting and conception — Reid, Essay 4, chap. 1

Conception in general — Stewart, vol. i., chap. 3.
- Attended with belief — Stewart, vol. i., chap. 3.
- Power of description depends on — Stewart, vol. i., chap. 3.
- Improved by habit — Stewart, vol. i., chap. 3.

Conception — Abercrombie, Part 3, sect. 1.
- Clear or obscure — Abercrombie, Part 3, sect. 1.

In conception neither truth nor falsehood — Locke, Book 2d, chap 22 sects. 1—4, 19, 20.
- Clear or obscure — Locke, Book 2, ch. 29, sect. 1

CHAPTER II.

CONSCIOUSNESS, ATTENTION, AND REFLECTION.

SECTION I.—CONSCIOUSNESS.

CONSCIOUSNESS is that condition of the mind in which it is cognizant of its own operations. It is not thinking and feeling, but that condition in which we know that we think or feel. Thought, however, is necessary to consciousness, for unless thought existed, we could not be conscious of it. We may nevertheless suppose a mental act to be performed of which we have no consciousness. In such a case we should have no knowledge of its present existence, and should only know that it had existed by its results.

On this subject, however, a considerable diversity of opinion obtains. Sir W. Hamilton and many philosophers of the highest authority believe that consciousness cannot properly be separated from the act to whose existence it testifies, and that to make a distinction between the assertions, "I perceive" and "I am conscious of perception," is impossible. They hold that when we are not conscious of an act, the act is not performed; and that when consciousness does not testify to anything, it is because there is nothing concerning which it can testify.

In answer to this, it may be granted that when it is said "I perceive," the meaning is the same as when I say "I am conscious of perceiving." When I say "I perceive," there is involved, by necessity, in this assertion, the evidence of consciousness. The question still returns, Is there a state of mind which involves perception, of which we are not conscious, and which is not expressed by the words "I am conscious that I perceive"?

Let us, then, proceed to examine the facts. A person may be engaged in reading, or in earnest thought, and a clock may strike within a few feet of him without arresting his attention. He will not know that it has struck. Let, now, another person ask him, within a few seconds, if the clock has struck, and he will be conscious of a more or less distinct impression that he has just heard it; and, turning to observe the dial-plate, finds such to have been the fact. What, now, was his state of mind previous to the question? Had there not been a perception of which he was not conscious?

But we may take a much stronger case. While a person is reading aloud to another, some train of thought frequently arrests his attention. He, however, continues to read, until his opinion is requested concerning some sentiment of the author. He is unpleasantly startled by the reflection that he has not the remotest conception of what he has been reading about. He remembers perfectly well up to a certain point, but beyond this point he is as ignorant of the book as if he had never seen it. What, then, was the state of his mind while he was reading? He looked upon the page. He must have seen every letter, for he enunciated every word, and observed every pause correctly. No one had a suspicion that he did not cognize the thoughts which he was enunciating to others. Yet, the moment afterwards, he has not the least knowledge either of the words or the ideas. Can we say that there was no perception here? Could a man read a sentence aloud without perceiving the words in which it was written? Yet, so far as we can discover, this state of mind was unattended by consciousness.

Another case of a very striking character, was related to me by the person to whom it refers. A few years since, while in London, I became acquainted with a gentleman who had, for many years, held the responsible office of short-hand writer to the House of Lords. In conversation one day, he mentioned to me the following occurrence. Some time during the last war with France, he was engaged in taking minutes of evidence in a court of inquiry respecting the Walcheren expedition. In this duty he was incessantly engaged from four o'clock in the afternoon until four o'clock the next morning. At two o'clock in the morning he was aroused from a state of unconsciousness by Sir James E., one of the members of the court, who asked him to read the minutes of the evidence of the last witness. It was the testimony of one of the general officers who had described the fortifications of Flushing. My friend, Mr. G., replied, with some embarrassment, "I fear I have not got it all." "Never mind," replied the officer, "begin, and we will help you out." The evidence consisted of two pages of short-hand, and Mr. G read it to the close. He remembered it all perfectly excepting the last four lines, of which he had no recollection whatever. These last lines were, however, written as legibly as the rest, and he read them without difficulty. When he came to the end, he turned to General E., saying, "Sir James, that is all I have." "That," replied the other, "is all there is; you have the whole of it perfectly." He had reported the evidence with entire accuracy up to the very moment when he was called upon to read, and yet the last four lines had been written, and written in short-hand, so far as he knew, during a period of perfect unconsciousness.

The condition of the mind which we term derangement conveys some instruction on this subject. Here, it is not uncommon for the patient to suppose that he is not the person speaking or acting, but some other, and that some other mind than his own is occupying his body and performing the intellectual operations, of which he is conscious. Thus, Pinel mentions the case of a man in France who imagined that he had been sentenced to death and guillotined; but that, after his execution, the judges reversed their decision, and ordered his head to be replaced; the executioner replaced the wrong head, and hence he was ever after thinking the thoughts of another man instead of his own. We have said that consciousness is that condition of the mind in which it becomes cognizant of its own operations; that is, we are cognizant, not only that certain intellectual operations are carried on, but that they are our own. In this case of deranged consciousness, the individual was aware that there were thoughts, desires, remembrances, &c., going on within him, but he could not recognize them as the operations of his own mind.

These cases would seem to show that a distinction may fairly be made between consciousness and the faculties to the operation of which it testifies. Yet it would scarcely seem proper to denominate it a faculty; I prefer to call it a condition of the mind.

Such being the nature of consciousness, it is of course unnecessary to specify the various kinds of knowledge which we cognize by means of it. If it be the condition necessary to the cognition of our mental operations, then all forms of thought are made known to us through this medium. Hence, as I have before suggested, to say I know, and to say I am conscious of knowing, mean the same thing: since the one cannot be true without involving the other.

Consciousness always has respect to the state of the mind itself, and not to anything external. We are not conscious of a tree, but conscious that we perceive the tree. We may be conscious of hearing a sound; we are not conscious of a sound. Those writers who deny the existence of consciousness as a condition distinguishable from the act to which it testifies, of course, adopt a different form of expression. They would say that I am conscious of a tree, or of a sound, assuming that perception in all its varieties is but so many forms of consciousness. I have no desire to enter upon a further discussion of this subject. So far, however, as I am able to observe the operations of my own mind, I am constrained to believe that the form of expression which I have used represents my act in perception more accurately than the other.

Consciousness has respect to the present, never to the past. We can be conscious of nothing that does not exist now and here. We may be conscious that we now remember the sunset of yesterday, but we cannot now be conscious of the perception of the sunset of yesterday. We may be conscious that we remember the appearance of an absent friend, but we cannot be conscious of the appearance of an absent friend.

In the normal condition of the mind, consciousness, without any effort of the will, is always in exercise, and is always bearing witness to the existence of our own mental acts. It may be turned off involuntarily from the object directly before us to some other, but, during our waking hours, it always bears witness to something. Hence, consciousness, united with memory, gives rise to the conviction of personal identity. We know by means of this faculty that certain thoughts and feelings exist, and that they are the thoughts and feelings of the being whom I denominate I, myself. Memory connects these various testimonies of consciousness into a connected series, and thus we know that our intellectual acts, from our earliest recollection, proceed from the same being, and not another. I thus know that the thoughts and feelings which I remember to have been conscious of yesterday are the thoughts and feelings of the same being who is conscious of other intellectual acts to-day; that is, that through all the changes of the present state, the *ego*, myself, is the same individual and continuous subject.

There have been observed occasionally abnormal cases of what may be termed double consciousness. In such a case, the present existence of the individual is at one time connected with one period of his life, and at another time with another. A young woman in Springfield, Mass., some years since, was affected in this manner. She was at first subject to attacks of what appeared to be ordinary somnambulism. These were then transferred from the night to the day-time, and during their continuance her powers of perception were in a strange manner modified. With her eyes thickly bandaged, in a dark room, she could read the finest print. She was removed to the hospital for the insane at Worcester, in order to be under the care of the late Dr. Woodward. Here it was immediately observed that her normal and abnormal states represented two conditions of consciousness. Whatever she learned in the abnormal state was entirely forgotten as soon as she passed from this state to the other, but was perfectly remembered as soon as the abnormal state returned. Thus she was taught to play backgammon in both states. What she learned in the abnormal state was entirely disconnected from what she learned in her natural state, and *vice versa*. The acquisition made in one state was lost as soon as she entered the other: and it was remarked that she learned more rapidly in the abnormal than in the normal state. The first symptom of her recovery was the blending together of the knowledge acquired in these separate conditions. As the cure advanced, they became more and more identified. until the testimony of consciousness became uninterrupted, and then the abnormal state vanished altogether. Several cases are also on record in which persons have been subject to this double consciousness without any manifestation of somnambulism. In such instances, the individual has suddenly awaked to a recollection of his former life, with the exception of a portion immediately preceding, of which he has no recollection. A period of his existence seems perfectly parenthetical, and his present consciousness connects itself only with that portion of his life which preceded the change in his condition. This peculiar affection will be best illustrated by an example. A few years since, a theological student, represented to be a person of unexceptionable character, was suddenly missing from a city in the interior of New York. All search for him was fruitless, and he was supposed to have been murdered. A few months afterwards, his friends received a letter from him, dated Liverpool, England. He stated that a short time before, he had found himself on board of a vessel bound from Montreal to Liverpool, without the least knowledge of the manner in which he came there. He recollected nothing from the time of his being in the city where he had last been seen by his friends. He however learned from his fellow-passengers that he had embarked on board the vessel at Montreal,— and he must have walked about two hundred miles in order to arrive there,— that he sometimes seemed peculiar on the passage, but that there had been nothing in his conduct to excite particular remark.

Consciousness suggests to us the notion of existence. When we are conscious of a sensation there immediately springs from it the idea of self-existence. The consciousness of a perception suggests the idea of the existence both of the object perceived, of the subject perceiving, and frequently of some particular condition of that subject. Thus, suppose I am looking upon a waterfall. I am conscious of cognizing an external object; I am conscious of the state of mind called perception, and I am conscious of the emotion of beauty or sublimity occasioned by the object which I perceive.

It is obviously in our power to contemplate at will either of these objects of thought. I may direct my attention to the external object, or to the internal mental act, or to the emotion which the object occasions. Thus, in the instance just mentioned, I may direct my whole power of thought to the observation of the waterfall. I may examine it so carefully and minutely, that its image is fixed in my remembrance forever. Or, on the other hand, I may turn my attention to my own intellectual state, and analyze the nature of the act of perception. Or, still more, after having become deeply impressed with the external object, I may contemplate my own emotions, and, following the train of thought which they awaken, may lose all consciousness of the perception of the object, wholly absorbed in the sensibilities which it has called into action. We may do either of these in any particular instance. We may from natural bias, or from the circumstances of education, form the habit of pursuing either the one or the other of these trains of thought.

Hence arises the distinction between objective and subjective writers. The objective writer describes with graphic power the appearances of external nature, the march of pageants, the shock of battles, and whatever addresses itself to the perceptive powers. This habit of mind is also of special importance in all the researches of physical science The subjective writer turns his thoughts inward, and either as a metaphysician, analyzes his own mental phenomena, or pours forth in the language of poetry the emotions of his soul. Thomson and Scott, especially the latter, are eminently objective. Young and Byron are equally subjective No one can compare a canto of the Lady of the Lake with a canto of Childe Harold, or with one of Young's Night Thoughts, without observing the difference which I am here attempting to illustrate.

It is, however, obvious that no writer can be either wholly objective or wholly subjective. Were two writers wholly objective, their representations of external nature would be exactly alike. But how dissimilar are the most objective passages of Scott, Thomson and Moore! Each one tinges every description with the hues of his own subjectivity. Nor, on the other hand, can the most subjective writer be wholly subjective. He needs some objective starting-point, and he will choose it in conformity with the peculiar bias of his mind, and pursue that line of thought which best harmonizes with his general temperament. Thus Young commences a train of subjective reflection by reference to an external object.

> " The bell strikes one ! We take no note of time
> But by its loss. To give it then a tongue
> Is wise in man. As if an angel spoke,
> I feel the solemn sound ! If heard aright,
> It is the knell of my departed hours."

Minds of the very highest endowment have the objective and the subjective equally at their command. Not only the descriptions of Shakspeare and Milton, but their delineations of human emotion, are the theme of universal eulogy. And we may also remark that for its power over the human heart genius depends less upon the circumstances by which it is surrounded, than upon its own inherent energies. Cowper has so described the bogs and fens of Olney, that we seem to have been contemplating a picturesque landscape; and "the turning up of a mouse's nest with the plough" is reflected back in images of affecting loveliness from the bosom of Burns.

SECTION II. — ATTENTION AND REFLECTION.

I HAVE remarked in the previous section that consciousness, in the ordinary states of the mind, is involuntary. We are sensible of no effort of the will when we either observe the objects around us, or are conscious of the mental changes taking place within us. I have also above alluded to the fact that we may make either the object perceived, or the state of the perceiving subject, an object of thought.

But, besides this, our consciousness may be accompanied by an act of the will. We may, for instance, will to examine, with the greatest possible care, an object of perception, as a mineral, or a flower, or some particular work of art. Excluding every other object of thought, the effort of the mind is concentrated upon the act of perception. We thus may discover qualities which we never before perceived. But in what respect does this state of mind differ from ordinary consciousness? The effort of the will cannot change the image formed on the retina; for it can exert no influence whatever on the laws of light to which this image is subjected. It must consist in a more intense consciousness, by which every impression made on the organ of sense is brought more directly before the mind. Our perception is excited and directed by an act of the will. This condition of mind, when directed to an external object, is properly called *Attention.*

The difference between consciousness and attention may, I think, be easily illustrated. In passing through a street, we are conscious of perceiving every house within the range of our vision. But let us now come to a row of buildings, one of which we desire to find, and which has been previously described to us. We examine every one of these houses earnestly and minutely. We can, if it be necessary describe every one of them with accuracy, while of the others which we have passed in our walk we can give no account whatever. We say that we have observed every house in that row *attentively*, but that on the others we bestowed no attention. Or, to take a too common instance; we read a book carelessly, we see every letter and form a conception of every sentence; but all is done listlessly, and we close the book hardly aware of a single idea that we have gained while we have been thus occupied. Let, however, our whole mental effort be directed to the subject on which we are reading, and we fix it in our recollection, and we can, at will, recall it and make it a matter of thought. We say of ourselves, that in the former case we read without and in the latter case with attention.

We sometimes, I think, speak of attention as practically distinguished from every other act of the mind. Thus, suppose we are striving to catch an indistinct sound that is occurring at intervals, we then listen with attention. We say to another person, "Give all your attention that is possible, and you may hear it." He may possibly reply, "I am all attention." Here we seem to recognize the condition of attention directed to no present object of perception, bu we merely place ourselves in a condition to perceive any object which presents itself.

Sometimes the object to which our thought is directed is internal; that is, it is some state of the mind itself. Ordinary consciousness testifies to the existence of these states without any act of the will; nay, it is not in the power of the will to arrest this continuous testimony. But we sometimes desire to consider some particular mental state, as the act of perception or memory; or some emotion, as that of the beautiful or sublime. It is in the power of the will to detain such mental state, and hold it up before us as an object of thought. When, by volition, we make our own mental states objects of observation, we denominate this act *Reflection*. As the etymology of the word indicates, we turn the mind backwards upon itself, so that it contemplates its own states and operations, very much as in the case of attention it concentrates its effort upon objects of perception.

I do not pretend that the words attention and reflection are always used in this restricted sense. Attention is frequently used to designate voluntary consciousness both objective and subjective. Reflection is not so commonly used to denote both mental states. It has, however, seemed to me that these mental states should be designated by different terms, and that the etymology of the two words, as well as the general current of good use, tends in the direction which I have here indicated.

This general power of rendering the various faculties of the mind obedient to the will is of the greatest possible importance to the student. Without it, he can never employ any power of the mind with energy or effect. Until it be acquired, our faculties, however brilliant, remain undisciplined and comparatively useless. From the want of it, many men, who in youth give, as is supposed, great promise of distinction, with advancing years sink down into hopeless obscurity. Endowed with fertility of imagination and unusual power of language, they are able to follow any train of thought that accident may suggest, and clothe the ideas of others with imagery which seems to indicate original power of scientific research. But the time soon arrives when the exigences of life require accuracy of knowledge, soundness of judgment, and well-placed reliance on the decisions of our own intellect. The time for display has passed, and the time for action — action on which our success or failure depends — has come. Such men, then, after perhaps dazzling the circle of their friends with a few wild and fanciful schemes, which gleam at intervals amid the approaching darkness, sink below the horizon, and are seen no more forever.

One of the greatest advantages derived from early and systematic education is found in the necessity which it imposes of learning thoroughly and at stated periods certain appropriate lessons. We are thus obliged to direct our attention for a time to the earnest pursuit of some object. By being placed under this necessity for a few years, the power of the will over the faculties, if we are faithful to ourselves, becomes habitual. What we learn is of importance, but this importance is secondary to that of so cultivating and disciplining our faculties that we are ever afterwards able to use them in enlarging the boundaries of science, or directing the courses of human thought and action. If a system of education, besides cultivating the habit of attention, cultivates also the habit of reflection and generalization, so that the student learns not only to acquire but from his acquisitions to rise to general principles, observe the operations of his own mind, and compare what he has learned with the instinctive teachings of his own understanding, the great object of the instructor will be successfully accomplished.

To acquire habits of earnest and continued attention and reflection, is one of the most difficult tasks of the student. At the beginning, he finds his mind wandering, his attention easily turned aside from the object to which he would direct it, and disposed to yield to the attraction of external objects, or to seize upon every fancy that the memory or the imagination may present. Much of that time is thus spent in dreamy idleness, which he had really determined to employ in laborious study. It is evident that his success must depend wholly on the correction of these habits. Our minds are comparatively useless to us, unless we can render them obedient servants to the will, so that, at any time and under any circumstances, we can oblige them to think of what we wish, as long as we wish, and then dismiss it and think of something else. We should strive to attain such a command of all our faculties that we can direct our whole mental energies upon the most abstruse proposition, until we have either solved it, or ascertained that, with our present advantages, a solution is impossible.

Perhaps the section cannot be more profitably closed than by the suggestion of some means by which the power of the will over the other faculties may be increased.

1. Much depends upon the condition of the physical system. Our intellectual faculties are in more perfect exercise in health than in sickness, and as the condition of the body tends to sickness our power over them is proportionally diminished. Every one knows how difficult it is to command his attention during a paroxysm of fever. In recovering from illness, one of the first symptoms of convalescence is a return of the power over the mind, and a disposition to employ it in its accustomed pursuits. Now, it is obvious that anything which interferes with the normal condition of the system, during the continuance of its action, produces the same effect as temporary indisposition. Such causes are over-feeding, either occasionally or habitually, the use of indigestible food, the want of sleep, or of exercise, undue mental excitement, or excessive fatigue. Every one in the least attentive to this subject must have observed the effect of some or all of these causes upon his power of mental concentration. A large portion of the life of many men is spent in habitual violation of the laws by which the free use of the mind is conditioned. If, by accident, they for a short time obey the laws of their nature, their intellectual powers recover their tone, and they enjoy what they call a lucid interval. They postpone all important mental labor

until this favored period arrives, without ever suspecting that it is owing to their own folly that they are not in this condition continually. Our Creator manifestly intended that our intellectual light should shine with a clear and steady brilliancy, not that it should gleam out occasionally, after long periods of mist and gloom and darkness. But, if we would obtain the power of using our intellect to the greatest advantage, we must habitually obey those laws which have been imposed upon us by our Creator.

The diet of a student should be light, and rather spare than abundant. A laboring man needs nutritious and abundant food, to supply the waste caused by physical exertion. The diet which is indispensable to the one is exceedingly injurious to the other. A student also requires regular and sufficient daily exercise, which should generally be carried to the point of full perspiration. His sleep should be all that health requires, and he should invariably retire at an early hour. His study and sleeping room should be well ventilated, and his ablutions should be daily and abundant. To specify more minutely in detail the treatment of the physical system, would be out of place here; and, besides, no rules which could be given would be applicable to every case. Every man, observing the laws of the human constitution, should apply them honestly to his own case. All that is required is that the student form all his physical habits with the direct and earnest purpose of giving the freest scope and the most active exercise to all his intellectual faculties.

It is, however, the fact that students are liable to err in almost all of these particulars. They pay no attention either to the quantity or quality of their food. Though, perhaps, in early life, accustomed to labor, as soon as they commence a course of study, they forsake, not only labor, but all manner of exercise. If anxious to improve, they study until late at night, thus destroying the power of application for the following day. They live in heated and ill-ventilated rooms. Measuring their progress by the number of hours employed in study, they remain over their books until the power of attention is exhausted. Much of their time is thus spent in ineffectual efforts to comprehend the proposition before them, or, after they have comprehended it, in equally ineffectual attempts to fix it in their recollection. The result of all this it is painful to contemplate. Broken down in health and enfeebled in mind, the man in early life is turned out upon society a confirmed and mediocre invalid, equally unfitted for the habits either of active or sedentary life. This is surely unfortunate. There can be no good reason why a student, or the practitioner of what are called the professions, should be an invalid. To study, violates no moral or physical law. A student may, then, be as healthy in body and vigorous in mind as any other man. If he be not, his misfortune is the result, not of mere mental application, but of the violation of the laws under which he has been created.

2. I have already intimated that the power of prolonged and earnest attention depends upon the will. But we find that until the mind becomes in some manner disciplined, the influence of the will is feeble and irregular. Of course, our first attempt must be to increase the power of the will over the other intellectual faculties.

Here, however, I am aware that probably great differences exist in mental constitution. The will in some men is by nature stronger than in others. Some men surrender a deliberately-formed purpose at the appearance of a trifling obstacle; others cling to it with a tenacity which nothing but death can overcome. In this latter case, every physical and mental energy is consecrated to the accomplishment of the purpose to which the life of the being is devoted. When such a will, moved by high moral principle and guided by sound judgment, is directed to the accomplishment of a great enterprise, it wins for its possessor a name among the benefactors of the race. John Howard was an illustrious example of this class of men. The most masterly delineation of this form of character found, so far as I know, in any language, is contained in John Foster's Essays; a book which I should fail in my duty did I not recommend to the thoughtful perusal of every young man.

Such instances of energetic will are, however, rare, and it becomes us to inquire whether the control over our faculties can be obtained by those who are less happily constituted. The most important means of cultivation, if we desire to improve ourselves, lies in the will itself. The more constantly we exercise it, the greater does its power become. The more habitually we do what we resolve to do, instead of doing what we are solicited to do by indolence, or appetite, or passion, or the love of trifles, the more readily will our faculties obey us. At first the effort may yield only a partial result, but perseverance will render the result more and more apparent, until at last we shall find ourselves able to employ our faculties in such manner as we desire. If, then, the student finds his mind unstable, ready to wander in search of every other object than that directly before him, let him never yield to its solicitations. If it stray from the subject, let him recall it, resolutely determining that it shall do the work that he bids it. He who will thus faithfully deal with his intellectual faculties will soon find that his labor has not been in vain.

But, in order to arrive at this result, we must be thoroughly in earnest, and willing to pay the price for so invaluable an acquisition. We must forego many a sensual pleasure, that the action of our faculties may be free and unembarrassed. We must resolutely resist all tendencies to indolence, both physical and mental. We must learn to be alone. We must put away from us all reading and all conversation that would encourage the tendencies which we wish to suppress. By doing this, and exerting to the full the present power of our will, we cannot fail to make progress in mental discipline.

It may not be improper to add a remark respecting a kind of reading in which a student is, at the present day, strongly tempted to indulge. I have no disposition here to discuss the advantages and disadvantages of the reading of works of fiction. It is sufficient for my purpose to observe, first, that this kind of mental occupation evidently requires no effort of the will to arrest the attention. The mind follows pleasantly and unconsciously the train of conceptions presented by the author. Disquisitions requiring mental effort are always considered blemishes in a romance, and are, I believe, generally passed over unread. And, secondly, the mind becomes filled with interesting and exciting images, which remain with us long after the reading has been finished. From these causes, reading of this character must enfeeble the will, and create a tendency to wander from a course of thought which follows entirely different laws of association. These reasons seem to me sufficient for advising any person desirous of cultivating the habit of attention, either to abandon the reading of fiction altogether, or, at least, to indulge in it with such severe discretion as shall prevent it from fostering those habits which we desire to eradicate After we have accomplished our object, and the victory of the will over our other powers has been acknowledged, we may allow ourselves a larger liberty. Until this is done, the stricter the discipline which we enforce upon ourselves, the more rapid will be our attainment in the habit of self-government.

3. The power of the will over our other faculties s

greatly assisted by punctuality; that is, by doing everything in precisely the time and place allotted for the doing of it. If, when the hour for study has arrived, we begin to waste our time in frivolous reading or idle musing, we shall find our real work more distasteful, the longer we procrastinate. If, on the contrary, we begin at once, we the more easily conquer our wandering propensities, and our minds are fully occupied before trifles have the opportunity of alluring us. The men who have accomplished the greatest amount of intellectual labor have generally been remarkable for punctuality; they have divided their time accurately between their different pursuits, have rigidly adhered to the plan which they have adopted, and have been careful to improve every moment to the utmost advantage.

4. The control of the will over our faculties is much assisted by the use of the pen. The act of writing out our own thoughts, or the thoughts of others, of necessity involves the exercise of continuous attention. Every one knows that, after he has thought over a subject with all the care in his power, his ideas become vastly more precise by committing them to paper. The maxim of the schoolmen was *studium sine calamo somnium.* The most remarkable thinkers have generally astonished their contemporaries by the vast amount of manuscript which they have left behind them. I think that universal experience testifies to the fact that no one can attain to a high degree of mental cultivation, without devoting a large portion of his time to the labor of composition.

It is a very valuable habit to read no book without obliging ourselves to write a brief abstract of it, with the opinions which we have formed concerning it. This will oblige us to read with attention, and will give the results of that attention a permanent place in our recollection. We should thus, in fact, become reviewers of every book that we read.

The learned and indefatigable Reinhardt was thus able to conduct one of the most valuable reviews in Germany, by writing his opinions on every work which came under his perusal. The late Lord Jeffrey commenced his literary career in precisely this manner. When a youthful student at the university, he not only wrote a review of every book which he read, but of every paper which he himself composed. His strictures were even more severe on his own writings than on the writings of others. He thus laid the foundation of his immense acquisitions, and attained to so great a power of intellectual analysis, that for many years he was acknowledged to be the most accomplished critic of his time.

REFERENCES.

Consciousness — Reid, Essay 1, chap. 1 ; Abercrombie, Part 2, sect. 2 ; Locke, book 2, chap. 6, sect. 2 ; chap. 9, sect. 1.

Is consciousness distinguished from perception? — Stewart, vol. i., chap. 2.

Cases of Abnormal Consciousness — Abercrombie, Part 3, sect. 4 ; part 2

Attention and Reflection — Reid, Essay 1, chap. 5 ; Essay 4, chap. 4 Stewart, vol i., chap. 2. Abercrombie, Part 2, chap. 1.

Improvement of Attention and Reflection, Part 2, chap. 1.

Consciousness — Cousin, sect. 1, p. 12, 8vo : Hartford, 1834. **Henry translation, and note A, by Prof. H.**

CHAPTER III.

ORIGINAL SUGGESTION, OR THE INTUITIONS OF THE INTELLECT.

SECTION I.—EXAMINATION OF THE OPINIONS OF LOCKE.

We have thus far considered those powers of the human mind by which it obtains a knowledge of the existence and qualities of the external world, and of the existence and energies of the thinking subject. This knowledge, as I have said, is all either of individual existences or of individual acts, or states of the subjective mind. It is, of course, all concrete, and the conceptions derived from it are of the same character. This knowledge is original, direct and immediate. It is the constitutional testimony of our faculties as soon as they are brought into relation to their appropriate objects. It always contemplates as an object something now existing, or something which at some time did exist.

Let us, then, for a moment consider what would be the condition of a human being possessed of no other powers than those of which we have thus far treated. He would be cognizant of the existence and qualities of the objects which he perceived, and of the state of mind which these objects called into exercise; and, if endowed with memory, he could retain this knowledge in recollection. Here, however, his knowledge would terminate. Each fact would remain disconnected from every other, and each separate knowledge would terminate absolutely in itself. No relation between any two facts would be either discovered or sought for. The questions why, or wherefore, would neither be asked nor answered. The knowledge acquired would be perfectly barren, leading to nothing else, and destitute of all tendency and all power to multiply itself into other forms of cognition. The mind would be a perfect living daguerreotype, on which forms were indelibly impressed, remaining lifeless and unchangeable forever.

It was the opinion of Locke, that all our knowledge either consisted of these ideas of sense or consciousness, or was derived from them by comparison or combination. Thus, says he, "First, our senses, conversant about particular sensible objects, do convey to the mind several distinct perceptions of things, according to those various ways in which those objects do affect them. Thus we come to those ideas we have of yellow, white, heat, cold, soft, bitter, and all those which we call sensible qualities; which, when I say the senses convey to the mind, I mean they from external objects convey into the mind what produces these sensations. This source I call *Sensation*." — Book 2, chap. 1, sec. 3.

Secondly. "The other fountain from which experience furnisheth the understanding with ideas, is the perception of the operations of our own minds within us, as it is employed about the ideas it has got; which operations, when the soul comes to reflect on and consider, do furnish the understanding with another set of ideas, which could not be had from things without. Such are perception, thinking, doubting, believing, reasoning, knowing, willing, and all those different acts of our own minds, which, we being conscious of and observing in our ownselves, do from these receive into the understanding as distinct ideas as we do from bodies affecting our senses. I call this *Reflection*." — Ibid. sect. 4.

"The understanding seems to me not to have the least

glimmering of any ideas which it does not receive from one of these two. External objects furnish the mind with the ideas of sensible qualities, which are all these different perceptions they produce in us, and the mind furnishes the understanding with ideas of its own operations." Again: "Let any one examine his own thoughts, and thoroughly search into his understanding, and let him tell me whether all the original ideas he has there are any other than of the objects of his senses, or of the operations of the mind considered as objects of his reflection, and how great a mass of knowledge soever he imagines to be lodged there, he will, upon taking a strict view, see that he has not any idea in his mind but what one of these two have imprinted, though, perhaps, with infinite variety, compounded and enlarged by the understanding, as we shall see hereafter."—Ibid. Sec. 5.

Again: "If we trace the progress of our minds, and with attention observe how it repeats, adds together, and unites its simple ideas received from sensation and reflection, it will lead us further than perhaps we should have imagined. And I believe we shall find, if we warily observe the originals of our notions, that even the most abstruse ideas, how remote soever they may seem from sense or from any operations of our own minds, are yet only such as the understanding frames to itself by repeating and joining together those ideas that it had from objects of sense, or from its own operations about them."—Book 2d, chap. 12, sec. 8.

From these extracts it appears evident that Locke believed all our original knowledge to proceed from perception, or, as he calls it, sensation, and consciousness. Whatever other knowledge we have, is produced secondarily by adding together, repeating, and joining together, the simple ideas derived from these original sources. I have before remarked that these ideas are of individuals and are concrete. If, therefore, the theory of Locke be correct, all our other knowledge is created by adding, repeating, and joining together these individual and concrete conceptions.

Now, if this be so,—if it be the law of our nature that the human intellect is incapable of attaining to any other knowledge than the ideas of sensation and reflection, that is, of perception and consciousness,—in other words, than the knowledge of the qualities of matter and the operations of our own minds, then it follows that all our notions which cannot be reduced to one or the other of these classes, is a mere fiction of the imagination, unworthy of confidence, and is, in fact, no knowledge at all. But it is obvious that there are in our minds many ideas which belong to neither of these classes; such, for instance, are the ideas of relation, power, cause and effect, space, duration, infinity, right and wrong, and many others. Can these be produced by the uniting, joining, or adding together our conceptions of the qualities of matter, or of our own mental acts? Let any one try the experiment, and he will readily be convinced that they can be evolved by no process of this kind. It will follow then, if the theory of Locke be admitted, that these notions, which I have above specified, and all others like them, are mere fancies, the dreams of schoolmen or of fanatics, having no real foundation, and forming no substantial basis for science, or even valid objects for inquiry. Nothing, then, can be deemed worthy of the name of science or knowledge, except the primitive data either of perception or consciousness, or what is formed by adding, uniting, joining together, these primitive cognitions. Hence, the ideas of which I have spoken, such as those of space, duration, infinity, eternity, cause and effect, all moral ideas,—nay, the idea of God himself,—are the figments of a dream, and all that remains to us is merely what we can perceive without and be conscious of within. This was the conclusion at which many men arrived at the close of the last century.

Inasmuch as their principles were said to be derived from Locke, he has sometimes been considered the founder of the sensual school.

It is, however, to be observed, that Locke did not perceive, much less would he have admitted, the result to which his doctrines led. He speaks of the ideas to which I have alluded, such as space, power, &c., as legitimate objects of human thought, and gives quite a correct account of their origin. Thus, speaking of power, he remarks: "The mind being every day informed by the senses of the alteration of those simple ideas it observes in things without, and taking notice how one comes to an end and ceases to be, and another begins to exist which was not before; reflecting, also. on what passes within itself, and observing a constant change in its ideas, sometimes by the impression of outward objects on the senses, and sometimes from the determination of its own choice; and concluding, from what it has always observed to have been, that like changes will for the future be made in the same things by the same agents, and by the like way considers in the one thing the possibility of having any of its simple ideas changed, and in another the possibility of making that change, and so it comes by that idea which we call power."— Book 2, chap. 21, sec. 1.

Here we perceive that Locke acknowledges the existence of ideas or knowledges derived neither from sensation nor reflection, and gives a very intelligible account of their origin. It is obvious that the idea of power is not derived from the senses; we neither see, nor feel, nor hear it. It is not an operation of the mind, therefore is not derived from reflection. And, besides, comparing, adding together, uniting, are acts of the mind, wholly different either from perception or consciousness. It is evident, therefore, that Locke, when he examined the ideas in his own mind, observed among them many which neither perception nor consciousness could give; and he, perhaps carelessly, accounted for their origin by the use of the indefinite expressions, "takes notice of," "concludes," "comes to the idea," &c. We see, therefore, that Locke went beyond his own theory, and really saw what his theory declared could not be seen. Had he pursued a different method, and first observed the ideas of which we are conscious, and afterwards investigated their origin, his system would probably have been greatly modified. He, however, pursued the opposite course; first determining the origin of our ideas, and then limiting our ideas by the sources which he supposed himself to have exhausted.

The manner in which Locke was led into this error is apparent. He had been at great pains to refute the doctrine of innate ideas, and to show that the human mind could have no thought until some impression was made upon it from without. It was also obvious to him that the only objects which we are able to cognize are matter and mind. He compared the mind to a sheet of white paper, entirely blank until something is written on it by a power external to itself. This, however, although the truth, is only a part of the truth. As I have before remarked, if the sheet of paper had the power of uniting the letters written upon it into words, and these words into discourse, and of proceeding forever in the elimination of new and original truth, it would much more accurately represent the intellect of man. This illustration of a sheet of white paper evidently misled our philosopher, and prevented him from giving due prominence to the originating or suggestive power of the mind.

This brief notice of the opinions of Locke seemed necessary, especially since so great and important conclusions have been deduced from his doctrine. The whole subject has been treated in a most masterly manner by Cousin, in his Review of the Philosophy of Locke, to which I would specially refer the student.

But to what conclusion are we led by this brief examination of the theory of Locke? We have seen that, on the supposition that all our ideas are derived from perception and consciousness, a large portion of the most important ideas of which the human soul is conscious must be abandoned as the groundless fictions of the imagination, having no foundation in the true processes of the understanding. On the other hand, we know from our own consciousness that these ideas are universally developed in the human intellect as soon as it begins to exercise independent thought. We must, therefore, conclude, that the theory of Locke is imperfect, and that it does not recognize some of our most important sources of original knowledge. It is, then, our business to inquire for some other sources besides those recognized by Locke.

REFERENCES.

Sources of our knowledge — Locke, Book 2, chap. 1, sec. 3, sec. 4, sec. 5 ; Book 2, chap. 12, sec. 8, chap. 22, sec. 1, 2, 9.

Suggestion a power of the mind — Reid, Inquiry, chap. 2, sec. 7 ; Int. Powers, Essay 3, chap. 5 ; Essay 2, chap. 10, 12.

Examination of Locke's Theory — Stewart, vol. i., chap. 1.

Before all others. — Cousin's Examination of Locke's Philosophy, chap. 1, 2, 3, 4.

SECTION II. — THE NATURE OF ORIGINAL SUGGESTION, OR THE POWER OF INTUITIVE COGNITION.

LOCKE has truly stated that all the substances to which in our present state we are related are matter and mind. By perception we obtain a knowledge of the qualities of the one, and by consciousness a knowledge of the operations of the other. Each is distinct and complete within itself, and each terminates definitely at its own appropriate limit.

The thought, however, thus awakened, does not thus terminate. The mind of man is endowed not only with a *receptive*, but also with what may be called a *suggestive* power. When the ideas of perception and consciousness terminate, or even while they are present, a new series of mental phenomena arises by virtue of the original power of the intellect itself. These phenomena present themselves in the form of intuitive cognitions, *occasioned* by the ideas of consciousness and perception, but neither produced by them nor in any respect similar to them. They may be considered acts of pure intellection. To the ideas of perception or consciousness there by necessity belongs an object either objective or subjective. To those ideas of the intellect I think no such object belongs. Hence they could not be cognized originally either by perception or consciousness. They could not exist within us except we were endowed with a different and superior intellectual energy. We can give but little account of these intellections, nor can we offer any proof of their verity. As soon as they arise within us, they are to us the unanswerable evidence of their own truth. As soon as we are conscious of them, we know that they are true, and we never offer any evidence in support of them. So far as our powers of perception and consciousness are concerned, the mind resembles in many respects a sheet of white paper. Here, however, the analogy terminates. There is nothing in the paper which in any respect resembles this power of intuitive knowledge of which we here speak.

What we here refer to may, perhaps, be best illustrated by a familiar example. A child, before it can talk, throws a ball and knocks down a nine-pin. By perception aided by memory, it derives no other ideas besides those of a rolling ball and of a falling ninepin. This is all that the senses could give it. It might be all that would be apparent to the mind of a brute. But is this the case with the child? Far otherwise. There arises in his mind, by virtue of its own energy, the notion of cause and effect; of something in the ball capable of producing this change, and of something in the ninepin which renders it susceptible of this change. He instinctively cognizes a most important relation existing between these two events. Still more, he has an intuitive belief that the same event can be produced again in the same way. Relying on this belief, he sets up the ninepin again, and throws the ball in the confident expectation that it will produce the same result as at first. There has thus been created in his mind, not only the relation of cause and effect, but the important conviction that like causes will produce like effects. In consequence of the relations which have thus been revealed to him, he sets a value upon his toys which he did not before. The same idea is developed as soon as the infant puts his finger in the candle. He will not try the experiment a second time. He immediately obtains a knowledge of the relation of cause and effect, and that the same cause will again produce the same effect. He does not *see* this relation; it is not an object of perception, nor is it an operation of the mind. He does not *feel* it when he is burned. As soon, however, as he cognizes the relative ideas, the relation in which they stand to each other presents itself to him as an intuitive cognition.

I have here used an illustration from external objects. I, however, by no means assert that in this manner we first arrive at the knowledge of cause and effect. The same idea is evidently suggested by every act of voluntary motion. A child wishes to move his hand; it moves, but perhaps not in the right direction. He tries again, with better success. At last he accomplishes his object. Here is, perhaps, the most striking instance of this relation which he ever witnesses, and it is brought home directly to his own consciousness. He is conscious of the act of volition, he knows that he wills; this mental act is followed by a change of position in his hand, and by motion in something with which his hand comes into contact. This succession of events, the former of which is within the cognition of his own consciousness, and the latter of his perception, would be sufficient to give occasion to this intuitive knowledge at a very early period.

It may be proper to observe, that although this power of original suggestion is developed and perfected with advancing years, yet it commences with the first unfolding of the intellect. Both the perceptive and the suggestive powers belong to the essential nature of a human mind Were a child destitute of the power of intuitive cognition, even at a very early age, we should know that it was an idiot. If, for instance, it manifested no notion of cause and effect, but would as soon put its fingers into a candle the second time as the first, we should be convinced that it was not possessed of a normal understanding. Nay, we form an opinion of the mental capacity of a child rather by the activity of its suggestive than of its perceptive powers. It may be blind or deaf, or may suffer both of these afflictions together; that is, its perceptive powers may be at the minimum, and yet we may discover that its intellect is alert and vigorous, and that it discovers large powers of acquisition and combination. Such a case occurs in the instance of Laura Bridgman, a blind mute, whose suggestive powers are unusually active, and who has, with admirable skill, been taught to read and write, so that she is at present able to keep a journal, and correspond with her friends by letter.

With respect to these ideas of suggestion, or intuition, two important remarks are made by Cousin. I give his ideas here, rather than his words.

1. "Unless we previously obtained the idea of perception and consciousness, we could never originate the suggested or intuitive cognitions. If, for instance, we had never observed the fact of a succession, we could never have obtained the idea of duration. If we had never perceived an external object, we should never have obtained the idea of space. If we had never witnessed an instance of change, we should have had no idea of cause and effect. As soon, however, as these ideas of perception and consciousness are awakened, they are immediately either attended or followed by the ideas of suggestion. We perceive, then, that, *chronologically* considered, the ideas of perception and consciousness take precedence. They appear first in the mind, and, until they appear, the others could have no existence. It was this fact which probably gave rise to the error of Locke. Because no other ideas could be originated except through means of the ideas of perception and consciousness, he inferred that our knowledge could consist of nothing but these ideas, either in their original form, or else united or added to each other. The fact, on the contrary, seems to be, that our suggested ideas are no combination or modification of our receptive ideas ; they form the occasions from which the mind originates them by virtue of its own energy. We are so made, that, when one class of ideas is cognized, the other spontaneously arises within us, in consequence of the constitution of the human intellect.

2. "But, secondly, when we have thus obtained these ideas of suggestion, we find that their existence is a necessary condition of the existence of the very ideas by which they are occasioned. Thus, as I have said, the notion of an external world is the occasion in us of the idea of space but, when we have obtained the idea of space, we see that

it is a necessary condition to the conception of an external world; for, were there no space, there could be no external world. If we had never witnessed a succession of events, we should never have obtained a conception of duration. Having, however, obtained the conception of duration, we perceive that it is a necessary condition of succession; for, were there no duration, there could be no succession. And again, had we never observed an instance of change, we should never have attained the conception of cause and effect, or of power. But the conception of power once gained, we become immediately sensible that, had there been no power, change would have been impossible. We thus learn that, *logically* considered, the suggestive idea takes the precedence, inasmuch as it is the necessary condition of the idea by which it is occasioned."

With these remarks of this most acute and very able metaphysician I fully coincide, so far as they apply to a large portion of our ideas of suggestion. I think, however, that there is a large class of our intuitive cognitions, of which the second of these laws cannot be affirmed. Take, for instance, our ideas of relation and degree, arising from the contemplation of two or more single objects. I do not see how it is true that the relation is a necessary condition to the existence of the bodies which occasion it, or that the idea of degree is a necessary condition to the existence of the qualities by which it is occasioned. I dissent with diffidence from an author so justly distinguished; nevertheless, in treating on this, as on any other subject, I am bound to state fully the truth as it presents itself to my individual consciousness.

In order the more fully to illustrate this subject, I have thought it desirable to present a number of instances in which these original suggestions or intuitions are occasioned by the ideas of perception and consciousness. I by no means attempt an exhaustive catalogue. It will be sufficient for my purposes, if I am able to present such a view of the subject as will direct more definite attention than has generally been given to this part of our intellectual constitution.

It has seemed to me that these intuitions might be classified as follows:

I. Those unaccompanied by emotion.

II. Those accompanied by emotion.

I. Those unaccompanied by emotion are,

1. Those occasioned by objects in a state of rest.
2. Those occasioned by objects in the condition of change.

II. Those accompanied by emotion are,

1. Æsthetic ideas.
2. Moral ideas.

REFERENCES.

Cousin, chaps. 2, 3, and 4.

SECTION III. — IDEAS OCCASIONED BY OBJECTS IN A STATE OF REST.

WE may contemplate objects in a state of rest either as one or many. Let us, in the first place, examine a single object.

Suppose, for instance, a solid cube is placed before me. I look at it, and perceive its color and form; I handle it, and perceive that it is hard and smooth, and that its form is the same as I have discovered by sight; I strike it, and it gives forth a sound; I attempt to smell it and taste of it, and thus derive all the knowledge of its qualities which I am able to discover. I reflect on these various acts of perception, and thus obtain a knowledge of the state of my mind when performing these mental acts. I have then all the knowledge which I can derive from perception and consciousness. Had I no other mental energies, my knowledge would here arrive at an impassable limit. If, however, we reflect upon our own cognitions, we shall be conscious of much important knowledge *occasioned* by these mental acts, which the acts themselves do not give us.

I look upon the cube; I perceive it to be extended; I remove it to another place. What is there where the cube was a moment since? What is that which the cube occupies, and in which it is contained? It can be occupied by matter, or left vacant. I become conscious of the fact that it is a condition necessary to the existence of all matter. Abolish it, and I abolish the possibility of an external universe. I call it space. What is it? It has no qualities that can be cognized by the senses. It is neither an act nor an affection of the mind. It is not matter; it is not spirit. It differs from both in every conceivable particular. The existence of matter is made known to us by the senses. Space is cognizable by none of them. It is neither seen, nor felt, nor heard, nor smelled, nor tasted. Matter is a contingent existence; it may or may not exist here, or it may not have existence anywhere. I can conceive of an era in duration when it never existed. I can conceive of another era when it will cease to exist. Not so of space; as soon as I form a notion of it, I perceive it to be necessary. I cannot conceive of its non-existence or annihilation. This cube and all other matter is limited, and is so from necessity; space is by necessity unlimited. Matter, being limited, of necessity has form; space has no form, for it has no limitation. The conception of a body, however vast, suggests an image; space suggests to us no image. We find ourselves, therefore, in possession of a conception, revealed to us neither by perception nor consciousness, which, nevertheless, is cognized by the mind, from the necessity of its own nature. Without perception it would never have been cognized. Chronologically, it is, therefore, subsequent to it. As soon, however, as I obtain this conception, I know that it is a necessary condition to the existence of that which is perceived. It is necessary physiologically; for without space there can be no matter. It is necessary psychologically; for we cannot in our minds conceive of matter without conceiving of space as a necessary condition of our conception.

But let us reflect upon this idea somewhat more attentively. We all have a knowledge of what is meant by space; we cannot easily confound it with any other idea; yet no one can describe it. It has no qualities. It holds no relation to our senses, or to our consciousness. What are its limits? As I have before said, it has none. The house in which I am writing occupies space, and is contained in space. The earth and the whole planetary system move in space. The whole sidereal system either moves or reposes in space. We pass to the utmost verge of the material universe—space still stretches beyond, unmeasured, immeasurable. We have approached no nearer to its confines than at first; for, were such creations as now exist to be multiplied forever, space would be yet inexhaustible. What do we call this idea, which, by the constitution of our minds, emerges necessarily from this conception? It is the idea of the boundless, the immensurable, the infinite. It is an idea which we cannot comprehend, and yet from which we cannot escape. We may, perhaps, remember how, in childhood, we wearied our feeble understandings in the attempt to grasp it. It is at present as far beyond the power of our comprehension as at first, yet we find the mind ever tending towards it. It is an idea neither of perception nor consciousness, nor can it be evolved from any union or combination of those ideas. It evolves itself at once, on our conception of space, from the energies of the mind itself. Having been once formed, it holds its place independently in the mind, and depends not for its existence on any other idea.

Again; I cannot be conscious of my own existence without being conscious at the same time that I am an individual, separate not only from the rest of the material, but from the other individuals of the spiritual universe. I am, in myself, a complete form of existence, distinct from every other form that has existed, or that may exist. When I observe the cube, it suggests to me the same idea, that of unity. I retain this idea of oneness, apart from any object which at first suggested it. It cannot be called a quality. It is not an energy of the mind; yet it is an idea which immediately arises within us, on such occasions as I have suggested.

It may, however, be proper to remark, that this idea of unity is always relative. It always has respect to the relation in which we contemplate an object. An individual human being is one; yet it possesses one body and one spirit, and without both of these, in our present state, it would not be a human being. A human soul is one; but, in order to be a human soul, it must be possessed of various faculties, each one of which may be considered distinctly. A regiment is one, and yet it could not be a regiment, unless it were composed of several distinct companies united under a single commander. A company is one; but it is made up of single individuals, as privates, subalterns, captain, etc. We thus see that, in speaking of unity, the relation in which we contemplate the object is always to be taken into view; and that there is no absurdity or contradiction in saying, that it is *one* in one relation, and *many* in another relation.

Let us look once more upon our cube. We perceive in it form, solidity, divisibility, color, etc. These we call qualities of matter, or the powers which it possesses of affecting us in a particular manner. But is either of these qualities matter? Are all of them combined matter? Were we to say that color and form and divisibility, etc., are matter, or substance, would this assertion express the idea of which we are conscious when we reflect upon this subject? So far is this from the fact, that the assertion would seem to involve an absurdity. We always say of a material object, it is something divisible, solid, colored, etc.; plainly distinguishing, in our conceptions, the something in which the qualities reside, from the qualities which reside in the something. We thus find ourselves possessed of the two ideas, essence and attribute, substance and quality. We know that there must be one, whenever we perceive the other. But where does this idea of substance come from? Surely neither from the senses nor from consciousness; yet we all have attained it. It must have originated in the mind itself. We perceive the quality. The mind affirms the existence of the substance, and affirms it not as a contingent, but as a necessary truth.

It is almost superfluous to remark, that we arrive at the same idea from consciousness. Consciousness testifies to the existence of mental energies. From this knowledge, the mind at once asserts the existence of an essence to which these energies pertain. Were there no mental energies, we could never become cognizant of a spiritual substance; but, having been cognizant of it, we know that it is a necessary condition to the existence of the energies of which we are conscious.

2. These instances are sufficient to illustrate the nature of the cognitions which are suggested by the energies of the mind itself, when we contemplate a *single* object. Let us now suppose several objects, some of similar and others of

dissimilar qualities, to be present before us. Suppose them, for instance, cubes, pyramids, cylinders, etc.

If I observe them singly, each will furnish me with all the primary and suggested ideas to which I have just now referred. I observe several to be of one form. I compare their aggregate with unity, and there arises in my mind the idea of number. As soon as I have formed this notion, I find myself abstracting it from the cubes, and from every other object, and treat it as a conception by itself, capable of enlargement or diminution at my will. So readily does this conception separate itself from the objects which gave occasion to its existence, that, in the rudest conditions of society, men give names to the several ideas of number, and very soon form a symbolical language to represent them. Every one knows that his ideas of number were originally derived from the observation of a plurality of objects; and yet no one, thinking of ten, twenty, thirty, to say nothing of thousands and millions, ever associates these ideas with any actual existences. We always consider them as abstract ideas, yet ideas of the most fixed and determinate character. But these ideas are not objects of perception. We neither see nor feel nor taste number; yet perception occasions these ideas. We know number as soon as the occasions which suggest it present themselves.

In enumeration, we always proceed by unity. We repeat unity until we arrive at a certain aggregate, which we then consider as a unit. Thus, in our enumeration, we repeat unity, giving a different name to every increasing aggregate, until we arrive at ten. We then make this our unit, and add to it other similar units, until we arrive at a hundred; in the same manner, we make this our unit until we arrive at a thousand, then to a million, etc. Suppose, now, I carry on this process to any assignable limit, can I exhaust my idea of number? Suppose I proceed until my powers of computation fail, have I yet proceeded so far that I cannot add to the sum millions upon millions? Can I conceive of any number so vast that I cannot add to it as many as I choose? We perceive this to be impossible. Here, again, we recognize the same idea which lately evolved from our notion of space. It is the idea of infinity. We see that it springs at once, by the operation of our minds, from every conception capable of giving occasion to it.

Again; we cannot observe a number of objects at the same time, without recognizing various relations which exist between them. I see two cubes possessing in every respect the same qualities. Hence arises the relation of identity of form, color, etc. Others possess different qualities; hence the relation of diversity. When the forms are precisely the same, or when they occupy exactly the same space, there arises relation of equality. When they occupy different measures of space, there arises the relation of inequality. These latter relations are specially used in all our reasonings in the mathematics. All our demonstrations in this science are designed to show that two quantities are either equal or unequal to each other.

Still further, I perceive that two or more objects are not in contact. Space intervenes between them, and we recognize the relation of distance. Each one has a definite relation in space to all the others. Hence arises the relation of place. Place always refers to the position which a body holds in respect to other bodies. Were there but one body in space, we could not from it form any notion of place. As soon as other bodies are perceived, and their relation to it recognized, we obtain this idea respecting it. Thus, I say this paper lies where it did ten minutes since. Here I refer to the table and the objects upon it, whose position in relation to the paper is the same as it was before, leaving out of account altogether the fact that the table has moved with the diurnal and annual revolution of the earth. A man in a railroad car will say that he has not changed his place for half a day, when he knows that he has been moving at the rate of thirty or forty miles an hour.

Again; we perceive that, of several cubes, the first occupies a larger portion of space than the second, and the second a larger portion than the third. All of them are red, but the tinge of one is deeper than that of another. Hence arises the relation of degree. This idea is so universally recognized, that, in all languages, it is designated by a special form, entitled degrees of comparison.

But it is not necessary that I pursue this subject further. I think that every one must recognize in his own mind a power of originating such knowledges as these, as soon as the occasion presents itself. They are not ideas of perception or of consciousness, but ideas arising in the mind, by its own energies, as soon as we cognize the appropriate objects which occasion them. Having once obtained them, they immediately sever themselves from the objects which occasion them, and become ideas of simple intellection, which we use as abstract terms in all our reasonings.

REFERENCES.

Space — Locke, Book 2, chap. 13; Cousin, chap. 2; Reid, Essay 2, chap. 19.

Space and body not the same — Locke, Book 2, chap. 13; Cousin, chap. 2.

Infinity from space — Locke, Book 2, chap. 13; Cousin, chap. 3; Reid, Essay 2, chap. 19.

Unity — Locke, Book 2, chap. 7.

Substance and solidity — Locke, Book 2, chap. 4; Cousin, chap 3.

Number — Locke, Book 2, chap. 16, 17; Cousin, chap. 3.

Relation — Locke, Book 2, chap. 25.

Identity and Diversity — Locke, Book 2, chap 27.

Place — Locke, Book 2, chap. 13.

SECTION IV. — SUGGESTED IDEAS OCCASIONED BY THE CONSIDERATION OF OBJECTS IN THE CONDITION OF CHANGE.

EVERY one must be aware that motion, change, progress, and decay, are written upon everything within us, and upon everything without us. It is natural to suppose that a variety of suggestions, or intuitive cognitions, would be occasioned by the development of this universal law.

Our thoughts are in a condition of perpetual change. Thought succeeds thought; one conception follows another without a moment's cessation, at least, during our waking hours, from the commencement to the close of our present existence. The idea of incessant change is essential to our notion of life. Abolish it, and the result is universal death.

Destitute of memory, we should be unconscious of these changes, and cognizant only of the thought or emotion of the present moment. Endowed with memory, however, we become aware of the fact that the thought of which we are now conscious is not the thought of which we were conscious a few moments since; and that the thoughts of yesterday, or of boyhood, are very different from the thoughts of to-day.

The same knowledge is also derived from the acts of perception in connection with memory. We perceive a cloud overspreading the heavens. When last we looked upward all was clear; now all is lurid. Again, the cloud is dissipated, and all is sunshine. We arise in the morning, and light is gradually stealing over the heavens. Soon, the sun arises, and all nature is aroused to life. In a few hours it is mid-day, and animal and vegetable droop with the excessive heat. Soon, the sun declines; it sinks beneath the horizon; we are fanned by the breezes of the evening, and behold the blue expanse above us dotted with innumerable stars. Had we no memory, we should be cognizant of the existence of but one phenomenon,— that which presented itself to us at a particular moment. Our existence in consciousness would be limited to the smallest conceivable portion of duration. Constituted as we are, we become aware that one event succeeds another; and we hold the fact of this succession distinctly within our knowledge.

From both consciousness and perception, then, united with memory, we acquire a knowledge of succession; that is, that some other event or events preceded that of which we are now cognizant. But another idea is immediately occasioned in a human mind by the idea of succession, different from it, and from any which we have thus far considered It is the idea of duration. I cannot define it. I cannot explain it. Yet it belongs to the very elements of human thought. We can neither think nor act without taking it for granted. It is a condition of existence; for, were there no duration, nothing could exist. It is neither an idea of perception nor of consciousness. We cannot cognize it by our senses, nor is it an operation of the mind. The intellect seizes upon it as soon as we recognize the fact of succession. No one can give any further account of its origin. No one can enumerate its qualities, for it has no qualities. Yet, every one has the idea, and no one can conceive of its non-existence.

We perceive, in this case, the difference between the chronological and the logical order of these two ideas. Chronologically, the idea of succession takes the precedence; for, unless we had first cognized the fact of succession, we should never have obtained the idea of duration. But when both have been acquired, we immediately perceive that duration is the necessary condition to succession; for, without duration, succession would be impossible. Logically, therefore, duration takes the precedence.

The first measure of duration seems naturally to be the succession of our own thoughts. A portion of duration seems long or short, in retrospect, according to the number of events to which we have attended, and the tone of mind or the degree of earnestness with which we have observed them. But it is obvious that these elements vary greatly with the same individual at different times, and with different individuals at the same time. We, therefore, seek for some definite portion of duration, as the unit by which we may measure with accuracy any other limited portion. Such natural unit is found in the revolution of the heavenly bodies; and hence we come to measure duration by days, and months, and years, or by some definite portion of these units. Duration measured in this manner we call time. If I do not mistake, we mean, by time, that portion of duration which commences with the creation of our race, and which will terminate when "the earth and the things therein shall be dissolved."

But let us take a year, and add to it by unity. We soon arrive at a century. Taking this as our unit, we add again, until we arrive at the era of the creation. We go backward still, until we even find ourselves in imagination at the commencement of the sidereal system. Duration is still unexhausted; it is yet an unfathomable abyss. We conceive of ages upon ages, each as interminable as the past duration of the material universe, and cast them into the mighty void; they sink in darkness, and the chasm is still unfathomable. We go forward again, and add century to century, without finding any limit. We pass on until the present system is dissolved, and duration is still immeasurable. We add together the past and the future term of the existence of the universe, and multiply it by millions of millions and we have approached no nearer than at first to the limits of duration. We are conscious that it sustains no relations either to measure or limit. It is beyond all computation made by addition of the finite. It is thus, from the contemplation of duration, that the idea of the infinite arises in a human intellect from the necessity of its nature.

This idea of the infinite, to which the mind so necessarily tends, and which it derives from so many conceptions, is one of the most remarkable of any of which we are cognizant. It belongs to the human intelligence, for it arises within us unbidden on various occasions, and we cannot escape it. Yet it is cognized by none of the powers either of perception or of consciousness. It is occasioned by them; yet it differs from them as widely as the human mind can conceive. The knowledge derived from these sources is by necessity limited and finite. This idea has no relations whatever to anything finite. It has no qualities, yet we all have a necessary knowledge of what it means. Is there not in this idea some dim foreshadowing of the relation which we, as finite beings, sustain to the Infinite One, and of those conceptions which will burst upon us in that unchanging state to which we are all so rapidly tending?

Of cause and effect, and of power.

I proceed to the consideration of this important subject. I have no expectation of adding anything new to a discussion, which, from the earliest history of philosophy, has engaged the earnest thought of the ablest men. I shall not enter upon the consideration of many of those questions which emerge out of it. Were I to attempt to present them ever so briefly, I should transcend the limits to which a work of this kind must be restricted. I shall content myself with stating the views which, after some reflection, have presented themselves to my own mind.

Let us, then, commence with the observation of a single

phenomenon; that is, a case of change. Suppose, for instance, I observe that water, which a few minutes since was fluid, has now become solid. I find myself unable to think of this change as an isolated fact, or as the commencement of a series. It must have had antecedents. Nor is this all. The antecedents must have stood in a certain relation to it. Suppose I attempt to think of this change as occurring while all the conditions of the existence of the fluid remained throughout just as they were at the beginning. I cannot think it. There is a book on one end of my table. I leave the room for a moment, and, on my return, I find it at the other end of the table. I ask what moved it. I am answered, nothing. I am told that all the conditions of the existence of that book had been absolutely the same during its change of place; that no agency of any kind had been exerted upon it, and yet the book had been removed from one place to another. I am obliged to reply I cannot think it. It is as unthinkable as the proposition that two straight lines can at the same time be parallel and at right angles with each other, or that two circles can cut each other in more than two points. I intuitively know that there must have been a cause which rendered the water hard, which an hour ago was fluid; and a cause which removed the book from one place to another. If I am asked why I think in this manner, I can give no account of it. I am obliged to say I am so made. To think in this manner seems to me necessary to the normal condition of a human intellect.

This, however, is but one form of causation; the case in which the antecedent and consequent, the cause and effect, are both brute matter. A variety of other cases deserves to be considered.

2. Brute matter may be the cause of change in spirit. Thus, I open my eyes and see a tree. A sonorous body is struck, and I hear a sound. Here brute matter produces in

me a change. A new condition of mind is produced within me, which I denominate a knowledge. This could not have existed but for the presence of the material objects which have caused it. Under some circumstances, the effect is as inevitable as when both cause and effect are material. The effect, however, is here modified by conditions unknown in the former case. For instance, a considerable portion of my life is spent in sleep, during which time the effect of ordinary agents upon my mind is suspended. Again; no knowledge is created in my mind except through the medium of consciousness. But consciousness is indirectly subject to the will. If, by the effort of the will, it is earnestly directed to another object, the tree may be present, or the sonorous body may be struck, and no appropriate knowledge is created in my mind. Here, we see that a new element enters into the conditions of cause and effect, by which the universal relation of the one to the other is considerably modified.

3. Spirit or mind may be the cause of change in matter. The simplest instance of this mode of cause and effect is in the movement of the limbs. I put forth my hand and take a pen between my fingers. I dip it in the ink and proceed to write a sentence. Here, I am conscious of an effort of the will. I perceive the movement of my hand, and I observe on the paper precisely the words which I intended to write. In the normal condition of my spiritual and material faculties, this effect is universal. But I observe here another peculiarity. The event to be produced is foreseen by the mind, and it takes place precisely according to its predetermination. I ought, however, to add that, though this event is always foreseen and intended, yet, by education, the connection between the volition and the material result is rendered more perfect. Thus, when I began to write, I at first made nothing but straight lines, and could not for some time make them as correctly as I intended. By prac-

tice, however, I rendered the connection between the volition and the physical act more and more perfect, so that they came at last to correspond with considerable accuracy to each other.

4. Spirit may be the cause of change in spirit. This includes two cases: First, when we effect changes in the condition of our own minds; and, secondly, when we effect changes in the minds of others.

1. When we effect changes in our own minds. For instance, I am thinking of some subject; I resolve to banish it, and think of something else; I succeed. The first thought is displaced; it is to me, for the time, as if it had never existed, and I now think of something entirely different. Here, however, we may observe a considerable range in the conditions of the phenomena. In the first place, much depends on the general, and, also, on the particular energy of my will. It may be constitutionally feeble, or, by neglect, I may have lost the power of self-control. I try to banish the present thought, and it will not leave me, or, if it leaves me for the moment, it immediately returns. Again, I may know that I ought to banish the thought which now occupies me, and I resolve to do it; but, on the other hand, the thought is pleasant to me, and I am unwilling to relinquish it. Either no result, or a very imperfect one, is accomplished. Or, again, some peculiar thought has seized upon me with overwhelming power, and, under my present circumstances, I cannot displace it by any effort of my will. For instance, suppose I am a miser. I have cultivated within myself the habit of esteeming wealth the greatest of earthly blessings, and have given it the first place in my affections. By a sudden calamity, a large portion of my property is destroyed. Thinking of it will not restore it. I desire to banish the subject from my mind. I cannot; it is present with me by day and by night, tormenting me, and I

cannot help it. Here the power of the will is conditioned by the present state of the mind itself, which state is the result of successive previous volitions. We hence perceive that the act of the will here is subject to conditions wholly unknown in the third case considered; that is, where the mind acts on material substances.

2. The mind may produce change in other minds. Here the conditions become more complicated. I will suppose myself in the possession of some truth, which is, in its nature, adapted to effect a change in the mind of another; for instance, a change in his course of action. Now, the effect produced will depend both on the state of my own mind and the state of mind in those whom I address. Thus, I may conceive the truth imperfectly, feebly, so as to leave an indefinite impression on others. I may conceive of it adequately, but I may be unaffected by it myself, and may have no particular desire to affect others. Or, again, having a clear conception of it myself, I may have an all-absorbing desire to cause others to be affected as I am affected myself. Each of these conditions will probably vary the effect produced on the minds of others. Or, in this last case, supposing myself to be ever so much in earnest, the effect of my communication may be different in the case of each auditor. The effect will, in each case, be determined by the state of every man's mind. In one I may create joy, in another sorrow; one may be pleased, another displeased; one may resolve to take the course which I recommend, and another to resist it to the uttermost. Here, the same cause produces diametrically opposite effects; the effect in each individual case being determined by the present condition of the mind, and its relation to the truth which I exhibit.

Now, concerning these various cases, I would offer a few suggestions.

1. So far as I am able to discover, these are all legiti-

mate instances of cause and effect. Whether I have included them all, I pretend not to determine, but I think no exhaustive classification can be formed without including those which I have mentioned.

2. The link which binds together the cause and the effect is, in all cases, hidden. This is, I believe, universally granted. We may observe the cause and then the effect, but a veil is in all cases spread over the nexus between them, which it has not been given to the human mind to penetrate.

3. When I examine these several cases, they seem to me very unlike. The matter affecting and affected is, in the different instances, exceedingly dissimilar, and the results produced are very widely different. What can be more unlike than the freezing of water by cold and the change of the moral character of a human being by the presentation of truth?

4. Hence, I would ask, may there not be different kinds of causation? May not causation in matter be a totally different nexus from causation in mind? Were we endowed with faculties capable of knowing perfectly all the phenomena, might we not find them as dissimilar in themselves as they are in their effects?

5. Such being the possibility, can it be legitimate to reason from causation in the one case to causation in the other; that is, to conclude that because causation in matter is one thing, therefore causation in spirit is the same thing? Is not the argument for fatalism deduced from a view of the indissoluble nature of cause and effect founded on this assumption?

6. Granting, what is evidently true, that, under precisely the present conditions, any given cause must inevitably produce, whether in matter or spirit, a definite and certain

effect; are there not many things predicable of the inevitableness in the one case which cannot be predicated of it in the other? For instance, I present to a miser a case of distress, precisely calculated, in its nature, to awaken benevolent emotions in the mind of an intellectual and moral being in a normal condition. But, by a course of previous voluntary action, he has so changed his mind from its normal condition, that the recital serves no other purpose than to harden his heart against suffering. In his present condition, this result as inevitably follows from my appeal, as his death would follow from plunging a knife into his bosom. Now, granting the inevitableness in both these cases to be the same, is the nexus between the two events of the same character? Suppose me to know the inevitableness to be the same, is the moral character of the two actions equal?

If, then, finally, the nature of causation in matter and causation in mind be so unlike, when finite beings alone are concerned, that we cannot reason from the one to the other; how much greater must be the disparity when the cause is infinite, and the effect produced is on the finite! How, especially from causation in matter, can we reason respecting the acts of the Infinite Spirit, whose thoughts are not as our thoughts? It would surely be a humbler and wiser philosophy, if we believe in a Universal Cause of perfect holiness and perfect love, to receive the facts of his government as he has revealed them, assured that in the abysses of his wisdom, far past our finding out, mercy and truth go before his face, and justice and judgment are the habitation of his throne.

The notion of cause, by the constitution of the human mind, involves the idea of power. It is the logical condition to this idea; without it, the idea of cause could not exist. It is that in the cause by virtue of which it produces its effect.

It is a cause simply, and for no other reason, than that in it resides the power.

The notion of power is always fixed and invariable. We cannot conceive of it as, under the same circumstances, sometimes producing an effect and at other times producing none. When we find such an antecedent, we at once determine that it is destitute of power, and that it is not, in this case, a cause. It is essential to our conception of power, that under the same conditions it shall invariably produce the same change.

Hence, we perceive the difference between invariable succession and cause. Cause is invariable succession with the additional idea of power. Cousin's illustration here is apposite. "I sit in my room," he observes, "and wish that I could hear a certain air. Some one in another room plays it. I wish for it again, and it is played again. But this is a very different thing from taking up an instrument and playing it myself. The one is a case of succession, the other of cause and effect. In the latter, I recognize my own volition, not merely as the antecedent, but the cause of the sounds." And we may observe, still further, that the power, by reason of its invariableness, is the sole reason of the invariableness of the succession. Were not power such as I have suggested, the succession might intermit, vary, and fluctuate, indefinitely.

This idea of cause and effect, and power, is not derived from experience, as some philosophers have asserted. It springs by necessity from the original constitution of the human mind. When we observe a change we cannot do otherwise than think of the cause. The change furnishes the occasion for the creation of this idea; but, as soon as we have arrived at it, we know that the existence of the power residing in the cause was the necessary condition to the existence of the effect. It arises as truly on the first observation of a change, as on the thousandth. It is as obvious to the apprehension of children as of adults. If it was not apparent in the first instance, it could not be in the thousandth. If, in the first instance, we recognize nothing but succession, and had no idea of cause and of power, the second instance would be precisely like it, and the third, and thus indefinitely. Every one remembers the case reported of Dr. Beattie. He wrote, on the prepared soil of his garden, the name of his son, a very young child, and sowed some delicate seeds in the lines which he had thus traced. In a few days the child came running to inform him of the wonder which he had discovered — his own name plainly growing in the flower-bed. The father, for a while, pretended to believe that there was no cause for the phenomenon, but that the letters had grown in their present form of themselves, and he attempted to create this belief in his son. It was all in vain; the child could not believe it. The necessary relation of cause and effect was as deeply fixed in his mind as in the mind of his father. Dr. Beattie then made use of this illustration to teach him the necessary existence of a First Cause. The same incident, I observe, has been related of the father of Gen. Washington.

But, it may be asked, has experience nothing to do with our investigation of the laws of cause and effect? I answer, nothing whatever with our original idea of cause and of power. This is given us in the very constitution of our intellectual nature. If it were not so given, we should have no conception of a cause, and should, of course, have no occasion to institute any inquiries concerning it.

But, although experience, or more properly experiment, furnishes us with no original ideas of causation, yet, when this idea has been given us, and we know that by necessity the cause of a certain phenomenon must exist, it is by experiment alone that we are able to discover what that cause is. Experiment, therefore, follows directly upon the suggestion of causation in any particular instance. This may be clearly illustrated by observing the principles which govern us in carrying forward a case of philosophical investigation. The steps in such a process are, I think, the following:

1. We observe an instance of obvious and manifest change, or, in the language of philosophers, a phenomenon. We are so made that we cannot think of this change without also thinking of the cause which produced it. Every one knows that to speak of a change producing itself, or of a change occurring with no relation whatever to any other event, is not only to speak nonsense, but to utter what is unthinkable.

2. This notion of cause, which, in these circumstances, has arisen within us, involves the idea of power. It is, in fact, this power which makes it a cause. But, since power is a fixed and unchangeable idea, we cannot conceive of it without conceiving of it as always acting in the same way under the same circumstances. Hence, we know that in whatever antecedent the power resides, that antecedent must be the cause of the phenomenon. And, on the other hand, when we observe any antecedent to be fixed and invariable, in that we suppose the power to reside; that is, we affirm this antecedent to be the cause of the consequent effect.

3. In order, then, to ascertain the fixed and invariable antecedent, we institute our experiments. We place the phenomenon under every variety of antecedents. When we find an antecedent which, under all circumstances, invariably precedes the change, we assume this to be the cause. Henceforth, these two events hold this relation to each other.

4. Hence, we perceive that if two distinct and separate events were the stated and invariable antecedents of another

event, it would be impossible to determine which of the two was the cause. One would fulfil the conditions of the problem as well as the other. Hence we see that our knowledge of causation is never absolute, being always conditioned by the actual progress of human knowledge. Thus, so far as human observation has gone, the event A has always been the invariable antecedent of the event B. But subsequent investigations may reveal the fact that A is not the invariable antecedent, or that the antecedency of A is conditioned by some other event with which it must be combined in order to produce the effect. Thus, it was observed that water boiled at 212° of Fahrenheit, and it was, for a long time, supposed that this law was universal. It was, however, subsequently ascertained that it boiled on the tops of high mountains at a lower temperature. Hence it was necessary to condition the former law by the pressure of the atmosphere, and say that water boils at 212° at the level of the sea. If it should be found that the electrical condition of the atmosphere had any power to modify the result, it would be necessary to add this new condition to the original law.

It may be useful to illustrate these remarks by observing the manner in which we proceed in determining any particular cause. I will take, for example, the freezing of water.

I perceive, on some occasion, for the first time, that water, which I left fluid at sunset last evening, is solid this morning. I, first of all, inquire whether it be the identical substance which was a short time since fluid. I examine the vessel in which it is contained; I ascertain that no human being has approached it; that all the other water in the same vicinity has undergone the same transformation. I am satisfied that here is a case of legitimate change.

From the constitution of my mind, I am unable to conceive that this change could have been produced without an adequate cause. Had the water remained through the night, with all its relations to all other things unchanged, it must by necessity have continued in its original condition. This is to me as obvious as that if a body be at rest, it must forever remain at rest, unless some power from without compel it to assume the condition of motion. There must, therefore, be some cause for this event. The instinctive impulses of my nature lead me to inquire for this cause. This inquiry I conduct by experiment or trial. In what manner shall I proceed?

I first observe all the antecedent events which I am able to discover. For instance, the water was fluid in daylight; it became solid in darkness. Darkness may have been the cause of its solidity. It became solid in the open air; it returned to its former fluidity as soon as it was brought into the house. Change of place may have been the cause of the phenomenon. Or, again, I observe that there was a sudden change of temperature during the night, and that the mercury in the thermometer fell from 40° to 20°. This change of temperature may be the cause of which I am in search. I proceed to institute a series of experiments for the purpose of determining which of these is the invariable antecedent of the phenomenon. I find that water, in various instances, becomes solid in light as well as in darkness, and that again it becomes fluid in darkness when it had become solid in daylight. Darkness cannot, then, have been the cause. I examine the other hypothesis. Was change of place the cause? I find that, without any change of place, the water which was solid at sunrise becomes fluid at noon. Change of place will not, therefore, account for the phenomenon. Was the cause, then, the change of temperature? I subject water to this trial. I find that everywhere, and under all circumstances, when the temperature falls below 32° Fahrenheit, water becomes solid, whether by day or by night, and without any regard to locality.

therefore arrive at the conclusion that the temperature of 32° is the cause of the freezing of water, and that water has the susceptibility of being frozen at this temperature The two events thus stand to each other in the relation of cause and effect. I have discovered the cause of the event, or, in other language, I have accounted for a phenomenon. It is on these principles, and in this manner, that we proceed in any legitimate case of philosophical investigation.

Having thus obtained the idea of causation and of power, and having learned how to determine the cause in any particular case, the necessity of our intellect obliges us to proceed a step further. As we look about us, we observe that everything bears witness to the exertion of power. The universe is subject to perpetual change, and change without the idea of power is unthinkable. Day and night, sunshine and storm, summer and winter, spring and autumn, are names indicative of changes and classes of changes more numerous and more complicated than the human mind can comprehend. Power is, then, one of the most universal ideas of which we are able to conceive. But let us look at the case a little more carefully. We say that atmospheric air, moisture, and sunlight, are the causes of vegetation. Let us, then, examine the growth of a vegetable, from the putting forth of its first leaf, through all the changes of its development, to its beautiful flower and its ripened fruit. Let us examine a single leaf, and investigate all its functions, and their exquisite adaptation to coöperate in the general design. Let us generalize this case, and we find the surface of our globe to be thickly covered with just such instances. We cannot fail to observe that the beauty and adaptations of the effect infinitely transcend any attribute possessed by the physical cause. We cannot conceive of the gases of the atmosphere, the drops of water, and the rays of the sun, as adequate causes of all these wonderful results.

We conceive by necessity of some cause or causes unseen, beyond, directing, controlling, energizing, those perceived causes, in which, at first view, this power seemed to reside.

To ascend thus from apparent to unseen causes, from physical to supernatural power, seems to be the necessary tendency of our intellectual nature. The human mind is hardly capable of so intense degradation as not to recognize the existence of some power unseen, by which all that is seen is governed and sustained. Hence have arisen the innumerable systems of idolatry which have prevailed among men. Every nation recognizes some invisible powers as the causes of visible changes, and hence as objects of worship. The very absurdity of many of these systems teaches us this tendency in the clearest possible manner. The more absurd the object of worship, the stronger is the proof that the necessities of the human intellect demand some cause to which the changes of visible nature can be referred; and that it will accept the most preposterous notion of an ultimate cause, sooner than believe that no such cause exists.

But the human mind, having advanced thus far, proceeds by necessity a step further. As we contemplate the various phenomena of the universe, we observe that no class of facts, nor any single fact, is isolated. All are parts of one plan, the development of one idea. The vegetable and animal kingdoms, the laws which govern organic and inorganic nature, and the relations which subsist between them, all represent portions of one idea, which must have been conceived by a single intelligence before anything visible was created. Hence we are called upon to account for this perfect harmony in this infinite variety of parts, the perfect order which exists among beings in themselves so diverse from each other. We can account for it only on the supposition that the cause of causes is not many, but one, infinite in power and wisdom, the sufficient reason why every thing is, and why it is as we now behold it. That this opinion has universally prevailed among men who have addicted themselves to thinking, is manifest. The philosophers who paid an outward respect to the classic mythology acknowledged and reverenced the Supreme Divinity. And everywhere, among men of reflection, it has been acknowledged that, if there are causes beyond those which we perceive, there must be one universal Cause, all-powerful, all-wise, all-good, self-existent, and, of course, eternal.

But, supposing this to be granted, other questions emerge from this belief. If there be a universal, all-pervading Cause, what is the nature of his agency? In material causation, is he the sole operator in every change, so that every event is an immediate act of the Deity, or the result of such an act? Or, on the other hand, has he constituted matter with such attributes and relations that all which we see is the necessary consequence of the original creation, from which the Creator has withdrawn, and over which he now exerts no agency? And, again, in spiritual changes, similar questions arise. Does the free will of man act independently of any controlling agency of the Deity, or is the Deity the cause of spiritual change, as in the first supposition above in regard to matter? Or has he so created spirits that the changes of which we are conscious proceed by necessity from the elements of our original creation? These questions, and many more, arise from the conception of an universal, all-pervading, and all-powerful Cause.

With respect to these inquiries, I would remark, in general, that I believe the most opposite answers to either of them can probably be proved to be true, by arguments which it would be difficult to confute; and that the clearest reasoning may lead us to results at variance with the simplest dictates of our moral and intellectual nature. To what conclusion, then, shall we arrive? I answer, to the belief that the subject is clearly beyond the reach of our understanding. The point in which the infinite and the finite come in contact has been, and must ever be, hidden from mortal eyes. It is the dictate of reason and religion that the Deity is all-wise, all-good, and all-powerful, and therefore that he is the only being capable of governing the universe which he has made. It is not possible that such a being should govern it too much. On the other hand, we have the evidence of our own consciousness that we are perfectly free. We know that such a being as the Deity must carry on his wise and just and merciful intentions, and that he must carry them on through the agency of his intelligent creatures; we know, also, that we are perfectly free to act as we choose, and that this freedom is an essential element of our moral responsibility. Of the manner in which these agencies coöperate, I think we must be content to remain in ignorance.

REFERENCES.

Idea of power — Locke, Book 2, chap. 7, sec. 8.
Power, active and passive — Locke, Book 2, chap. 21, sec. 2.
Cause and effect — Locke, Book 2, chap. 26.
Idea of a God — Locke, Book 4, chap. 10, sec 1—8.
Cause and effect — Reid, Essays on In. Powers, Essay 6, chap. 6.
Power, cause and effect — Reid, Essays on Active Powers, Essay 1.
Locke's idea of power examined — Cousin, chap. 4.
Notion of power derived either from the objective or subjective — Cousin, chap. 4.

SECTION V.—SUGGESTED IDEAS ACCOMPANIED BY EMOTION.

We have thus far considered those ideas which are suggested to us by the contemplation of objects which produce in us no emotion. They are purely intellectual, and have no other effect upon us than to increase our knowledge. Thus, the ideas of duration, cause and effect, space, and a variety of others, are simple knowledges, and produce in us no ulterior state of mind.

Were we merely intellectual beings, these would be all the suggestive ideas of which we need be conscious. But we find the case to be otherwise. We are made not only to *know*, but to *feel*. As we look abroad upon the world, we find ourselves not only capable of knowing that things are or are not, but also of deriving pleasure or pain from the contemplation of them. Who does not know with what eager gaze the eyes of the child are turned towards the rainbow? Who has not been deeply moved at beholding the glory of a summer's sunset? Again, it is undeniable that we are variously affected by our observation of the actions of our fellow-men. Some of them awaken in us admiration, respect, gratitude and love; others fill us with disapprobation, disgust and abhorrence. These various cognitions, and the emotions which they create, belong, I suppose, to the class of original suggestions. They may be divided into two classes: 1, Ideas of the beautiful and the sublime, or ideas of taste; and, 2, Moral ideas.

1. *Ideas of the beautiful and sublime.*

Let us commence the exposition of this subject by an example. Suppose there were placed before us an antique marble vase of exquisite workmanship. We look at it, and observe its color, and form, and proportions. We feel of it, and discover that it is solid, smooth and heavy. We test it by our other senses, and ascertain whether or not it possesses any qualities which they can recognize. When we have done this, we have obtained all the knowledge concerning it which our perceptive faculties can give.

Let us now place by the side of it a rough block of marble, of a similar magnitude. The senses give us, as before, a knowledge of its color, form, solidity, roughness or smoothness, sonorousness, taste and smell. This knowledge is all that our perceptive faculties can give us in either case. Were we merely intellectual, that is, unemotional beings, no other impression besides that of knowledge would be produced upon us. Both of these objects would be contemplated with equal indifference; nay, the rough block might be preferred, if we could devote it to a purpose of utility of which the other was not susceptible. Thus, we are told that, not unfrequently, the remains of a beautiful statue are found imbedded in mortar, in the wall of a peasant's hovel, in the neighborhood of an ancient city on the plains of Asia Minor.

Let us now observe these objects together, and remark the feelings which they awaken within us. We cannot fail to observe that the one has a power of affecting us very differently from the other. As we look upon the one, we are conscious of an emotion of exquisite pleasure. We attach to it a value such as wealth can scarcely estimate. We look upon the other with total indifference, or, it may be, with disgust, and cast it away as an incumbrance. To the one we are powerfully attracted, while from the other we are repelled. We recognize in the one the quality of beauty, of which we perceive the other to be destitute. A child at an early age would make this distinction. Every one knows how strongly even very young persons are attracted by brilliant colors and agreeable forms. Yet this emotion cannot be defined. It arises unbidden at the contemplation of outward objects of a particular character, under such circumstances as have been appointed by the Creator to occasion it within us.

This idea is not, however, cognizable directly by the senses. We neither see, nor hear, nor feel, nor taste beauty; nor is it an energy of our minds. Yet, whenever we perceive certain external objects, there arises within us the knowledge that they are beautiful, and we are conscious of the subjective emotion which this quality occasions. In this respect it resembles the other suggested ideas. They, as we have seen, are not cognized by the senses, but the cognitions derived from the senses are the occasion of their existence. So, in this case, as soon as we are conscious of the perceptions, we are conscious of the cognition of this quality, and of the emotion which this quality produces.

The emotion of the beautiful is suggested by an infinite variety of objects in the external world. It arises from the contemplation of form, of color, of motion, of proportion, and, in fact, from almost every object in nature. I shall not here enter into an illustration of these obvious facts. It is sufficient merely to allude to them, reserving the more extended discussion to another place.

If we observe the various objects which give occasion to this emotion, we shall observe them to be exceedingly dissimilar. The objects are unlike, but the emotion is the same. We thus learn to distinguish the emotion produced, from the causes which produce it. Having done this, we ascribe to any object this quality, if it produces in us this particular emotion. Thus, the mathematician speaks of the beauty of a demonstration; the critic, of the beauty of a metaphor; the moralist, of the beauty of a social relation; and the mechanic of the beauty of a machine. In each case, the emotion of the beautiful is awakened in the mind of the speaker, and he ascribes the quality of beauty to that which produces it.

There is also another emotion, suggested by the contemplation of material and immaterial objects, in many respects similar to the emotion of beauty. The mode of its origin is the same. It is suggested, in the first instance, by objects in nature; it is a source of exquisite pleasure; it arises on a great variety of occasions; but yet the emotion itself is always the same. Its character may perhaps be best illustrated by an example. He who has stood by the sea-side in a storm may perhaps remember the ceaseless roar of the waves, the rude shock of the surge, which, heaving itself against the cliff, made the solid rock to tremble beneath him, and the tossing of the white foam as it flew from the crest of the billow. All this might have been equally well perceived by the dog at his feet, or the wild sea-bird, as, screaming in gladness, it dashed into the thickest of the spray. But these are not all the ideas that arise within the bosom of the man. Besides all these, he feels an emotion of awe, and yet of exultation; of solemnity, and yet of excitement; of humility when he thinks of his own littleness, and yet of greatness when he yields himself up to the conceptions which crowd upon him. His imagination roams over the ocean; he muses upon its matchless power, its vast extent, its deceitful smiles, and its sudden wrath, until he is bewildered in the throng of his thick-coming fancies. Every one recognizes in this the emotion of sublimity.

Here, as before, we perceive that this idea, and the emotion which accompanies it, are entirely different from the simple perceptions by which they are occasioned. They could not arise without the perceptions, and the perceptions would be perfect without them. They are called forth under peculiar circumstances in obedience to the principles of our constitution, and, having once arisen, they remain with us, irrespective of the circumstances that gave them birth.

Having, however, obtained this idea, with its corresponding emotion, we find that it is excited by a variety of spiritual conceptions, as well as external perceptions. The infinite in space and duration, immaculate justice, heroic self denial, self-sacrificing love, and a large variety of the more majestic moral qualities, excite this emotion in a very high degree. How dissimilar soever they may be in themselves, if they awaken this emotion we class them under the same designation, and call them all sublime. Hence we speak of the sublime in nature and in art, of the sublime in eloquence, in poetry, and in action. The external objects which awaken this emotion are dissimilar, but, producing a similar effect, we comprehend them all under the same classification.

Of moral ideas derived from suggestion.

Thus far we have observed chiefly those suggested ideas which may be derived from irrational objects. It would be natural to expect that suggestions of a peculiar character would be occasioned by observing the actions of our fellow-men, intelligent and accountable agents.

Thus, for instance, I find myself in possession of a certain amount of power. I can move my limbs in any direction. I know, however, that these motions are not uncaused; they are consequent upon, and caused by, the energy of my own will. I look further, and find that my will does not act at random. I will to perform an action, in order to accomplish a certain purpose. So long as I am sane, that is, governed by the established laws of my being, I find these two antecedents, will and motive, always preceding every act of power which I exert.

If I observe the acts of others, I come to the same conclusion. I cannot conceive of an act of a man in a normal condition, without considering it as emanating from his will; nor can I conceive of an act of the will uninfluenced by any motive. Hence, when we contemplate the act of an intelligent being, we always involve in our conceptions not merely the outward change, but also the will in which it originated and the motive by which the will was governed

15*

But our acts commonly influence the happiness, or affect the rights of our fellow-men. Whenever we observe such an act, there arises in the mind a wholly new idea, unlike any which we have thus far examined; it is the idea of right or wrong. A particular quality in that action is immediately recognized. Perception gives us nothing but the external act; but by virtue of our constitution there is suggested to us a moral quality, something very different from the external action itself; and the cognition of this quality is always attended by certain subjective affections. These subjective affections are the most important of any of which we are susceptible. The faculty of the mind which gives rise to these objective cognitions and subjective affections is called conscience. It belongs to moral philosophy to treat of this subject at large.

I might mention various other instances of original suggestion, but the above will suffice to illustrate my meaning. It will, I think, be obvious, from what I have said, that, by virtue of this power, we possess a distinct and most important source of knowledge. The ideas which we derive in this manner are unlike those either of perception or consciousness, yet they are no less truly clear and definite, and really lie at the foundation of all our subsequent knowledge. They seem, more than any other of our ideas, to result from the exertion of the pure intellect. We know them to be true, without the intervention of any media. The intellect with which we are created vouches for their truth, and we cannot conceive them to be false.

If it be asked how we may improve this faculty, I answer that in a matter so simple, when our knowledge is intuitive, rules seem almost useless. A few suggestions may, however, not be wholly without advantage.

It must be obvious to every one, that our train of thought may follow in the line of our perceptions, or of our suggestions. We may pass from perception to perception without heeding the suggestions to which they give occasion; or, detaining every perception, we may follow out to their utmost extent the suggestions which spring from it. The former is the habit of the superficial, the latter of the reflective mind. The one cognizes only the facts which are visible on the surface; the other arrives at a knowledge of the hidden relations by which all that is seen is united together and directed. Millions of men, before Sir Isaac Newton, had seen an apple fall to the ground, but the sight awakened no suggestion; or, if it did, the suggestion was neither retained nor developed. He seized upon it at once, followed it to its results, and found that he had caught hold of the thread which could guide him through the labyrinth of the universe.

If, then, we would cultivate the faculty of original suggestion, we must exercise it by patient thought. Suggestions will arise in our minds, if we will only heed them, and they will arise the more abundantly the more carefully we heed them. We should attend to our own intuitions, examine their character, determine their validity, and follow them to their results. We should have due respect for the teachings of our own individual intelligence. What other men have thought is valuable, but its chief value is, not to save us from the labor of thinking, but to enable us to think the better for ourselves. If, with patient earnestness, we thus follow out the suggestions of our own minds, we shall find them enriched and invigorated. Instead of drinking forever at the fountains of other men, the mind will thus discover a fountain within itself. "If," said Sir Isaac Newton, "I am in any respect different from other men, it is in the power of patient thought."

REFERENCES.

Origin of moral ideas — Locke, Book 2, chap. 2, secs. 1, 2 ; book 2, chap. 21, sec. 42 ; book 2, chap. 28, sec. 5.

Cousin, chap. 5.

Necessity of patient thought in cultivating original suggestion — Locke Book 4, chap. 3, sec. 22—30.

Abercrombie, Part 4, sec. 1.

CHAPTER IV.

ABSTRACTION.

In order the more definitely to understand the nature of Abstraction, let us review the ground which we have passed over, that we may the more distinctly perceive the point from which we are about to proceed.

We have seen that by perception we cognize external objects, and that by consciousness we cognize our internal energies. Our knowledge, however, derived from both of these sources, is individual and concrete. I perceive a tree; it is an individual tree. I perceive fifty trees; they are all individuals, differing in various respects from each other but each a distinct and unique object of perception. So, also, I am conscious of an act of memory, that is, of remembering a particular object. I am conscious of remembering another. Each act is numerically, and as I think of it, distinct from every other act. Our conceptions of these acts are of the same character as the acts themselves, and, with these powers alone, every idea would be as distinct from every other idea as the grains of sand on the sea-shore, without either cohesion or fusibility.

The same remark applies in substance to the ideas derived from original suggestion. Of these ideas some I know are general, and can be referred to no particular object. Such are the ideas of space, duration, infinity, and perhaps some others. These are cognized as universal and necessary a soon as the mind begins to think; and, as they are at the beginning, so they remain forever, unsusceptible of either change or modification. Another class of our suggestive ideas is, however, of a different character. I perceive, for instance, a case of change, as the rolling of a ball, or the falling of a pin. The idea of cause and power at once suggests itself, but it is of the power requisite to produce this effect, and this only. It is the idea, not of causation in general, but of causation in this individual instance. Should I see another case of change, the same notion of causation would arise, but it would again be of an individual change, and would be wholly disconnected from that which I observed before. That is, every idea of causation would be indissolubly connected with that change by which it was occasioned, and thus our knowledge of causation would be nothing more than the remembrance of these several isolated and separate facts.

If, then, our intellectual powers were limited to those which we have already considered, it is easy to imagine what must be our condition. We could perceive individual objects, and be conscious of the exertion of individual energies, or of the putting forth of certain intellectual acts. Every object of perception would be distinct and disconnected, and equally so the conceptions which it originated. Our knowledge would be all of individuals, and every object must have its own proper name, or that which is equivalent to it. When we speak of different men, we call them John, James, William, meaning by each of these terms to designate an individual unlike every other in existence. Such would be our knowledge if we had no other faculties than those already examined.

But, if we look into our own minds, and observe the minds of other men, we find our condition to be the reverse of all this. Proper names, or those used to designate individuals, are the rarest words in a language. We use them only to point out persons and places, and when these are not alluded to such words are never employed. In works of science they have no place whatever, unless we find it necessary to refer to some historical fact. Language is made up altogether of words designating classes of things, as book, house, tree, idea; or of qualities, as red, white, blue, warm, cold; or of actions, as walk, ride, think, give, take; or of relations, as by, to, upon, &c. When we use these words we have no reference to individuals, and desire merely to indicate classes of things, actions, qualities or relations, signified by these terms. So universally is this the case, that, when we wish to individualize a particular object, we are obliged to use several descriptive terms, in order to distinguish it from its class. Thus, if I wish to direct attention to a particular table, I am obliged to refer to it as my table, of such a color and size, or standing in such a place, or bought of such a person. In this manner we select an individual from a class, in order to make it an object of particular attention.

We observe, then, what our conceptions *would* be, were we endowed with no other powers than those which we have thus far considered. We see, on the other hand, what our conceptions actually *are*. With no other powers than those of perception, consciousness, and original suggestion, our ideas would be all of individuals. But we find, in fact, that they are the reverse of this—that they are all of classes. We naturally inquire, How does this change take place? How do we pass from the conception of individuals to the conception of generals? How, from single, isolated, concrete facts, do we form notions of classes, or of genera and species? It is to this subject that we are now to direct our attention.

Abstraction is that faculty of the mind by which from

individual, concrete conceptions, we form general and abstract ideas.

Though I speak of abstraction as a faculty of the mind, I am aware that it is, in many respects, unlike those of which I have thus far treated. It gives us no new knowledge, like perception, consciousness and original suggestion; it only modifies the knowledge which we have acquired by these faculties. It does not, like them, perform its office by a single act. On the contrary, it accomplishes its object by a succession of acts, each one different from both the others. Yet, as it performs a function which could be performed by no other power,—as it actually *does* something, and as a faculty is the power of doing something,—I think we cannot err in designating it by the same general name which is given to the other intellectual energies.

In the mental process by which we pass from individuals to generals, three separate acts can be distinctly perceived; these are *analysis*, *generalization* and *combination*.

1. *Analysis*. I have remarked, when treating of conception, that we have the power of retaining a notion of any object of perception after the object is removed, precisely similar to that which we formed when we were perceiving it. For instance, I saw a rose yesterday. I cognized it then as present, and observed its color, form, magnitude, as a distinct and concrete object, uniting in itself these various and dissimilar qualities. I retain to-day a notion of it as an object absent, uniting in itself all the various qualities which I cognized in it as present. The difference, subjectively, is merely between the notion of the object as present and the notion of it as absent. Now, when I make the conception of this rose an object of reflection, I am able to separate, in thought, these qualities from each other; that is, to think of each quality separately, without thinking of the others. Thus, I may think, exclusively, of

its color, then of its form, its weight, &c.; at each time banishing from my mind the conception of all the other qualities. I look upon a lily; I form a conception of it in the same manner, and in the same manner can I, in thought, separate its qualities one from the other, making each one of them the exclusive object of attention. I behold a mountain as present. I form a conception of it as absent. I can think exclusively of its form, or its magnitude, or its color, or its trees, or of the strata of which it is formed. The act by which we thus, in thought, separate the elements of a concrete conception from each other, and consider each one by itself as a distinct object of thought, is commonly termed abstraction. I prefer to call it analysis, as this word sufficiently designates its character, and distinguishes it from the other acts which with it go to make up the process of abstraction.

I wish it, however, to be distinctly remembered, that this act, in every case, has for its object an individual conception. I have analyzed my conception of a rose, and considered its qualities separately. But they are the qualities of this particular rose, and nothing more. The case is the same when I analyze a lily, or a mountain; it is not the analysis of any and every lily, or mountain, but only of that one which I saw, and of which I now form a conception. The color is not the color of roses, or lilies, but only of this particular rose, or of that particular lily. The same remark applies to the form, fragrance, or any other of its qualities. It is just the same as if I, for the first time, saw one of these objects, and were never to see it again. In thought, I separate each one of its qualities from the other, and then the mental act terminates.

2. *Generalization.* By analysis I have separated the qualities of an individual rose. Suppose I were called upon to give to each of them a name; I could do it in no other

manner than by designating each of them by the name of the object from which the concrete conception was derived. I must call them, for instance, the color, the form, the fragrance, the weight, of the rose A. But suppose, now, another rose is presented to me. I analyze the conception which I have formed of it as before, and find it made up of color, form, fragrance, etc. These qualities now cease to be the qualities of the rose A; they become the qualities of the roses A and B. I see a hundred roses. I analyze the con ceptions which I form of them, and find the same qualities in each. These qualities cease, then, to be the qualities of the roses A and B, but become the qualities of roses.

But I proceed further, and analyze the conception I have formed of other objects, as, for instance, of a carnation, a peony; and I find that the color of the rose is also the color of these flowers. I observe again, and find that cherries and other fruits present the same color. It ceases, then, to be the color of roses, or flowers, or fruits; and, by necessity, separating it from every object in which I perceived it, I designate it by a particular name, and call it red. Again; I observe a violet; I analyze the conception which I form of it, and call the color, the color of this particular violet. I see several violets, all having the same color, and then this color becomes to me the color of violets. I observe monks-hood, and various other flowers, different kinds of fruit, the heavens above me, and many other objects clothed in the same color; and it is no longer the color of a violet, or of violets. I give it a name to designate this particular quality, and call it blue. Henceforward I think of it by itself, without any reference to all, or any, of the objects in which I at first detected it. It forms, in my mind, a distinct conception. Again; I find that every object which I perceive has a particular mode of addressing the eye Some are red, some are blue, some are brown. I consider this impression, aside from the various objects which produce it, and give it a general name, color.

In this manner we form simple abstract ideas of the several qualities which we observe. We derive them originally from individuals, in the manner above stated; but we conceive of them without respect to any individuals whatever.

When these simple abstract ideas are thus formed, they constitute the alphabet which we use in thinking. As we unite the letters of the alphabet into syllables, syllables into words, and words into sentences and discourse, so these simple abstract ideas, combined into the various forms of complex conceptions, form the matter which we use in the exercise of the powers of reasoning and imagination.

3. *Combination.* The process in this case is exceedingly obvious. Having obtained these simple abstract ideas, disconnected from any subject in which they originally existed, it is manifestly in our power to unite them together so as to form any complex conceptions that we may desire. Thus, to refer to the previous instances, I have formed simple abstract ideas of red, blue, the form and the fragrance of a rose, the color, form, and fragrance of a lily, or violet, the magnitude and form of a mountain. It is evident that I may recombine these different simple ideas just as I choose. I can, in conception, unite the form of a rose with the color of a lily, and the fragrance of a violet. I should, then, have the conception of a white rose with the perfume of a violet. I can unite the idea of the form of a mountain with the color red, and I then have a red mountain. I may combine the notion of red with the leaves and green with the petals of a rose, and I have a green rose with red leaves, &c.

In this manner we are every moment forming conceptions by means of language, either written or spoken. A few days since I read in a newspaper an account of a new variety of roses which had been discovered in North Carolina; its peculiarity consisting in this, that the petals of the flower were green. I unite together the simple abstract ideas indicated by the words, and I have almost as definite conception of it as if I had seen it. So, when any new plant, or animal, or work of art, is described to us, we immediately unite the several simple ideas in the manner indicated by our informer, and the conception stands before our minds like a reality.

From this view of the subject, we see that abstraction — meaning by this term the three several acts entering into this process — is indispensable to the formation of language. To make the most simple affirmation by the use of proper names, or individual concrete conceptions, such as they are delivered to us by perception, consciousness, and original suggestion, is manifestly impossible. We must, by such combinations as I have mentioned, form ideas designating classes; or language could not exist. If we examine the words of a language, we shall find that, except such as designate simple ideas, they are all used to express a group of ideas united under a single term. The definition of a word analyzes it, and shows the various simple ideas of which it is composed. Thus, if we take any words at random, as debtor, creditor, father, brother, friend, country patriotism, treachery, murder, robbery, &c., we shall find that each of them is composed of several distinct ideas. A correct definition gives us every element that essentially belongs to the compound conception.

We thus learn the manner in which the communication of thought is rendered practicable. A single word is made the vehicle of ever so large a group of conceptions. If, instead of using such words, we were obliged at length to enumerate all the ideas which they designate, human intercourse by language must cease. The thought now expressed m a single sentence would require pages for its development, and the multitude of apparently disconnected ideas would render the comprehension of an ordinary statement almost impossible.

From these illustrations of the nature of abstraction, it appears that the exercise of this faculty may give rise to two different classes of conceptions. The first class is formed entirely in obedience to our own will. Having formed simple abstract ideas, we have the power to unite them together in just such compound conceptions as we please. We may conceive of the magnitude of a mountain with the form and color of a rose; we have then a conception of a rose as great as a mountain. We may unite the form of wings with that of a horse, and we have the conception of a winged horse. We may go further, and unite in one complex conception various distinct images of beauty. Thus, Milton, from various scenes which he had beheld, selected those portions best adapted to his purpose, and formed the complex conception of the Garden of Eden. So the sculptor, from several specimens of the human form, selects those features which seem best suited to his purpose, and unites them in one conception more perfect than any which he has seen in actual existence. When we use this faculty for these purposes, we call it Imagination.

But we use this faculty for another purpose. By means of it we form all our classifications of the objects of nature, and hence it lies at the foundation of all natural science. Here, however, we find it acting under different conditions from those which we have last considered. The elements of our complex conceptions were then subject to nothing but the will. Our object was to please, and, if this was accomplished, our whole end was attained. Here, our object is to instruct. We desire our classifications to coincide with objects in nature, and if they do not our labor is worse than thrown away. We are, therefore, restricted in our materials to the matters of fact before us. In forming a complex conception from nature, we must combine precisely those elements which nature herself has combined, and neither more nor less. In just so far as my conception departs from the fact in nature, it is imperfect, superfluous, or monstrous. If I am forming a scientific conception of a lion, I must admit into it precisely those elements which nature has united in this class of animals. If I form a conception of a lion at will, I may add to it wings, any color that pleases me, and any magnitude that will answer my purpose. In the one case, we have the conception of a physiologist; in the other, of an imaginative sculptor, such as designed the winged lions in the temples of Nineveh.

The manner in which we form the classifications of science may, then, be easily illustrated. Suppose a physiologist wishes to form a scientific conception of a horse. A specimen is presented to him; he examines the outward appearance of the animal, its form, color, motion; he dissects it, and examines its internal structure, the peculiarities of its skeleton, the number of its bones, their position and relations to each other. He takes note of these elements with all the care in his power. These various simple ideas belong to nothing but this individual specimen, the horse A. Let another specimen be in a similar manner examined. He notes, as before, all its elementary ideas, and proceeds until he has satisfied himself that further investigation is useless. But these various elements have now ceased to be the elements of any particular horse; they are the elements of the class of animals whose character he is investigating.

He is now desirous of uniting these several ideas into a conception that shall apply not to one or another horse, but to all horses. He compares these elementary ideas, and finds some of them constant; that is, belonging to all the horses he has seen. Others of them are inconstant; that is, they belong to some, and not to others. He separates the one from the other, uniting in one complex conception all the constant elements, and leaving out of his conception all that are variable. For instance, the form of the skeleton, the number of vertebræ, the structure and number of the teeth, the organs of digestion, etc., are constant. These are found to be the same in all. On the other hand, color, size, and many other elements, are variable. It is by the union of these constant qualities that he forms his general abstract idea of a horse, referring to no horse in particular, but being the conception which answers in his mind to that word when it is used either by himself or others. In this manner all our general conceptions, that is, conceptions comprehending a number of similar objects, are formed. That we are always conscious of every step of the process, I do not affirm. We are so continually performing this mental operation, that we give no heed to the manner in which we proceed. If, however, any one will pause, and observe his own mental operations, I think he will find them such as I have attempted to describe.

I have spoken of the mode in which our general abstract conceptions are formed in matters of science. It is proper to remark that all men, whether learned or unlearned, proceed precisely in the same manner. A common man, in forming his notion of a horse, acts just like a physiologist. The only difference is, that the one is able to detect a greater number of elementary ideas, and is the better able to distinguish the constant from the variable. The one observes merely the elements which are obvious to the senses; the other, by dissection, examines the organs which perform the functions necessary to the existence of the animal. The difference, then, is, that the observation of the one covers a larger field, and is made with more minute accuracy, than the other. Both, however, depend on the same principles, and obey the same intellectual impulses.

It will be readily seen, from what has been remarked, that abstraction, or the faculty by which we form classes, is indispensable to enumeration. Whenever we speak of any number of objects, we must first reduce them to a class. Thus, if I were asked how many are there in this room, how would it be possible to reply? I ask how many what? — how many persons, or books, or chairs, or tables, or things? Until I know the class to which the objects to be enumerated belong, I can never reply to the question.

I have thus explained the manner in which we form general abstract conceptions, or conceptions of classes. Let us examine the manner in which we proceed when we form our conceptions of genera and species.

Let us take, for instance, our conception of horse; it is a conception formed by the union of all the constant elements which we have found existing in that animal. Suppose I proceed, and examine a zebra, an ass, an elephant. I form general conceptions of these, as I did of the horse. I now compare these several conceptions together, and find that there are certain elements in which they all agree, while each one has additional elements peculiar to itself. I combine in one conception the elements which they all possess in common, and gave to it the name pachydermata, which includes all these several classes. This general name distinguishes the genus, while the additional elements, by which these subordinate classes differ from each other, mark the species. Thus it may be said that these several classes of animals form species, included in the genus pachydermata.

As we proceed in our investigations, we observe various other classes of animals, as carnivora, rodentia, and a multitude of others. We compare these genera together, and find that in certain elements, gradually growing less numerous, they all agree. I form a larger class by uniting those less numerous elements into a simple conception, and give to that conception the name mammalia. Pursuing my examination further, I find other classes of animals, as numerous as mammalia, differing from them in many important respects, yet having one or more elements in common; for instance, they all have vertebræ. I then form a generic class, by uniting in one conception the few and simple elements which they all hold in common. This forms my widest and most comprehensive generalization.

We see, then, that vertebrate comprehends under it an immense number of individuals; that is, every one endowed with this form. Under this are several subordinate classes, each one possessing this element, and also something additional peculiar to itself, as mammalia, fishes, etc. If I now take one of these second classes, I find that under it are several sub-genera, each one possessing all the elements of the genus, and also some other elements by which it differs from every other sub-genus. In this manner I descend, until I come to the lowest species or variety, in which all the individuals are, in all constant elements, similar to each other. In this manner we form the genera and species of science. We of course find that, the greater the number of elements which enter into the idea of a class, the smaller is the number of individuals under it; and, on the other hand, the smaller the number of elements in the idea of a class, the greater the number of individuals which it comprehends.

From what we have here observed, we perceive the difference between the process of investigation and of instruction. In investigation, we proceed from particulars to generals; we discover particular facts and reduce them to classes, and then, going still further, comprehend these classes under more general classes, until we have arrived at the widest generalizations in our power. But, when we wish to instruct, or communicate knowledge to others, this process is reversed. We then begin with the simplest and most universal principles, comprehending the greatest number of individuals under them. From these we proceed to the largest subordinate genera, from these to sub-genera or species, until we have mastered the whole class of objects which our most generic classification comprehends. At each step, as we proceed downwards from the more to the less general, we add some new elements, until we at last arrive at the conception of the individuals, with which, in the labor of investigation, we commenced.

And hence we learn the nature of a definition in science.

When we define any scientific conception, we first mention the genus to which it belongs, and then the specific difference, or those other elements, which, being added to the conception of the genus, designate its peculiar species. Thus, in geometry, we define a figure as "any combination of lines which encloses space." Here "combination of lines" is the generic idea, and "enclosing space" is the specific difference, or the element added to the generic idea which makes out our conception of a figure. Again; "a plane triangle is a figure bounded by three straight lines." Here, again, "figure" denotes the genus, and "bounded by three straight lines" is the specific difference, or the element added to the conception of figure which gives us the conception of the species, triangle. So, again, "a right-angled triangle is a triangle one of whose angles is a right angle." Here, again, "triangle" is the genus, and "one of whose angles is a right angle" is the specific difference, or the element added to the idea of triangle which creates the conception of a right-angled triangle.

Hence, we see that simple objects, or those which have

no parts, or into the conception of which no plurality of elements enters, can never be defined. They can furnish no specific difference, nor can they, by analysis of elements, be classed within any genus. In such cases, we are obliged merely to describe the circumstances under which the object is presented to our cognition, or else place the subject himself under these circumstances. Thus, if we wish to make known to any man a simple energy of the mind, we mention the circumstances under which it arises; he refers to his own experience, and instantly recognizes our meaning. If he has had no such experience, he can never arrive at the knowledge. Thus, I cannot define seeing to a blind man, for it is a simple act. I describe to him the circumstances under which it occurs to me, but under the same circumstances he receives no impression. There is, therefore, an impassable gulf between us, so far as this cognition is concerned. The case is similar in all our simple cognitions.

The question has arisen, and formerly it was argued with great bitterness, what is the object of our thought when we form a general conception? Thus, I think of animal, quadruped, mammal, man, tree, etc. There is nothing in nature answering to this conception, for every individual possesses all the elements which enter into my conception, and also many more. What, then, is the object of thought, when we think any of these ideas? Some philosophers asserted that there was an actual object corresponding to this conception; and others, that, when we formed a general conception, the only object was the word which designated it. The one class was called realists, the other nominalists. It is needless to enter into this discussion at present. It is evident that conception is a mode of thought, and that there is in this act nothing numerically distinct from the mental act itself. It is true, as Sir W. Hamilton has observed. that we may in thought make a distinction between the faculty or state of the mind in conception, and the concept or notion in which this act exhibits itself. But there is no existing thing numerically different from the act, and, therefore, it seems evident that both nominalists and realists were equally wide of the truth.

From these illustrations, I hope that the manner in which we form classes and general conceptions will be sufficiently understood. It is, however, evident that this process may be employed in a great variety of ways. Abstraction enables us to classify, but we may classify for different purposes, and thus, under different circumstances, select different elements as the basis of our classification.

It may be useful to mention some of the more common and obvious principles by which our classifications are determined.

1. We very frequently form classes from our observation of the external appearance, the form, color, magnitude, etc., or from an examination of the internal structure. Thus, as I have before remarked, men classify the objects which they behold, as animals, birds, etc., according to their external appearance; the physiologist classifies them by an examination of their internal structure, and the manner in which they perform the various functions necessary to life. Such are, in general, the classifications in the various departments of natural history.

Here it is proper to remark that, having once formed our classification, we naturally refer a new specimen to some one of the classes which we have found already existing. It seems, however, strange, that, while knowledge is ever advancing, men are disposed to believe, at every successive step, that they have arrived at its ultimate limits. Yet such is manifestly the infirmity of man. Hence it is that our classifications are frequently incorrect. Supposing, incautiously, that the classes which we have recognized include all the specimens or all the facts that can exist, we are liable to refer a new specimen or a new fact to a class to which it does not belong. Thus the islanders of the Pacific, who had never seen any other quadrupeds than hogs and goats, upon seeing a cow, declared that it must be either a large goat or a horned hog. These being the only classes they had ever observed, they naturally supposed that this new specimen must be referred to either the one or the other. This was the error of savages, but the same error is liable to occur among philosophers. What is called accounting for a phenomenon is nothing more than referring it to some law, or general classification, under which it is comprehended. Thus, if I am asked why a stone falls to the earth, I account for it by replying that all matter is reciprocally attractive; that is, I refer this individual fact to a general law, or the expression of a more general fact. From the disposition to refer a new phenomenon to some established law, philosophers as well as savages are exposed to error. In the case of philosophers, however, the error is liable to be carried a step further. When they cannot account for a phenomenon,— that is, when they know of no class to which to refer it,— they not unfrequently deny its existence; taking it for granted that if they cannot account for a phenomenon, it could not have occurred. It is for this cause that every new discovery is obliged to fight its way to a place in science, against the whole influence of philosophic incredulity. So far as this leads to a more thorough investigation of whatever claims to be a discovery, it is well and reasonable; but so far as it rejects whatever cannot be accounted for as unworthy of examination and deserving only of ridicule, it is neither well nor reasonable, and is directly opposed to all true progress in science. Philosophers would frequently be wise would they bear in mind the instruction of the poet:

"There are more things in heaven and earth, Horatio,
Than are dreamed of in your philosophy."

2. Individuals may be classified by similarity of cause Here we neglect entirely all consideration of external appearance or of internal structure, and, forming the conception of a particular cause, combine into one class every individual to which that cause gives origin. Thus, the geologist may arrange rocks into two classes, the one of which has resulted from the action of fire, and the other from the action of water. The physician may arrange diseases according to the causes which have produced them, one class resulting from the affection of the nerves, another from the affections of the lungs, the stomach, etc.

3. We may classify individuals from similarity of effects. Here, omitting all consideration of appearance, structure, and origin, we form a conception of a particular effect. Having formed this conception, we comprehend under it every individual which will produce the effects in question. The physician arranges all the substances in the materia medica on this principle. It matters not to him whether the articles which he is examining belong to the animal, vegetable or mineral kingdom. We classify them as narcotics, stimulants, sudorifics, emetics, etc., according, solely, to the effects which they are known to produce upon the human organism. Thus, the critic classes objects in nature or art according to the effect which they are known to produce upon the human mind. He calls a landscape, a metaphor, a picture, beautiful, graceful or sublime, as he observes it to produce these particular emotions on the mind of man.

It will appear, from these few illustrations. that the varieties of classification are as numerous as the principles on which classifications may be formed. Every art has its own principles, on which it classifies the substances on which its labor is exerted. The same individual may thus be comprehended under as many different classes as there are different conceptions formed in the minds of those who contemplate it. The physician, the botanist, and the poet, may all examine the same plant, and each will assign it to a different class, according to the controlling ideas by which his classification is governed.

It is obvious that a faculty, which enters so essentially into all the modes of thought, must greatly influence our intellectual character. This will be rendered the more evident if we consider the separate acts which form the process of abstraction, and observe the manner in which the predominance of either affects the elements of our intellectual constitution.

1. Analysis. This power to detect and distinguish from each other all the various qualities of an external object, and all the various changes of a material or a spiritual phenomenon, is frequently denominated acuteness of observation. It is essentially what we have spoken of under the name of analysis. Its importance to a thinker or discoverer is manifest. As every variety of external appearance indicates a modification of internal quality, and as every variation in the process of a change indicates some alteration in the condition of the cause, it is obvious that this power must be of prime importance to a philosopher. He who is best able to analyze the constituent elements of the objects to which his attention is directed, whether in the world within or the world without, is the most richly provided with the materials for accurate judgment. It is thus that an accurate observer frequently detects facts which result in important discoveries, that have always been within the reach of his contemporaries, but which had never before attracted their attention. From the want of this power, the effects of one cause are sometimes ascribed to another; important causes are undetected; cause and effect, antecedent

and consequent, are blended together; and, in general, research becomes vague, unsatisfactory, and unworthy of reliance. He, then, who desires to attain to accuracy of philosophical inquiry, should strive to cultivate this power to the greatest perfection. Nor is this all. By this instrument we are able to detect sophistry, and lay bare the insufficient foundations of all false reasoning. It was from want of acuteness of observation that Locke fell into many of his most important errors. The value of this endowment is also conspicuously seen in the review of his Philosophy, by Cousin, an author of surpassing mental acuteness. This power has always been largely developed in those favored individuals who have made the most important additions to our knowledge of the laws of nature.

2. Of different, but not inferior, importance to a cultivated mind, is the power of generalization. Acuteness of observation will discover new facts, and observe changes heretofore unknown; it will analyze what is concrete, and unravel what is complicated; but it will do no more. If we possess only this power, we may do important service to science by collecting valuable materials; but we shall collect them only that they may be wrought into philosophical laws by the genius of others. Besides this, therefore, an inquirer after truth needs a power which, having discovered an important relation, shall enable him to detect it under whatsoever changes of condition it may be hidden. He will thus be able to arrange under each class those individuals which the Creator himself has arranged under it, and trace out a given cause through all the diversities of time and place to which its influence may have extended. Probably no power of the human mind has been so fertile in discovery as this. From a single observation of an hitherto unnoticed phenomenon, or from the minute and almost microscopic experiments of the laboratory, the philosopher is

able frequently to enunciate a law which controls the most important changes of the universe. It was thus that Sir Isaac Newton, having accurately determined the law which governed the fall of an apple, at once began to generalize this idea. If this law governs bodies at small distances from the earth, why should it not govern bodies at great distances? If it governs bodies at great distances from the earth, why may it not reach to the moon, and govern her motion in her orbit? and if the moon in relation to the earth, why not the earth and planets in relation to the sun? Thus, by following out this elementary law, the germ was evolved of the greatest discovery recorded in the annals of science. In a similar manner, Dr. Franklin made himself acquainted, by experiment, with the laws of the electric fluid. He observed the phenomena of lightning in the thunder-cloud. Comparing them together, and making due allowance for the difference between the vastness of nature and the littleness of man, he detected the same elementary phenomena in both, and the question at once occurred to him, Are they not identical? A simple experiment decided the question in the affirmative, and added a wide domain to the empire of human knowledge. It was also a rare combination of these two powers of observation and generalization that gave to Cuvier the first place among the naturalists of his own, and, perhaps, of every age.

3. Intellectual character is also affected by the degree in which we are endowed with the power of combination.

I have already remarked that the power of combination may be either poetic or scientific; that is, that we may form our combinations at will, or they may be limited by the objects in nature from which they are derived. This difference of endowment distinguishes the class of Milton and Shakspeare from that of Newton and Franklin.

But, passing this general distinction, it is evident that

the power of scientific combination is possessed by men in very unequal degrees. Suppose a philosopher to have observed with accuracy a series of phenomena. He has them before him,— the facts and the order of their succession. He knows that under the same conditions the same succession will be repeated. But this is not enough. What are the unseen changes of which these phenomena are the manifestations; and what are the relations which they sustain to each other? In a word, what is the rationale of these several changes? As, for instance, he places a piece of wood on the fire; it inflames and burns to ashes. The facts are visible and common, and he knows that another piece of wood, under the same conditions, will be subject to the same changes. But what is the rationale of these changes? What is combustion? What is flame? What is ashes? What are the combinations formed and dissolved during the change of wood to a substance so utterly unlike itself? Here, then, is a demand for philosophical combination. The next step is to form a conception of such unseen causes as will be sufficient to account for the phenomena.

The power of forming such conceptions exists in very different degrees. Some men merely observe the facts, and give themselves no trouble to ascertain the cause. Others, in seeking for a cause, form conceptions after the manner of the poets, which have no relation to established laws, and can never be verified by observation or experiment. He who is endowed with true philosophical genius seems instinctively to originate combinations analogous to truth, which become the immediate precursors to discovery. I do not say that there is anything of the nature of proof in a conception of this kind, only that it serves to direct the inquiries of the original investigator. Having formed his conception, his next business is to prove it to be true. When he has done this, his discovery is made. Without proof, nothing has yet been determined; but without some conception to direct investigation, there could be no proof, for there would be nothing to prove. Sir Isaac Newton and Sir Humphrey Davy seem to me to have been richly endowed with the power of scientific combination. On the other hand, Dr. Priestley, though an eminent philosopher, seems to have possessed it in a very imperfect degree. Though his discoveries were numerous, and of the highest importance, yet all his theories of the changes which he observed have long since been exploded.

The power of philosophical combination, of necessity, improves with the progress of science. As the laws of nature and her modes of operation are better understood, we form conceptions more and more analogous to truth. We learn to think more and more in harmony with the ideas of the Creator; and, from a larger and more accurate acquaintance with the known, we are the better able to unravel the mysteries of the unknown. When it was observed that water would rise in a pump, the solution of the phenomenon at first said to be given was that nature abhorred a vacuum. When it was found that it would not rise more than thirty-two feet, this fact was explained by the theory that nature did not abhor a vacuum for more than thirty-two feet. Can it be that any of the hypotheses of the present day will seem as strange to our successors as this theory does to us?

With regard to the improvement of this faculty, a few words may be added at the close of this chapter. Let us refer to each of the three acts into which abstraction has been divided.

Analysis, or the power of distinguishing and separating from each other things which differ, may be employed either objectively or subjectively, as we are inquiring into the qualities and relations of the world without us, or the energies and relations of the world within us.

So far as the accurate observation of the external world is concerned, much depends upon the delicacy of our senses, but probably no less upon the earnest attention with which we use them. A listless, careless observer never discovers anything. It is only by an intense direction of the mind to the objects of our inquiry, that we are able to detect changes and relations which have been hidden from preceding observers. Truth reveals herself not to those who pay her mere formal and perfunctory service, but to those who render to her the earnest and heartfelt homage of the whole soul.

Acuteness in the analysis of mental phenomena requires an equal earnestness, though it is differently directed. We here find it necessary to cultivate the habit of withdrawing from all external objects, and fixing our attention on the revelations of our own consciousness. Few men can do this without long-continued and patient effort. With such effort, however, most men can attain to it. We must learn to look calmly and steadily upon a mental phenomenon. If there appear in it the slightest indications of complexity; if, when examining it from different points of view, the least shade of difference be cognizable in our consciousness; or, if, on comparing two forms of thought, which seemed to us identical, there arises within us the intellectual feeling of dissimilarity, we must pause until we are thoroughly satisfied on the subjects of our inquiry. It is by listening to the first suggestion of a difference, that we learn to determine the character and relations of our mental phenomena.

If we would enlarge our power of generalization, I know of no better method than to study the generalizations of nature. Admirable lessons of this sort are found in the natural sciences,— chemistry, physiology, geology, etc. No finer exercise for the power of generalization can be desired, than to take a single important chemical law, and trace out its operations on the vast and the minute throughout the kingdom of nature. Having become familiar with these wide-spreading classifications, we shall be the better able to pursue the generalizations of the subjective. We may then take an intellectual or moral law, and, having clearly marked out its nature and limitations, follow out its effects on the character of individual and social man. The light which will thus dawn on the mind will frequently astonish the student himself. Patient thought in this direction will furnish explanations of phenomena, and suggest rules of conduct, which would hardly reveal themselves to any other mode of investigation.

To improve the power of philosophical combination, we need, most of all, to study the actual combinations of nature. The more familiar we become with them, the clearer will be the light shed upon the unknown. Much may also be learned from the lives of those who have been so fortunate as to extend the limits of human knowledge. By observing the manner in which they have labored, we may hope to be able to follow their example. This subject will, however, come again under consideration, when, in a subsequent chapter, we treat of scientific imagination.

REFERENCES.

Abstraction — Locke, Book 2, chap. 11, sections 9, 6, 10, 11 ; chapter 12, section 1 ; Stewart, vol. i., chapter 4 ; Reid, Essay 5, chapters 2, 3, and 4.

Why most words general — Locke, Book 3, chap. 3, sections 1—10 Reid, Essay 5, chap. 1.

Simple words not definable — Locke, Book 3, chap. 4, sections 4—11.

Nominalism and Realism — Cousin, sect. 5, last part ; Stewart, vol. i., chap. 2, sections 2 and 3

CHAPTER V.

MEMORY.

SECTION I.—ASSOCIATION OF IDEAS, OR A TRAIN OF THOUGHT IN THE MIND.

The next faculty which we shall consider is Memory. As, however, its nature cannot be unfolded without a knowledge of the laws which govern the succession of thought in the mind, we shall devote to this subject a preliminary section.

Every person is conscious of the fact that, during his waking hours, his mind is continually engaged in thinking. Were any one to ascertain that an hour, or even a few minutes, had elapsed, in which he had been conscious of no thought, he would know that, unless he had fallen asleep, he must have been affected with some disease which had for the time paralyzed his intellectual powers.

And yet more; we are all conscious that it is impossible, without severe and long-continued effort, to fix the mind continuously upon any particular thought. It naturally, and without effort, passes from one idea to another, and it requires a determination of the will to detain it upon any one subject. No interval seems to intervene between one thought and another. They succeed each other without any volition on our part, and frequently take a direction which we strive in vain to control. A train of thought will sometimes seize upon the mind, and we are unable to disengage it. We strive to turn our attention to other objects, and after repeated and strenuous efforts, succeed but imperfectly. And in general it may be remarked, that he has attained to uncommon intellectual self-discipline who is able to think at will, and for any considerable length of time, upon any subject that he chooses.

But, while all this is true, it is, on the other hand, true that our thoughts do not follow each other at random. There are what may be called laws of connection, by which their succession is governed. Whenever an unusual idea occurs to us, nothing is more common than to inquire for the reason of its appearance at that particular time and place. We take it for granted that it could not have occurred to us without being related to some other idea previously existing in the mind. We, therefore, refer back to the thoughts which were just before present to our consciousness, and endeavor to trace some connection between them and that for whose origin we are inquiring.

This fact may be abundantly illustrated by our own experience. The following examples will recall other instances to our recollection. Mr. Hobbes relates, in his Leviathan, that, upon some occasion, several gentlemen were engaged in a conversation respecting the civil war. One of them abruptly inquired the value of a Roman denarius. The question sounded oddly, and strangely at variance with the subject under discussion. Mr. Hobbes relates that, on a little reflection, he was led to trace the train of thought which led to the inquiry. The subject of conversation, the civil war, naturally led the mind to the history of Charles I. The remembrance of the king suggested the treachery of those who delivered him up. The treachery in this case introduced the treachery of Judas Iscariot. The crime of Judas was at once associated with the price for which it was committed, and hence the question what was the value of a Roman denarius.

Stewart gives an illustration from the voyage of Captain King, the companion of Cook, of the power of a single object to awaken a train of reflection. "While we were at dinner in this miserable hut, on the banks of the river Awatska, the guests of a people with whose existence we had before been scarcely acquainted, and at the extremity of the habitable globe, a solitary half-worn pewter spoon, whose shape was familiar to us, attracted our attention; and, on examination, we found it stamped on the back with the word *London*. I cannot pass over this circumstance in silence, out of gratitude for the many pleasant thoughts, the anxious hopes, and tender remembrances, it excited in us. Those who have experienced the effects that long absence and extreme distance from their native country produce on the mind, will readily conceive the pleasure such a trifling incident can give."

A touching incident, illustrative of the same principle, is related by Mrs. Judson in her reminiscences of her late husband. During Dr. Judson's long captivity, in the death prison at Ava, his heroic wife, intending to create an agreeable surprise, had taken great pains to prepare an article of food that might cheer his spirits by reminding him of home. "In this simple, homelike act, this little unpretending effusion of a loving heart, there was something so touching, so illustrative of what she really was, that he bowed his head upon his knees, and the tears flowed down to the chains about his ankles. Presently the scene changed, and there came over him a vision of the past. He saw again the home of his boyhood. His stern, strongly revered father, his gentle mother, his rosy, curly-haired sister and pale young brother, were gathered for the noonday meal, and he was once more among them. And so his fancy revelled there.

Finally, he lifted his head, and O the misery that surrounded him! He moved his feet, and the rattling of the heavy chains was as a death-knell. He thrust the carefully prepared dinner into the hands of his associate, and, as fast as his fetters would permit, hurried to his own little shed."—Vol. i., pp. 378–9.

It is unnecessary to illustrate more fully the general fact that our ideas thus follow in succession independently of our will. We may remark, still further, that when thought follows thought without any connection, we recognize it immediately as a proof of insanity. To say of another that he talks *incoherently*, is to say that he is not in his right mind. Without any knowledge of the laws of mental association, we, in this manner, intuitively distinguish a normal from an abnormal state of the intellect. Thus, in the annual report of the Massachusetts General Hospital for 1853, one of the patients is referred to as continually talking after the following manner: "I have a commission as a justice of the peace, and an asparagus bed. I like lightning best at a distance. Whoever puts his name on paper in the Wiscasset Bank, has a mark on his forehead, and is worse off than if he was dining with one of the selectmen. Look out."

It is obvious, then, that our thoughts follow each other in a train subjected to certain general laws, and that they only move at variance with these laws when the mind is in an abnormal state.

The laws by which the train of thought is governed, or, as they are called, the laws of association, are of two kinds, objective and subjective. The objective laws are those arising from the relations which our thoughts sustain to each other; the subjective arise from the relations which our thoughts sustain to the thinking subject. Among the objective laws are numbered resemblance, contrast, contiguity, and cause and effect; among the subjective are, interval of time, frequency of repetition, coëxistent emotion, and the mental condition of the particular individual.

I. *Of the objective laws of association.*

1. *Resemblance.* Every one knows that when we are thinking of any interesting object or event, other objects or events in any respects similar to it, naturally present themselves. If we look, for the first time, upon a river in a foreign land, we instantly recall some river in our own country which it resembles; and we are never as well satisfied as when we find a marked similarity between them. We never pass over ridges of snow-clad mountains without being reminded of the Alps. When we visit a battle-ground, we find rising up within us the recollection of other battles which may have resembled it in the fierceness of the contest, the number of the slain, the principles which nerved the different combatants, or the results which flowed from the action over the destinies of humanity. This universal tendency is seen in the manner in which we designate remarkable events by giving to them the name of some remarkable event of a similar character. Thus any battle in which a small number of patriots have resisted a host of invaders is called a Thermopylæ or a Marathon. A distinguished general is called an Alexander or a Julius Cæsar, a patriot is a Washington. These instances all illustrate the facility with which one event suggests to us another which resembles it.

If, however, we examine the cases which we associate by resemblance, we shall find them to be of two kinds. Sometimes we associate objects by resemblance in their external qualities. Thus, when we see a vast mountain, we think of Mont Blanc, Chimborazo, or the Himalayas. We compare a vast river to the Mississippi or the Amazon. So, when distinguished men are mentioned, we are continually comparing them together, if, in their character or circum stances, there be any elements of similarity. Hence Cromwell and Napoleon, Charles I. and Louis XVI., Pitt and Fox, Scott and Byron, are so commonly spoken of in connection. In fact, a large portion of our conversation consists of comparisons of this character.

Another mode of association belonging to the same class, but a source of far greater pleasure, is that in which objects and events are connected, not by resemblance in their external appearances, but by their effects. Here the mind is delighted, not simply by the addition of another image in itself beautiful, but by the peculiar effect of novelty and unexpectedness. Thus Ossian describes the music of his minstrel by saying, "The music of Caryl, like the memory of joys that are past, was pleasant yet mournful to the soul." Here the objects themselves, music and a recollection, are entirely unlike; but, agreeing in the effect which they produce, we derive a peculiar pleasure from associating them together, and we are conscious that the pleasure is greater from the fact that the resemblance is unexpected. Thus Job compares his friends to a brook in the desert, which, in summer, when it is most needed, is dried up, and disappoints the hope of those who relied upon it for succor. There is no similarity here in the objects themselves. A man cannot resemble a brook. In one thing, however, they are alike: they disappoint hope. Hence the beauty of the figure. It is on this circumstance that the success of metaphorical language depends. Hence the rule of rhetoricians, that those metaphors are most beautiful in which the objects themselves are most dissimilar, while in the effects which they produce, or the point in which they are compared, they are the most alike. Hence the beauty of the passage in Longinus, in which he compares the Iliad of Homer to the meridian sun, and the Odyssey to the sun at his setting, when the magnitude is increased, but the effulgence is diminished.

2. *Contrast.* We find ourselves frequently associating ideas on the principle of contrast; that is to say, one idea at one time suggests to us another which resembles it; at another, an idea exactly opposite to it. Thus, happiness frequently recalls to our mind the idea of misery, as in the verse of Young: "How sad a sight is human happiness!" Height and depth, power and weakness, greatness and littleness, poverty and riches, the palace and the hovel, the cradle and the grave, are mutually suggested by each other. Hence in rhetoric the frequent use of antithesis.

As I remarked respecting resemblance, that it may be either in external appearance or in effect, the same is true of contrast. We here derive pleasure from contemplating similarity of external appearance, while the effects are exceedingly unlike. Thus, in the beautiful passage from Milton's Comus:

"I have often heard
My mother Circe, with the sirens three,
Amidst the flowery kirtled naiades,
Culling their potent herbs and baleful drugs,
Who, as they sung, would take the prisoned soul
And lap it in Elysium. Scylla wept
And chid her barking waves into attention,
And fell Charybdis murmured soft applause.
Yet they in pleasing slumber lulled the sense,
And, in sweet madness, robbed it of itself;
But such a sacred and homefelt delight,
Such sober certainty of waking bliss,
I never heard till now."

COMUS, 254—262.

3. *Contiguity.* This may be either of time or place.

1. Of time. When we reflect upon any event, we naturally find our attention called to other events which occurred at the same period. When we think of a distinguished man, we always recall his cotemporaries. Whoever thinks of Johnson without finding him surrounded, in our conception

by Boswell, Goldsmith, Garrick, Burke, and Sir Joshua Reynolds? When we think of Napoleon, we surround him with his marshals, and the sovereigns whose destinies he so greatly changed. An event of historical importance suggests the events contiguous to it in time. The advent of our Saviour could hardly be thought of without leading us to reflect upon the condition of Rome, and of the then civilized world. Hence we learn the appropriateness of the rule, in the study of history, to fix definitely in our minds the culminating events in each particular era, and then the contemporaneous occurrences will easily group themselves in their proper places.

2. Contiguity in place. When any important place is visited or thought of, it at once suggests to us the other places in its vicinity. Who can think of Jerusalem, and not think of the hills of Calvary, the mount of Olives, the garden of Gethsemane? Who can think of Waterloo without thinking of Brussels, and Quatre Bras, and the localities in the neighborhood, on the possession of which the issue of the contest so frequently turned? It is on this account that we survey with such impassioned interest any spot from which, at an earlier age, have emanated influences which have been deeply felt in the history of our race. The sentiments of Johnson at Iona find a response in the bosom of every cultivated mind. "We were now treading that illustrious island which was once the luminary of the Caledonian regions, whence savage clans and roving barbarians derived the benefits of knowledge and the blessings of religion. To abstract the mind from all local emotions would be impossible if it were endeavored, and would be foolish if it were possible. Whatever withdraws us from the power of the senses, whatever makes the past, the distant, or the future, predominate over the present, advances us in the dignity of thinking beings. Far from me and from my friends be such frigid

philosophy as may conduct us indifferent and unmoved over any ground which has been dignified by wisdom, bravery, or virtue. That man is little to be envied whose patriotism would not gain force upon the plain of Marathon, or whose piety would not grow warmer among the ruins of Iona." — *Journey to the Western Islands.*

Hence we perceive the reason why names of places, persons, etc., frequently add so much vivacity to style. Instead of an abstract and it may be disconnected idea, they present us with a visible image, surrounded by a multitude of associate ideas. Thus, when we wish to render impressive the idea of successful resistance to oppression, we refer to particular localities, as Runnymede, Naseby, Lexington, Bunker Hill, or Yorktown. And hence we learn that the study of history should always be connected with that of geography; that is, we should study history with the map before us. We thus associate events with localities, and remember them more perfectly, as well as comprehend them more accurately.

4. *Cause and effect.* I have already, when treating of original suggestion, referred to the fact that the observation of a change always leads us to ask for the cause. In the same manner, when we observe the manifestation of power, we instinctively ask for the results which have followed it. We associate in obedience to this universal tendency. If we think upon the reformation by Luther, we naturally think of the causes which led to it, and strive to trace out its consequences. If we think of the landing of the Pilgrims, we ask ourselves what causes could have led them to forsake the comforts of a civilized home, and plant themselves, in midwinter, upon a continent inhabited only by savages; and, before we have answered this inquiry, we find ourselves turning to the changes which this event has wrought upon the destinies of the world. So, when, for the first time, I

observe a philosophical experiment, I am wholly unsatisfied until I understand the rationale of the changes which it presents. I see, for instance, a taper lighted, when placed in the focus of one concave mirror, if a heated cannon-ball is placed in the other, though the taper is carefully protected from the direct rays of the ball. It is a disagreeable puzzle until the doctrine of the radiation of caloric is explained to me. As soon as this is done, my mind is at ease, and I proceed at once to explain other phenomena by the application of the same principle. Now, it is obvious that, this connection having been thus established, either one of these ideas will almost infallibly suggest the other. The law of caloric radiation will suggest the effect which has been mentioned, and the effect will suggest to us the law. So, having examined the causes which led to the first settlement of this country, and the consequences which have flowed from it, either one will bring to our mind the other, almost as a matter of necessity. It will readily occur that, as this is a permanent relation, like causes always producing like effects, this mode of association must be one of the most important means of enlarging and retaining our knowledge.

It will be easily perceived that these various forms of objective association intermix with and modify each other. Thus, the relation of cause and effect would naturally associate two events together; the association by resemblance would recall similar causes, and that by contrast, causes and effects of a dissimilar character; while events connected by the relation of contiguity of time and place would be more likely to occur to us than events remote and long since passed away. Thus, were I thinking of the landing of the Pilgrims, I would naturally think of the causes which led to this event; resemblance would lead me to think of similar cases of colonization, and contrast would bring to my recollection other instances in which men had left their native country, for love of adventure or thirst for gold. As I traced the results, I would naturally compare those which resembled the enterprise of the Pilgrims with those originating in a dissimilar cause; and, as the most contiguous in time and place, I would naturally turn to the states of South America, and contrast the causes and effects of these two modes of colonization together. In this manner, by the blending of these various forms of association, a vast range of thought is opened before us; while, at the same time, it is always under the control of established and recognized laws.

II. *Of the subjective laws of association.*

The laws commonly comprehended under this class are, as I have remarked, interval of time, frequency of repetition, coëxistent emotion, and the mental state of the particular individual.

1. *Interval of time.*

Every one knows that if two ideas are associated together from any cause whatever, the one readily recalls the other, if only a short interval of time have elapsed. But, if both of the ideas have been for a long time absent from our recollection, the association becomes indistinct, and the suggestion occurs less readily. To the truth of this remark every one's experience bears testimony. The events of a journey, by the relations of contiguity of time and place, readily suggest each other in regular succession, immediately after our return. But, if we enter upon our usual avocations, and have no occasion, either by writing or conversation, to recall the scenes which we witnessed, all but the most prominent events fade from our recollection. We forget most of the localities, and those which we remember cease to suggest the events connected with them. All becomes blended together in one confused remembrance; we forget both when and where we saw particular persons or things, and nothing remains to us but a recollection of the most important events, and a general impression made by the facts, which are themselves fast sinking into oblivion. The same truth is illustrated by the reading of a book, and in a thousand other instances.

2. *Repetition.*

It is obvious that an association which has been frequently recalled presents itself to us much more readily than another which has only once or twice, and at long intervals, passed through the mind. By every successive act of repetition, the connecting link between the two ideas is strengthened, until, at length, the association between the two becomes indissoluble. Hence it is that the beliefs of childhood are with so great difficulty eradicated, and that, even after the belief has passed away, the association still remains. Thus, many persons who in youth have been taught the belief in goblins, and night after night have listened to the recital of ghost stories and spectral appearances, although now perfectly convinced of the groundlessness of their former belief, never pass by a grave-yard, in darkness, without a tremor. They have so firmly associated a grave-yard with ghosts, that, in spite of the most deliberate conviction, the one idea recalls the other with its former unpleasant emotions.

The value of this power of rendering associations permanent by repetition is seen in the acquisition of practical skill. He who has been in the habit of performing the most complicated operations never finds himself at a loss; each step in the process instantly suggesting that which is immediately to succeed it, and each successive emergency calling to mind the means by which it has been previously encountered. Hence, we see the difference between theory and practice, and the peculiar advantages of each. He who is only acquainted with the theory is obliged to pursue a course of reasoning in order to arrive at a result; while, to a practical man, the result is suggested by the principle of reiterated association. A man may have studied thoroughly the theory of navigation, and may understand the laws by which a vessel is governed in moving through the water, both in fair weather and foul. But let him be called on to reduce his knowledge to practice in any trying emergency, and he will be obliged to compare and reason, and form a judgment from various conflicting elements, so that he will probably not arrive at a result until the time of action is past. He, however, who has been long in the practice of navigation, who has witnessed storms in all their variety, and has frequently been called upon to employ the means necessary to escape their violence, finds that at the critical moment the course proper to be pursued suggests itself spontaneously. He will, therefore, have taken all the measures necessary for safety, before the theoretical navigator has determined what they are. The extent to which practical skill may be carried, without any knowledge of principles, is often remarkable. A very intelligent captain of a steamer once told me that he had, for several years, employed an engineer, in whom he reposed entire confidence, and whom he had found, on every occasion, perfectly competent to the discharge of his duties. It happened that on one occasion the engineer made some remark which led him to ask the question, what makes an engine go. The man replied, at once, that he never knew, and he never could understand it, although he knew the several parts perfectly, and could, by the sound of the machinery, tell in an instant the nature and place of any irregularity, and the manner in which it should be rectified.

By these remarks, however, I do not wish it to be understood that I consider practical skill preferable to theoretical knowledge. Were events always to follow each other in the same succession, and always to require the same mode of treatment, practice would seem nearly all that was necessary in education. But the reverse is the fact. Cases are continually occurring which can only be provided for by a knowledge of general laws; and here, if we have no guide but practical skill, we must be inevitably disconcerted. When a new emergency arises, nothing but general laws will enable us either to understand or to provide for it. The perfection of education requires that both of these elements be combined,—that is, that we learn the laws by which changes are governed, and acquire so thorough a knowledge of the modes of their application, and, by repeated practice, associate so strongly the steps of the process we perform, that, while we act with the promptitude of the practised artisan, we may comprehend the reasons of our action, and be able, on the instant, to form a correct judgment under the pressure of an untried emergency. Thus the affairs of a government, under ordinary circumstances, may be sufficiently well conducted by a mere official, guided solely by precedent, provided he be familiar with the routine of daily administration. But when new combinations arise, and events transpire, for which official rules furnish no direction, there is demanded, besides a knowledge of the forms of proceeding, a comprehensive acquaintance with general principles, which shall unfold the true relations of things, under what conditions soever they may present themselves. Thus says Mr. Burke, in his speech on American taxation: "It may truly be said that men too much conversant with office are rarely minds of remarkable enlargement. Their habits of office are apt to give them a turn to think the substance of business not to be more important than the forms in which it is conducted. These forms are adapted to ordinary occasions, and therefore persons who are nurtured in office do admirably well so long as things go on in their common order; but when the high roads are broken up, and the waters are out,—when a new and troubled scene is opened, and the file affords no precedent, —then it is that a greater knowledge of mankind, and a far more extensive comprehension of things, is requisite than ever office gave, or than ever office can give."

It has frequently been observed that military commanders have generally succeeded remarkably well in the administration of civil affairs. As examples of this, the founders of dynasties may be referred to; or, if particular instances need be given, we may mention the names of Frederick the Great, Washington, Napoleon, Wellington, General Jackson, and a multitude of others. The reason of this may be found in the remark made above, that the perfection of education consists in the combination of theoretical knowledge with practical skill. The duties of a military commander give him this education. He is obliged to form for himself the plans which must be carried out upon his own responsibility. Hence, he must study them thoroughly for himself, understand their bearings, and take no step which he has not decided upon after the most mature reflection. He must then execute his decisions himself, and thus the relation of theory and practice, of the conception and the execution of it, must be constantly present to his reflection. The advantage which this habit of mind must confer, over that of theorists who never practise and practical men who never reason, must be apparent. India has been called the cradle of great men, and for this same reason. In the immense empire of Great Britain in the East, the government of so many provinces must create a vast number of situations in which almost the sole authority must reside in the chief administrative officer of the district. He must learn to decide for himself, and decide wisely, and also provide the means for carrying his decisions into effect. In such a school as this, talent is rapidly developed, and thus not unfrequently a man of thirty-five attains the clearness of mind, fertility of resources, and promptness of action, of a man, under ordinary circumstances, of fifty.

3. *Coëxistent emotion* is the third law of subjective association.

By the law of coëxistent emotion, it is meant that whenever an event awakens in us strong emotion, it becomes deeply fixed in the memory, and is more readily associated with any other event to which it is related.

Of the existence of such a law in our mental constitution our own experience will furnish us with innumerable examples. The events of several days will frequently pass away, without leaving more than a dim and shadowy trace of their occurrence. But if on any particular day a fact has been communicated to us by which we were strongly excited, as the death of a friend, the unexpected arrival of a relative, or an event of great importance to our country, that day will long stand out vividly before us. The place where and the time when we first received the intelligence are indissolubly associated with the event itself, and the fact, with all its attendant circumstances, is engraven on the mind forever. So, in travelling over a country for the first time, its ordinary features, awakening no emotion, are soon forgotten; but if we chance to pass by a celebrated river, an overhanging precipice, a magnificent waterfall, or any other object that awakens the emotion of novelty, beauty, or sublimity, we find it indelibly fixed in our recollection, with all its attendant circumstances; and it is ever afterwards ready to be associated with similar scenes which we witness ourselves, or which are described to us by others. The power of emotion is here two-fold; — in the first place, it rivets the event on the memory, and, in the second, it recalls it whenever, on a subsequent occasion, the same emotion is awakened.

It is on this principle that felicity of style, splendor of imagery and power of description, become important aids in

19

all our efforts to convince men by argument. When we desire to change the opinions of men, it is necessary that our reasonings be retained in their recollection, and frequently dwelt upon in reflection. When an argument is associated with emotion it is more easily retained; and when the emotion is pleasant it is more readily recalled, and more earnestly considered. Under these circumstances it will produce a more distinct impression on the judgment, and the judgment itself is associated with agreeable emotions. Every one will remember, after hearing a discourse, that different passages present themselves to his recollection with different degrees of distinctness; and he always finds that those which affected him most strongly during delivery are those which fix themselves, afterwards, most firmly on his memory. Of the thousands who have read Burke's speech on the nabob of Arcot's debts, probably very few have any distinct conception of the argument, while all remember his magnificent description of the descent of Hyder Ali upon the Carnatic, commencing, "When, at length Hyder Ali found," etc. The facts and the reasonings may have long since passed away, but we remember the scene of devastation which the orator describes, and, whether justly or unjustly, hold in abhorrence the men whom he stigmatizes as the authors of the calamity.

4. *Peculiarities of mental character*. Some of these are permanent, and some accidental.

Men differ very greatly in mental constitution. In some the reasoning element predominates, in others the imaginative, and in others the practical. These intellectual biases must modify very materially the train of thought. Let, for instance, a poet and a philosopher, on a clear night, go out to survey the vault of heaven, studded with innumerable stars. The trains of thought which will arise in the minds of the two men will be exceedingly unlike.

The one would associate all that he saw with various ideas of moral sublimity with which he is familiar, and would perhaps express his emotions in a hymn of praise, or an ode to a planet. The astronomer would think of the distances, magnitudes and revolutions, of the heavenly bodies, and would find himself striving to solve some problem which their present position suggested. A devout man, on the other hand, would probably give utterance to his emotions in the words of David: "When I consider the heavens the work of thy fingers, the moon and the stars which thou hast ordained, what is man, that thou art mindful of him, or the son of man, that thou visitest him?" To a mind like that of Newton the fall of an apple might give rise to a train of thought which would lead to the most magnificent discoveries; to a boy it might suggest no other idea than the desire of eating it; while to the botanist it would recall the class and order of plants to which the tree belonged. Agassiz and Coleridge would be very differently affected by a view from the vale of Chamouni. On the other hand, in an uncultivated mind, none of these trains of thought would be awakened. Thus, the poet, describing a mind of this order, tells us,

> "A cowslip, by the river's brim,
> A yellow cowslip was to him;
> And it was nothing more."

Besides these intellectual differences, there are permanent varieties of character depending on the tone of mind of the individual. Some men are always cheerful, the present and the future being always tinged with the roseate hue of hope. Every change seems to them indicative of prosperity. Such is, more commonly, the character of youth. To others the present, but more especially the future, seems clothed with gloom; and the prospect of change awakens no other emotion than apprehensiveness. Such is the character of the melancholy man, and such is apt to be the tendency of age. Milton, in his L'Allegro and Il Penseroso, has, with striking beauty, illustrated these two forms of character.

These are permanent varieties; but there are accidental varieties, depending on the circumstances of the individual. The mind, deeply affected by any train of reflection, will pursue it for some time, though at variance with its natural bias. Thus, an astronomer, fresh from the reading of Milton, might look upon the heavens for a time with the emotions of a poet; and a poet, rising from the study of the Principia, might look upon them with the eye of an astronomer. And then, again, our tone of mind frequently varies from its accustomed bias. A cheerful man is sometimes sad, and a melancholy man is sometimes mirthful. Images exquisitely ludicrous occasionally flitted across the gloom which habitually shrouded the mind of Cowper. We all know how different are the trains of thought which press upon him who walks abroad for the first time after the death of a friend, and him who, after confinement by sickness, rejoices in the freshness of invigorated health.

These subjective laws again modify each other. Thus, for instance, lapse of time is modified by coëxistent emotion; that is to say, an event which has strongly interested us will much more readily be associated with surrounding circumstances, even after a long interval, than an event which awakened no emotion, though of more recent occurrence. Or, again, the objective and subjective laws may modify each other. Thus, we know that we associate ideas in obedience to the laws of resemblance or contrast, but whether we shall associate by the one, or the other, may depend upon the permanent or accidental tone of mind of the individual. Thus, if a cheerful scene be presented to a happy man, he associates by resemblance, a melancholy man by contrast. The loveliness of spring to a mourner suggests only images of disappointed hope and speedy dissolution To the cheerful man even the gloom of winter awakens the anticipations of returning spring, and he thinks only of the contrast which, in a few months, will renew the whole face of nature.

It is, in this manner, by the combination of these several laws, that the train of thought is directed. As these various causes operate with unequal power at different times, and are modified by each other, and by the present circumstances of each individual, there arises an infinite variety in the modes of mental association. Hence we should consider it almost miraculous if two men should be affected in exactly the same manner in precisely the same circumstances, so that they should give utterance to their sentiments in the same language. Yet, while all this diversity is known to exist, we are conscious that it is still governed by laws; for we recognize in an instant an abnormal or incoherent association, and attribute it at once either to idiocy or insanity. So delicate are our mental instincts, that he who knows nothing of the laws of association is intuitively aware when they are violated.

It is on the perfection of this delicate instinct, which spontaneously recognizes all the laws of association, that the power of the dramatist essentially depends. He forms conceptions of a variety of characters, and places them in circumstances designed to call forth the intensest emotion. But these circumstances will affect each individual according to his peculiar idiosyncrasy. The dramatic poet has the power of throwing himself into each character, and of feeling instinctively the emotions to which such a human being, under such circumstances, would give utterance. This is one of the rarest gifts with which genius is ever endowed. It is to this power that Shakspeare owes his preëminence. Considered simply as a poet, there are other men of genius with whom he may come into comparison; but in dramatic exhibition of character he stands, by confession, without a rival.

> "Our Shakspeare's magic could not copied be;
> Within that circle none dare walk but he."

It may seem, from what I have said, that association evinces a power beyond our control, and that hence we are not responsible for our trains of thought, or the consequences to which they lead. This inference, it is almost unnecessary to add, is unwarranted. By association ideas are suggested, but it still depends on our own volition to determine whether the suggestion shall be heeded. A thought is presented by the law of association; we may accept or reject it. Two dissimilar thoughts are suggested, and we may select either of them at our option. When a particular association is followed repeatedly, we form the habit of thinking in that particular train; but the formation of that habit depended, at each successive step, upon our own will. It is, then, evident that the formation of our characters, whether intellectual or moral, is dependent on ourselves. Hence it is that circumstances are said to form men; that is, the conditions in which we are placed accustom us to certain modes of thinking, which, becoming habitual, render our character fixed and determinate. Hence, also, we see how much character depends upon energy of will, by which the development of our own powers ceases to be the result of accident, and follows in the line marked out for it by reasonable and predetermined choice.

It has been truly remarked, that our associations are frequently the cause of great errors in judgment. When we repeatedly associate two ideas together, we are prone, without examination, to consider the connection by its nature indissoluble. Thus, in youth, having observed many good men members of our own religious sect, we associate the idea of goodness with that sect, and, going further, consider piety exclusively confined within its limits. Having, again, experienced innumerable benefits arising from a republican government, we not only associate the idea of freedom and intelligence with our own institutions, but suppose that these advantages can be enjoyed under no other conditions of humanity. A multitude of cases of a similar kind will readily suggest themselves. These errors are manifestly to be removed by a larger knowledge of the world, and a more careful and frequent examination of the reasons of our opinions. This subject is treated with great beauty and sound discrimination in Stewart's chapter on Association.

REFERENCES.

Stewart — Vol. i., chap. 5 ; Locke — Book 11, chap. 33 ; Reid — Essay 4, chap. 4.

SECTION II. — THE NATURE OF MEMORY.

MEMORY is that faculty by which we retain and recall our knowledge of the past. I saw a tree yesterday. I know now that I saw it then and there. I have a conception of a tree, with a certain knowledge that I saw the tree which corresponds to this conception, at some previous time. How I know this I cannot tell, but my consciousness reveals it to me as positive and reliable knowledge.

I have, in the above definition, ascribed but two functions to memory,— the power by which we retain, and that by which we recall, our knowledge of the past. The distinction between these powers is easily observed, for they are not always bestowed in equal degrees. Some men retain their knowledge more perfectly than they recall it. Others have their knowledge always at command, and make even small acquisitions eminently available.

Stewart divides the first of these functions into susceptibility and retentiveness. A foundation for this distinction evidently exists. Some men acquire with great rapidity, but they very soon forget whatever they have learned. Others acquire with difficulty, but retain tenaciously the knowledge which they have once made their own. Others, again, as I have just remarked, have a remarkable command of their knowledge on all occasions. It must be evident that memory is perfect in the degree in which it is endowed with all these attributes. Men of the highest order of intellect are often preëminently gifted in all these respects. It will be sufficient to mention the names of Leibnitz, Milton, Johnson, Scott, Napoleon, Cuvier, Goethe, Sir W. Hamilton, in order to confirm the truth of this remark. Such men acquire with incredible facility, rarely forget anything which they have learned, and, at will, with remarkable accuracy, concentrate all their knowledge upon the point which they are at the moment discussing.

The knowledge which we obtain by memory may properly be called, in the words of Sir W. Hamilton, representative and mediate, in distinction from presentative and immediate knowledge. When I see a tree, I am conscious of an immediate knowledge, the object being presented directly before my mind. When I remember a tree, there is no external object presented. The tree is represented by the act of the mind itself. I know the tree through the medium of this representation. The immediate object of my thought is this conception of the thing, while, by a power inherent in my intellect, I connect this image with the idea of past reality. That this is true, is evident from the fact that the mental state is precisely the same whether the object at present is or is not existing. I remember a house which I saw a year ago. The image of it is distinctly before my mind. I am told that the house has been burned down, and that nothing remains where it stood but a heap of smouldering ruins. This does not at all affect the image I have in my mind. The only difference in the two cases is, that before I contemplated it as the representation of something existing, now only of something that did exist.

Concerning this faculty, as thus defined, several important facts may be observed.

1. I have before remarked, when treating of the perceptive faculties, that our knowledge derived from this source is of two kinds, simple and complex. Simple knowledge is merely a state of mind, a consciousness of a peculiar impression made upon our sensitive organism, without giving us an intimation of anything external; a mere affection of the *me*, without any relation to the *not me*. The other kind of knowledge is complex; that is, together with this affection of the *me*, there is communicated to us a knowledge of the *not me*, in some of its modifications. In this latter case, we form a notion of the *not me* as something numerically distinct from the *me*.

Whenever our knowledge is of the latter character, our recollection of it is always attended by a conception, and this conception forms a part of the act of memory. Sir W. Hamilton, on this account, happily describes memory as a recollective imagination. We have before us an image of the object remembered, and are conscious that it represents some past existence. Thus, when we remember a visible object, we form for ourselves a distinct conception of its appearance. We never consider an act of memory complete until this conception is created. Thus, if I am asked whether I remember a village which I passed through some years since, if I can recall the conception of the locality, I answer in the affirmative; if I only know that from the route which I took I must have passed through it, but have no conception of its appearance, I answer in the negative. If, however, after an interval, I am able to recall it as I perceived it, I reply that now I recollect it.

With respect to simple knowledge, or that which is limited to sensations, the case is different. We here form no conception, and the act of memory is imperfect. I remember, for instance, the visible appearance of a peach, its color, magnitude, form, etc., and I represent it to myself in thought. I have, however, no such recollection either of the smell or taste of the peach. I form no representation of these qualities, nor, so far as I know, am I able to do it. My recollection amounts to no more than this: I know that I have, at various times, both smelled and tasted of peaches, and that I should instantly recognize these qualities were they present; but I can do no more. An exception to this remark is, however, to be made in the case of hearing. Here, though the knowledge is simple, that is, merely an affection of our sensitive organism, it is, however, capable of forming a conception. Hence, our recollection of it is remarkably perfect. After once hearing a tune, we can, if skilled in music, recall it with perfect accuracy, and can do it in perfect silence, merely forming a conception of the sounds by the memory.

2. A complete act of the memory is always attended by belief. He who remembers, is conscious of an original conviction that the conception which he forms is the true representative of some preëxisting knowledge. He knows it to be, as has been said, a recollective imagination. How we know this, how we are able to distinguish a simple imagination from a recollective imagination, we are unable to explain. Consciousness reveals to us the difference, and we can discover nothing beyond the simple fact. It has been said that we learn to rely upon the testimony of memory by ex

perience. This, however, must be incorrect, for we evidently rely upon it anterior to experience. And, besides, the very experience on which we are here said to depend, presupposes the validity of the testimony of memory. Unless I rely on memory to give me a knowledge of the past, I can gain no experience respecting the character of memory itself.

I am, however, aware that there are frequent cases in which, while we have a clear conception of an act, our recollection is imperfect, so that we doubt whether the state of mind be merely a conception or a recollection. Thus, I intended several days since to write a letter, and formed a purpose to write it at a particular time. The question now occurs to me, did I write it or not? When I think of the act, is my mental state that of recollection, or only of conception; in other words, did I actually do it, or did I only resolve to do it? Here our consciousness enables us to distinguish between certainty and doubt, though it does not enable us to resolve the doubt. So far, however, as I have observed, it is generally the fact that when we doubt the doubt is entitled to precedence, and we find on inquiry that the thing was not done. When, on the other hand, the testimony of consciousness to our recollection is perfect, we rely upon it with as much certainty as on the present evidence of our senses. I am as sure that I saw a certain tree yesterday, as I was sure yesterday that I was then seeing it. It is upon this attribute of memory that all our belief of the existence of the past and the distant depends. We repose the same confidence in the memory of competent witnesses as in our own. I just as fully and perfectly believe in the existence of Constantinople as of London, though the one I have seen and the other I have not seen. On this belief in the veracity of memory, all the evidence of testimony depends; and hence, with entire confidence in its validity, we proceed to decide questions involving property, reputation, and life itself.

It is proper here to remark, that this consciousness, by which we determine a representation in our minds to be a recollection and not an imagination, is liable to be greatly impaired. He who forms the habit of deliberate lying, or of affirming that his conceptions are recollections, will gradually lose the power of distinguishing the one from the other. By passing from truth to falsehood and from falsehood to truth, without moral consciousness, the line which separates them from each other becomes more and more indistinct, until it is at last obliterated. I have known men who would utter the most absurd falsehoods, without seeming to be conscious either that they were lying or that their hearers knew them to be liars. A more just retribution for the abuse of our moral faculties cannot be conceived.

Another peculiarity connected with this part of our subject deserves to be remarked. We are sometimes led into innocent mistakes concerning our recollection. If we hear an event frequently related, until every minute incident is engraven on our recollection, we may, after a considerable period has elapsed, seem to ourselves to have witnessed it. I think it is Burke who says, "Never let a man repeat to you a lie. If he tell you a story every day which you know to be false, at the end of a year you will believe it to be true." A distinguished justice of the Supreme Judicial Court of Massachusetts once related to me a case which pertinently illustrates this remark. He was once trying a cause relating to a will, and a lady testified most distinctly to some occurrences which she had witnessed when she was a child. Her evidence was distinct and minute as to all the circumstances of person, time, and place. She was a person of mature age, of a character above suspicion, and incapable of testifying to what she did not believe to be true. It however appeared, in the course of the trial, from incontestable documentary evidence, that the events had transpired several years before she was born. When a girl she had heard the occurrence so frequently related, with great particularity, that in mature years it presented itself to her as a matter of personal knowledge rather than of recollection of the narrative of others.

Lastly; the act of memory involves two subordinate beliefs. First, it presupposes a belief in the past existence of the object recollected; and, secondly, in the past and present existence of the subject recollecting. From both of these we derive the idea of duration, for were there no duration, there could be no past existence; that is, the idea of duration logically precedes the idea of memory. From the second of these beliefs we derive the idea of personal identity. The belief that we, who are now existing, cognized an object at any previous point in duration, supposes both the cognitions to appertain to the same subject; that is, that the *ego* in both these cognitions is one and the same.

3. The power of recollection in different individuals differs greatly, both in degree and in kind.

Some men are so remarkably gifted in this respect, that without apparent effort they seem to remember whatever they have read, and every person whom they have even casually seen. Others, though possessing many eminent qualities of intellect, find difficulty in recollecting the persons and things which daily surround them. Cyrus is reported to have been able to call by name every soldier in his army, and Themistocles to have known individually every citizen of Athens. I have been told that General Washington never found it necessary to be twice introduced to the same person. Boswell records of Dr. Johnson, that once, when riding in a stage-coach, he repeated with verbal accuracy a number of the Rambler, some ten or twelve years after its publication; at the same time stating that he had not seen it since he corrected the original proof-sheets. In his life of Rowe he criticizes the poet's works with a very accurate conception of their merits, frequently quoting whole passages as though he were transcribing them from the printed page. When he had finished it, he said to a friend, "I think this is pretty well done, considering that I have not read a play of Rowe's for thirty years." On the contrary, Montaigne, though a man of original genius, and one of the marked men of his age, was always complaining of the badness of his memory. "I am forced," says he, "to call my servants by the names of their employments, or of the countries where they were born, for I can hardly remember their proper names, and if I should live long, I question whether I should remember my own name." In this case there seems to be some peculiar idiosyncrasy; for while he forgot so readily the individual, he was able to remember the class to which he belonged.

Differences of memory exist not only in degree, but in kind.

I have already observed that some men are more remarkable for susceptibility, others for retentiveness, and others for readiness of memory. Every one who has observed the minds of young persons, must have seen frequent illustrations of the truth of this remark. But these differences do not terminate here. There exist what may not inappropriately be termed objective differences of memory; that is, this power seems in different individuals to manifest an affinity for different classes of objects. Some men remember numbers and dates with remarkable accuracy, and easily retain not only figures, but even long and complicated algebraic formulæ. Other men remember permanently and without effort, localities, the faces of persons, and every form of external nature. Some have great facility in recollecting words and their relations to each other; and hence at an early age manifest a fondness for the study of language and the pursuits of philology. Others again, who are possessed of none of these powers in a remarkable degree, acquire principles and general laws without effort, and will frequently remember the law, while they forget the facts by which it is established. It is said that the late Dr. Gall was first led to the investigations which terminated in his system of phrenology, by observing that some boys possessed peculiar skill in finding their way out of a forest, while others, under the same circumstances, would be completely bewildered. He remarked, that those of the first class were marked with a protuberance in the forehead just above the eye. He also observed that those who displayed a remarkable aptitude for languages were formed with a depression of the roof of the orbit of the eye, which gave to the eye the appearance of unusual fulness. Generalizing these observations, he was led to conclude that every modification of mental character was accompanied by some corresponding peculiarity in the form of the brain. Whether there be the connection between the mental and physical organization which phrenologists assert, I will not determine; but that they have aided us in remarking with greater exactness many peculiarities of mental constitution, may, I think, be fairly admitted.

That these differences may be accounted for, in some degree, by education, I have no doubt. In the most remarkable instances, however, they seem to depend chiefly on natural endowment. I have known several persons who have been gifted with some of these forms of recollection in a very uncommon degree, and they have uniformly told me that the things which they remembered cost them no more pains than those which they forgot. All the account which they could give of the matter was, that some classes of facts, without any special effort, remained permanently fixed in their recollection, while others were as readily forgotten by them as by other men. A highly-esteemed clergyman of Massachusetts, lately deceased, who could tell the year of the graduation of every alumnus of his university and the minutest incidents relating to every ordination in his vicinity for the last half-century, assured me that it cost him no labor, but that it was, so far as he knew, a mental peculiarity.

The large development of any particular form of memory is not, of necessity, accompanied by any other remarkable intellectual endowments. Instances have frequently been noticed of men, with prodigious powers of recollection, whose abilities in other respects were even below mediocrity. Very remarkable memory has even been observed in persons of so infirm an understanding that they did not even comprehend what they accurately repeated. In this case, probably, the power was mere susceptibility of memory; that is, the power of acquiring on the instant, without the ability of permanent recollection. A very remarkable case of this one-sided power is mentioned in the life of the late Mr. Roscoe, of Liverpool. A young Welsh fisherman, of about the age of eighteen, was found to have made most remarkable progress in the study of languages. He was not only familiar with Latin and Greek, but also with Hebrew, Arabic, and other oriental dialects. Some benevolent gentlemen, in that city, provided means for giving him every literary advantage, in the hope that his vast acquisitions might be made useful to society, and also that he might unfold the processes by which his singular attainments had been made. The attempt was, however, unsuccessful. He seemed not to be peculiarly capable of education, but, with the exception of this peculiar gift, his mind partook entirely of the character of the class with which he had been associated.

4. The character of memory changes materially with age.

Memory is one of our faculties which is developed at a very early age, specially in the characteristics of susceptibility and retentiveness. Of this any one will be convinced who will observe the prodigious number of particulars which a human being acquires almost in infancy. A child of four or five years old has already learned the names and uses of the ordinary objects which he sees around him; and has acquired a tolerable knowledge of his native language. A boy, before he goes to school, is better acquainted with his mother tongue, than he will be with Latin and Greek after ten or twelve years of study. Nor is this all. Children educated in a family in which several languages are spoken, learn them all with equal facility.

As might, however, be expected, this faculty, which first comes to maturity, is also the first to decline. The first intellectual indication of advancing years is a conscious failure in the power of recollection. When the memory becomes impaired from this cause, we do not forget so much the knowledge acquired in youth, as that acquired at a later period. Hence, old men recite the deeds of their youth, not those of maturer years. Horace describes an old man as *laudator temporis acti.* The heroes of our revolution are never so well pleased as when relating the events of that illustrious struggle, and the reminiscences which they have treasured up of the career of Washington. The reason for this is two-fold. An event which transpires in youth awakens in us a deeper coëxistent emotion than in age; and, secondly, the social character of youth leads us frequently to relate the incidents which please us, and hence every interesting event becomes more deeply engraved on the mem ory. To an old man, the later period of his life resembles a dream; the period of youth and early manhood alone seems like reality.

As old men are naturally inclined to recite the events of their youth, so this very recital is most pleasing to the young. A child wearies his parents with the request that they will tell him what they saw and did when they were young. We are all conscious of the eagerness with which we listen to the relation, by eye-witnesses, of occurrences which transpired sixty or seventy years since. The final cause of this arrangement is as obvious as it is beautiful. These corresponding dispositions were conferred upon us for the sake of binding together the young and the old by the tie of mutual sympathy. The tedium and infirmity of age is beguiled and alleviated by the society of youth; and the young are taught those lessons of experience, which they would seek for in vain from those who, like themselves, are just commencing the warfare of life.

From these facts, we learn the more correctly to appreciate the importance of a diligent and well-spent youth. If the spring-time of life is consumed in frivolity and sin, the mind, in the winter of age, must sink into decrepitude; and nothing will present itself to the memory, but the recollection of deeds which tinge the cheek with shame, and goad the conscience with remorse. If, on the other hand, the memory is stored in youth with valuable knowledge, and the faculties are disciplined by strenuous exertion, we sow the seeds of a green old age; that condition in which, without the vigor and elasticity of youth, there exist the accumulated knowledge of a laborious life, and the calm, ripe wisdom of a large experience. If to these be added the consciousness of purity of motive, and the beautiful simplicity which results from a virtuous life, old age becomes one of the most favored periods of our present state. It may then be worth while for the young to remember, that while diligence and mental discipline afford the only reasonable hope for success in manhood, they present the only security against the evils of an imbecile, unhappy, and neglected old age.

It is to be remarked, further, that the memory of youth differs in kind, as well as in degree, from that of maturer life. In youth, as might be expected, we remember facts; as we advance in age, we observe, appreciate, and remember laws and their relations. In the early period of life, we collect the materials; as we grow older, we learn to use them. In youth our tendency is to the objective and concrete; in maturer years we tend to the subjective and the abstract. If we were to be more particular, we might affirm, that in childhood susceptibility seems more active; in youth, retentiveness; and in manhood readiness. In childhood, as I have said, we learn a multitude of things which we soon forget. The ordinary events of the first four or five years of our lives soon pass into oblivion. In advancing youth, while we lose in some degree the power of committing to memory, we retain what we have learned much more tenaciously. I have remarked on the facility with which young persons will learn several languages at the same time, and, what is scarcely possible for an adult, they will learn them idiomatically.* It is, however, a singu-

* A singular confirmation of this remark is found in the life of Dr. Carey, the pioneer Protestant missionary in India. Dr. Carey had a decided talent for languages, and acquired them with great facility before he left England. When he arrived in Bengal with his family, he commenced the study of the native tongues with his usual perseverance, assisted by the best helps, both printed and oral, which the country then afforded. His children, without any instruction, were left to amuse themselves with natives of their own age. It was not long before the father was obliged to call in his children to explain to him phrases and idioms which he was unable to understand. They had learned, by playing with their fellows, more rapidly than he by the combined aid of books and pundits.

lar fact, that if a young person studies an ancient language, as Latin or Greek, and, from change of residence, forgets his native tongue, he will remember the language which he acquired by grammatical study, longer than his vernacular. This difference may arise either from the fact that retentiveness of memory increases with age, or because whatever is learned by a protracted effort is more indelibly fixed in the recollection.

5. Memory may be improved in a shorter time, and to a greater extent, than any of our other faculties.

The change that may be produced in this respect is frequently remarkable. Pupils in a school may, in a few months, be taught to commit to memory an amount which, at first, would have seemed incredible. It is not difficult to teach a class to recite from beginning to end the acquisitions of a whole term, without any aid from the instructor. A gentleman with whom I am well acquainted, informed me that he once determined to ascertain the extent to which the improvement of his memory could be carried. He soon found himself able to repeat verbatim, two or three pages of any book after it had been read to him only once. He was able to go into a legislative assembly, and write down from recollection, after its adjournment, the proceedings of the day, with as much accuracy as they were reported by the stenographers.

While, however, it is generally true, that the memory may be greatly and permanently improved by judicious practice, it is probable that the rapid improvement, of which we have frequent instances, has respect more to susceptibility, than either to retentiveness or readiness. What we acquire so suddenly is learned only for a particular occasion; and when the occasion has passed away, all we have learned has passed away with it. Clergymen, who with ease commit their sermons by once or twice reading them over, are obliged to commit them anew as often as they are called to deliver them. When we desire to cultivate the memory in general, and render our knowledge permanently available, greater care is necessary. The process is more difficult, and must be conducted on principles which depend on the general laws of the human mind.

The following case, related by Dr. Abercrombie, illustrates the extent to which the susceptibility of memory may be increased by the pressure of circumstances. "A distinguished theatrical performer, in consequence of the sudden illness of another actor, had occasion to prepare himself, on very short notice, for a part which was entirely new to him; and the part was long, and rather difficult. He acquired it in a very short time, and went through it with perfect accuracy, but, immediately after the performance, forgot every word of it. Characters which he has acquired in a more deliberate manner he never forgets, and can perform them at any time without a moment's preparation; but, in regard to the character now mentioned, there was the further and very singular fact, that, though he has repeatedly performed it since that time, he has been obliged each time to prepare it anew, and has never acquired in regard to it that facility which is familiar to him in other instances. When questioned respecting the mental process which he employed the first time he performed this part, he says that he lost sight entirely of the audience, and seemed to have nothing before him but the pages of the book from which he had learned it; and that, if anything had occurred to interrupt this illusion, he should have stopped instantly." — Abercrombie, Part 3, section 1.

6. The power of recollection depends much on the manner in which our knowledge has been acquired.

Knowledge acquired by the assistance of our perceptive faculties, is much longer remembered than that acquired by conception through the medium of language. And, further, a proposition which can in any manner be represented by an image is more easily remembered than a purely abstract proposition, of which no image can be formed. We remember a landscape far better by having seen it, than by the most elaborate description. Every one knows that the scenery depicted in the writings of travellers and novelists leaves scarcely a trace on the recollection. A machine may be described to us with the most careful particularity, and we may be able distinctly to comprehend it; yet, if we see neither it nor a model of it, we soon find that our recollection has become exceedingly shadowy and vague. The use which may be made of this fact is evident. It teaches us the importance of illustrating, by figures, diagrams, or experiments, whatever we desire to communicate to others, wherever the subject admits of it. Hence the use of a black-board in a class-room; and hence the value of skill in drawing, to an instructor, in every branch of physical science.

7. It is, however, the fact, that, in our present state, time gradually obliterates the impressions made upon the memory. What we learned yesterday, may be fresh in our recollection to-day, but we shall remember it much less perfectly in a month. If a year elapse without having had occasion to recall it, it will in a great degree have faded away from our recollection. I say, in a great degree; for, although the principle which it involves, or the conclusion which it establishes, may remain, the sharp and definite outline of the facts will have dissolved into forgetfulness. In this respect, we are all the victims of a perpetually recurring delusion. It seems to us that what we remember so perfectly, and understand so clearly, to-day, can never be forgotten. Though repeated trials, and lamentable ignorance of what we have once known, might seem sufficient to convince us of

our error, we press blindly onward, ever learning, and yet ever failing permanently to treasure up what we have already acquired.

While this, however, is the general fact, it is subject to several modifications. Some of these are the following:

1. Exact and definite knowledge is much longer remembered than vague and indefinite conceptions. A proposition but half known, and indistinctly conceived, is almost immediately forgotten; while that which we have thoroughly thought, and adequately comprehended, does not easily escape us. Hence we see that our progress in knowledge does not so much depend upon the amount which we read as upon the manner in which we study. He who reviews his past history will observe that his present acquisitions are the sum of all that he has at some time thoroughly learned. That which was only imperfectly understood is lost in the mass of confused and useless reminiscences.

2. An isolated proposition is soon forgotten, while one of which we perceive the connections and relations is more easily remembered. A single number, as the height of a mountain, the area of a field, the page of a book, a law of mechanics expressed in abstract terms, or any truth viewed without relation to any other truth, easily eludes our recollection. We obviate this difficulty, if we can establish any relation, even though it be but fanciful, between the fact which we desire to remember, and some other truth permanently known. Thus, if we wish to remember the height of a mountain, we associate it with the height of some well-known object, and we find our power of recollection increased. If we associate a law with the facts for which it accounts, the same effect is produced. It is on the principle of associating something to be remembered, with something else well known, that the systems of artificial memory are constructed.

3. Knowledge which is beginning to vanish from our recollection is rendered more permanent by even a cursory review. By occasionally repeating this review, the truth becomes incorporated with our permanent knowledge. It is a good rule never to commence the reading of to-day, until we have carefully reviewed the reading of yesterday; and never to lay aside a book until we have leisurely imprinted on our minds its most important truths. Conversation on what we have read is of great service in this respect. I think it is Johnson who mentions that it was his custom, in youth, as soon as he had finished a book, to find some one to whom he could explain its principles. Full and free discussion upon the truths which we have acquired, gives not only permanency but definiteness to our knowledge. It is on this account that studious men derive so much advantage from associating together, and communicating the result of their researches for the benefit of each other.

8. From remarkable and well-authenticated facts, it appears that, probably from some unexplained condition of the material organs, the recollection of knowledge long since obliterated may be suddenly revived. These cases have been observed to occur most frequently in extreme sickness, and on the near approach of death. May it not be that, in our present state, the material and immaterial part of man being intimately united, our failure of recollection is caused by some condition of the material organism; and that, as this union approaches dissolution, the power of the material over the immaterial is weakened, and the knowledge which we have once acquired is more fully revealed to our consciousness, indicating that when the separation is complete it will remain with us forever?

A variety of cases are mentioned by writers on this subject, a few of which are here inserted:

An instance is mentioned by Coleridge of a servant-girl

in Germany, who, in extreme sickness, was observed to repeat passages of Greek, Latin and Hebrew, though she was known to have no acquaintance with these languages. Upon inquiry into her history, it was found that, many years before, she had been a domestic in the family of a learned professor, who was in the habit of repeating aloud passages from his favorite authors while walking in his study, which adjoined the apartment in which she was accustomed to labor. This case is the more remarkable, inasmuch as the person had never been conscious herself of having acquired the knowledge which she, under these circumstances, exhibited.

The Rev. Mr. Flint, a very intelligent gentleman, who, in a series of interesting letters, has related his experiences in the valley of the Mississippi, informs us that, under a desperate attack of typhus fever, as his attendants afterwards told him, he repeated whole pages from Virgil and Homer, which he had never committed to memory, and of which, after his recovery, he could not recollect a line.

Dr. Abercrombie, in his work on intellectual philosophy, mentions a variety of cases in which persons in extreme sickness, and under operations for injuries of the head, conversed in languages which they had known in youth, but had for many years entirely forgotten.

Dr. Rush mentions the case of an Italian gentleman, who died of yellow fever in New York, who, in the beginning of his sickness, spoke English; in the middle of it, French; but on the day of his death, nothing but Italian. A Lutheran clergyman informed Dr. Rush that the Germans and Swedes of his congregation in Philadelphia, when near death, always prayed in their native languages, though some of them, he was confident, had not spoken them for fifty or sixty years.

Dr. Abercrombie mentions another case, of a boy, who, at the age of four, received a fracture of the skull, for which he underwent the operation of the trepan. He was at the time in a state of perfect stupor; and, after his recovery, retained no recollection either of the accident or of the operation. At the age of fifteen, during the delirium of a fever, he gave his mother a correct description of the operation, and the persons who were present at it, with their dress and other minute particulars. He had never been observed to allude to it before, and no means were known by which he could have acquired a knowledge of the circumstances which he related.

What conclusion we are authorized to draw from these facts, it is difficult to determine. They, however, indicate that what we seem to forget, can never be irretrievably lost to the percipient soul. The means for recalling it in some inexplicable manner appear to exist, and when, under some unknown conditions, they are called into action, all or any part of our knowledge may, on the instant, be brought to our recollection.

The moral lesson which these facts inculcate is obvious. If every impression made upon the mind is to remain upon it forever, if the soul be a tablet from which nothing that is written is ever erased, how great is the importance of imbuing it with that knowledge which shall be a source of joy to us as long as we exist! And, again; since knowledge which lies so long dormant may be revived unexpectedly, under conditions which we cannot foresee, and at times when it may have the most important bearing upon our decisions and our destiny, it is of the greatest consequence to us to store the mind with such knowledge as shall invigorate our principles and confirm our virtue. He who reads a corrupting book for pastime may thoughtlessly lay it down, and suppose that in a few days all the images which it has created will have passed from his remembrance forever. But these latent ideas may be recalled by some casual association or some physical condition of the brain, and give that bias to his mind, in the hour of temptation, which will determine him to a course that shall tend to his final undoing.

It may not be inappropriate here to suggest the harmony between this condition of memory and the scripture doctrine of a general judgment. The teaching of the New Testament on this subject is, that the whole race of man will be summoned before God, to be judged according to the deeds done in the body. We can easily perceive how all this may be done, if the view which we have taken on this subject be correct. Suppose every being to be perfectly conscious of all the events of his past life, and of all the obligations which he has violated, and his character in a spiritual world to be as manifest to others as it is to himself; and the judgment concerning every individual must be immediately formed by the whole universe. No examination is needed, for the facts which in each case form the basis of the condemnation are apparent to all. Like choosing its like, the good would be separated from the bad; and the decision pronounced by the Judge would be reëchoed back from the conscience of every individual, with the assent of every moral intelligence.

It may be well, in closing this section, to refer to some singular effects produced on memory by disease. They do not come under any law with which I am acquainted, yet they deserve to be recorded for the purpose of directing attention to the subject. It is by the observation of anomalous cases in science, that we are led to the discovery of new and important laws.

Sometimes, in consequence of injury or disease, the memory of a particular period is lost altogether, while what occurred both before and after that period is remembered with accuracy. Dr. Beattie mentions the case of a clergyman who, in consequence of an apoplectic attack, lost the recollection of precisely four years.

Sometimes the loss of memory relates to particular persons. Dr. Abercrombie mentions the case of a surgeon who was thrown from his horse and carried into a neighboring house in a state of insensibility. From this he soon recovered, and gave minute and correct directions respecting his own treatment. In the evening he was so much relieved, that he was removed to his own house. The medical friend who accompanied him in the carriage made some observation respecting the precautions necessary to be observed to prevent unnecessary alarm to his family, when, to his astonishment, he discovered that his friend had lost all idea of having either a wife or children. It was not until the third day that the circumstances of his past life began to recur to his mind.

Cases have occurred in which, from an injury to the head, the knowledge of a particular language has been lost. In other cases, not a language but a particular class of words has been dropped from the recollection. A case is mentioned, in which a patient suffered from an attack of apoplexy. On his recovery, he had lost the power of pronouncing or writing either proper names or any substantive, while his memory supplied adjectives in profusion. He would speak of any one whom he wished to designate, by calling him after the shape or color for which he was distinguished; calling one man "red," from the color of his hair, and another "tall," from his stature; asking for his hat as "black," and his coat as "brown." As he was a good botanist, he was acquainted with a vast number of plants, but he could never call them by their names. A similar instance occurred, lately, in Livingston county, New York.

A remarkable case is mentioned in the life of Rev. Wm

Tennent, a distinguished clergyman of New Jersey, about the middle of the last century. While prosecuting his studies preparatory to the ministry, he was taken ill and apparently died. After lying for some days without manifesting any signs of life, he was resuscitated and recovered. When he regained his health, it was found that he had lost all knowledge of the past, and was obliged to commence his studies anew, beginning at the alphabet. He had proceeded in this manner for some time, and had advanced as far as the Latin grammar, when, on a sudden, he placed his hand on his head, complaining of violent pain, and, on the instant, his former knowledge had returned to him just as it existed previous to his illness. The whole account is very remarkable, but I believe its authenticity to be above suspicion.

Of these, and a vast number of similar facts, I believe our present knowledge is unable to furnish us with any explanation. They deserve to be recorded as material for future investigation. Subsequent inquirers may be enabled to use them so as to point out more clearly the connection between the mind and the material organism, and thus enlarge our knowledge of our intellectual faculties and the conditions of their exercise.

REFERENCES.

Nature of memory — Reid, Essay 3, chap. 1; Stewart, vol. i., chap. 6.

Implies the power of retaining and recalling — Stewart, vol. i., chap. 6, sec. 1. Locke, Book 2, chap. 10, sec. 1, 2, 8; chap. 19, sec. 1.

Includes susceptibility, retentiveness and readiness — Stewart, vol. i., chap. 6, sec. 2.

An original faculty — Reid, Essay 3, chap. 2.

Involves conception — Reid, Essay 3, chap. 1; Stewart, vol. i., chap. 6, sec. 1.

Attended with belief of past existence and personal identity — Reid, Essay 3, chaps. 1, 4, 6.

Varies in different individuals — Abercrombie, Part 3, sec. 1, Stewart, vol i., chap. 6, sec. 1, 2.

Local and philosophical memory — Abercrombie, Part 3, sec. 1.
Greatly improvable — Stewart, vol. i., chap. 6.
Objects which awaken emotion easily remembered — Stewart, vol. i chap. 6, sec. 1.
Ideas fade from memory — Locke, Book 2, chap. 10, secs. 4, 5.
Reviewing fixes knowledge — Abercrombie, Part 4.
Effect of disease on memory — Abercrombie, Part 3, sec. 1.

SECTION III. — THE IMPORTANCE OF MEMORY.

In treating of this subject, I shall consider, first, the relation of memory to our other faculties; and, secondly, the importance of a cultivated memory to professional success.

I. *The relation between memory and our other intellectual faculties.*

Memory is not necessary either to perception or consciousness. We could see, and hear, and feel, and be conscious of all the operations of our faculties, as well without memory as with it. It is not necessary to some acts of original suggestion. Without it we might have a notion of existence, both objective and subjective. We could not, however, without it, form those original suggestions which involve the idea of succession. Thus, without it, we could have no notion either of duration or of cause and effect.

Memory, on the other hand, is essential to the existence of all those ideas into which the element of time enters. Without it our whole knowledge would consist of the impressions made upon us now and here. Our intellectual existence would thus be reduced to a single point. Whatever we had known previously to the present moment, whatever ideas had occupied our minds before the one which now occupies them, would be blotted out forever. Hence, though we could form a notion of that which was immediately before us, we could not retain that notion, or anything corresponding to it, after it was withdrawn. Being unable to form conceptions, we could perform no acts either of analysis, generalization, or combination. We could form no notion of classes, and could have no general ideas. We could exercise no power of association, for there would be nothing within the scope of our mental vision, except the single idea with which we were at the moment occupied. Equally impossible would it be for us to reason. We reason by the comparison of propositions; but every proposition involves two ideas, and one of these must designate a class; and without memory, as I have remarked, the notion of classes would be impossible. But if this be true of the single propositions which form a syllogism, how much stronger is the case when we consider the syllogism itself, and, still more, the series of syllogisms which form an argument.

Thus, memory holds an intermediate place between those mental acts into which time does and those into which it does not enter. It originates nothing; it gives us no new ideas; it merely retains the ideas given us by the originating faculties, and presents them to those other faculties whose office it is, by modifying, comparing, and combining, to enlarge our knowledge, and extend indefinitely the range of human intelligence. Thus, though memory originates nothing, yet, without it, the faculties which originate would be useless. Though it neither analyzes nor compares, yet, without it, the powers by which we analyze and compare might as well not exist. Were we possessed of this alone, our existence would be an absolute blank; yet, possessed of every other but this, our existence would be reduced to a single point. If this be the relation which memory sustains to our other faculties, it must evidently be one of the most invaluable of our intellectual endowments. The greater the perfection in which it exists, the broader foundation is laid for the exercise of our powers of analysis, combination, and reasoning. The more accurately we retain and the more promptly we recall our knowledge of the past, the richer is our supply of material for every form of intellectual exercise.

II. *The importance of a cultivated memory to professional success.*

By a cultivated memory, I mean a memory so improved by education that it can treasure up with ease, retain with firmness, and recall with promptitude, the knowledge acquired by the other faculties.

1. Without such a memory it is evident that reading must be, to a great degree, useless. Without it, a man may be what Horace calls a "*helluo librorum*," a devourer of books; but he will rarely be anything more. We sometimes meet with men of this class, omnivorous readers, who seize upon books with avidity, with no other object than, either present enjoyment, or the reputation of vast general knowledge. They are pleased with the images spread before them. These pass away to be succeeded by others, until the labor is completed, and nothing remains but a confused recollection of pleasant or painful emotions, and the consciousness that another unit has been added to the number of books which they have read. It is evident that a man may read, in this manner, forever, without any increase of mental energy, or any real addition to the amount of his knowledge.

2. A cultivated memory is also indispensable to a vigorous imagination. Imagination is the power of forming complex conceptions out of materials already existing in the mind. But it is evidently impossible to combine into images elements which we have never collected, or which, if we have previously collected, we are unable to recall. Hence, we find that those authors who have been remarked for boundless fertility of imagination have always been endowed

with the highest gifts of memory. Scott, Goethe, Coleridge, Milton, Macauley, might be easily referred to as illustrations. A distinguished poet must be an intense and accurate observer of nature, and the conceptions formed from actual observation must be the materials from which he creates the images of beauty or sublimity which please or subdue us. The case is similar in philosophical imagination. Unless we are possessed of all the facts in a phenomenon or a series of phenomena, we can never form any adequate conception of the rationale which binds them together in one scientific idea. Without an accurate knowledge of the facts in astronomy, Copernicus could never have formed his idea of the solar system.

3. The importance of a cultivated memory to reasoning is equally obvious. Reasoning is a series of mental acts by which we pass from the known to the unknown. Whenever a proposition is capable of being proved, there exist certain other propositions, which connect it indissolubly with truths already known. These intermediate propositions are called the argument or proof. Suppose, now, that we desire to demonstrate a particular proposition; if we can summon at will all that we have ever known on the subject, we can easily determine whether we possess the required media of proof. If, on the other hand, our knowledge is vague and undetermined, and we are unable to recall it to our recollection, we weary ourselves and perplex others by multiplying irrelevant truths by which nothing is determined. The value of this power is specially illustrated in the case of forensic or legislative orators. They are frequently obliged to construct an argument, or reply to an opponent, when there is neither opportunity for consulting authorities nor examining digests. All that can possibly avail a man is the knowledge which he has previously acquired, and he must be able to bring it to bear at once on the point at issue, or the op

portunity is lost forever. On this power must, therefore, frequently depend the skill of a debater, or the success of an advocate.

4. A cultivated memory is necessary to the attainment of accuracy of practical judgment.

By practical judgment I mean an ability to predict the future from a knowledge of the past, and to form an opinion of the doubtful from a knowledge of the true. This talent, more than almost any other, gives us influence among men; and sometimes seems, in the most favored individuals, to attain almost to the certainty of prescience. Burke, in his writings on the French Revolution, predicted the course of events almost precisely as they subsequently occurred. Other skilful statesmen have been able, from the present aspect of affairs, to anticipate the changes which were approaching in the distance. Several of Napoleon's predictions of the course of events in Europe, have been, in a remarkable manner, verified by the political revolutions that have occurred since his death.

The dependence of this talent upon memory is easily perceived. As our judgments respecting the future must proceed upon the supposition that the course of nature is uniform, how can we predict the future without a knowledge of the past? But mere general and indefinite knowledge will not here suffice. He who would attain to soundness of judgment must possess himself of facts in particular, with the circumstances by which they were surrounded, the limitations by which they were fixed, and the conditions under which they existed. This, of course, supposes an accurate and comprehensive memory. We shall find that the most eminently sagacious men have been favored with a memory of this character. Of this type of mind Dr. Franklin seems to present a remarkable instance.

But this, of itself, will not confer that eminence of practical judgment to which we here refer. We frequently observe men capable of amassing a vast collection of facts, but they are all thrown together at random, and ever remain in a state of chaotic confusion. Their knowledge has neither been associated by scientific relations, nor classified according to established principles; hence it is useless for the purposes of investigation, and can form the basis of no practical judgment. It consists of merely isolated facts, from which no general principles have been deduced, and hence it furnishes no rules for future conduct. Such a man, though ever so extensively read, will ever be incapable of the wise conduct of affairs. Men are frequently pointed out as walking libraries, to whom every one applies for the knowledge of a fact, but to whose opinion no one would defer in any case of practical importance. Thus, we see that those powers by which knowledge is rendered available must be cultivated, as well as those by which it is acquired, if we would attain to soundness of judgment in the practical affairs of life.

I am, however, aware that, to these, other elements must be added, in order to form the character of which we are treating. To a cultivated understanding, a retentive and ready memory, must be united great freedom from prejudices, invincible love of truth, decided moral courage, and firm reliance on the decisions of the human intellect, if we would realize that conception of practical wisdom which Locke somewhere happily denominates "large round-about common sense." Without freedom from prejudice we shall look upon the plainest facts through a distorted medium. If we have no real love of truth we shall never take the pains necessary to arrive at it. If we are deficient in reliance on the decisions of our own intellect, no matter how clearly we may comprehend our position, we shall never reach a deliberate conclusion. And without moral courage, whatever be our conclusions, we shall never dare to carry them into practice. In this, as in every other case, we perceive that moral qualities form the most important elements of human character. Hence we see that actual ability depends greatly upon the cultivation of our own nature; and is placed more within our own reach than might at first be supposed.

The distinction between mere learning and that practical wisdom by which all learning is made available to the purposes of science, or the exigences of practical life, is well illustrated by Cowper in his Task, one of the most delightful poems in the English language.

> "Knowledge and Wisdom, far from being one,
> Have ofttimes no connection. Knowledge dwells
> In heads replete with thoughts of other men ;
> Wisdom, in minds attentive to their own.
> Knowledge, a rude unprofitable mass,
> The mere material with which Wisdom builds,
> Till smoothed, and squared, and fitted to its place,
> Does but encumber what it seemed to enrich.
> Knowledge is proud that he has learned so much.
> Wisdom is humble that he knows no more.
> Books are, not seldom, talismans and spells,
> By which the magic art of shrewder wits
> Holds an unthinking multitude enthralled.
> Some to the fascination of a name
> Surrender judgment hood-winked. Some the style
> Infatuates, and, through labyrinths and wilds
> Of error, leads them by a tune entranced.
> While sloth seduces more, too weak to bear
> The unsupportable fatigue of thought,
> And swallowing, therefore, without pause or choice,
> The total grist unsifted, husks and all."
>
> WINTER WALK AT NOON.

If these remarks be true, it seems remarkable that the question should ever have arisen, whether a powerful memory is compatible with great soundness of judgment. We see, from the above considerations, that soundness of judgment, without a fair development of memory, is impossible. The mistake on this subject has probably arisen from two misconceptions. In the first place, a cultivated and disciplined memory has been confounded with a miscellaneous and unclassified collection of facts. In the second place, the abuse of memory has been confounded with the use of it. Memory is properly used when it is employed to recall our previous knowledge, in order to deduce from it laws which shall govern our future conduct. It is abused when we employ it merely for the purpose of recalling precedents which shall enable us blindly to follow our file-leader. Here it usurps the place of judgment, and renders us servile copyists and imbecile imitators. When we use it to furnish facts, which, by comparison and generalization, shall enable us to form judgments, we derive from it the benefit which the Creator intended.

That remarkable powers of memory are commonly associated with other distinguished endowments, might be easily shown by instances. I have already alluded to several men of genius, who possessed unusual retentiveness and readiness of memory. I do not, however, remember any individual in whom this combination was so remarkable as the late Emperor Napoleon. He used to say of himself, that his knowledge was all laid away in drawers, and that he had only to open the proper drawer, and all that he had acquired on that particular subject was at once presented before him. It was, I think, at the Congress of Erfurt, that he astonished the sovereigns of Europe by the minuteness of his knowledge of historic dates. When they expressed their surprise that he should have been able to attain such extraordinary accuracy amidst the pressure of business with which he had been so long overwhelmed, he replied, that his acquisitions of this kind were made when he was a lieutenant of artillery, and was for a considerable period quartered in the house of a bookseller; besides, added he, I had always great facility in the recollection of numbers. The diligent improvement of time, in youth, thus laid the foundation for the success of the future arbiter of Europe.

I have pursued this subject to a greater extent than might have seemed necessary, did I not suppose that the importance of this faculty is frequently underrated, especially by young men. If a man succeed in almost any department of intellectual labor, it is often said, by way of disparagement, that his effort is nothing but the result of unusual memory. Were this the fact, it would still be true, that the cultivation of memory to high perfection, so that our past knowledge is always available in every emergency, is neither an ordinary nor a contemptible attainment. But the assertion is commonly unfounded. While distinguished success, in any department, can rarely be attained by the exercise of memory alone, it is equally true that the noblest powers would be continually liable to mortifying failure without it. Let us, then, labor to cultivate this faculty by every means in our power, always remembering that we shall derive from it the greatest advantage, not by allowing it to supersede the use of the other faculties, but by training it to act in subordination to them. He who reasons without facts must always proceed in the dark; while he who relies on isolated facts, neither using his powers of generalization nor reasoning, must be willing to remain always a child.

SECTION IV. — THE IMPROVEMENT OF MEMORY.

From the preceding remarks, it is evidently of great importance to every educated man to be able to acquire knowledge rapidly, to retain it permanently, and to recall it with ease. To confer upon us this power, or, at least, to improve it, is one important object of intellectual discipline. I shall proceed to illustrate some of the general principles on which the improvement of memory depends. My object is purely practical. I desire merely to present such views of the subject as will enable us to give increased efficiency to this important faculty. The facts which we have to present are all within the range of every man's consciousness. But though nothing be added to our stock of knowledge, something may, perhaps, be gained, if what we already know can be directed more clearly to a valuable end.

1. Memory, whether we consider its susceptibility, retentiveness, or readiness, is strengthened only by habitual and earnest use. If unemployed, or not employed in diligent study, its power will gradually diminish. This may be illustrated in a variety of particulars.

Let a man find it necessary, for any particular purpose, to remember an event, a conversation, or some passage in a discourse, and he will find that the effort which he makes confers upon him in some degree the power which he needs. Let him be placed under the necessity of doing the same thing frequently, and statedly, and he soon becomes conscious that his power rapidly increases. It matters not what may be the class of objects which we are called upon to recollect, we recollect with ease what we find it necessary to recollect habitually. The civil engineer remembers, without effort, localities, the outline of a country, heights, distances, levels, water-courses, and whatever facts are important in the practice of his profession. The merchant remembers prices in different countries, the amount of production in each for a great number of years, the consumption under various circumstances, and the conditions by which it is affected, the rates of exchange, and the fluctuations of markets. The lawyer remembers, in the same manner, decisions, arguments, analogies, precedents, and cases. Neither of these could do more than very imperfectly what the other does with facility. The memory, strengthened by exercise in one particular department of knowledge, is left in other respects almost in its natural condition.

Nor is this all. The power of recalling our knowledge is materially affected by the circumstances under which the habit is cultivated. He who is accustomed to extemporary speaking will find his recollection more active when in the presence of an audience than in the retirement of his study. He has made that most valuable acquisition, the power of thinking upon his legs; and he will perceive truth more clearly, he will illustrate it more forcibly, and find all his knowledge more perfectly under his control, in these circumstances, than in any other. Another man, who has accustomed himself solely to writing, finds his power of recollection much more active when surrounded by his books and papers. The pen has become to him an almost indispensable instrument of thought, and, without it, he is frequently and strangely at a loss. Neither of these men could do the work of the other. Hence it is that so few men have been successful in both written and extempore discourse. Hence it is that, frequently, orations which have produced the deepest impression during delivery, have appeared so tame and lifeless when they have been committed to paper. The excitement of delivery, which enabled the speaker to associate so many images of beauty and sublimity with the subject-matter of his discourse, passed away when the orator attempted to write, and little remains but the plain appeal to the understanding. Cicero somewhere alludes to the difficulty of attaining to great perfection in both written and spoken discourse, and justly, if not wisely, compliments himself on having been successful where most other eminent men had failed.

The effect of society upon the character of our recollection has frequently been remarked. He who associates habitually with men of distinguished colloquial ability, is placed under the necessity of recalling his knowledge on the instant, and of recalling it on any subject that the occasion may demand. The peculiar kind of recollection is also greatly modified by the company with which we associate. If our companions are men of humor, we find ourselves involuntarily recalling humorous events and droll associations. If we consort with men of science, the mind takes a bias in a contrary direction Thus a man of great colloquial excellence transforms into his own intellectual likeness those who are much in his society. An illustration of this remark is found in Boswell's Life of Johnson. The associates of this great converser were remarkable for their colloquial talent, and every individual was more or less tinged with the peculiarities, whether good or bad, of their master. Men of quite opposite elements of character were assimilated in their modes of thought to him whom they all admired; and they thus formed a school, of which the lineaments were recognized throughout the contemporary literary world.

Instances of the power of recalling all our knowledge upon a given subject, are found in the lives of men who have been successfully employed in the conduct of affairs. We see them forming plans for the future, embracing a complicated variety of contingencies, for all of which provision must be made in advance. The motives of men must be weighed, the effect of measures upon different governments estimated; action and reäction must be subjected to deliberate calculation, and all the elements which would advance or retard the design must be distinctly present to the mind. The intellectual effort required in a great military commander is essentially the same. It is said that before the Duke of Wellington took the command of the army of the Peninsula, the plan of operations which he subsequently carried into effect had been thoroughly matured and resolved upon. Every one must perceive the vast knowledge of facts, and the wonderful accuracy of judgment, which were required in order to perfect a plan which could be carried into effect in the midst of so many and so complicated contingencies. Dumas also relates, that, when the Emperor Napoleon "decided to abandon the invasion of England, and attack the Emperor of Austria, it was necessary to confide to the chief of his staff not only the idea of the plan of the campaign which he meditated, but, likewise, to develop all the details. He dictated to M. Daru, off-hand, and without once stopping, those memorable instructions, that admirable plan of the campaign, which we saw executed precisely as he had fixed it, doubtless after profound meditation. In these instructions, the march of every day, the places at which the army should arrive at successive periods, and the place and almost the day on which the great battle should be fought, were minutely specified. With these previous instructions the actual result corresponded with astonishing accuracy. Every one must be amazed at the amount and the minuteness of the knowledge which could foresee and provide for every emergency that might arise in so extended and vast operations."

I have pursued these illustrations beyond the limit which the importance of the subject would seem to demand. The object which I have in view must plead my apology. I have desired to give prominence to the fact that the memory is readily improved by exercise, and that it improves in the precise manner in which it is earnestly and habitually employed. Every one must see that such command of knowledge as I have exemplified could be the result of nothing but assiduous and thorough cultivation. A lesson of practical value to the young may be learned from these considerations. We are thus taught that we may, by diligent and earnest effort, become equal to the discharge of duties which now seem out of our power. The Duke of Wellington, in early life, gave no indications of eminent ability. We are liable to error in supposing that because we do not now possess the practical skill which a particular situation demands, it would therefore be presumption in us to undertake it. It is generally safe to believe that what other men, in the same circumstances, do, we, if the duty be imposed upon us, can do also. But, while we adopt this rule, we shall greatly err if we suppose that we shall be qualified for any situation merely by being placed in it. Place confers no talent, and it communicates no knowledge; while, therefore, we may hope to do what other men have done, it must be under the conditions in which other men have done it. Unless we take the same pains, and subject ourselves to the same discipline, as those who have succeeded, we shall unquestionably fail. Inspiration is, at least, as rare now as it has been in past ages; and, if we would attain to success, we must form our rules of conduct, not on exceptions, but on general laws. To subject ourselves to the discipline necessary to success, will not interfere with the inspirations of genius; while, should it happen that we are not inspired, without such discipline our failure will be inevitable.

2. It is a well-known fact that the power of recollection depends greatly on attention.

The condition of mind which we denominate attention is that in which we direct our whole mental energies exclusively to one particular object. It may proceed either from without or from within; from an objective or a subjective cause. In the former case, the occurrence itself so entirely engrosses our thoughts that, without any volition, everything else is excluded from the mind. Let a traveller in Europe ride over a field rising and falling, now in regular and again in irregular slopes, with here and there a clump of trees, on one side a windmill, and on the other an old stone house, and it will leave no definite impression on his mind. He can look upon just such scenes anywhere, and he has seen just as impressive landscapes every day of his life. His thoughts may wander in the direction of home, and his conversation turn to such subjects as the humor of the moment may suggest. But let him be informed that this is the field of Waterloo, that this eminence is Mount St. Jean, that yonder is the farm-house of La Haye Sainte, that there is the thicket and villa of Hougomont, and near him the tree under which Wellington remained during the greater part of the action; that on the slopes beyond the French were posted, and there in the vale is the spot where, for the first time, the Imperial Guard faltered, mowed down in ranks, as they advanced to the charge; every other thought now vanishes from his mind, and it is not possible for him to think of anything but that terrible battle, on which the course of empire in Europe depended. Such an impression is engraven on the memory forever.

In these cases, as I have said, the occasion of attention is from without. It is arrested by objects around us, we are conscious of no special mental effort when it is excited, and we could not control it if we would. There is another and very different form of attention, which depends upon the exercise of our will. In this case, by an act of volition, we dismiss all thought irrelevant to the subject before us, and concentrate upon it all the mental energy of which we are capable. The more perfectly we do this, the greater will be our power of recollection; we shall thus acquire knowledge in the shortest time, and retain it with the greatest success. The men who have been remarkable for great powers of memory have possessed in a remarkable degree the power of abstract attention. The biographer of Johnson observes that while he was reading the appearance of mental effort which he exhibited was painful even to his companions. He seemed wholly unconscious of the existence of anything around him; his countenance was flushed, the veins of his forehead became distended, and his whole appearance betokened the intensest mental concentration. A portrait, by Sir J. Reynolds, presents him in precisely this attitude.

Of the nature of attention, and the means by which it may be cultivated, I have before treated; I need not, therefore, repeat what I have said on this subject. It will be sufficient to observe that, if we desire to improve the power of memory, it is here that we must always commence. Until we have learned to dismiss from our minds wandering and irrelevant thought, and fix our intellectual energies on the subject directly before us, we shall always suffer the evils of imperfect and feeble recollection. Attention, as we have before observed, obeys the commands of a determined will. It is thus in our own power to enlarge and strengthen our intellectual faculties. A weak memory may be rendered strong, and a fleeting recollection permanent, by resolutely laboring to improve it. The remedy, however, resides in ourselves, and it is the same for all. If we are willing to make the sacrifices necessary to insure success, observing the laws by which the improvement of our faculties is governed, there is no one of our intellectual powers which may not be improved far beyond what at the commencement we should have believed possible. The men who earnestly labor to improve themselves generally go beyond expectation; those who rely on their undisciplined powers almost always fall short of it.

But, beyond this, we should labor to acquire, not merely the power of occasional attention, but the habit of constant and wakeful mental earnestness. In this manner, alone, does our existence become in the highest degree valuable, since every portion of it brings forth the richest and most abundant fruit, and no hour and no occasion is suffered to run to waste. An oasis in the desert is, by contrast, exceedingly beautiful and picturesque; but how valueless it appears when compared with the broad acres of a cultivated land, clothed as far as the eye can reach with exhaustless fertility, the hills covered with flocks, the valleys loaded with corn, supplying with prodigal liberality the wants of every living thing that finds a home upon its bosom! So the transient efforts of genius may delight and surprise us; but it is the steady labor of earnest minds that works out those changes in public opinion, by which error is dissipated, truth discovered and promulgated, and a new impulse given to the progress of humanity in wisdom and virtue.

It is by acquiring this habit of constant and earnest attention, and the power of transferring at will our whole energy from one subject to another, that some men are enabled to perform an amount of intellectual labor which seems almost incredible. The duties of the Chancellor of Great Britain, in his judicial office the most important in the kingdom, as speaker and a leading member of the House of Lords, and frequently an active member of the cabinet, could be successfully discharged by no one whose intellect was not disciplined to incessant and intense exertion. The same remark is applicable to every man who stands in the front rank of any profession. The demand for eminent service is incessant; and nothing can meet this demand but a mind capable of putting forth its best efforts without either cessation or weariness.

3. In the third place, readiness, or facility in recalling our knowledge, depends mainly upon the principles by which it is associated. The thought which we at this moment need

is brought to our recollection, because it has been connected by some law of association, with a thought now present.

Our associations are of two kinds, those by casual, and those by permanent relations. The associations which we form from contiguity of time and place, or from mere external appearance, as color, size, etc., are casual; those from cause and effect are permanent. When we see an event occurring at a particular time and place, it by no means follows that a similar event will recur at the same place at a corresponding time; nor are similar events, by any tie whatever, connected with, or related to, that time and place. Hence, if we associate an event by these relations, there is nothing whatever to recall our analogous knowledge. If, on the other hand, we observe an event, and associate it with its causes and effects, we know that the same cause, under similar circumstances, will produce the same effect, and, under modified circumstances, will produce modified effects. Hence, this form of association connects with the event which we wish to remember a multitude of other events, any one of which, if present to the mind, may recall any one or all of the others.

Inasmuch, then, as casual associations furnish no bond of connection by which facts are associated together, they can furnish little aid to the memory, and can assist us but feebly in the investigation of truth. If a lawyer associated cases merely with the court-rooms in which they happened to be decided, his knowledge would render but little service in the practice of his profession. He must remember them by their connection with the principles of equity, if he wishes to recall them whenever an analogous case occurs in the course of his pleadings. Were they associated merely by time and place, the most dissimilar decisions would be grouped together, so that he could rarely call to mind those adapted to his purpose. If he associate them by the principles to which they are allied, each case would recall the principle, and the principle the cases which it controlled. Knowledge, in this manner, becomes linked together. A single fact brings with it the recollection of a multitude of other facts, and these form the basis of important generalizations, or the materials for apt and ample illustration.

Or, again, suppose we witness a philosophical experiment. By casual association, we should connect it with nothing but the place in which it was performed; and the various steps of the process would be thought of only in the order of their succession. All that would remain to us would be the naked facts, that, at such a time and place, in such a lecture-room, the first event was followed by the second, and the second by the third, and so on to the end. If, on the contrary, the relations of cause and effect were clearly explained, and every change referred to its appropriate law, we should know not only the succession of changes, but the law which governed each succession. Hence, each event will be associated with the others by a definite and unchanging connection. Ever afterwards, any event in the series will readily call to recollection those thus associated with it, and also the law on which the succession depended; and any one of these laws will also recall not only these effects, but many others which at any time we may have had occasion to observe.

From these illustrations it is evident that readiness, or the power of recalling our knowledge, depends greatly upon philosophical association In order to associate in this manner, we must form the habit of referring facts to the laws on which they depend, and of tracing out laws to the facts by which they are exemplified. If we observe a phenomenon, we should, if possible, ascertain its cause. If we examine a specimen, we should refer it to its class. If we study an event, we should observe its necessary relations to the events which preceded and which have succeeded it. So, on the other hand, if we have comprehended an abstract principle. we should not be satisfied until we have transformed it into a concrete expression, observed the facts by which it is illustrated, and the results to which it leads. If, for instance, we comprehend a general law in mechanics, we should work out problems which illustrate its mode of operation, until the law and the facts which depend upon it are so thoroughly associated together that they form one clearly defined and well digested conception. So, in political economy, if we are satisfied that a law is true, we should not rest until, if possible, we have exhausted the results to which it will, of necessity, lead; and, on the other hand, if we observe a new fact in the movements of commerce, or the operations of finance, we should trace it back to its legitimate cause, and determine the law to which it owes its existence.

In this respect, our systems of education are probably defective. We determine, in the first place, that a certain number of sciences must be learned in a given time. In the time allotted to each, it may be possible either to communicate to the pupil some of the facts without the general principles, or some of the principles without the facts; but not to associate the principles with the facts by the patient labor of tracing out their connections with each other. It is by this latter mode of acquisition that the mind attains power and alertness. He who has thus mastered a single science has gained far better mental discipline than by cursory attention to several. He who has learned one thing thoroughly knows how other things also are to be learned; and he who has proceeded as far as this has made no contemptible progress in his education.

But, though a system of education does not accomplish all that might be desired, it may yet be of great value. We may derive important advantage from a distinct knowledge of general principles, although we have but little power of carrying them into practice. If we have gained only so much knowledge that we are able, in subsequent life, to refer common facts to general laws, or even to understand the reference when it is made by others, we have laid the foundations of philosophical association. The observations occurring in our daily occupations will, from time to time, revive and enlarge our knowledge. Every general law acquired in youth thus becomes a nucleus, on which our additional attainments crystallize, and the mass increases by continued aggregation. Hence it is often observed that young men, who are well grounded in the severer studies, attain, in the end, to a larger intellectual growth, and succeed much better in professional life, than those of greater brilliancy, who aim at more general attainments, and devote their time to what is called universal reading.

From these remarks we learn the value of hypotheses in philosophy. An hypothesis is a conception of the causes of a phenomenon which has not yet been established by proof. Since it is not established, it is of no positive validity, and can neither be received as a truth, nor made the basis of scientific reasoning. Yet it is not, therefore, valueless. It offers to our consideration a conjectural law. If to this law we can refer a number of phenomena which were before isolated, we are the better able to retain them in the memory. Suppose, for instance, several isolated facts have been observed in geology, for which no cause has been discovered. A theory is proposed which, if it be allowed, will account for the whole, or a considerable part of them. This is an hypothesis. By grouping them together as the result of this supposed cause, an important aid is rendered to our recollection. Burke, I believe, remarks that an hypothesis is good for as much as it will explain. An hypothesis, moreover, presents a definite subject for investigation

If it be proved false, science is the gainer by the research which it has occasioned; if it be proved true, an addition is made to the knowledge of man.

4. Readiness of memory is materially assisted by methodical arrangement.

Every one knows the difficulty of remembering isolated and disconnected items, such as a number of words selected at random, or a column of miscellaneous figures. This difficulty is greatly diminished by arranging these several items according to some general conception, as, for instance, by placing the words in alphabetical order, or grouping them according to the subjects to which they relate. By such an adjustment some principle of connection is immediately established, and, as one suggests the following, we easily commit them to memory, and more readily recall them afterwards.

It is obvious that all sciences, from the necessity of the case, are susceptible of a natural arrangement. In the discovery of knowledge, as I have before remarked, we proceed from individuals to generals, and from less to more general, until we arrive at the most comprehensive genus which the present state of knowledge admits. In the communication of knowledge, this process is exactly reversed; we commence with the most comprehensive genus, and proceed step by step to the less comprehensive, until we arrive at varieties and individuals. So, when, in any case, we desire to communicate truths, by patient reflection we shall be able to discover the general principle on which the whole essentially depends. When this is clearly displayed, it suggests in natural succession whatever is to follow. The order in which science thus arranges itself, confers important assistance on the memory. When knowledge has no relation to time, we proceed from more to less general truth. When time enters into the development of a subject the order of cause and effect is to be preferred. Thus, in natural history, we proceed from genera to species; in history, we follow the order of time, which here is also the order of cause and effect. In political economy, we treat, in succession, of production, exchange, distribution, and consumption; because this is the order of the dependence of one class of actions upon another, and this is the order of changes through which any object passes that is modified by the industry of man. It is easy to perceive that our power of recalling our knowledge of any subject, must be greatly increased by the simplicity and clearness with which it was arranged, when it was treasured up in the memory.

When any branch of knowledge is thus reduced to method, we can readily commence with its more general and elementary principles, and trace them through their subsidiary ramifications, each genus suggesting the several species which it includes, until all our acquisitions on this subject are spread in one view before the mind. The want of such an arrangement is, not unfrequently, a serious embarrassment to a student. He sometimes finds important truths carelessly thrown together — principles and results, causes and effects, in a condition of hopeless dislocation; so that to treasure them up as available knowledge in their present form is almost impossible. In this case, if the knowledge is worth the trouble, our best method is to think the subject out and reärrange it for ourselves. This will require time, but it is the only way in which knowledge so inartistically presented can be rendered useful to the student. The great work of Adam Smith, which has wrought so wonderful changes in the policy of nations, would have achieved its triumph at a much earlier period if its effects had not been weakened by great want of systematic arrangement.

The power of clear and well-digested method is of great

value, not only to the student himself, but also to those to whom he communicates knowledge. The preacher, who will take the trouble to acquire it, will not so often complain that his teachings are forgotten, or that his audience is inattentive. The lawyer will thus be enabled greatly to abridge his proceedings, and at the same time leave a stronger and more durable impression on the court and the jury. In our addresses to our fellow-men, I hardly know of an acquisition of greater importance than this, or one that aids more powerfully our efforts to produce conviction.

From what has been said, we perceive the incorrectness of the opinion, that the memory resembles a store-house, which may be filled to overflowing, or so filled as to render further acquisitions more and more difficult. If the student have used his memory aright, the greater his acquisitions the easier will subsequent acquisitions become. If he have formed the habit of concentrated thought, the less effort will be required to fix his attention. If he habitually refer his facts to principles, he will successively arise to higher and higher generalizations, and the knowledge which he acquires will connect itself by more and more numerous associations. We are never embarrassed by the amount of our knowledge, but only by its miscellaneous and disorderly variety. If reflection upon a subject presents us with nothing but a multitude of irrelevant and disconnected facts, without generalization or arrangement, we may well complain of being overburdened with knowledge. But, when reflection yields the fruit of apposite principles and illustrative facts, the wider the range of our acquisitions the greater will be our intellectual power. It is in consequence of the formation of such habits that an accomplished public speaker frequently astonishes us, by discoursing with ample fulness, and with the clearest method, upon occasions which allowed no opportunity for previous preparation. The attainment of such a power is certainly worth all the labor which it can possibly demand.

Of artificial memory.

Besides the means for the cultivation of memory which I have suggested above, others, depending upon artificial association, have been frequently recommended. Cicero somewhere mentions the systems of this kind which were in use in his time. It may be well to indicate the principles on which such systems are founded.

When we wish to remember a particular fact, we frequently associate it with something which we cannot easily forget. We sometimes see men desiring to recollect an engagement tie a knot in their handkerchief, or bind a string around one of their fingers. In artificial memory, a regular system of signs is employed for a similar purpose. I remember a lecturer on mnemonics, who used for this purpose a sheet or two of paper, divided into a large number of compartments, in each of which was engraved a figure of some well-known object. When a number of items, as a column of words, was to be remembered, the pupil was taught to associate each word with an object in one of these compartments. In this manner a large number of particulars might be remembered for a short time. The system, however, which has maintained the most permanent reputation, is that of Gray, in his Memoria Technica, a work of which Dr. Johnson speaks somewhere with great respect. The nature of this system may be known from a single example. Suppose the object is to remember numbers. The vowels, diphthongs, and the most important consonants, are so arranged as to correspond with the nine digits and cipher, in the following manner:

a	e	i	o	u	au	oi	ei	ou	y
1	2	3	4	5	6	7	8	9	0
b	d	t	f	l	s	h	k	n	x.

This table may be used thus: Suppose that I wished to remember the fact that Julius Cæsar arrived at the supreme power in the year 46, B. C. I observe that the letter o is above 4, and the letter s under 6. Forty-six is then represented by the syllable *os*. I write Juli*os* for Julius, and thus recall this date to my recollection. Or, again: Alexander founded his empire in 331, B. C. The number 331, as before explained, may be expressed by the letters *ita*. I then write Alex*ita* instead of Alexander, and am thus reminded of the date in question. Various other systems have been devised, but they all depend upon similar principles.

Of the utility of this method of aiding the memory, I am unable to speak from experience. I have, however, observed, that, whatever may be the immediate effect of these systems, they are generally soon laid aside. It seems as difficult to remember the system as to remember the knowledge which it would enable us to retain. Whatever be its virtue, it can confer upon us no valuable mental discipline. It would seem better, therefore, to cultivate the memory by those methods which give increased vigor to all our other intellectual faculties. When a subject is capable of philosophical association, it is surely better to fix it in our recollection by philosophical arrangement. When the matter to be remembered is names, dates, or other isolated facts, it is better to refer to tables and books, where such knowledge is to be found, than to trust to our memory, unless we are endowed with special facility for this sort of acquisition.

There is, however, one mode of rendering our knowledge available, which seems to me of great value. It is a well-arranged common-place book, or a book made for the purpose of recording any important items of knowledge in such manner as to be easily accessible. The Rev. Dr. Todd, of Pittsfield, Mass., has prepared a work exceedingly well adapted to this purpose. It is called an "Index Rerum." It consists of blank leaves ruled and paged, with the letters of the alphabet, so that a student can readily insert a word designating a particular subject, and under this word record all the places in which he finds this subject treated. A student, by the use of such a book, would be able to refer to all the works which he had read on any particular subject, by glancing at a single entry in his index. His common-place book would thus be an index to his whole library; enabling him, in the shortest time, and with the least trouble, to render all his past reading available for immediate use whenever he should require it.

At the risk of some repetition, I shall close this part of the subject with a few directions for study, deduced from the preceding remarks:

1. We should employ our minds as little as possible in those occupations which require no effort of attention. He who spends much of his time in reading that which he does not wish to remember, will find his power of acquisition rapidly to diminish. Light reading is entitled to its place, and need not be proscribed altogether. But light reading need not be useless reading. Facts of all kinds, to him who is able to make a proper use of them, are always of inestimable value. But much that is called light reading tends to no result whatever except present amusement; and nothing is more destructive of every manly energy than amusement pursued as a business. Nor let it be supposed that the vigorous employment of our faculties is destitute of its appropriate enjoyment. Here, as everywhere else, happiness is found, not when we seek for it directly, but when, thoughtless of ourselves, we are honestly doing our duty. The weariness caused by labor is relieved either by rest or by a change of pursuits, and the mind returns with renewed relish to its appointed labors. But what change

can relieve an intellect jaded and worn down by excessive excitement, and vexed with the incessant craving of unsatisfied desires?

2. We should strive to observe accurately every fact, and comprehend clearly every truth to which our attention may be directed. In this manner alone can we attain to precision of thought and distinctness of conception. We shall thus learn the difference between what we know and what we do not know; an attainment of more value than might at first seem manifest. He whose mind habitually rejects crude and undigested conceptions, and vague and intangible theories, has made no inconsiderable progress in intellectual cultivation. Nor is it enough that a man can comprehend what an author has written while the book is under his eye. He should attain to such a knowledge of the subject that he can think it out for himself in his own language, and trace its connections and dependencies by means of illustrations of his own. In this manner he will be able to understand what he reads, to remember what he understands, and to recall what he has remembered whenever the occasion renders it necessary.

I am aware that this method of study will seem to require a much longer time, and restrict us to a much slower progress, than the course commonly pursued. A man will be obliged to select his books with greater care, and devote to his reading a more vigorous and protracted effort, than is generally thought necessary. He may thus lose, if he ever possessed it, the reputation of genius; but, what is more important, he may find the reality. By forming the habit of earnest and habitual attention, he may thus acquire that power which is the very element of genius. At first, the mind laboring in this manner may seem to act slowly; but, as soon as effort becomes its natural condition, vigorous action will be as rapid as any other. Those who think intensely, if they do it habitually, require less time than other men to perfect their mental operations. It is thus that the powers of the mind are carried to their highest perfection, and those intellectual labors are performed which to other men seem almost miraculous.

3. Our knowledge should, as far as possible, be philosophically arranged. Facts should be accounted for, that is, referred to their appropriate laws; and laws should be exemplified until the use of them becomes perfectly familiar. In this respect students are very prone to err. I have frequently seen young men, who could pass a creditable examination in the rules of rhetoric, who could not successfully construct a discourse on the simplest subject, and who were unable to write three consecutive sentences without a blunder. Every one perceives that knowledge of this kind is useless, and must soon be forgotten. It is this habit of combining theory with practice which, most of all, confers professional ability.

The importance of arranging our knowledge methodically, that is, in its relations to the general principles on which it depends, need not again be insisted on. I will, therefore, only add that, in all our efforts to improve our minds, we should be patient with ourselves. Bad habits cannot be corrected except by the formation of good ones; and to form habits of any kind is a work of time. Strenuous effort, if we give it time enough, will accomplish all that we could desire. We must not, however, be disconcerted at the imperfect success of our incipient efforts. Each one will accomplish something; and every effort accomplished, though but imperfectly, will render less difficult that which succeeds. Those who have been the most successful in the end have frequently confessed that their first attempts were marked by mortifying failure. It was thus with Demosthenes; and if more men were blessed with his determination to succeed, the world would not so often have complained of the small number of great orators.

The application of the preceding remarks to the duties of an instructor is apparent.

The object of a teacher is to communicate knowledge, and so to communicate it as to develop and strengthen the powers of the mind. Hence, in order to succeed, he must observe the laws to which the mind is subjected. The mind of the pupil is similar to the mind of the teacher, age only excepted. The course which has proved most successful with the one, will prove the most successful with the other. If we bear this in mind, we shall perceive the importance of the following suggestions:

1. I have remarked that our power of recollection depends greatly upon the clearness of our conceptions. Now, the ability of young persons to comprehend complicated relations is, of course, much less than of adults. It is, therefore, the duty of the instructor to analyze what is complex and simplify what is intricate, or else so to direct the mind of the pupil that he can do it for himself. In this manner every kind of knowledge adapted to the age of the pupil may be brought within his intellectual grasp. The instructor should not merely hold forth to the pupil what is laid down in the books, but think it out for himself, observe its elements, and separate them from each other, so that he may place them in the clearest light before the conception of the pupil. In these respects instructors frequently fail. Sometimes they have no clear idea of a subject themselves, and, of course, can convey none to others. They merely inculcate by rote what they have learned by rote themselves. Sometimes an instructor, who understands a subject himself, forgets the labor by which his knowledge was acquired, and becomes unconscious of the difference between himself and his pupil. What is very simple to him now, appears to him,

of course, simple to every one. What became familiar to him only by severe and protracted effort, seems capable of being learned by his pupil in a shorter time than is actually possible. In these respects it becomes an instructor to be on his guard. He should consider, not what he can do now, but what he could have done when under the circumstances of his pupils. He should, therefore, be careful to assure himself that what he teaches is understood. He who will bear these things in mind will not often have to complain of the stupidity of his pupils. When an instructor finds all his pupils blockheads, the indication is certainly ambiguous; there is a blockhead somewhere, but whether it be either the teacher or the pupil becomes a proper subject of inquiry.

2. What has been rendered simple may be easily illustrated. Skill in illustration, therefore, is of great importance to a teacher. He perhaps presents to a pupil a new idea which is not readily comprehended. The conception of the one is not grasped by the other; or, if it is, the pupil does not certainly know that the idea in his mind is that which the teacher means to communicate. The teacher must, therefore, call up some analogous idea with which the pupil is familiar, so that, from ground common to both, he may pass by easy gradation to that which is new and uncomprehended. Things dissimilar in themselves frequently stand to each other in similar relations, thus affording wide range for analogies. In this manner the known is made to teach the unknown. Nor is this all. The illustration associates a new with a familiar idea. An interesting and apposite image is presented, and thus whatever is learned is more easily remembered. An illustration addressed to the eye is always the most successful. Hence, maps, diagrams, experiments, are among the most indispensable aids of an instructor.

3. It is scarcely necessary to add that the progress of the pupil will be greatly accelerated by reducing his knowledge, as far as possible, to practice. From the necessity of the case, it is evident that much of the pupil's time must be occupied in learning rules. If, however, the teaching is confined to these alone, it becomes intolerably irksome. The mind struggles against it, and is willing quickly to forget what is associated with nothing but pain. These difficulties, however, may in a great degree be removed, by teaching the pupil, as soon as he has learned a rule, to put it into practice. He then discovers that the knowledge of rules is a means of power, for it enables him to do what he could not do before, and he becomes conscious of progress and increased ability. Every step in advance brings with it an immediate reward, and he proceeds to the next step with new consciousness of power, and more earnest desire for other acquisitions. It was formerly the practice to carry a boy through the Latin grammar before he began to translate a word; and months were consumed in this dry and repulsive labor. It would be no wonder if, under such a discipline, he learned to abominate the grammar, the language, and the instructor, together. But if, as soon as he has learned a single rule, or mastered a single inflexion, he is taught to use it in the construction of easy phrases, and when, with the knowledge thus gained, he proceeds to the next rule, and finds the increased power derived from adding these knowledges together, further progress becomes desirable in itself, and learning is no longer a drudgery. While it would be absurd to say that, in all respects, our modes of teaching are preferable to those of our fathers, it is delightful to a benevolent mind to contemplate the improvements which have been introduced in the modes of instructing the young. The labor required is better adapted to the faculties of the learner, though here, it must be confessed, we yet

need improvement. Study ministers more to the growth of the mind, instead of being a barren exercise of memory; and a vast amount of misery has been lifted off from the human race — certainly no trifling consideration.

REFERENCES.

Relation of memory to philosophical genius — Stewart, vol. i., chap 6, section 8.

Improvement of memory — Stewart, vol. i., chap. 6, section 3.

Effect of practice in formation of habits — Stewart, vol. i., chap. 2.

Theory and practice — Stewart, vol. i., chap. 4, section 7.

Attention connected with memory — Locke, Book 2, chap. 10, section 8; Abercrombie, Part 3, section 1.

Connected knowledge easily retained — Stewart, vol. i., chap. 6, section 8; sections 1, 2, 4; Abercrombie, Part 3, section 1.

Memory aided by method — Stewart, vol. i., chap. 6, section 3; Abercrombie, Part 3, section 1.

Nature and use of hypothesis — Locke, Book 4, chap. 12, sections 12, 13; Abercrombie, Part 3, section 4; Stewart, vol. i., chap. 6, section 7.

Artificial memory — Stewart, vol. i., chap. 6, section 6.

Rules for study — Stewart, vol. i., chap. 6, section 5.

Effects of writing on memory — Stewart, vol. i., chap. 6, section 5.

Visible objects easily remembered — Stewart, vol. i., chap. 6, section 2.

Memory a storehouse — Reid, Essay 3, chap. 7.

CHAPTER VI

REASONING.

SECTION I. — THE NATURE AND OBJECT OF REASONING, AND THE MANNER IN WHICH IT PROCEEDS.

We now come to the consideration of that series of mental acts denominated reasoning. Before, however, we enter upon this branch of our subject, it may be useful to review again, very briefly, the ground which we have gone over, that we may distinctly perceive the point from which we proceed, and learn the relation which this form of mental action holds to the other acts of the mind.

By our perceptive powers, we become acquainted with the qualities of external objects, and, in general, with the facts in the external world. By our consciousness, we learn the facts existing in the world within us. By original suggestion, various intuitive truths and relations become objects of cognition. By abstraction, conceptions of individuals assume the form of general ideas; and by memory, all this knowledge is retained and recalled to our consciousness at the command of the will.

Were we endowed with no other powers than these, we might enjoy the pleasures of knowledge. Whatever we had observed or experienced, and whatever had been observed and experienced by others, might be retained, generalized and combined, and thus our acquisitions might be both extensive and valuable. But, with no other faculties, we could only know what we or other men had actually observed or experienced. We could never make use of this knowledge to penetrate into the unknown. In a word, we could observe, and feel, and generalize, and classify, and remember, but we could not reason.

But such is not the condition of the human mind. As soon as we acquire any knowledge whatever, we are prompted to use it for the purpose of acquiring other knowledge. We are continually saying to ourselves, if this be thus, then this other must be so; or this must be so, because this and that are so. If this be so, what must of necessity follow? This is the language of human beings, young and old, savage and civilized, learned and ignorant. It is the impulse of our common nature, and one of the endowments with which we have been blessed by a merciful Creator. He has enabled us to cognize relations existing between certain truths, from which emanate other truths different from the preceding, but which, without a knowledge of them, could never have been discovered.

The results of the exercise of this faculty have been most astonishing. Unlike our other endowments, every one of its acts provides a wider field for its future employment, and thus its range is absolutely illimitable. The perception of one color gives me no additional power to perceive another color. A fact remembered furnishes only accidentally a basis or an aid to wider recollection. But every truth discovered by the reasoning power, and, in fact, every truth, however acquired, becomes, by use of this power, the means for proceeding to further discovery. Through the elementary cognitions in geometry, our reason at first discovers certain truths concerning lines, angles and triangles. Using these increased means of knowledge, it proceeds to discover truths concerning circles and squares and, using these again, it discovers those concerning solids, spheres and spherical triangles; and, using these again, it has been able to reveal to us the magnitude, distances and motions, of the heavenly bodies, and thus unfold the wonders of modern astronomy. The knowledge which we thus obtain is original knowledge; that is, it is given us specially by this faculty, and could be given us by no other. How could we ever learn the distance or magnitude or motion of the planets, either by perception, or consciousness, or original suggestion, or abstraction, or memory? The same remark is true respecting the other sciences. Every science which presents to us knowledge which could not be attained by the powers above mentioned, must rely for its discoveries wholly on reasoning.

We see, then, the nature of this faculty. It cognizes nothing directly and immediately. It neither perceives the facts of the outward nor is conscious of the facts of the inward world; it furnishes no original suggestions, and neither abstracts nor remembers; but it receives these data as they are delivered to it by these preceding faculties, and, by a process of its own, uses them to discover new truths, to which none of them could ever have attained. The manner in which this is done, we shall attempt to explain.

Reasoning consists in a series of mental acts, by which we show such a relation to exist between the known and the unknown, that if the former be true, the latter must also be equally true. Thus, in geometry, the known with which we commence is the definitions and axioms. Our first demonstration shows such relations to exist between them and the first proposition, that if those be true this must be true also. This first proposition is thus added to the known, and becomes as firm a ground from which to reason as the definitions and axioms from which we at first proceeded. In our next step we again show, by our reasoning powers, that

24*

if this increased known be true, the second proposition must be true also. We then add our second proposition to the known, and with this increased material of knowledge proceed to the third proposition; and so on continually. In each act of reasoning, we observe first the known, reaching to a definite limit, beyond which all is uncertainty. We observe, secondly, a proposition in the unknown which may be true or may be false, of which nothing can with certainty be affirmed, separated from the known by a chasm, so to speak, of thus far impassable ignorance. The reasoning power projects a bridge across this chasm, uniting them indissolubly together, transforming the unknown into the known, adding a new domain to science, and enlarging by every such act the area of human knowledge.

If such be the nature of the mental process which we denominate reasoning, it suggests to us three distinct topics for consideration:

First, the nature of the truths from which we proceed.

Secondly, the validity of the results at which we arrive.

Thirdly, the nature of the process by which we pass from the one to the other.

To the consideration of these subjects the remainder of this section will be devoted.

I. *The nature of the truths from which we proceed.*

I have already said that, in reasoning, we design to show that if certain things are true, certain other things, whose truth is now unknown, must be true also. We then must, of necessity, proceed from the true to the doubtful, from the known to the unknown. The premises are always, at the commencement, *better* known than the conclusion at which we propose to arrive. From this it is evident that we can never reason unless from what is either known or conceded; and, further, that we can never prove any proposition unless we can find some other proposition better known by which to prove it. If any proposition is to be proved, all other possible propositions must stand to it in one of three relations, either *less known*, *equally known*, or *better known*. To attempt to prove what we *know* by what we *do not know*, or to prove what we *know* by what we do *not know as well*, is absurd. Inasmuch as proof brings the conclusion to precisely the level of the premises, a process of this kind would diminish instead of increasing the certainty of our conclusion. That an error of this kind cannot be committed, I would not, however, assert. We not unfrequently hear men attempt to prove, what every one at the beginning allows, but which, at the conclusion of the argument, every one is disposed to doubt. Such must always be the result when we attempt to prove self-evident truths. Secondly; to attempt to prove either what we know or what we do not know, by what we only know *equally well*, is nugatory. We of course know no better at the end than at the beginning of our argument, and all our labor is by necessity thrown away. We could not, by a life's labor in this manner, advance a single step in knowledge. Hence we can never prove any proposition, unless we can find some propositions better known than that which we desire to prove. Hence it follows, that, when we find a proposition so evident that no proposition more evident can be discovered, the truth of such a proposition cannot be established by the reasoning faculty. If it be true, its truth must be determined by some other power of the mind. Hence, all reasoning must commence from truths not made known by the reason, that is, which the intellection perceives to be true previous to all reasoning, and from which all the deductions of reason proceed. Let us consider the nature of some of these elementary beliefs, which lie at the foundation of all reasoning.

Were nothing more required than that a man should convince himself of the truth of any proposition, nothing more would be necessary than that he himself was satisfied that his premises were true. I do not, of course, say that he would thus, of necessity, arrive at truth, but he would be able to convince himself of the truth of the proposition in question. But, if we reason for the purpose of convincing another man, it is obvious that he also must admit with us the truth of our premises, or the propositions from which we proceed. Unless the two can agree in the premises, argue as long as they may, they can make no progress towards a conclusion. The argument which convinces the one has no effect on the other, since he denies the premises on which it is founded. No argument, then, can have any power over the mind of another, unless both equally admit the truth of the premises on which the conclusion rests. But what is true of any two men, is true of all men collectively. We can never convince the human mind of the truth of our conclusions, unless there be some truths from which we proceed, which all men equally with ourselves admit prior to all argument. If such truths did not exist, all reasoning addressed to the human race would be nugatory and useless. When men reason at great length, without coming to a conclusion, the cause of their difficulty generally is, that they have no principles in common. Hence, when we find ourselves in this condition, the proper course to be pursued is to refer back to the premises from which we proceed, and determine whether they be the same. When men agree in premises, and reason logically from them, it cannot be long before some conclusion is reached.

But it is evident that in all matters of science, and, in fact, in all our reasonings (those only excepted which are technically termed *ad hominem*), we address ourselves not to one man, or one class of men, but to the whole human race.

We proceed upon the belief that what convinces one man, of fair understanding and in a normal condition of the intellect, will convince all men under the same circumstances that is, that there are common truths which all men admit, and that, reasoning from them, they must all arrive at the same result as soon as the argument is fairly presented. And this anticipation is justified by universal experience. The conclusions of mathematics, astronomy, mechanics, of geology, chemistry, magnetism, of political economy, and social philosophy, from the time of their first promulgation, have established themselves gradually in the mind of man, until, by the force of their own evidence, they are admitted as acknowledged truths. Every man who has been convinced of the truth of the reasoning on which their conclusions depend, feels assured that every other man who contemplates them without prejudice will be convinced also. Hence the universal confidence that is felt in the maxim of Bacon, "*Magna est veritas et prevalebit.*" Such unanimous consent to conclusions could not be predicted, and could not exist, unless there were principles lying at the foundation of the reasonings, which all men admit, and from which conclusions follow, by irresistible sequence, which all men must allow. Such truths, made known to all men by the original constitution of the human understanding, must lie at the foundation of all science, and of all knowledge established by reasoning. They have been called, by Buffier and Dr. Reid, first truths, and they are said by these philosophers to emanate from the common sense of mankind.

It may reasonably be demanded whether there is any mode by which we may determine whether or not any proposition is a first truth. Is there any test by which they may be practically distinguished from mere propositions that are inferred from them? To this I answer,

First, *they are incomprehensible.*

Secondly, *they are simple.*

Thirdly, *they are necessary and universal.*

Fourthly, *they are so evident that nothing more evident can be discovered by which to prove them.*

This subject has, however, been already considered under the head of the Reality of our Knowledge, pages 95—97, to which pages the reader is referred.

The axioms of geometry are acknowledged to be the foundation truths of that science; but other self-evident truths lie equally at the foundation of all other knowledge established by reasoning. For instance: that I exist; that an external universe exists; that the testimony of my perceptive and my reasoning powers is to be received; that a change presupposes a cause; that the course of nature is uniform, or that the same causes under the same conditions will produce the same effects; that rational beings act from motives, and that a change of action must proceed from a change of motives, and a multitude of others, may be placed in the number of first truths.

Between the truths that are acknowledged by all as self-evident, as I have before remarked, a distinction may be observed. The first truths of geometry, for instance, are perceived to be such unconditionally. Thus, we could not conceive of any circumstances in which the whole of anything would not be greater than its part, the reverse of this truth being manifestly unthinkable. This, as we perceive, must be true *semper et ubique.* But that I exist, that an external world exists, is only a conditional first truth. Neither I nor the external world have always existed, and it is not impossible to suppose them to cease to exist. It is not, however, possible to conceive them not to exist, *things being as they are;* that is, I being conscious of the acts of thinking, perceiving, etc. Thus also, things being as they are, it is impossible to conceive of an intelligent being as acting without motive, but it is not impossible to suppose beings constituted so differently from us as to act in this manner, or to suppose that no intelligent beings had ever been created. *But, things being as they are*, the opposite of these truths is utterly inconceivable.

On these first truths all our reasonings ultimately depend. They are rarely stated in language, because every man instinctively takes them for granted, and he knows that all other men do the same. It would, however, be a very valuable service to science, if the first truths of all knowledge in general, and of the separate sciences in particular, could be plainly stated and accurately classified. In this manner a large amount of useless discussion would be prevented, and truth arrived at with much greater facility. Dr. Reid, in the sixth chapter of his sixth Essay on the intellectual powers, has stated several of the necessary truths in grammar, logic, mathematics, in taste, in morals and metaphysics, together with many contingent truths which are admitted in all our efforts after knowledge. The subject, however, demands a more extended and minute examination. Whenever it shall have been done, the labor of intellectual research will be greatly diminished, and its results more easily verified.

2. I have stated above that the end to be accomplished by the reasoning faculty is to render the conclusion at which we arrive, of precisely the same validity as the premises. From this it is evident that whatever the reasoning faculty has logically deduced from first truths is just as valid matter from which to proceed as the first truths themselves. Thus, in geometry, from the axioms and definitions we prove a proposition; that proposition, when logically proved, is as certainly true as the axioms from which we at first proceeded. The proposition that the angles at the base of an isosceles triangle are equal, is just as valid a premise, in a

geometrical demonstration, as the truth that things equal to the same are equal to one another. And, still further, whatever is by logical process proved from this proposition is just as valid matter as the proposition itself. And this will be the case to any extent whatever.

The only abatement to be made to this statement is the uncertainty arising from the imperfection of our faculties. We may, from this imperfection, reason illogically without perceiving it. If there be this liability, the greater the number of arguments, the greater the probability that in some one there will be error. And this liability increases with the complication of the relations which we are called to consider. This liability is reduced to the smallest practical value when the various steps of an argument have been examined by men skilled in the discovery of truth, and their validity has been allowed by all succeeding philosophers.

3. Besides these truths given us in the original constitution of our intellect, and the truths following from them by logical deduction, other truths are valid matter in our reasonings. Such are the acknowledged laws of nature, established by incontestable observation. Thus, it has been ascertained that the sensation of hearing, under normal conditions, is caused by the vibration of the air; the perception of external objects, by the formation of an image on the retina; that water boils at 212° and freezes at 32° Fahrenheit, under ordinary conditions of barometrical pressure; that the atmosphere is a mixture of oxygen and nitrogen gases, and water a compound of oxygen and hydrogen, both always in definite proportions; that atmospheric air is necessary to animal life. These, and all other laws and general facts, which at any time have been discovered by experiment or observation, whether in matter or mind, are valid matter from which to proceed in our reasonings. We thus see the

connection between those powers of the mind which we have previously considered and the reasoning faculty. The former observe and retain and generalize, and thus change individual facts into general laws. These become the premises from which, by our reasoning power, conclusions are drawn; and thus knowledge is increased, and the dominion of man over nature extended.

4. I have thus far treated of premises, or propositions from which we proceed in reasoning, of which the truth is incontestable. Wherever such propositions can be discovered we always are bound to use them, for thus alone can we arrive at pure truth, and enlarge our positive knowledge. Frequently, however, in our practical conduct, such propositions cannot be discovered, and we are obliged to form our reasonings on mere probability. In this case we can arrive at nothing higher than probability, but this probability is in many cases far preferable to ignorance, and may furnish a valuable guide for our conduct. Thus, we say, concerning a coming event, men under certain circumstances generally act thus or so. A, is under these circumstances, therefore he will probably act thus or so. Under such or such conditions of the atmosphere it generally rains; such are the conditions this morning, therefore it will probably rain to-day. Or, again: if there be a war in Europe, there will be a demand for American grain; there will probably be a war in Europe, therefore probably there will be such a demand. It is obvious that much of our reasoning concerning future events is of this character. It does not furnish us with certain knowledge, but yet with knowledge which may be of great value in the practical business of life, and the management of affairs.

II. Such are some of the truths from which we proceed in the use of our reasoning powers. I proceed to inquire, secondly, what is the state of mind at which we arrive provided the reasoning faculty has been employed in obedience to the laws to which it has been subjected.

The states of mind of which we may be conscious in regard to any proposition, are, I think, the following:

1. We may be in perfect ignorance concerning it, neither believing nor disbelieving it in the slightest degree. Thus, were it affirmed that the sun is inhabited, I must say, I know nothing about it. I have no facts from which to reason, and am therefore in absolute ignorance; I have not even an opinion either in favor of, or in opposition to, the proposition. It is to me precisely the same as if the affirmation had not been made.

2. I may know that a proposition is true. Here I express my state of mind by saying that I believe it, or I know it. Thus, I know that the exterior angle of a triangle is equal to the two interior and opposite angles. I believe that there are such cities as London, Paris, and Washington.

3. I may know a proposition to be false. Here my state of mind is expressed by the words, I disbelieve it. Thus, if the proposition were presented to me, that the angles at the base of an isosceles triangle are unequal, I know it to be false, and I say I disbelieve it.

4. Without being able to arrive at either belief or disbelief, I am capable of forming an opinion concerning the truth or falsehood of a proposition. I weigh the several considerations presented, and I find my mind inclined in one direction or the other; though I am fully aware that this inclination may be reversed by subsequent and more accurate knowledge. Thus, in the present state of knowledge, I am unable either to believe or disbelieve that the planets are inhabited, yet I may have an opinion on the subject inclining either to the one view or the other. I therefore

wait for further information, prepared to change my opinion with the progress of knowledge.

The object of reasoning is to advance our certainty, and to move the mind onward from the extreme of ignorance on the one hand, to the opposite extreme of belief on the other. Hence it may change our mental state from ignorance to opinion, from opinion to more confident opinion, or from either of these to certainty or confident belief. Its movement is all in one direction, from a lower to a higher degree of certainty.

From what has been said, it is evident that, when our premises are indubitable, we arrive, by reasoning, at absolute belief or indubitable truth. When our premises are merely matters of opinion we arrive only at opinion. In every case we raise the conclusion to precisely the same degree of certainty as the premises from which we proceed; we make what was before unknown, or less known, exactly equal to what was before more known. Our conclusion can never be more certain than our premises, but if our process be logical, it can never be less certain.

III. We now come, in the third place, to inquire what is the process by which this relation between the known and the unknown is rendered apparent, so that we are enabled to raise the one to the certainty of the other.

We do this by syllogism. A syllogism is a series of judgments or propositions, the last of which affirms the conclusion at which we have arrived. Before considering syllogisms, it will be proper to consider the nature of judgments, or the propositions of which they are composed.

Judgment is an act of the mind in which we affirm one thing of another; that is, we affirm a predicate of a subject, or judge that a particular individual or species is included in a particular genus or class. Thus, I judge snow to be white, grass to be green, avarice to be contemptible; that is, I judge these particular individuals to be comprenended within the class which I predicate of them.

Our judgment may be either clear and distinct, or obscure and confused.

A judgment is formed from two conceptions, and it affirms that one of these may be predicated of the other. Now, if we have a complete comprehension of both these conceptions, our judgment must be clear and distinct. On the other hand, if my knowledge of the conceptions involved be imperfect, vague, and obscure, my judgment must be of a similar character. Thus, when the proposition is announced that the three angles of a triangle are equal to two right angles, I comprehend the terms employed both in the subject and predicate, and my judgment is definite and unambiguous. If it be said that the rings of Saturn are chaos, I find myself to have a very incomplete idea of the rings of Saturn, and a very indistinct idea of chaos. Hence, I am unable to form anything more than a very indistinct idea of the proposition.

It is hardly necessary to remark that judgment enters as an element into almost all our mental acts. We think in judgments; that is, we are always affirming one thing of another, and we do not consider anything else to be thinking. To conceive of things without forming judgments, is to make no progress. We can only be said to think when we form a judgment, respecting two conceptions, in which one is affirmed of the other.

The expression of a judgment in words, is called a proposition. A proposition, therefore, must consist of a *subject*, or that of which we affirm, a *predicate*, or that which we affirm of it, and a *copula*, or that which affirms the relation existing between them. Thus, if I say, man is a vertebrate, here *man* is the *subject*, *vertebrate* is the *predicate*, and *is* is the copula, or that which affirms the one of the other.

The subject is that of which we discourse, the predicate is the class to which we affirm that it belongs, or under which it is comprehended, and the copula is that which affirms the existence of this relation.

When we thus affirm a predicate of a subject, we affirm that all the qualities of the predicate are possessed by the subject. When I say, man is a vertebrate, I affirm that all which is comprehended by the predicate *vertebrate* is possessed by *man*.

In every proposition it is obvious there must be two conceptions. Of these one must be a general idea, or one designating a class. To affirm of two individuals is either nugatory or false. To say John is John is nugatory, for the proposition does not advance our knowledge. To say John is Peter is false, for it affirms something to be different from what it is.

The subject may be either an individual or a species; the predicate must be a genus; that is, it must designate a larger class than the subject. In a proposition, we therefore affirm that a particular individual is included within a particular class. Hence, every proposition must be either true or false. The subject is either included within the class designated by the predicate, or it is not. It cannot be neither within nor without it. Thus, if I say horse is a vertebrate, it is either true or false, for horse is either included within this class, or it is not.

We may now proceed to the subject of syllogism.

A syllogism, in the language of Aristotle, is a speech in which certain things (the premises) being supposed, something different from what is supposed (the conclusion) follows of necessity, and this solely in virtue of the suppositions themselves.

The principle on which a syllogism depends is the following: Whatever is affirmed or denied of a class is affirmed or denied of every individual under that class. Thus, when

I say snow is white, I mean that snow is comprehended under the class white, and I affirm this also of all snow whatever. When I say snow is not black, I exclude snow from the class black, and I exclude all snow from this class; that is, I deny black of snow.

It will be seen, from what has been said, that logic, or the science of syllogisms, is formal; that is, it must proceed from premises conceded. It of itself takes no cognizance of either their truth or falsehood. Supposing them to be true, it governs the forms of propositions, and their relations to each other, and merely assures us that the conclusion which we infer in obedience to its rules is as true as our premises. It renders us no other aid than this, but this it renders most effectually.

It has sometimes been supposed that syllogism was a mode of reasoning, and a mode of reasoning employed by philosophers, while other men reasoned in some other and simpler manner. It has even been said, that, much as philosophers talk about syllogism, when they come to reason, they neglect it all, and reason like common men. To this it may be replied, that syllogism is not *a* mode, it is *the* mode of reasoning. It is the peculiar process of the reasoning faculty. The reasoning power forms syllogisms just as the imagination forms pictures, each being the purpose for which these different powers were respectively designed Philosophers and other men must, therefore, if they reason at all, reason in the same way, for they have no other method by which to proceed. I do not, of course, pretend that either of them draws out every argument in the form of a syllogism. One or both of the premises are frequently so well known as to be taken for granted, and we need only state the conclusion which must follow from what is conceded by all. But, in this case, our reasoning, though ever so much abridged, may always be reduced to the form of a syllogism, and we always so reduce it, if we desire to test its truth and examine it with accuracy.

In forming a syllogism in the first proposition we affirm that a species is included under a genus. By the second proposition we affirm that an individual or a sub-species is included under this species. In the third proposition, or the conclusion, we affirm the proposition which, of necessity, follows from the conjunction of the two first propositions or premises.

Thus, for example, I affirm,

1. All tyrants are detestable.
2. Cæsar was a tyrant.
3. Cæsar was detestable.

Here, by the first proposition, I affirm that the species tyrant is included under the genus detestable; by the second proposition, I affirm that the individual Cæsar was included under the species tyrant; and, by the third proposition, I affirm the conclusion which of necessity follows, namely, that Cæsar is included under the class detestable.

In order to illustrate this subject, let us suppose that the proposition to be proved is, Cæsar was detestable. The predicate is called the major term, the subject the minor term. When we make this assertion, it is denied by an opponent; that is, he asserts, on the contrary, that this predicate, detestable, cannot be affirmed of the subject, Cæsar. In what manner is it given us to proceed? Assertion is confronted by assertion equally decided. In what manner shall we arrive at the truth, so as to convince an opponent, or mankind in general, of the validity of our proposition?

We do this by seeking for what is called a middle term, or for some class which is included in the class detestable, and which also includes the subject Cæsar. Suppose I choose the term dictator, and say,

1. All dictators are detestable.

2. Cæsar was a dictator.
3. Cæsar was detestable.

My opponent refers to Fabius, and other dictators, who were not detestable. I am, therefore, obliged to change the first premise, and say, some dictators are detestable. But, as all dictators are not included in the class detestable, the conclusion will not by necessity follow, and this argument must be relinquished.

I seek for another middle term, and select that mentioned above, the term tyrant. I show by facts that Cæsar was comprehended under this class. I then proceed as before, and the conclusion follows by necessity, in virtue of the suppositions themselves.

The above is an affirmative syllogism. In a negative syllogism the process is modified as follows: We first affirm that a certain species is wholly excluded from a particular genus. In the second place, we affirm that the individual or sub-species is included in this excluded species. The conclusion follows, by necessity, that the individual or species is excluded from the first mentioned genus.

For example, suppose it were to be proved that Cæsar was not detestable. This is denied, and we must seek for a middle term which shall include Cæsar, and be excluded from the class detestable. I choose the term dictator, and then say,

1. No dictator is detestable.
2. Cæsar was a dictator; therefore,
3. Cæsar was not detestable.

Here, however, I am met by the fact that some dictators were detestable, and for this reason my argument fails, since some dictators are not excluded from this class.

I must, therefore, select another middle term. I say therefore,

1. No brave and generous man is detestable.

2. Cæsar was a brave and generous man.

3. Cæsar was not detestable.

If these premises are granted, the conclusion, as before, follows by necessity. If any of our premises is denied, we are obliged to form a syllogism in the same manner, and prove our premise before we can proceed. But, having established the premises, the conclusion cannot be evaded.

The above instances will illustrate the general nature of syllogisms. Sophisms are arguments purporting to be syllogisms, in which the essential laws of syllogism are violated. Thus,

1. All quadrupeds are animals.
2. Birds are animals; therefore,
3. Birds are quadrupeds.

Here it is seen at once that the class quadrupeds, which is included in animals, does not include birds. Therefore, nothing is concluded. So again,

1. Black is a color.
2. White is a color; therefore,
3. White is black.

Here, as before, both white and black are included in the same genus, but there is no species included in the class color, which also includes the subject of the conclusion.

I have thought that this subject might be illustrated by a few simple diagrams. I, therefore, add them in this place, for the sake of representing the doctrine of syllogism to the eye. To those learned in logic, they will, I know, be deemed superfluous; but, as this work is designed for those who are entering upon this study, they may not be wholly without advantage.

The affirmative syllogism may be represented by the following diagram. For instance,

All vertebrates are animals.

Horse is a vertebrate; therefore,

Horse is an animal.

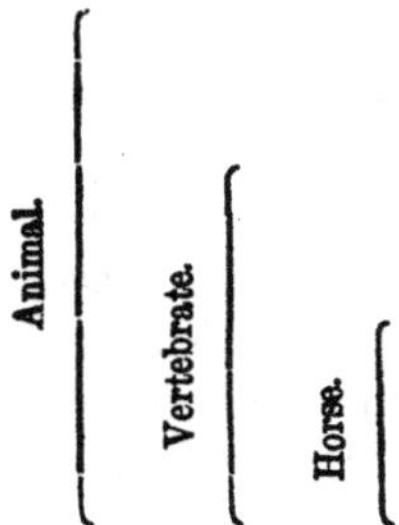

That is, vertebrate is included in animal, horse is included in vertebrate; therefore, horse is included in animal.

Take, again, a negative syllogism; for instance,

No predaceous animals are ruminant.

Lion is a predaceous animal; therefore,

Lion is not ruminant.

This may be represented by the following diagram:

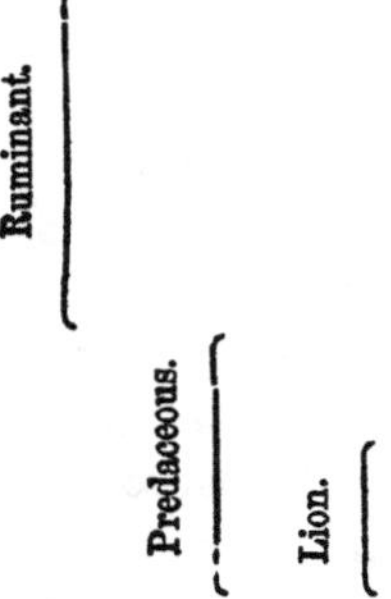

That is, predaceous is excluded from ruminant, and lion is included in predaceous; therefore, lion is excluded from ruminant.

This is the regular form of syllogism. The nature of sophisms or false syllogisms may be illustrated by similar diagrams. For instance,

All quadrupeds are animals.
Birds are animals; therefore,
Birds are quadrupeds.

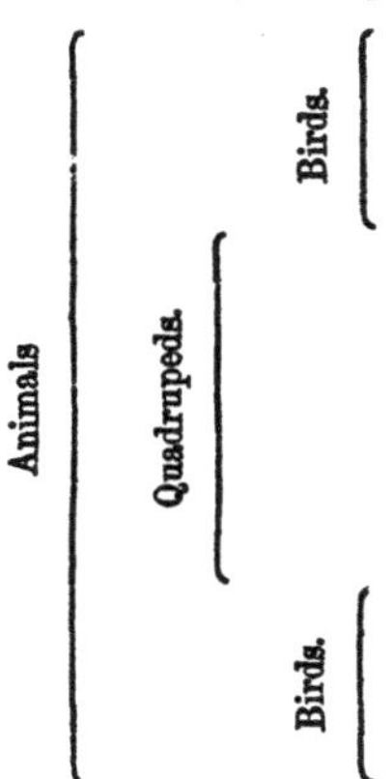

That is, quadrupeds are included in animals; birds are included in animals, but are not included in quadrupeds; therefore, nothing is concluded. Again,

Food is necessary to life.
Corn is food; therefore,
Corn is necessary to life.

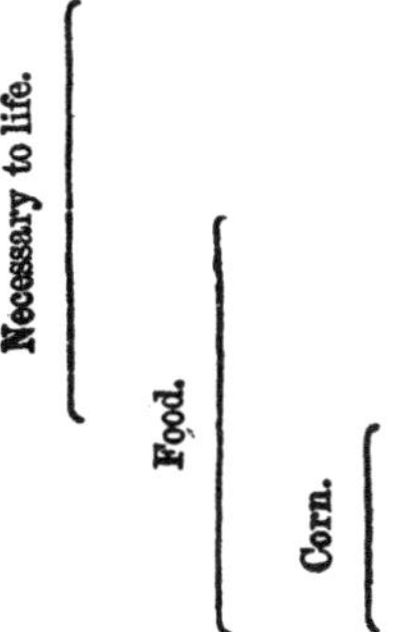

That is, necessary to life includes some food, but not all

food includes corn, but, as necessary to life does not include all food, so corn is not of necessity included in necessary to life. So, again,

Black is a color.
White is a color; therefore,
Black is white.

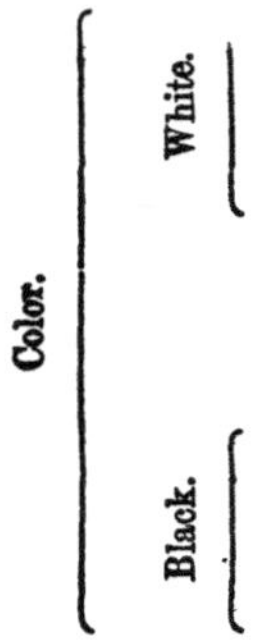

White.

Color.

Black.

Here color includes black and also includes white. Both are colors, but we see at a glance that nothing is concluded.

In this manner we may represent various forms of syllogisms and sophisms. The above examples will, however, sufficiently illustrate the nature of both.

In some cases we are able to discover a middle term which is intuitively true and fulfils all the conditions of proof. Here our course is plain. But suppose we are unable to do this, what course remains for us? We are then obliged to construct a conjectural syllogism, which will prove our proposition, provided we can show its premises to be true. We then take the conjectural premise, and construct a syllogism by which it can be proved. If here one of our premises is conjectural, we construct another syllogism, until we have arrived at some proposition which we are able to prove. In this manner the premise in question is established. When both the original premises are proved, the work is done, and the original conjectural syllogism is shown to be true. Or, on the other hand, if, attempting to prove either of our premises, we find the foundation on which it rests to be false, we abandon it altogether, and seek for some other media of proof.

This process may, I think, be illustrated by the proposition commonly known as the 47th of the first book of Euclid's elements, or that which proves that in any right-angled triangle, the square of the side subtending the right angle is equal to the sum of the squares of the sides containing the right angle. I presume every reader to be familiar with the proposition, and, therefore, I need only indicate briefly the illustration which I have to offer.

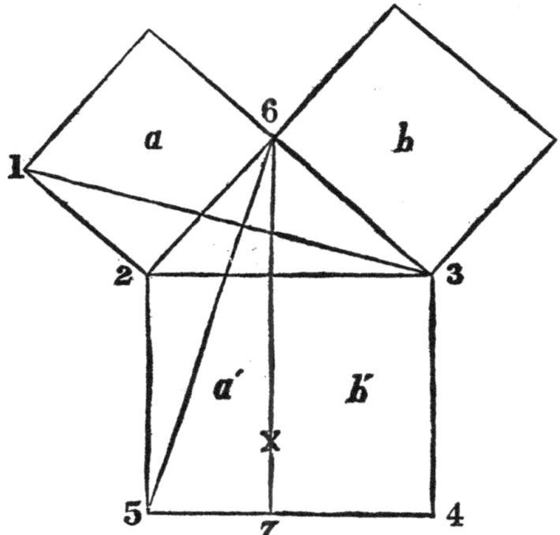

The proposition to be proved is that the squares a and b are together equal to the larger square x.

Here I can find no middle term of acknowledged truth by which to prove this proposition. I proceed, therefore, and construct an argument which will prove it provided the premises can be shown to be true. Having divided the larger square, x, into two parts, by the line 6, 7, I say,

Things equal to the same are equal to each other.

The square x, and the sum of the squares a and b, are equal to the parallelograms a' and b'.

Therefore, the square x is equal to the sum of the squares a and b.

Now this syllogism will prove the proposition if I can show the premises to be true. But it is not proved that the squares a and b are respectively equal to the parallelograms a' and b'. This is, in the next place, to be proved.

I say, then, again,

The doubles of equals are equal.

The parallelogram a' and the square a are each double of the equal triangles, 1, 2, 3, and 6, 2, 5.

Therefore, the parallelogram a' and the square a are equal.

But it is yet to be proved that these two triangles are equal. This has been taken for granted.

I proceed again.

Triangles having two sides equal, and the angle contained by these two sides equal, are themselves equal.

These triangles have these sides and angles equal;

Therefore, these two triangles are equal.

The equality of the triangles proves the square and parallelogram to be equal, and thus my conjectural syllogism is proved to be true.

The conjectural syllogism with which I commenced, proved the proposition, provided its premises could be proved. I have proved the premises, and, therefore, the proposition is proved.

But, having discovered this truth, suppose I wish to communicate it to another. I then reverse the process, and commence with the proposition with which I just now concluded.

I first show that the triangles are equal;

Then, that a rectangle and a triangle being on the same base and between the same parallels, the rectangle is double of the triangle;

Hence, the triangles being equal, the rectangle and the square must be equivalent.

And, hence, the two smaller squares and the greater square being both equal to the two parallelograms, the two smaller, and the greater square are equal to each other.

In this instance the example is taken from the mathematics. But the case is essentially the same in all cases where we attempt to prove a proposition. We first construct a syllogism, which, if true, will prove it. But one or both the premises may be doubtful. We take the doubtful premise and form a syllogism, which, if true, will prove it. If, here, one of our premises is conjectural, we make a third proposition, which, in like manner, we attempt to prove, until we arrive at some acknowledged truth from which it proceeds. We then construct our argument, beginning with the fundamental truth at which we last arrived, and proceed outwards, reversing our process, until we show that our original proposition depends upon truth which all must acknowledge.

Thus, when one of our premises is denied, we must prove our premise. If the premise of this proof is denied, we must prove this premise. Going backward, in this manner, we at last arrive at first truths, or those which every mind, in a normal condition, perceives by intuition to be true. Thus, in the proposition just taken for an example, if our premises were continually denied, we should at last arrive at the definitions and axioms of geometry. And thus, in any other reasoning, we arrive, by the same process, at truths equally obvious to a sound understanding. When we have arrived at these, reason can go no further. If these are denied, the party denying must be wanting in ordinary intellect, or we must have taken as true what is obviously false. Whichever be the case, there is an end of argument.

We hear it frequently said that all mathematical reasoning depends upon definitions and axioms. This is true; but their importance depends upon different principles. It may be well to consider briefly the nature of each.

A definition is a conception expressed in language. Thus, if I am about to prove to another person a proposition in which I use the conception of lines, angles, triangles, squares and circles, it is evident that my argument will be useless to him, unless, when I use these words, he have the same conceptions as myself. If, when I say "line," he has the same conception that I have when I say "triangle," we could never understand each other. It is necessary, therefore, that I explain, as clearly as possible, the conception which I form when I use these terms. Having done this, and it being certain that we have the same conception when we use the same words, we are prepared to proceed in our argument.

An axiom expresses an intuitively perceived relation between our conceptions. Thus, having defined what we mean by lines, angles, and other elements of quantity, we say "Two straight lines cannot enclose space." "Things equal to the same are equal to one another." These relations being conceded by both parties, and the same conceptions being common to both, we have the elements necessary for reasoning.

When it is said, therefore, that we cannot reason without definitions and axioms, the impossibility arises from different causes. We cannot reason without definitions, because we cannot reason together unless the terms which we employ create in the minds of each other the same conceptions. But this cannot be known unless the terms which we use are adequately explained; that is, unless they are defined.

The reason for the necessity of axioms is different. We must agree as to the laws to which these conceptions are subjected, or else we can never arrive at a common conclusion. If I show that what I assert is true, for otherwise two straight lines must enclose space, or that the whole be less than its part, I can proceed no further. But, if my opponent does not admit these axioms or laws of quantity to be true, he will never feel the force of my reasoning, and will, of course, not be convinced.

This is manifestly true in the mathematics. But it is obvious that the same principles must govern all our reasonings. Unless men attach the same meaning to the same term, that is, unless a term awakens in each the same conception, they can no more reason together than they could if each spoke a language unknown to the other. In ordinary discourse, the meaning of terms is sufficiently established by usage to prevent any serious difficulty. It is found, however, necessary, when accuracy of reasoning is attempted, to proceed further, and define our terms with the greatest precision. Were this more frequently done, much valuable labor would be saved, and differences of opinion among honest men would be found less important than they seem to be. And so of axioms. Unless the relations which exist between these conceptions are admitted, men may reason together forever without coming to any conclusion. Thus, were two men arguing together on the nature of human rights, they might define *man* as accurately as they pleased, but, unless they agreed upon the relation which man sustains to individual man and to society, they could never come to any conclusion. Neither would be pressed by the arguments of the other, and what seemed to the one perfectly conclusive, would to the other seem destitute of all show of reason. It is to be regretted that much of our reasoning is apt to be of this character.

The whole subject of syllogisms, their nature and classification, the rules to which they are subjected, and the distinction between true and false syllogisms, is treated of in the science of logic. To these the reader is referred for a further development of the doctrines here briefly alluded to. I ask leave to commend this study to all persons who aim at the attainment of mental acuteness, and the thorough cultivation of their reasoning power.

REFERENCES.

Reasoning, its nature — Reid, Essay 7, chap. 1.

Reasoning, instinctive — Reid, Essay 7, chap. 1.

Reasoning rests on first truths — Reid, Essay 1, chap. 2; Essay 6, chap. 2.

This denied — Locke, Book 4, chap. 2, secs. 7, 8; chap. 7, secs. 8, 10, 19, 20.

Cousin's Review of Locke — chap. 9.

Buffier, first truths.

Test of first truths — Reid, Essay 6, chap. 4.

Classification of first truths — Reid, Essay 1, chap. 2; Essay 6, chaps. 5, 6.

Judgment, its nature — Reid, Essay 6, chap. 1.

Judgment distinguished from testimony and conceptions — Reid, Essay 6, chap. 1.

Judgments necessary and contingent — Reid, Essay 6, chap. 1.

Common Sense, Reid, Essay 6, chap. 2.

Syllogism not the great instrument of reasoning — Locke, Book 4, chap. 17, secs. 4—7; Cousin, chap. 9.

Aristotle's logic examined — Stewart, vol. ii., chap. 3, sec. 1.

Effects of study of logic on intellectual habits — Stewart, vol. ii., chap 3, sec. 2.

Use of definitions — Stewart, vol. ii., chap. 2, sec. 3.

Nugatory propositions — Locke, Book 4, chap. 8, sec. 4.

Propositions true or false — Locke, Book 2, chap. 32, secs. 1—4.

SECTION II.—OF THE DIFFERENT KINDS OF CERTAINTY AT WHICH WE ARRIVE BY REASONING.

I HAVE remarked that by the process of reasoning, if properly conducted, we always render the conclusion as certain as the premises. This is the sole object of syllogism, and this it invariably accomplishes. I have also observed that our conclusions may be either certain, or only probable, according to the nature of the premises from which they proceed.

Dismissing the consideration of the cases in which we establish probability, and confining our attention to that in which we arrive at certainty, we perceive that this certainty is of two kinds. We may arrive, first, at metaphysical or absolute, or, secondly, at practical certainty. Let us attempt to distinguish these from each other, and show the peculiarities of each.

I. *Of metaphysical and absolute certainty.*

When we arrive at this kind of certainty, the matter of our reasoning is wholly conceptions, or the notions which we form in our own minds, representing no actual reality. These are, of course, precisely what we make them, neither greater nor less, nor in any possible respect different from our thoughts; for they are our thoughts themselves, and nothing else. Hence, when they are distinctly comprehended, and formed into syllogism according to the rules of logic, they must lead to a conception of the same character as the premises, and be inevitably as true. There is no liability for misconception or ambiguity. The result must be as true as our thoughts themselves.

The most remarkable example of this mode of reasoning is found in the pure mathematics. Here the matter about which we reason is pure conceptions. We demonstrate truth about lines, angles, triangles, circles, etc., not as actual existences, but merely as conceptions. By our definitions, we announce distinctly the ideas intended by the terms which we employ. These ideas we continue to use without change throughout our reasonings, and the results at which we arrive are concerning these alone.

I have said that in this mode of reasoning we have nothing to do with actual existences. This is evident from the fact that the pure mathematics might have been carried to any conceivable degree of perfection, had a material universe never been created. All that is required for this mode of reasoning is a thinking mind. Hence we never, in geometry, attempt to prove anything respecting an existing figure. We may use a diagram for the sake of concentrating our attention, but our reasoning is not concerning it, or any other thing visible or tangible. No actual figure exactly corresponds with our definitions, and, if it did, we have no faculties by which to ascertain the correspondence. We say the angles at the base of an isosceles triangle are equal. This we show to be unconditionally true. But it is true of our conceptions only, and not of the diagram on the blackboard. We do not know that the lines of that triangle are perfectly straight, or the sides equal; nay, we know that it is beyond our power to make them so. But this in no manner affects our demonstration. If any one should attempt to convict us of error, by measuring the triangle and showing that one angle was greater than the other, we should smile at his ignorance. We know that our proposition is true concerning the conception existing in our minds, and this is all we ever attempted to prove.

I have said that the most striking example of this species of reasoning is observed in the case of the pure mathematics. I know of no reason, however, why it should not exist in anv other case in which the matter of our argument is pure conception. All that is necessary is that our terms be accurately defined and clearly apprehended, and that they be subjected to the laws of syllogistic reasoning. The result must be as purely truth in the one case as the other. Thus,

1. All accountable beings are entitled to freedom.
2. Sylphs and gnomes are accountable beings.
3. Sylphs and gnomes are entitled to freedom.

Suppose the first proposition clearly understood.

Sylphs and gnomes are imaginary beings, of which I form a conception just as I please. The conclusion must follow as clearly and inevitably as in mathematical demonstration.

It must, however, be manifest that the range of subjects of this character is extremely limited, and, therefore, its utility by no means extensive. We live in a matter-of-fact world. We desire to enlarge our knowledge, not of mere conceptions, but of realities. We wish to know the laws of things actually existing, and so to use them as to ascertain other laws of which we are ignorant. In order to do this, we must come forth from the region of conceptions into that of realities. Thus, the pure mathematics themselves would be utterly useless, except as a discipline, unless we combined them with existing facts, when they assume the form of mixed mathematics. Here, however, we arrive not at absolute, but practical certainty. Let us observe the manner in which II. *Practical certainty* is attained.

In this kind of reasoning, either one or both of our premises is some general law, or particular fact, established by observation or experiment. Our conclusion, then, approaches no nearer to absolute truth, than our fact or observation represents the pure and absolute verity. But no one pretends that our faculties are capable of arriving at pure and absolute truth. It has often been remarked that a perfect circle, or triangle, or square, never was constructed, and that no instrument ever made, could claim to be absolutely accurate. Our processes may be as perfect as the present condition of the arts will allow, but we can go no further. Progress in the arts may enable us to exclude additional causes of error, and thus arrive at greater accuracy. But when we have done all, our powers are limited and imperfect; and, to use the words of Johnson, "a fallible being must fail somewhere." The eye is incapable of discerning objects below a certain magnitude, or differences which do not exceed a certain degree. The sensation of touch can only detect impressions when their impulse attains to a certain force. Our nerves are easily fatigued, and fatigue impairs their accuracy of observation, and their control over our muscles. The various passions to which we are subject influence our whole sentient organism, and frequently unfit us for observation at a time when their perfect accuracy is the most needed. It is said that when Sir I. Newton had arrived very nearly at the close of that calculation which has made his name immortal, and saw the result to which he was tending, he was seized with so violent a fit of trembling, that, unable to complete the work, he surrendered his papers to a friend, by whom it was finished. It is told of one of the observers sent many years ago to the Pacific Ocean to observe the transit of Venus, that, at the precise moment when the transit occurred, he fainted from excess of excitement. Perfect accuracy can, therefore, never be predicated of a being in whose organization are involved so many liabilities to error.

Thus, for instance, in the *mixed* mathematics we arrive at only *practical* certainty. Here we first establish the relations existing between the lines of a figure of which we have conceived. This is pure mathematics, and our result is absolute truth. We then apply these relations to a figure actually existing, and as nearly identical with the figure which we have conceived, as we are able to make it, and proceed to our result. This result is obviously not absolute truth; it is only proximate; that is, just as near to absolute truth as the actual figure is near to the perfect conception which forms the basis of our reasonings.

Let us take an example. I demonstrate by pure mathematics that the homologous sides of similar triangles are proportional. Availing myself of this law, I proceed to ascertain the height of a steeple. I measure a base line, and observe the angle formed between the extremity of this line and the highest point of the object. I find a corresponding tabular triangle in the tables, and by a single proportion arrive at the result. But is this a perfect result? Its accuracy depends upon the accuracy of my measurements of the base line and the angle. But are these infallible? Was my chain perfectly true? Was the temperature such as to have effected no change upon it? Was the surface perfectly level, and was my muscular tension precisely such as to ensure perfect accuracy, and, at every movement of the chain, was that tension precisely the same? Was the instrument with which I measured the angle, of perfect construction and in perfect order? Was there no tremor in my muscles, and was my sight of the object absolutely true? No one of these things can be asserted, and, unless they can all be asserted, perfect accuracy is impossible. But what then? Are our results valueless? By no means. They are perfect for any and every practical purpose. If we have taken every precaution in our power to exclude the liability of error, we have arrived at all the certainty which the present condition of knowledge admits. We know that our result cannot, except by accident, be perfectly accurate; but it is so accurate that neither ourselves nor any one else can detect any error This is, to all intents and purposes, precisely as good to us as absolute certainty. In the one case we know that there is no error; and, in the other, although we admit there may be error, yet neither we nor any one else is able to detect it.

The case is illustrated in the study of astronomy. We here first conceive of spherical triangles, and determine, by demonstration, the relations between them. Here we arrive at absolute truth. We then measure degrees on the earth's surface, we take the measure of angles, we make observations on the times and places of planetary bodies, and, by constructing triangles as far as possible identical with those which we have before conceived, we determine the distance of the sun, and the diameter of the orbit of the earth. But does any one pretend that these calculations are absolutely correct? Their accuracy depends wholly on the perfection of the observations, which, of necessity, enter as elements into our calculations. Were our measurements of lines and angles absolutely perfect? Were our observations absolutely infallible? This, from the nature of our faculties and the imperfection of instruments, is manifestly impossible. Our conclusions must, therefore, share in, or must greatly magnify, these imperfections. We say the sun is so many millions of miles from the earth; but, thus speaking, do we intend to be understood as enunciating an absolute truth? Do we mean that it may not be a hundred or a thousand miles either nearer or more distant? All we know is that we are unable to discover any error; that we have arrived at as near an approximation to truth as is possible in the present condition of science. We can do no more, and we pretend to do no more. This is as far as our Creator has permitted us, in our present state, to proceed, and with this we must be content. When we have approached so near to the truth that we can discover no error, we have arrived at practical certainty, and we need ask for no more.

Now, if I do not mistake, this is precisely the method of our reasoning respecting any matters of fact. We reason by conceptions. If our premises, matters of fact, the result of observation, precisely correspond with these conceptions, our reasonings are true absolutely. But we cannot be sure that there is this perfect correspondence. We may, however, be convinced that this correspondence is so nearly exact that the human faculties can discover no error, and here, as before, we arrive at practical certainty, or the limit marked out for us by our intellectual constitution. When our premises have been established with all the accuracy of which our Maker has made us capable, and our conclusion from them follows by the laws of reasoning, we have arrived at as near an approximation to truth as is possible in our present state. If neither we nor any one else can point out any error, we may well be satisfied; for we may know that the error can never be appreciated by the faculties which God has given us; and, therefore, to us it is precisely the same as if it were absolutely true.

Thus, suppose we say,

When men can have no motive for testifying falsely, their testimony is worthy of belief.

A and B can have no motive for testifying falsely; therefore the testimony of A and B is worthy of belief.

The truth of the first of these propositions would, I presume, be admitted; it being one of the acknowledged laws of human action, since no man acts without a motive. The second only can admit of doubt. We, therefore, make it the object of special examination. We survey all the motives by which men are known to be influenced. We inquire whether any of these motives could have induced them to speak falsely. We are unable to discover any. We then rely with firmness on the conclusion that they have testified truly. It may be said that motives for falsehood may exist which have never been discovered. Be it so. But, inasmuch as we have been unable to discover them, we have arrived at the nearest approximation to truth which our faculties admit, and we must rely on such faculties as we possess. When, in the full and free exercise of our intellectual powers, we can discover no error in our premises, and no error in our reasoning, we must receive as true the conclusions which they necessitate. We have no other resource. If we deny this, there is an end to all reasoning, and everything beyond our own observation is a delusion.

If we now compare these two kinds of reasoning, we observe the following facts:

1. The process which we employ is, in both cases, precisely the same. When we attempt to discover truth by reasoning, we use syllogism; for this is the mode of action imposed upon our reasoning faculty. We use this, for we have no other to use.

2. The one kind of reasoning treats only of conceptions both in its premises and its conclusions. With actual existences, *res gestæ*, it has nothing to do. Of course, it is excluded from all cases which involve matters of fact. The other has to do with actual existences, and to them its conclusions refer. Hence, this is the mode of reasoning which we must, of necessity, employ in all the business of life, and in all those investigations of science which contemplate things as actual existences.

3. By the one we arrive at absolute certainty respecting things not existing except in our conceptions. By the other we arrive at practical certainty respecting things as existing wholly distinct and separate from ourselves. In the one case we arrive at absolute truth; in the other, we approach as near to absolute truth as the limited and imperfect nature of our faculties admits. We approach so near to it that we are unable to detect any error.

It will be observed that these two kinds of reasoning correspond in general to those commonly termed demonstrative and moral reasoning. I have used different terms from those commonly employed, because I suppose them better adapted to the subject. It will be seen, if what I have said be true, that the difference between these two kinds of reasoning is much less than has frequently been supposed, both as to the mode in which they are conducted, and the results at which they arrive.

From what has been said, I think it will appear that but little ground exists for the superiority which has been claimed for demonstrative reasoning, or that which treats purely of conceptions. It is granted that in this species of reasoning we arrive at absolute truth; but then, from its conditions, it excludes all actual existences, and can, therefore, furnish no guide to conduct. As soon as demonstrative reasoning has to do with matters of fact, it reposes, by necessity, upon moral reasoning, and, specially, on the evidence of testimony. Thus, suppose I have demonstrated the distance of the sun from the earth. It is evident that the facts which form the elements of my reasoning must be established by what is called moral evidence. I am told that such and such observations have been made by different men, through a succession of years. Now, here is a two-fold liability of error. In the first place, how do I know that these observations were ever made at all? I have nothing here to rely on but the testimony of men, which is said to be so vastly inferior in certainty to demonstration. In the second place, what assurance have I that these observations were correctly made? How shall I be sure that all the instruments were perfect, or that proper skill was employed in the use of them? Important errors have frequently been made by scientific men. Sir Isaac Newton's discoveries were for several years postponed, by an error in measuring a degree of the earth's surface. What shall guard us against similar error? Now, if these are not reliable grounds of belief, all our demonstration is useless; for, on the facts which they deliver to us, all our calculations rely. Our demonstrations, then, as soon as they affect any matter of fact, are limited in their certainty by moral evidence, and they attain to no higher certainty than moral evidence confers. By the evidence of testimony, however, we are assured that these observations were made. From the known characters of the observers, we have every reason to believe that they were made correctly. On these assurances our calculations proceed, and they arrive at a degree of accuracy so great that neither we nor any one else can discover any error.

From these remarks we perceive the absurdity of demanding what is called demonstrative evidence to substantiate a matter of fact. Men sometimes tell us, for instance, that a revelation from God, being a matter of so great importance, should have been attested by mathematical demonstration. We see that to ask this is to demand what is absolutely impossible. Being a matter of fact, it must come under the laws of evidence which belong to matters of fact. To attempt to prove a fact by mathematical demonstration is as absurd as to attempt to prove a mathematical proposition by testimony.

REFERENCES.

Conclusions either certain or probable — Reid, Essay 6, chapter 4; Essay 7, chap. 1.

Metaphysical and mathematical reasoning — Reid, Essay 7, chapter 1; Locke, Book 4, chapter 4, section 6.

Nature of demonstrative evidence — Stewart, vol. ii., chap. 2, secs. 3, 4.

Superiority of mathematical reasoning — Stewart, vol. ii., chapter 2, section 3; Reid, Essay 7, chap, 2.

Morality capable of demonstration — Locke, Book 4, chap. 2, sections 16, 18; chap. 3, section 18; chap. 4, section 7.

Conclusions in mixed mathematics as sure as data — Stewart, vol. ii, chap. 2, section 4.

SECTION III. — OF THE EVIDENCE OF TESTIMONY.

In demonstrative reasoning our premises rest upon truths intuitively perceived by every intellect in a normal condition, or else upon truths proceeding from these by necessity. In reasoning concerning matters of fact, many of our premises are general laws, established by observation and experience. But this observation and experience must be established by many witnesses. A single individual can observe but little. We must all rely upon the labors of others. But how shall we distinguish true from false testimony? Many things have been recorded as true, which have subsequently been found to be false. We need, therefore, to ascertain the laws by which testimony may be established, so that we may be able to proceed with certainty in our reasonings. It is, therefore, proper to examine this part of our subject, and determine, if possible, the principles on which the evidence of testimony rests.

Testimony is of two kinds, direct and indirect.

I. *Of direct testimony.*

It must be admitted that the testimony of man is a source of as certain knowledge as any that we possess. If we refer to our own consciousness, we find no difference between the strength of our belief in matters of fact and matters of demonstration. We as perfectly believe that such persons as Julius Cæsar, Cicero, Alexander, Martin Luther, Washington, and Napoleon, existed; that the battles of Marathon, Bunker Hill, Austerlitz and Waterloo, were fought; and that there are now standing the cities of London, Paris and Vienna, as we believe that the three angles of a triangle are equal to two right angles. If we ask ourselves which do we most confidently believe, we can discover no shade of difference. In any practical matter we should proceed upon the belief of one as readily as upon that of the other. This is true of mankind universally. If this be so, then both of these grounds of belief must rest equally upon the laws of human thought. There must exist elementary first truths, acknowledged by all men, on which our confidence ultimately reposes. That this is true of mathematical reasoning is universally admitted. It must, however, be equally true of any other mode of proof which produces the same results.

Let us take another case. We are told that, a few years since, an eclipse of the sun occurred on a Sunday, a little after noon. It had been predicted by astronomers, and their predictions concerning it had been extensively published. Men in every place on this continent declared that they witnessed it. The daily newspapers, immediately after it is said to have occurred, were filled with accounts of the phenomena that were said to have been observed. Every fact respecting it was minutely recorded, and the statements of its various phases were inserted in the transactions of learned societies throughout the world. Now, granting these facts to be so, could we any more doubt that an eclipse really occurred, at the time and in the manner specified, than we could doubt a proposition in geometry? Suppose that one man, under these circumstances, should doubt the fact of the eclipse, and another should doubt a demonstration in mathematics, should we not decide that the mind of the one was in as abnormal a state as that of the other?

Yet I am aware that there are differences in the belief in the two cases. In the one case our belief is in the truth as universal, as true at all times and in all places. In the other, it is particular; that is, it is not true of every time and every place, but only of this time and this place. In the one case our knowledge is perfect and complete; that is, we know the whole of the truth affirmed, and nothing can be added to render our knowledge more adequate. When I am convinced that the three angles of a triangle are equal to two right angles, nothing can be added to the proposition by which my knowledge can be increased. If I fully comprehend the terms, I have precisely the same knowledge of the truth as Newton himself. He might have seen consequences derivable from it which I do not see; but our knowledge of the proposition itself is entirely the same. In the case of the other proposition, that at a given time and place there was an eclipse of the sun, it is not so. We all may be equally confident of the main fact; but of various circumstances respecting it, our knowledge may be dissimilar and unequal. Men who observed the eclipse may have been more or less influenced by their imaginations; they may have dissimilar appreciations of the temperature, of the degree of darkness, of the time and duration of the event. Hence their narratives may in these respects differ; and it may require much labor to obtain a complete idea of the eclipse; and there may, after all, remain many circumstances which we know but imperfectly. All this may be granted, and yet it does not in the least affect our belief of the main fact. Nay, all these variations must exist if the main fact be true. They follow from the differences in the subjective nature of man. Hence the rule in testimony is that the best evidence to any fact is, agreement of witnesses as to the main event, and difference as to the minor particulars.

The following striking illustration of these remarks is worthy of notice. I presume that no one can doubt that the battle of Waterloo was fought on the eighteenth of June, 1815, between the French and the allies, under the command respectively of Napoleon and Wellington. It may certainly be taken for granted that men believe this fact as undoubtingly as they do any proposition in geometry. Yet the time of the commencement of the battle cannot even now be settled with precision. In Maxwell's life of Wellington, I find the following statement:

"The time when the battle began has been stated with marked contrariety. The Duke of Wellington says it commenced about ten o'clock, and further observes that when his troops discontinued the pursuit, at night, they had been engaged twelve hours. In this General Gneisenau concurs, but, of course, only from information he had received. General Alava, who was by the side of the duke the whole day, fixes it at half-past eleven. Napoleon and General Drouet state twelve as the hour; while Marshal Ney names one o'clock. Without tracing minuter contradictions, this may suffice to show the difficulty of attaining exact knowledge when it might have been presumed no difficulty could exist. With one exception, which I think ought to be decisive, I was equally bewildered by the intelligence I received from officers whom I had an opportunity of consulting. By one I was told that the battle began soon after mid-day, by another exactly twenty minutes past eleven, and by a third at ten o clock. But Sir George Wood — and his information is what I conceive cannot be disputed — gave me the following statement. The action commenced about half-past ten or a quarter to eleven. There had been skirmishing, before, all the morning. A column of the enemy was advancing against Hougomont, and the first gun that was fired was from our lines against that column. I gave the order by the command of the duke. The gun did immediate execution, and killed six or eight. This column then retired, and went round the wood."— Maxwell's Life of Wellington, vol. 3, note to page 479.

We perceive, from this incident, how dissimilar is the adequateness of our knowledge in a matter of fact, from that in an abstract geometrical proposition; and yet our confidence in the truth of the main fact is as great in the one case as in the other.

But, it may be very properly demanded, is testimony of all kinds equally worthy of belief? Are we not very often the dupes of false evidence? We reply, that in this respect we are all very liable to be deceived. But the case is the same with mathematical evidence or demonstration. How often has it been announced that men have demonstrated the quadrature of the circle; but, upon examination, it has been discovered that either they have been deceived, or that they desired to deceive others. Either they had commenced with false principles, or they had reasoned incorrectly from true ones. So in the mixed mathematics, innumerable errors have from time to time been discovered and corrected. This, however, presents no objection to the validity or reliability of mathematical reasoning. It only teaches us the necessity of examining our arguments with care, and assuring ourselves that our reasonings are conducted strictly according to the laws of mathematical proof. When they are so conducted, they never did and they never can lead to error. So in the case of evidence. It is granted that we are liable to be deceived by reliance upon testimony. But this by no means proves that testimony is worthless; or that testimony, when given strictly according to the laws of evidence, is not as reliable as demonstration. It only teaches us the necessity of subjecting testimony to its own appropriate laws, that we may thus separate the true from the false. If, therefore, we can establish the elementary laws of evidence, and apply them strictly to any case of testimony, we receive the result to which they lead us with unquestioning confidence.

The essential and self-evident truths on which the evidence of testimony rests, seem to be two. The *first is the law of perception*, to which allusion has been made when treating of that subject. It may be expressed as follows: Whenever, in the normal condition of our faculties, we are conscious of a perception, then there exists an object, such as we perceive, as the cause of that perception. I cannot perceive what I will. The consciousness of perception must be excited from without, and it cannot exist under normal conditions, unless a corresponding object from without give occasion to it. I am conscious that I perceive the paper on which I now write, and the table at which I am seated. I could not, by the laws of my being, be thus conscious, unless there existed here and now these objects which give rise to it.

Under the term normal conditions, as here used, several things are to be supposed. For instance, the external circumstances must be such as to admit of no liability to error. If I testify to an object of sight, the light must be sufficient to allow me to see correctly. If I testify to an object of sound, I must be near enough to hear it distinctly. The same remark applies to the other senses.

The mind must be in a normal condition. The witness must be sane. He must be free from any violence of passion or excitement of imagination, which would lead to erroneous observation. Thus, if a man were habitually terrified in passing by a grave-yard, we should receive with great suspicion his testimony respecting a ghost which he believed he had seen seated on a tomb-stone. Intense prejudice, which affected the matter in question, would lead to similar suspicions.

The senses must be in a normal condition. No one would repose perfect confidence in the testimony of a man to a visual fact, whose eyes were either partly blind or subject to optical illusions.

Here, however, two remarks deserve attention. First, we always take it for granted that men are in a normal condition unless there is evidence to the contrary. No man is ever called upon to prove his sanity. The very fact that he is thus called upon, must proceed upon the supposition that he is able to construct a proof; that is, that he is sane. He who affirms that another is insane, must himself furnish the evidence; and, in the absence of such evidence, the contrary is to be taken for granted.

Secondly, it is to be remarked that abnormal cases are extremely rare. We may meet a thousand individuals, without finding one among them whose condition is, in any respect, so abnormal as to affect his testimony. And hence, when a number of persons agree in testifying to the same fact, the supposition of abnormal action is excluded. Thus, if only one person had testified that he saw an eclipse, we might suppose that his mind or his organs were diseased. But to suppose that so large a number of persons, in different places, were in an abnormal condition, and in precisely the same condition, at the same time, is manifestly absurd.

The second general law is derived from the nature of the active powers of man. It may be stated as follows:

1. *Every human action is the result of motive.* That is to say, when there is no motive there is no action.

2. *When there is no motive for speaking falsely, men always speak the truth.* The motive which leads men to speak falsely may be very unreasonable or insufficient. They will sometimes speak falsely against their own permanent interest; but they always speak from a present motive, as fear, vanity, desire of applause, etc.

3. *When no motive can be conceived why men should testify as they do, but the love of truth; and every other conceivable motive would impel them to testify differently, then they testify from the love of truth; that is, they affirm what they believe to be true.* To suppose the contrary is absurd. For, if no motive but the love of truth

could impel them to their present testimony, to suppose the love of truth removed,—that is, suppose them to testify falsely,—is to suppose men to act without any motive, and in opposition to every conceivable motive. This is diametrically opposed to the laws of human action. To suppose any one to act in this manner, is to suppose him not to be endowed with proper human faculties.

But it may be said that motives for speaking falsely may exist, though we cannot conceive of them. Granted. But then we have arrived at the point previously mentioned; that is, we have come so near the truth that we can discover no source of error. We have, therefore, attained to that practical certainty which is all that is given to us in establishing any matter of fact. When we have gone so far, we have reached the limit which the Creator has assigned to our faculties, and we can proceed no further.

Again; in the case supposed, when many witnesses testify, this motive which no one can assign, which no one ventures to announce, and which no one has yet discovered, must have influenced a number of persons, against every conceivable interest, to testify to the same thing. To make such a supposition the ground either of belief or disbelief, is manifestly absurd; but to make it the ground of either, in opposition to testimony established by the laws of evidence, exhibits a state of mind for which it is difficult to find a name.

But suppose that on such ground as this the evidence of testimony is to be disregarded, what is the result? Evidently, that no fact in history or science could be believed, unless we had seen it with our own eyes. The past would be a universal blank. Books would be useless, and the whole of human knowledge must be limited to our own individual experiences. There is here no middle path. Either we must receive everything established by the strict laws of evidence, or we must receive nothing. Which is the alternative to be chosen by a reasonable intelligence, it is not difficult to discover. He who desires to see this subject treated with great acuteness and admirable humor, should read Archbishop Whately's "Historical Doubts relative to Napoleon Buonaparte."

At some risk of prolixity, I will illustrate this subject by an example to which I have before referred.

It is granted that a great number of persons, of different ages and pursuits, and in various places throughout this country, testified that on a particular day they witnessed a total eclipse of the sun. In what manner shall we examine this evidence, in order to ascertain whether their testimony is worthy of belief?

In the first place, we appeal to the law of perception. Was this an event which they were all capable of observing? Could they have been conscious of perceiving it, unless the event had actually occurred? On this subject there cannot exist the shadow of a doubt. Every one will admit that if these persons were all conscious that they perceived the eclipse, the eclipse must have taken place.

Secondly, were they really conscious that they perceived it; that is, did they testify truly?

Here we turn to the law of human motive. We say no motive but the love of truth could have impelled all these persons, of different ages, habits, culture and prejudices, in many different places, to unite in this testimony. Take away the love of truth,— that is, suppose them to speak falsely,— and we must suppose them to act individually without any motive; and, still more, that without any motive they all, and without concert, united in giving the same testimony. The absurdity of this supposition is, I think, obvious.

This testimony would be still more irresistible, if the

persons who testified were, in consequence of their evidence exposed to contempt, obloquy, persecution, loss of property and of life. In this case, to suppose them to testify falsely, would be to suppose them to act not only without any motive, but in opposition to every motive. It is impossible to suppose an intelligent being with a human constitution to act in this manner.

In such a case as this, we show that what is testified to is true, or else an intuitive law of perception, or an intuitive law of human action is violated. When we have done this, we have done all that reasoning can do. This is all we do in demonstrative or mathematical reasoning. We there show that unless a proposition be true, an axiom, or an intuitive law of quantity, is violated. We can go no further. In either case, where we have shown this, the proposition in question has been proved. Facts thus established have never been shown to be false. Indeed, they never could be disproved, for we can never be more certain of anything than of the intuitive laws of our own nature. Suppose that the opposite of what we have thus proved was also proved, it could not show the first proposition to be false. It would only establish an opposite proposition on equivalent evidence, and we should be perfectly unable to choose between two contradictory propositions, both being perfectly entitled to belief.

From these remarks it will appear, that, in establishing any fact by testimony, two points, and but two, are of necessity to be made evident. First, that if the witnesses were conscious of perceiving it, it really must have occurred. Here we show that the event was one properly cognizable by the senses, that the witnesses were in proper conditions, objective and subjective, for observing it; that is, that the impression on their senses must have been made under the ordinary laws of perception. In the second place, we show that the witnesses testify to what they really believe to be true; that is, they really believe themselves to have been conscious of the perception in question. We here show that there can be no motive for testifying falsely; that is, to suppose them to testify falsely, is to suppose them to act without motive. If we can proceed further, and show that if they testify falsely, they not only act without any motive, but in opposition to every motive, we have then the same evidence as if every witness was on oath.

In this manner we prove any fact in history; as the death of Cæsar in the senate-house, his conquest of Britain, or any other event. On these principles trials are conducted every day in our courts of law. I do not know of any method by which a student will improve his knowledge of the science of evidence more advantageously, than by analyzing carefully the evidence in important trials, when the decision depends upon the establishment of matters of fact. If the above remarks be correct, they will enable him to carry on this examination and analysis with some degree of success.

II. *Of indirect or circumstantial evidence.*

In the preceding remarks I have considered the case in which the witnesses testify directly to the fact in question; that is, they declare that they themselves perceived the fact which they relate.

But cases are continually occurring in which it is important to establish a fact to which there were no witnesses. How, in the absence of witnesses, shall such a fact be proved? This is done by indirect or circumstantial evidence. The principles on which we here proceed are as follows:

It is obvious, from the regular succession of cause and effect, to which all the changes in the universe are subjected, that no event can occur isolated and alone. I do not know that, as we are constituted, it is possible for us to conceive of such an event. Every phenomenon is indissolubly connected with other phenomena, to which it stands in permanent relations. When we see water changed into ice we know that it must have been exposed to a temperature as low as 32°. When water boils, we know that its temperature has been raised to 212°. If a body at rest begins to move, or if, when moving, it changes suddenly its direction, we know that some force must have been applied to it. These changes could not have produced themselves; they are the result of some stated antecedent. Now, if we can show the existence of a train of facts, so related to the fact in question, that unless this fact occurred the laws of cause and effect must have been violated, then we have proved the main fact by indirect, or circumstantial evidence.

The rules which govern us in this kind of evidence are the following:

1. When we are not inquiring for a fact, but for the cause of it, the fact itself must first be established. Thus, if it be required to prove that A murdered B, we must first prove that B was murdered, and prove it by direct evidence.

2. In the second place, all the facts, on which we rely to prove the fact in question, must be established by direct evidence. Thus, if we rely on the facts A, B, D, to prove the fact C,—that is, these facts being proved, that the fact C must have existed,—we must prove the facts A, B, and D, by the personal knowledge of witnesses themselves.

3. We must show that the facts A, B, and D, could not have existed unless the fact C had existed. When we have established these facts, and shown that they can be accounted for on no other supposition than the existence of the fact C,—that is, that unless the fact C occurred, a law of nature has been violated,—then we have proved this fact by indirect evidence.

This, however, will be rendered more eviden by an example. Take the following case. B is found alone in a room, dead, stabbed in the back, and his skull fractured by the stroke of a bludgeon. The first thing to be established is that the man is dead; and, secondly, that his death was occasioned by the wounds upon his person; and, thirdly, that the wounds could not have been inflicted by himself; that is, that he died by the hands of another, and not by his own. These facts must be proved by direct evidence. It is thus shown that the man was murdered. The question next to be answered is, who was the murderer?

Here it is shown that A and B unlocked the door and entered the room together. A noise, as of altercation, was heard. No one entered the room until A left it, and the first person who entered it after his departure found B dead in the manner described. Now, these facts having been established, it is proved that A is the murderer. The man is dead. He died of these wounds. They could have been inflicted by no person except A or B himself. They are so situated that B could not have inflicted them on himself; they must, therefore, have been inflicted by A.

But, besides these, other antecedent and subsequent facts may confirm the supposition of the guilt of A. For instance, men do not commonly commit such a crime without a violent motive. If such a motive existed, it gives confirmation to the supposition of his guilt. And, again, when a man has committed so atrocious a crime, he is commonly apprehensive, and takes means to escape the consequences. If B was known to enter the room with a purse of gold and was found with his pockets rifled, and if this purse was found in the possession of A, this will furnish a motive for the deed. If A immediately afterwards changed his name, disguised his person, and was preparing immediately to escape from the vicinity, and no reason but his guilt can be

28*

assigned for his conduct, this is a strong confirmatory circumstance. The supposition that he was the murderer can alone account for all his subsequent conduct.

Hence, we see the points which are to be made out by the prosecution in any trial where the evidence is circumstantial. First, the crime must have been committed. For instance, if it be a case of murder, the body must be found, and it must be proved that the death was caused by violence. Second, the facts must be such as can be accounted for on no other supposition than that the accused was the murderer. If they can be accounted for on any other reasonable supposition, then the case is not proved. And, on the other hand, the ground of the defence is, first, that the deceased did not die by violence; or, in general, that he was not murdered; or that, if murdered, the facts can be accounted for on some other supposition. The facts in all cases must be established, as I have said, by direct testimony.

In every trial, where the evidence is circumstantial, we hear much said about the uncertainty of this kind of evidence, and various cases are mentioned in which the lives of innocent men have been sacrificed in consequence of this uncertainty. This may have been the case when the principles of evidence were less perfectly understood than at present. But, if a trial is conducted according to the rules of evidence as at present established, circumstantial proof may be relied on with as much certainty as direct. Men may be mistaken as to a fact, or they may swear falsely; but a well-connected chain of circumstances can rarely deceive us. It is somewhat remarkable, that, in a late trial for murder in Boston, where the evidence was circumstantial, the circumstances proved, all led to the true result; while the direct evidence, intended to prove an alibi, was absolutely, though innocently, erroneous.

This kind of evidence is frequently resorted to in scientific investigations. Certain facts are observed. In what manner are they to be accounted for? that is, what must have been the nature and the order of the changes by which these appearances were produced? When we have conceived of a cause, or succession of causes, which will account for all the facts, and which alone can account for them, we may consider such cause or causes as matter of established truth Thus, a geologist observes that a river has cut its way through banks a hundred feet high. Some thirty feet below the surface of the soil a layer of vegetable matter is discovered, the stumps of trees, standing upright, imbedded in the soil where they grew, and the trees broken off lying upon and by the side of them. Some thirty feet lower. another stratum of a similar character is observed. From the position of these trees it is evident that they also must have grown on the spot where they are found, and, of course. that each of these layers must have been, at the time of its growth, on the surface of the earth. There is but one way in which these facts can be accounted for. After the lower layer of trees had grown to its present size, the surface of the earth must have subsided until they were covered with drift for thirty or more feet. The subsidence was then arrested until another forest grew up. Another subsidence must have occurred until the drift covered the timber again to a similar depth. Then the whole surface must have been upheaved to its present position, and, afterwards, the river must have cut its way through the mass, thus laying bare the mode of its formation. As no other cause can be assigned for these effects, we are warranted in believing that such events as these actually existed.

It will be seen that direct and circumstantial evidence may frequently be found corroborating each other, and they then present the strongest possible ground of belief. If any marked event occur, not only will it be seen by witnesses but it will be preceded by its appropriate causes, and followed by its appropriate effects. Thus, the death of Cæsar is proved by the testimony of eye-witnesses, and contemporary writers. But, besides this, the civil wars in the Roman empire, and the character of the parties that were formed immediately after that event is said to have taken place, can be accounted for on no other supposition than that of his violent death. So the invasion and occupation of Britain by the Romans is proved by the testimony of historians. But if such an event had occurred, we should naturally expect that some traces of their occupation would be observed in that island. Hence, we examine, and find there the remains of Roman encampments, walls, roads, Roman coins of that age, and inscriptions which could have been made by no other people. These facts can be accounted for on no other supposition than that of the conquest and permanent occupation of Britain by the former conquerors of the world. This coïncidence of direct and indirect evidence furnishes the most perfect ground of belief which we can conceive to any matter of fact.

REFERENCES.

Evidence of testimony — Reid, Essay 7, sec. 3 ; Stewart, vol. ii., chap 2, sec. 4 ; Abercrombie, Part 2, sec. 3.

Different kinds of evidence — Reid, Essay 2, chap. 20.

Testimony of others a source of knowledge — Locke, Book 4, chap. 16, secs. 6—8 ; Abercrombie, Part 2, sec. 3.

Laws of testimony — Abercrombie, Part 2, sec. 3.

Natural bias to truth — Abercrombie, Part 2, sec. 3 ; Reid's Inquiry, chap. 6, sec. 24.

Hume's argument against miracles — Abercrombie, Part 2, sec. 3

Case when witnesses are numerous — Abercrombie, Part 2, sec. 3.

Circumstantial evidence — Abercrombie, Part 2, sec. 3.

SECTION IV. — OTHER FORMS OF REASONING.

I. *Of probable evidence.*

Thus far I have treated of those modes of reasoning in which our premises are acknowledged to be true, and our conclusion is equally, that is, absolutely true. But all of our reasoning is not of this character. It frequently happens that our premises rise no higher than probability, and our conclusions can only reach the same level. Our process is, however, precisely the same, the only difference consists in the degree of certainty to which we arrive.

When the reasons for believing a proposition to be true are not such as to establish belief, but only to show that it is more likely to happen than not, we say that such a proposition is probable. Thus, if the wind is in a certain quarter, I say that it probably will rain. I examine the evidence that may be adduced in favor of the proposition that the planets are inhabited, and I say that it is or is not probable. It may require the coöperation of several causes to render an event certain. If, however, only a part of these causes unite in a particular case, the event may occur, though we cannot expect it with confidence. So, if an intelligent being has several times, under given circumstances, acted in a particular manner, we form a distinct anticipation that he will act in the same manner under similar circumstances. But here our anticipation only amounts to a probability, for we know not what changes may have taken place in his character since we last observed him; and there may have arisen circumstances which affect him of which we are ignorant. When, in this manner, we attain to mere probability, we call our state of mind opinion; that is, we judge a proposition more likely to be true than false.

We take such opinions as the grounds of our reasonings

in a large number of cases in practical life. Thus, we say,

It is probable that the character of a human being will be improved by affliction.

A. B. has suffered affliction; therefore,

A. B. is probably improved in character.

Or, again:

If there be war in Europe, the price of breadstuffs will rise.

There will probably be a war in Europe; therefore,

It is probable that the price of breadstuffs will rise.

When only one of our premises is a doubtful and the other a certain proposition, the probability of our conclusion is equal to that of our doubtful premise. Thus, it being granted that if there be war in Europe prices will rise, the probability of our conclusion is precisely as great as the probability of a war. When, however, both of our premises are mere probabilities, the probability of our conclusion is greatly reduced, and can rarely furnish a ground for an opinion. Thus,

If the south wind blow to-morrow, it will probably rain

The south wind will probably blow to-morrow; therefore

It is (very slightly) probable that it will rain.

When so slight an indication of an event is given, it is manifestly of very little use in forming a judgment.

From the fact that we reason from probabilities, very commonly, in the practical business of life, it has happened that this mode of reasoning has sometimes been confounded with that by which we arrive at practical certainty. It has sometimes been said that moral reasoning, or reasoning concerning matters of fact, is nothing else than a succession of probable arguments, each one reducing the liabilities of error, until they become so small as to be inappreciable. The cases, however, are dissimilar. In the one case, we proceed from an approximation to truth so near that neither we nor other men can discover any error, and the result is of the same character. In the other case, we proceed from an approximation to truth, but so distant that we can appreciate our liability to error; we know the uncertainty of our premises, and the result is a mere approximation similar to them, producing not belief, but merely opinion. For instance, suppose we endeavor to ascertain whether the battle of Waterloo was fought on the 18th of June, 1815. We proceed according to the laws of evidence as before stated We apply the rule of perception, and the rule of human motive. We can discover no error, and no other man can discover any. I rely upon the result at which I have arrived with perfect confidence, and the state of mind of which I am conscious is belief, full, entire, and unquestionable. Again; the question is asked, when did the battle commence? I find that here the accounts vary. The best authorities differ, some placing it as early as ten o'clock, and others as late as one. I form an opinion, by comparing the accounts, and balancing the probable motives which would lead men into error. I form an opinion as to the time, but it is not belief. I am conscious of a state of mind very dissimilar to that in the preceding case.

Or, again; from the data established by observation as accurate as the faculties of men will permit, we determine the distance and magnitude of the planet Jupiter. No error can be discovered either in our data or our reasoning. We know that there may be error, but that it cannot exceed a certain amount, and we rely on the result under this condition with absolute certainty. But when it is said the planet Jupiter is inhabited, we collect our data, and they give us nothing but a probability to reason from, and we arrive at nothing but an opinion. The states of mind differ not in degree but in kind. The one proceeds from data in which no error can be discovered by the faculties which

God has given us. The other proceeds from data which we know to be uncertain, and the uncertainty of which we are able to appreciate. They, of course, lead to an entirely different subjective result, and a line of distinct demarcation must ever separate the one from the other.

II. *Reasoning from induction.*

The object of this mode of reasoning is to establish a general law, from the observation of particular instances. The principle on which it depends has been already explained, when treating of cause and effect. See pages 153—158.

It is in conformity with our intuitive beliefs, that, from observing a change, we proceed to ascertain its cause. We know that, wherever the cause exists, the effect must necessarily follow, and that wherever an event always follows a given antecedent, this antecedent must be the cause. We therefore observe all the various phenomena which precede a change. We ascertain, so far as possible, which of them is the invariable antecedent; in other words, that which being present the effect exists, and which being removed the effect ceases. When this has been done, we consider ourselves to have ascertained the cause.

Having thus determined, by experiment, the cause in this particular case, we proceed as follows:

What is the cause of this effect in one case must be the cause in all cases.

The event A is the cause in this case; therefore,

The event A is the cause in all cases.

It frequently happens that there are several antecedents, and the greatest skill and the most persevering sagacity are requisite in order to determine which of them is invariable. We are obliged to try every variety of combinations, in order to ascertain with perfect precision the cause, and to sever it from every occasional and variable antecedent. When, however, this is done, we generalize with entire confidence, and consider the law as established.

The manner in which we proceed, in such a case, is illustrated most happily in the process employed by Sir Isaac Newton to discover the cause of the solar spectrum. The full account may be found in the third chapter of Sir David Brewster's life of this great philosopher.

III. *Of reasoning from analogy.*

In this form of reasoning, we do not attempt to prove a proposition true, and we may not even attempt to prove it probable. All that we generally desire is to prove it not improbable.

In the other cases of which we have treated, we proceed upon the supposition that the same cause, under the same conditions, will produce the same effects. Here we proceed upon the supposition, not that the same cause will produce the same effect, but merely that similar causes may produce similar effects, in the absence of evidence to the contrary.

If this mode of reasoning were reduced to a syllogism it would take substantially the following form:

1. Similar causes may produce similar effects.
2. The cause A is similar to the cause B;
3. Therefore the cause A and B may produce similar effects.

The principal uses of analogical reasoning are the following:

1. It is frequently employed with success in answering an *a priori* objection. It is thus used with great acuteness and unanswerable force, by Bishop Butler, in his Analogy. Thus, if men deny the existence of God, and hence infer that there can be no future state of rewards and punishments, his answer is as follows: It is granted, even by atheists themselves, that in the present state we are rewarded for some actions and punished for others; that is, that we

find ourselves under a moral government. But, if we exist under such conditions now, when, by the supposition, there is no God, there can be no reason assigned why we may not continue to exist after death, and exist under the same conditions as at present; that is, under a moral government, in which we shall be rewarded and punished according to the character of our actions. The whole of this admirable treatise, one of the most remarkable that any language can produce, is intended to show that the principles of moral government taught in the Scriptures are strictly analogous to those everywhere exhibited in the government of the world, as seen by natural religion. Hence, it is evident that if God has adopted these principles for our government in one case, there can be no *a priori* reason why he should not adopt them in another case. "It will here be found," says he, "not taken for granted, but proved, that any reasonable man, who will thoroughly consider the matter, may be as much assured as he is of his own being, that it is not so clear a case that there is nothing in it."

While, however, analogy claims to do no more than this, it, in many cases, in fact, does much more. It is evident that the greater the similarity of cause the greater is the probability of the similarity of effects. It may thus, in some cases, approximate to proof; at the least, it furnishes grounds for a decided opinion. Thus, the similarity of many of the effects of electricity and galvanism created the opinion that they were the same agent, before their identity was discovered.

2. It will readily appear that an important use of analogy is to aid us in scientific investigation. Suppose, for instance, that we have discovered the cause for a well-known effect. We observe another effect of a similar character, and we instinctively are led to inquire, may it not arise from the same or a similar cause? Hence, in our search after

causes, we are greatly aided, and much useless labor is saved, by such an indication. Thus, Sir H. Davy discovered the metallic basis of potash. But there are other alkalies in many of their sensible properties nearly allied to potash. How natural was it for him to expect that the same laws governed them all, and that they all were formed in the same manner from metallic bases!

3. Analogy is frequently used by the orator with great effect. Thus, if it is admitted that a man has acted in one way at one time, there is no reason why he might not be expected to act in the same way at another time. Or, if it is honorable for one man to act in a particular manner in one case, there can be no reason why it is not honorable for another man, in a case essentially alike, to act in a similar manner. This mode of reasoning is used with the happiest success by Erskine, in the introduction of his argument for Stockdale. He commences by alluding to the fact that, though connected by ties of the closest intimacy with the political party who had directed the prosecution, yet, Mr. Stockdale had not hesitated to entrust him with his defence. He adds, "This, however, is a matter of daily occurrence. So unsullied is the character of the English bar, that no political bias ever interferes with the discharge of the duty of an advocate; that, whatever may be our public principles, or the private habits of our lives, they never cast even a shade across the path of our professional duties. If this be characteristic of the bar of an English court of justice, what sacred impartiality may not every man expect from its jurors and its bench." Many similar instances may be found in the speeches of this eminent orator, perhaps the most consummate advocate of modern times.

It is, however, obvious, that this mode of reasoning is liable to great abuse. The whole force of the argument depends on the similarity of the cases. But if an advocate can present cases seeming to be similar, while, in fact, they are widely diverse, he may draw from them the most erroneous conclusions. It is, therefore, the business of an opponent, or of an inquirer after truth, to examine reasoning of this kind with the closest scrutiny; and, when it is defective, point out the dissimilarity of the cases, and show the result to which such analogies would lead, if we allowed them to form the foundation of our judgment.

REFERENCES.

Probable evidence — Stewart, vol. ii., chap. 2, sec. 4; Locke, Book 4, chap. 15; Abercrombie, Part 2, sec. 3.

Induction — Reid, chap. 6, sec. 24; Stewart, vol. ii., chap. 4, sec. 1; Cousin, chap. 9.

Analogy — Reid's Inquiry, Essay 1, chap. 4; Stewart, vol. ii., chap. 2, sec. 4, chap. 4, sec. 4; Locke, Book 5, chap. 16, sec. 12; Abercrombie, Part 3, sec. 4.

Herschel's Discourse on the Study of Natural Philosophy.

Remarks on Analogical Reasoning in Whately's Rhetoric.

Bacon's Novum Organon.

SECTION V. — ON THE IMPROVEMENT OF THE REASONING POWERS.

It is appropriate to close this chapter with a few suggestions on the manner of improving the reasoning powers.

If the remarks in the preceding pages are correct, it will appear that the process which we employ in reasoning is, in all cases, essentially the same. Our object is to show such a relation between the known and the unknown, that, if one be true, the other is equally true; or, if one be only probable, the other is equally probable. If our premises are denied, we proceed to show their relation to something better known and more universally admitted, and thus fall back, step by step, until we rest upon those elementary truths which are given us in the constitution of the human intellect. From these, in the first place, all our knowledge proceeds.

The manner in which we accomplish this is by syllogism. We show that what is true of a class is true of every individual under that class. By making it evident that individuals or species are included under classes to which they were not supposed to belong, or that a predicate can be affirmed of a subject which could not have been affirmed of it before, new knowledge is evolved, and the domain of science is enlarged.

To proceed in this manner is, I suppose, the instinct of our nature. A human being begins to reason almost as soon as he begins to think; and were he incapable of reasoning, that is, of inferring a conclusion from premises, we should at once perceive that he was destitute of a rational soul, or deficient in an important element of our intellectual nature. Logicians unfold the process and develop the laws by which reasoning is performed, and thus enable us the better to distinguish between valid arguments and sophisms. To be able to do this is of great utility in the work of mental cultivation. We thus are rendered capable of determining whether our reasonings are, or are not, in accordance with the laws of the human mind. When this attainment has been made, we can rely with confidence upon the decisions of our own understanding. This is an important condition of all intellectual progress. We can never proceed boldly in the work of investigation, until we can say, with Sir Isaac Newton, "When I see a thing to be true, I know it is true."

If, then, we would cultivate our reasoning power with success, it is important to understand the nature of the human mind, and especially the process by which it establishes truth by reasoning. The first of these is treated of in works on intellectual philosophy. This, however, is not alone sufficient for our purpose. The whole subject of reasoning, in all its ramifications, is unfolded in the science of logic. By a diligent study of this science, our acuteness will be greatly sharpened, and, what is probably of greater consequence, the mind not only becomes accustomed to all the forms of reasoning, but learns instinctively to reject every conclusion not warranted by logical principles.

I lately met with the following curious illustration of the utility of the study of logic in cultivating the power of the mind:

"The Asiatic Journal, 1827, records the following instance of acuteness in a young brahmin. After the introduction of juries into Ceylon, a wealthy brahmin, whose unpopular character had rendered him obnoxious to many, was accused of murdering his nephew, and put upon trial. He chose a jury of his own caste; but so strong was the evidence against him, that twelve out of thirteen of the jury were thoroughly convinced of his guilt. The dissentient juror, a young brahmin of Camisseram, stood up, declared his conviction that the prisoner was the victim of a conspiracy, and desired that all the witnesses should be recalled. He examined them with extraordinary dexterity and acuteness, and succeeded in extorting from them such proofs of their perjury, that the jury, instead of consigning the prisoner to an ignominious death, pronounced him innocent. The affair made much noise in the island, and the chief justice, Sir Alexander Johnston, sent for the juror who had so distinguished himself, and complimented him on the talents he had displayed. The brahmin attributed his skill to the study of a book which he called 'The Strengthener of the Mind.' He had obtained it from Persia, and had translated it from the Sanscrit, into which it had been rendered from the Persian. Sir Alexander Johnston expressing a curiosity to see the book, the brahmin brought a Tamil manuscript, on palm leaves, which Sir Alexander found, to his infinite surprise, to be the 'Dialectics of Aristotle.'" I regret that I am not able to verify this anecdote by a reference to the original work. I give it as I found it in a periodical on education.

The study of rules and the comprehension of principles will, however, be of very little value, unless our knowledge, as we have before recommended, be reduced to practice. By the habitual practice of earnest investigation, without any knowledge of the rules of logic, a man will become an able reasoner; while, without this practice, no matter what be his understanding of the rules, he will never acquire the power of convincing others.

2. I, therefore, remark that the power of ratiocination may be improved by the study of works of a syllogistic character. Among these, it is common to assign the first place to the pure mathematics. A geometrical demonstration is composed of a succession of pure syllogisms, free from any admixture of contingent truth, and receiving as premises only what every human mind must necessarily admit. The appeal is made exclusively to the understanding; the conceptions are definite and precise, and the conclusions follow from their own intuitive evidence. This, then, would seem to present the simplest and purest exercise of the reasoning power. For this cause, the mathematics have always formed an important branch of a liberal education. They give exercise to the reasoning power, and they may be pursued at an early period of life, when other reasoning could not be so easily comprehended.

On the use of the mathematics for the purpose of intellectual cultivation, however, the highest authorities on the subject of education differ. Sir W. Hamilton * contends,

* On the Study of the Mathematics as an Exercise of the Mind.— Discussions on Philosophy, etc. London, 1852: pp. 256—327.

with great power and exuberance of learning, that they are, of all intellectual pursuits, the least adapted to produce the effect so commonly ascribed to them. It must be admitted that they discuss the relations of nothing but quantity, and the simplest of these relations; and that the matter of which they treat, and the mode in which they treat it, are entirely unlike those which must be employed in the affairs of life and the investigations of the other sciences. Whoever will read this very able discussion will at least be convinced that the ordinary opinion on the universal adaptedness of the mathematics to mental discipline requires a thorough reëxamination. It is also a duty manifestly imposed upon teachers to consider this question with a mind unbiased by preconceived opinions, and observe carefully the effect of this study on the reasoning powers of their pupils. In all our institutions of learning we require that every candidate for a literary degree shall devote a considerable portion of his time to the mathematics, not for any practical purpose, but purely as a means of special intellectual culture. It surely cannot be inappropriate to inquire whether it actually produces the anticipated results.

3. In the mathematics, our reasoning concerns nothing but the necessary relations of quantity, and, therefore, we arrive at absolute truth. A very small part of our practical reasoning is, however, of that character. We desire to have the truth, not concerning abstract conceptions, but concerning matters of fact, or that into which fact enters as a necessary element. Hence, were we to confine our reasoning to the mathematics, it may be doubted whether we should increase our power of general ratiocination. It has been frequently remarked that persons who have addicted themselves exclusively to this science, have been singularly deficient in the reasoning power which is required in the several professions, and in the ordinary affairs of life. I

have not perceived that original ability in young men was at all measured by proficiency in the mathematics. Men of decided talent generally succeed well in anything, and, of course, in abstract science. The general reasoning power is not more closely connected with special talent for mathematics, than with special talent for philology, philosophy, physics, or any other branch of learning.

It will, therefore, be necessary for us to accustom ourselves to reasonings concerning matters of fact, or, as it is called, moral reasoning. In order to do this, it will be useful to examine argumentative treatises, discourses, sermons, pleas at the bar, or anything which, by consecutive proof, professes to arrive at a conclusion. I hardly know of any work better adapted to such a purpose than Butler's Analogy. It will aid us in this labor, first, carefully to read the work which we attempt to examine, taking notes of every step of the argument, and thus, in the briefest manner, forming for ourselves an analysis of the whole. Then, fixing our minds distinctly upon the thing to be proved, we should examine the general syllogism by which it is established, and the proofs on which the several propositions rest. Where an argument is abbreviated, we should supply the propositions that are suppressed, and the conclusions that are omitted. In this manner we shall be able fully to appreciate the value of the whole argument, yielding an intelligent conviction to its proofs, and rejecting whatever is sophistical. A practice of this kind will have a marked effect upon our power of ratiocination.

By pursuing the course here indicated, we may be enabled to understand, appreciate and verify, the various forms of argument. We thus become skilful in detecting sophistry, and distinguishing truth from falsehood. This may be termed passive syllogistic power. It is an important preparation for further progress, but is in itself only a partial development of the reasoning faculty. We need the ability, not only to understand and appreciate the arguments of others, but also to originate and construct arguments for ourselves. This is the great purpose which this power was intended to accomplish.

4. We may improve ourselves in this respect by mathematical study. As soon as we have acquired the command of a few theorems in geometry, we should attempt to demonstrate for ourselves. Problems for this purpose should be provided in our text-books. It would be well if the student should never make use of the demonstration in the book, until he had exhausted his ability to originate one for himself. In this manner, though he might seem at first to make but slow progress, his real mathematical power would rapidly increase. If mathematical studies are to be used as a means for mental discipline, the practice of original demonstration must be invaluable. Were it more frequently adopted, I have no doubt that it would add materially to vigor and alertness of mind. In this respect, algebraical problems possess a peculiar advantage. I know of no exercise that calls into more active use the power of grasping firmly a particular conception, and tracing it out unchanged through various and complicated relations, than the effort to form a difficult algebraical equation.

5. If we would educate our reasoning powers, we must pursue the same course in subjects not mathematical. We must learn to form arguments for ourselves on all matters of investigation that come under our notice. When a doubtful question arises, instead of avoiding it, we should earnestly bend ourselves to the labor of solving it. We should be in the habit of forming logical plans of thought on every subject of study. Whether we write or speak, we should always have an end in view, towards which every thought tends by a natural succession, and a logical arrangement. If a lawyer

makes a plea, he should not be satisfied with merely presenting a variety of considerations that have a bearing on the subject; his argument should be direct and conclusive. If a preacher construct a discourse, he should have in view a particular moral condition to which he desires to lead his audience, and every paragraph and every sentence should tend to lead them to this condition.

If, however, we desire to cultivate our intellect to the best advantage, two cautions are here to be observed. The first respects reliance on authority. Many men, when a proposition is to be proved, spend their time in hunting up authorities, and collecting the opinions of others. By these they expect men to be convinced, without once asking the question whether they are convinced themselves. I would by no means speak lightly of the learning of the past, or of the opinions of eminent men; but it must still be apparent that an opinion, whether of an ancient or a contemporary, is worth just as much as the reason on which it is founded. No matter how high the authority, we should never attempt to convince another by an argument the force of which we have not ourselves acknowledged. We may embarrass and confound men by an array of learned authorities, but we shall rarely convince them unless we have first convinced ourselves.

But it is hardly enough that we ourselves be convinced by the teaching of others. We should, if possible, convince ourselves by reasons drawn from the fountain of our own reflections. A student who desires to develop fully his own powers, must make his own mind his chief reliance in all his intellectual labor. If he cultivate this habit, he will frequently find it less laborious to think out an argument for himself than to seek for it in books. A man endowed with a ready memory and sufficient command of language, may, without any active use of his reasoning powers, speak or write upon a subject with fluency and elegance. Such men in youth create great expectation, but when the hour arrives for decided intellectual trial, they fail. On the other hand, he who thinks for himself and relies on his own resources, may at first seem slow of apprehension and wanting in richness of thought, but his powers are invigorated by every effort. The exercise of his faculties yields continually a richer and more abundant product, and thus confirms his confidence in his own intellectual power. We should, therefore, resolve in the beginning that whatever we produce shall be, as far as possible, our own; at least, that it shall have passed through the processes of our own thinking, and thus become assimilated with the working of our own intellect. No habit is so fatal as plagiarism to all vigor of the understanding. It inevitably induces indolence, mental imbecility, and utter inability to carry on a train of original thought.

6. In order to improve the reasoning powers, it is important that we always labor for truth. Many persons, in order to acquire skill in debate, are in the habit of defending the true or false indiscriminately, believing that they can cultivate their own understanding by misleading the understanding of others. A man may learn thus to embarrass and confound an antagonist, but he does it at great sacrifice. By earnestly seeking for truth, and rejecting all sophistry, the mind acquires a tendency to move in the right direction. Chemists speak much of the affinities of various substances for each other. There is a natural affinity in the human mind for truth, and this affinity is strengthened by seeking for it with an honest and earnest purpose. If we in our investigations inquire for nothing but truth, it spontaneously reveals itself to us. The whole history of philosophical discovery illustrates this remark. Hence nothing can be more unwise than to destroy the original

delicacy of the faculty of reason by employing it indiscriminately in the support of truth or falsehood. We may thus gain the praise of acuteness or readiness in debate; but we lose what is of incomparably greater consequence, the instinctive love of truth, and the delicate discrimination between truth and error.

And, lastly; it is impossible for us to reason well, or so to reason as to increase the sum of human knowledge, without the possession of large and accurate knowledge. Reasoning is the process by which we pass from the known to the unknown. The known, then, lies at the foundation of our process. Unless there be something known, we cannot begin to reason; and the greater the amount of our knowledge, the larger is the material with which we labor. The more exact our knowledge is, the more successfully can we use it in the discovery of truth.

Able men, of marked independence of mind, and strong tendency for investigation, by failing to know what other men have discovered, are liable to waste their energies in search of that which has been already discovered. Hence, after arriving at valuable truth, they find themselves in the rear of their age. Though the cases are rare, able men sometimes fall into this error. If this be the case with men of unusual endowments, how much more does it deserve the attention of those who can boast of no extraordinary talent! He who would enlarge the field of human knowledge, must stand upon the limits of the known, before he can expect to enter the field of the unknown.

REFERENCES.

Cultivation of the reasoning faculties — Abercrombie, Part 3, section 4.
Mathematicians not good reasoners —Abercrombie, Part 3, section 4

Difference between sound judgment and ingenious disputation — Abercrombie, Part 3, section 4.

Power of reasoning depends on extent of knowledge — Abercrombie, Part 3, section 4.

Use of authorities — Locke, Book 4, chap. 20, section 17.

Advantage of clearness and exactitude of knowledge — Locke, Book 4, chap. 12, section 14.

CHAPTER VII.

IMAGINATION.

SECTION I.—THE NATURE OF THIS FACULTY.

THE next faculty of which we propose to treat is the Imagination. It is the power by which, from simple conceptions already existing in the mind, we form complex wholes or images. Thus, the painter, selecting several beautiful views from various landscapes which he has observed, forms them into a single picture. The novelist unites the elements of several characters which he has observed in the conception of his hero.

It is manifest that some form of abstraction must, by necessity, precede the exercise of imagination. Were we not able to analyze the concrete, and contemplate its several parts separate from each other, we could never unite them at will, so as to form an original image. The parts must be mentally severed before they can be reünited in a new conception. It is this power of reüniting the several elements of a conception at will, that is, properly, imagination. Imagination may then be designated as the power of combination.

There is, however, a difference in the manner in which the power of combination receives and modifies the materials derived from abstraction. In treating of abstraction I attempted to show that it included three acts; first, analy sis, by which the qualities of a concrete object are separated from each other; second, generalization, by which these simple elements of an individual become a general abstract idea; and, third, combination, by which these last are united in a complex conception, representing not an individual but a class. The act by which we form classes, may, perhaps, more properly be called conception than imagination.

The act of imagination proper, differs from that act by which we form classes. In the first place, the mode of abstraction in the two cases is unlike. In forming conceptions of classes we first separate qualities from each other. In collecting the elements for a picture in the imagination, we separate not qualities so much as parts. Again; before we can proceed to form classes, we must first generalize our individual abstractions, and thus form general abstract ideas. In imagination proper we do not generalize, but at once unite the ideas of individual parts which we have previously separated from each other. In the third place, the result is dissimilar. In the one case we form a notion of a class, meaning no particular individual; in the other, we form a notion of an individual, which is the more perfect in proportion to its distinct individuality.

The difference between these cases may be illustrated by a familiar example. Suppose that a physiologist were attempting to form a scientific conception of an animal, say, for instance, of a horse. He would examine the first specimen with all the accuracy in his power, taking note specially of all the qualities of its external appearance and internal structure. He would, in the second place, examine other specimens, taking note of each particular quality as before. These qualities would then not belong to one specimen, but to them all, or would become general abstract ideas. He would next distinguish those that were constant from those which were variable, uniting the constant into a single conception, and rejecting the others as valueless. This conception thus formed would represent the class, and would correspond to the word horse, whenever he or other physiologists used it.

But, were an artist required to paint the charger of a commander-in-chief on a battle-field, he would proceed in a very different manner. Observing several horses, he would perceive one remarkable for the beauty of its head. The body of another, and the neck of a third are distinguished for elegance of form and symmetry of proportions. Without any act of generalization, he would unite such of these several parts as he chose into one image, which he would transfer to the canvas. This picture would not be the representation of a class, but of an individual. The object of the painter would be, not to form an image which should stand for all horses, but a picture of a more beautiful horse than had ever existed, thus making this representation to stand out by itself, distinguished from every other that had ever been conceived.

Imagination proper is, therefore, the power of forming not general conceptions, designating classes, but particular images representing individuals. It is the power by which we form pictures in the mind, of some object or event. Hence, it would seem that those writers have erred who state that this act of the mind closely resembles the process of reasoning. The two acts are really remarkably unlike. The materials used in the reasoning process are always propositions, that is, affirmations respecting genera and species. The imagination, on the contrary, employs conceptions of separate parts, which it combines into an individual whole. The process which they employ is dissimilar; the one forming syllogisms, the other uniting elements. The result at which they arrive is different. The one ends in a proposition affirming a predicate of a subject; the other ends in a picture affirming nothing. The one asserts a truth, the other presents a conception. That the most gifted men are frequently endowed with both of these powers in a high degree, and that the possession of both is necessary to great intellectual efforts, is granted; but this no more proves them to be either identical or similar, than the necessity of reason and memory to intellectual effort proves these faculties identical.

If we examine the several acts of this faculty, we may, I think, observe a difference between them. We have the power to originate images or pictures for ourselves, and we have the power to form them as they are presented to us in language. The former may be called active, and the latter passive imagination. The active I believe always includes the passive power, but the passive does not always include the active. Thus we frequently observe persons, who delight in poetry and romance, who are utterly incapable of creating a scene or composing a stanza. They can form the pictures dictated by language, but are destitute of the power of original combination. Even this secondary and inferior form of imagination is possessed in different degrees. Every one in the habit of giving instruction, especially when description is necessary, must have been convinced of the great difference of individuals in this respect. Some persons create a picture for themselves as soon as it is presented in language. Others form it with difficulty, after repeated trials; and at last we are uncertain whether the conception in our own mind is the same as that awakened in the mind of another. It is on this power, chiefly, that the love of poetry and fiction depends. Hence, we frequently find persons of good sense and strong judgment, who never manifest any taste for imaginative writing. This type of character is most frequently observed in those who have not commenced their education until late in life. The imagination is most active in youth, and if it remain undeveloped until the period of youth be past, it rarely attains its full power or its natural proportions.

The active power of imagining is bestowed with still greater diversity. Some men are poets by nature. Hence the maxim, *poeta nascitur non fit*,— a poet is formed by nature, not by education. Men endowed with a creative imagination are continually perceiving analogies, forming comparisons, and originating scenes of beauty or grandeur, out of all that they observe and all that they remember. Johnson was sitting one evening by the side of a table, on which two candles were burning. The conversation turned on Thomson. "Thomson," said he, "could not see those two candles without forming a poetical image out of them." On the other hand, we are told of a celebrated mathematician, who, after reading the Paradise Lost, laid down the book in disgust, with the significant question, "What does it prove?" In the one case, the imagination had been exclusively cultivated; in the other, the reasoning power. The one had been accustomed to form pictures, the other demonstrations. Neither could have been interested in the labors of the other. Both would probably have derived advantages from a more generous and universal cultivation of their intellectual powers.

This distinction leads us to observe a mistake, frequently made, respecting the mode of cultivating the imagination. Young persons sometimes spend their time in reading works of fiction, and tell us that their object is to improve this power of the mind. This kind of reading produces an effect, but not the effect intended. It improves nothing but the passive power of the imagination; that is, it enables us the more readily to conceive of scenes presented to us by language. It cannot enable us to create scenes for ourselves.

If this passive imaginative power is exclusively cultivated, it is even liable to paralyze the power of creation by condemning it to perpetual inaction. Sir Walter Scott was, from boyhood, a vast reader of romances, but he was also an indefatigable story-teller, and would detain his school-fellows, by the half-day together, with fictions of his own creation, wrought out on the instant from the stores of his inexhaustible fancy.

Again; a distinction may be observed in the nature of the active power of the imagination. Some men instinctively employ this faculty in the creation of images of beauty or sublimity. They address themselves to the taste, and their object is merely to please. Such men are by nature poets Whatever they see or hear becomes at once materials for the exercise of the fancy. Analogies between the seen and the unseen, the relations of matter and the relations of mind, the objective and the subjective, are continually revealing themselves, and thus giving birth to comparisons, metaphors, similes and pictures. No one can read the poetry of Milton, Shakspeare, Burns, Cowper and Thomson, without observing this wonderful power of creating at will images of transcendent loveliness, from either the lowliest or the loftiest object that the eye rests upon.

But there is another and a smaller class of persons, richly endowed with imagination, in whom this faculty acts on somewhat different principles, and tends to a very different result. The materials which they employ are not scenes, or images of individual beauty, but laws of nature. They address not the taste, but the reason. Their object is not to please, but to instruct. The result at which they arrive is not a picture that can be painted on canvas, but a complex conception of truth united in one idea, and tending to a particular conclusion. Such men no sooner observe a phenomenon than they summon from the whole field of their knowledge every law that could relate to this particular case, and select and combine into one conception such of these laws as will reasonably account for the change. Most men, when they observe a phenomenon, know that it must have a cause, but never give themselves the trouble to seek for it. Others are perpetually searching after causes, but seem condemned to search forever in the wrong direction. Men who are preëminently gifted are generally endowed with this power of combination in a remarkable degree. Such were Archimedes, Plato and Aristotle, among the ancients, and among the moderns, Newton, Sir H. Davy, Cuvier, and many of the illustrious men yet spared to us. It has appeared to me that the study of chemistry, when pursued into the regions of original investigation, has a strong tendency to cultivate the highest exercise of this endowment.

As these two forms of the imagination are of special interest, and are to a considerable degree dissimilar, we shall in the following remarks consider them separately.

SECTION II. — POETIC IMAGINATION.

IMAGINATION, as we have said, is the power of combination. In poetic imagination, its elements are not general abstract ideas, but rather notions of the several parts of different wholes, which may be united at will. The pictures of the imagination are not representations of classes, but are individual images which the mind forms for itself from the conceptions which it has already treasured up.

Thus, when a painter would delineate on canvas an ideal landscape, he has recourse to the various elements of picturesque beauty which are present in his recollection. He has been in the habit of observing the aspects of nature in all their infinite variety Tree and shrub river and streamlet, meadow and hill-side, sunlight and shadow, at morning, noon and evening, are all vividly impressed upon his recollection. He forms, at first, a general conception of the picture which he is about to execute. He forms, perhaps, another and another, until the prominent features of his design are determined upon. When the elements of his combination are such as he approves, he proceeds to fill up the outline with such of the accessories as will best harmonize with his subject. When his conception is thus matured, he proceeds to give it form and coloring. The idea which at first existed in his own mind alone, now begins to appear in all the loveliness of a finished picture. It is said that Cole, the distinguished American landscape painter, never drew a line upon canvas until he had not only matured the whole scene in his mind, but even written out the description in full. From this written delineation he rarely made any variation when he transferred his conception to canvas. The case is the same in any other of the fine arts. One of the most impressive ideas that crowds upon the spectator, as he, for the first time, looks upon the interior of a gothic cathedral, is, that all this magnificence of beauty, even to its minute details, must have existed in the mind of the architect before the first stone of the mighty fabric was laid. It all appears like a gorgeous epic,—an Iliad, or a Paradise Lost, in stone.

In the preceding cases our design is simple. It is merely to present a conception which shall awaken the emotion either of beauty or sublimity in the minds of our fellow-men. Our labor is, in the first place, purely conceptual. It consists in creating in our own minds a picture. Suppose this to have been done; the next step is to give to this conception some external expression, by which we shall transfer to the minds of other men the very image which we have created in our own. Hence we see that two elements must be combined in the character of an eminent artist. First, he must be endowed with a rich and vigorous imagination, by which he may form beautiful and striking conceptions; and, secondly, he must be able to realize his conceptions in some material form, so that they may create their proper impression upon the minds of others. Artists may fail from the want of either of these elements. If a man be ever so highly gifted with imagination, but be deficient in power of execution, unable to establish any medium of communication between himself and other men, he will be forever exposed to mortifying failure. He may speak or lecture well on his art, but he can never become a successful artist. Such was apparently the case with Haydon. On the other hand, when imagination is wanting, the practitioner may be a skilful copyist; if a painter, he may draw with accuracy, or represent with fidelity, whatever he sees; but he can never attain to the highest conception of art.

The manner in which these two processes are united in art is various. Sometimes, as I have before remarked, the conception is elaborated and perfected in the mind, before it receives any external expression. Gray's Elegy and Burns' "Bruce's Address to his Soldiers," are said to have been completed before a word was written. In other cases, the rough draft is first committed to canvas, or written out in words, and this is elaborated and modified, until it has attained to all the perfection of which the author is capable Milton was for many years engaged in the plan of Paradise Lost, and there now exist in the Library of Trinity College, Cambridge, his various drafts, approaching nearer to the plan which he finally adopted. Which of these modes is to be preferred must be left to the mental habits of the artist. As a general rule, however, it may be remarked that the more thoroughly any work is excogitated in the beginning, the less will be the labor of composition, and the more marked and observable the symmetry of the whole.

But suppose that this first intellectual labor has been accomplished, and a conception has been formed which we desire to present to our fellow-men. What shape shall this expression assume? The answer to this question will depend upon the endowments special to the individual

If this conception has been formed in a mind endowed simply with the power of language, it will be expressed in prose.

Suppose, that, in addition to the power of language, an artist possess also an ear for rhythm, he will express it in poetry.

If, on the other hand, he be endowed with the power of delineating form, he will execute his conception in marble or stone, and become a sculptor or an architect.

If he have the power of expression, not only in form, but also in color, he will be a painter.

Thus, the fountain from which all the fine arts take their rise is precisely the same. It is the power of creating in our own minds images of beauty or sublimity. Hence flow the various forms of art in the channels marked out by our individual endowments. It is rare that an individual is gifted with more than one of these modes of expression, though, in highly favored instances, they are occasionally combined. Michael Angelo was equally distinguished in sculpture, painting and architecture; and was, besides, no mean poet. Washington Allston was both a painter and a poet. Such gifts are, however, uncommon, and success in a single department may well satisfy the ambition of any artist.

We see, then, the reason of the rule in rhetoric, that, in order to test the correctness of a metaphor, we should conceive of it as represented on canvas. We here recognize the principle that the spiritual part of the work is the same in both modes of expression; and we present it to the decision of taste, in any manner that will best display its form and proportions. Thus, Horace correctly remarks,

> "Pictoribus atque poetis,
> Quidlibet audendi semper fuit æqua potestas."

Hence a conception expressed in any one of the fine arts is readily transferred to the other. A group in painting is easily rendered in marble. Either of these also furnishes subjects for poetry, while the conceptions of Shakspeare, Milton, Scott and Bunyan, have supplied inexhaustible materials for the painter and engraver.

The relation of poetic imagination to taste is easily explained. By the imagination we create pictures in the recesses of our own consciousness. By poetry, painting, sculpture, and the other fine arts, we give to our conceptions an outward manifestation. By this outward manifestation we transfer our own conceptions to the minds of other men. They, by the passive power of the imagination, form for themselves the image which we represent. Hence, the imagination in us, addresses first the imagination of others. But this is not its ultimate object. Its design is to please the taste. Unless the emotion of beauty or sublimity is awakened, we fail to accomplish our object. If we do not form an impressive manifestation of our own conception, it will fail to create a corresponding conception in other men. After the conception has been awakened, if they look upon it with disgust or indifference, our labor has been thrown away. We see, therefore, that in order to form the character of a finished artist, there must be combined great vigor of imagination, and great delicacy ot taste. The author must be able instinctively to determine whether his conception is really beautiful, that is, whether it will give pleasure to the universal mind of man.

When taste is deficient and the imagination vigorous, a writer or artist will abound in conceptions; but they will be puerile, mean, disgusting, unnatural or misplaced; or, what is perhaps more common, beauty and deformity will be strangely and unaccountably mingled together. In such a case, the world sometimes passes them by in silence, sometimes overwhelms them with ridicule; or, provided the follies and eccentricities are strongly marked, at first it gazes upon them with wonder, then applauds them as original, and then consigns them to oblivion. In the words of Horace:

> "Humano capiti cervicem pictor equinam
> Jungere si velit, et varias inducere plumas
> Undique collatis membris, ut turpiter atrum
> Desinet in piscem, mulier formosa superne,
> Spectatum admissi risum teneatis, amici
> Crediti, Pisones, isti tabulæ fore librum
> Persimilem, cujus, velut ægri somnia, vanæ
> Fingentur species, ut nec pes nec caput uni
> Reddatur formæ."
>
> ARS POETICA, 1—9.

It is possible, however, that the cause of the failure of an author, or of an artist, may be precisely the reverse. His taste may be too far in advance of his contemporaries. In this case they will derive no pleasure from his conceptions, be they ever so perfect, and his works will fall dead from his hand, though ever so deserving of immortality. Painters have perished from want, the least deserving of whose pictures have since commanded a price which would have rendered the artist opulent. The manuscript of Paradise Lost was sold for five pounds; while, at present, the annual profits from the sale of his work would have been a fortune to the patriot-poet. The progress of taste may thus create a demand for a work of the imagination, which did not exist in the life-time of the artist or the author. Homer is said to have begged his bread while living; although, centuries after his death, seven of the most illustrious cities contended for the honor of having been his birth-place.

I have thus far treated of imagination as the power by which we form pictures at will. The object here is simple. The combinations thus formed address themselves to the taste. If they give us pleasure nothing more is demanded, and our object has been attained. If the painter execute a beautiful picture, or the sculptor a beautiful statue, we ask for nothing more. So, if the novelist or the descriptive poet present us with a succession of pleasing or exciting scenes, they may be entirely successful. More commonly, however, in writing, some other design is intermingled with this. Thus, when in earnest composition, we desire to lead the mind of the reader to a given result, some moral or intellectual idea, by the association of resemblance or contrast, suggests an event or object in nature or art to which it is analogous. We turn aside and form an image of the suggested idea. Here, however, our object is two-fold. To introduce an image merely because it was beautiful, might distract attention from the proper course of thought, and thus interfere with our principal design. Besides being beautiful, the image must illustrate and enforce the idea which suggested it. When both of these objects are accomplished, the great end of this form of imagination is attained, and to attain it is one of the most difficult achievements in literary labor. Those comparisons and metaphors which spring so spontaneously from the subject, that it appears impossible to have given utterance to the thought in any other manner, while they irradiate it with brilliant and unexpected light, have commonly been the result of intense labor, and are the product of the most exquisite artistic skill.

It may serve to illustrate this use of the imagination if we present a few examples. Moore, a writer of exuberant fancy, has occasion to allude to the fact, that the affections, by their nature, demand an object on which they may lean, and which they strive to appropriate to themselves. This idea naturally suggests the image of a vine, which can only be sustained by entwining itself around a support. This illustration, however, has been so often employed, that it has become trite. The poet looking more narrowly upon the object, observed that it clung to its support by means of a tendril. Hence he elaborates the following beautiful comparison:

> "The heart, like a tendril, accustomed to cling,
> Let it grow where it will, cannot flourish alone,
> But will lean to the loveliest nearest thing
> It can twine with itself and make closer its own."

Burke visited Versailles very soon after the marriage of Marie Antoinette. He saw what seemed the commencement of a brilliant and happy career, herself the most remarkable object in the court which she adorned. When, in his remarks on the French revolution, he had occasion to refer to this event, her position suggested to his rich and poetic imagination the appearance of the morning star. His mind turned at once towards the beautiful image, and he says, "It is now sixteen or seventeen years since I saw the queen of France, then the dauphiness, at Versailles; and surely never lighted on this orb, which she hardly seemed to touch, a more delightful vision. I saw her just above the horizon, decorating and cheering the elevated sphere she just began to move in, glittering like the morning star, full of life, and splendor, and joy."

Thus Longinus, when he is comparing the eloquence of Demosthenes and Cicero, turns to nature for analogies

By two very striking images he gives us an impression of the peculiar character of each, beyond the power of any mere description. He compares the one to the thunderbolt, which by a single stroke, scatters in splinters the giant oak leaving a second stroke superfluous; the other to a conflagration in a forest, spreading on every side irresistible destruction, furnishing for itself the material which it consumes, and gaining breadth and intensity at every step of its progress.

In these cases a two-fold object is accomplished. In the first place a new and beautiful image is introduced, to which the mind recurs with pleasure; and, secondly, the original idea is rendered vastly more definite and impressive. In this manner we render taste and imagination subservient to reason. We convince men, and make them pleased to be convinced, and thus rarely fail of success.

In the above instances it will be perceived that a visible image is presented to the mind, numerically distinct from the idea to which it owes its origin. In many cases, however, this is not done. The image is only casually and for a moment present to the mind of the writer, yet its presence suggests the use of words which belong rather to it than to the principal thought. Thus, he who resists successfully a host of enemies, naturally suggests the idea of a man making headway against a violent stream. We do not, however, introduce the image, but only use terms suggested by it, and say, he *stemmed the torrent* of opposition. When we think of the origin of our nation, its struggles with the aborigines, its exposure for years to universal destruction, we are naturally led to think of a tree just planted, which any hand may pluck up; or of childhood, which, in its helplessness, any assailant may overcome. We do not express the image in full, but its presence renders it almost impossible for us to speak upon the subject without employing the terms,--

"the germ of a nation," "the planting of a people," "the infancy of the republic," etc. So, when we reflect upon the progress of a great truth, first discovered by a retired philosopher, then modestly brought to the notice of the world, receiving testimony from kindred sciences, until, gaining strength at every step, it is universally acknowledged, we naturally think of a spring, which, rising in the recesses of the mountains, receives tributaries on every side, until it gradually spreads out into a mighty river. Hence, we speak of "ascending to the fountain head of knowledge," of "the current of opinions," of "a flood of evidence," and the like. Instances of this kind are found in abundance in the books on rhetoric.

There is another relation, somewhat different from the above, in which the imagination stands to the art of persuasion. By the imagination we form pictures of objects, scenes, events, characters, and the like. It is a well-known fact that our emotions are excited as truly by a conception as by the reality. We are moved by the incidents of a romance, we love one fictitious character and hate another, we grieve over the distresses of virtue, we rejoice in the punishment of crime, just as though what we read were veritable narrative. And this effect is produced by the conceptions themselves, for our emotions are not quelled even by the reflection that all this is fiction. In this manner, the imagination may be made to address our domestic affections, our passions,—worthy or unworthy,— our conscience, or our piety. Thus, the inimitable parables of our Saviour convey the most sublime and touching lessons of universal truth. The allegory of Bunyan overflows with religious instruction, and exquisite moral sentiment. Homer has instilled into the bosom of millions besides Alexander, the love of war, and the inextinguishable thirst for glory. We thus perceive that the passions and sentiments of mankind, either for good or for evil, are greatly under the power of the imagination.

The manner in which the orator avails himself of this principle is the following. In the attempt to convince men our first appeal is to their reason. We construct a train of argument which proves our propositions to be true, and we present such motives as should induce them to act in the manner we desire. If we are deeply in earnest ourselves, our earnestness will not fail to call into exercise every power of the mind. Notions of things material and immaterial, visible and invisible, related to our subject by all the laws of objective or subjective association, will with various degrees of distinctness rise before us. These various materials the orator uses in such manner as he perceives best adapted to accomplish his purpose. In the words of Shakspeare,

> "The poet's eye, in a fine frenzy rolling,
> Doth glance from heaven to earth, from earth to heaven;
> And, as imagination bodies forth
> The forms of things unknown, the poet's pen
> Turns them to shape, and gives to airy nothings
> A local habitation and a name."
>
> MID-SUMMER NIGHT'S DREAM.

When an image, a picture, or an event, presents itself to the imagination of the orator, better adapted to excite the emotion which he wishes to arouse than the naked statement of his argument, he spreads this picture before the mind with all the graphic power of which he is capable. We are, as I have said, affected by conceptions as truly as by reality. The emotion excited by the accessory is readily transferred to the principal idea, and thus we are sunk in sadness, melted into compassion, aroused to indignation, or inflamed to patriotism, as we listen to the earnest appeals of impassioned eloquence. It is by this combination of the reasoning power with the imagination, that the greatest triumphs of the art of persuasion have been accomplished.

Sometimes the imagination personifies an abstract principle, and, investing it with every element of grandeur and sublimity, awakens emotion which is at once transferred to the principle itself. Curran, in his defence of Rowan,— who had been indicted for the publication of a paper in which he pleaded for universal emancipation,— affirms that his client had claimed nothing more than was the birthright of every Englishman, and that universal emancipation is an essential element of the British Constitution. His imagination, fired with so noble a theme, at once conceives of universal emancipation as the genius presiding over British soil, and he proceeds to clothe this being with every attribute of majesty, thus transferring to the principle which he defends, the sublime emotions which his conception has inspired. "I speak in the spirit of British law, which makes liberty commensurate with and inseparable from the British soil, which proclaims even to the stranger and the sojourner, the moment he sets his foot on British earth, that the soil on which he treads is holy, and consecrated by the genius of universal emancipation. No matter in what language his doom may have been pronounced; no matter what complexion incompatible with freedom an Indian or an African sun may have burned upon him; no matter in what disastrous battle his liberties may have been cloven down; no matter with what solemnities he may have been devoted on the altar of slavery,— the moment he touches the sacred soil of Britain, the altar and the god sink together in the dust, his soul walks abroad in her own majesty, his body swells beyond the measure of the chains that burst from around him, and he stands redeemed, regenerated, and disenthralled, by the irresistible genius of universal emancipation." The effect of such a conception upon a hearer is obvious. He who before looked upon the doctrine as merely a matter of abstract right, now cherishes it as a sublime and most ennobling sentiment, and not only justifies, but honors and venerates the man who promulgates it.

It is obvious that the same means may be successfully used to arouse indignation against a person or an opinion. The same great orator, wishing to discredit the testimony of a government witness, presents before us an image which can awaken no emotion but those of loathsomeness and detestation. Referring to the confinement of this person in the Castle before the trial, he styles him "the wretch that is buried a man, who lies till his heart has time to fester and rot, and is then dug up a witness." He asks, "Have you not seen him, after his resurrection from that tomb, after having been dug out of the region of death and corruption, make his appearance upon the table, the living image of life and death, and the supreme arbiter of both? Have you not marked, when he entered, how the stormy wave of the multitude retired at his approach? Have you not marked how the human heart bowed to the supremacy of his power, in the undissembled homage of deferential horror? how his glance, like the lightning of heaven, seemed to rive the body of the accused and mark it for the grave, while his voice warned the devoted wretch of woe and death,— a death which no innocence can escape, no art elude, no force resist, no antidote prevent? There was an antidote,— a juror's oath; but even that adamantine chain, which bound the integrity of man to the throne of eternal justice, is solved and melted in the breath that issues from the informer's mouth. Conscience swings from her moorings, and the appalled and affrighted juror consults his own safety in the surrender of the victim."

From such instances as these it is easy to perceive the manner in which the orator may make even the imagination to aid in the work of persuasion. He may bring the past the present, and the future, before the mind of the hearer and awaken, by means of it, any train of sympathy that he desires. The pages of ancient and modern eloquence are studded with gems of this kind, illustrating the power of the consummate orator to wield the passions of men at his will, and too frequently, I must confess, to make the worse appear the better reason.

SECTION III. — ON THE IMPROVEMENT OF POETIC IMAGINATION.

IMAGINATION, as we have before said, is the power of combination, — the faculty by which, out of materials already existing in the mind, we form new and original images. Of course, our power of combination must be limited by the amount of the materials on which it may be exerted. Knowledge of all kinds is the treasury from which our power of combination must be supplied. The works of the classical poets of all languages furnish us with a great variety of beautiful imagery. But these poets themselves derived their images from nature. The same book is open to us, and we must study it for ourselves if we would attain to freshness and vigor of imaginative power. He, therefore, who would cultivate this faculty with success, must observe nature in all her infinite variety of phases, by day and by night, in sunshine and in storm, in summer and in winter, on the prairie and by the seaside, and delight himself in the beautiful and the grand wherever they may exist in every aspect of creation around him. Says Imlac, in Rasselas, "I ranged mountains and deserts for images and resemblances, and pictured on my mind every tree of the forest and flower of the valley. I observed with equal care the crags of the rock, and the pinnacles of the palace. Sometimes I wandered along the mazes of the rivulet, and sometimes watched the changes of the summer cloud. To a poet nothing can be useless. Whatever is beautiful and whatever is dreadful must be familiar to his imagination; he must be conversant with all that is awfully vast or elegantly little. The plants of the garden and the animals of the wood, the minerals of the earth and the meteors of the sky, must all concur to store his mind with inexhaustible variety; for every idea is useful for the enforcement or decoration of moral or religious truths, and he who knows most will have most power of gratifying his reader with remote allusions and unexpected instruction."—Rasselas, chap. 10.

The habits of those who have been most distinguished for richness of imagination will, I believe, confirm the truth of these remarks. The poetry of Homer, Shakspeare and Milton, is replete with images which could only have been derived from close observation of nature, as she presented herself to them in their dissimilar walks of life. But we may recur to more recent instances. It is recorded of the distinguished American, whose exquisite portraits of nature have rendered classic the banks of the Hudson, that he once invited a friend to visit his "studies." He led him to some of the mountains that overlook his favorite river, and remarked that he was accustomed to spend whole days, from sunrise to sunset, in those majestic solitudes, observing the never-ceasing changes wrought upon the scenery around him in every hour of the day, and that thus he labored to acquire a familiarity with every appearance of natural beauty. The boundless range of the imagination of Sir Walter Scott has been long acknowledged. Until, however, his memoirs were published, no one would have believed that he depended on minute observation for the materials of his fancy. Before he wrote Rokeby, he visited his friend Mr. Morritt, in whose grounds the scene of the poem was to be laid. "The Monday after his arrival, he said, 'You have often given me the materials for a romance, now I want a good robber's cave and an old church of the right sort.' We rode out and found what he wanted in the ancient slate quarry of Bignal, and the ruined abbey of Eglinstone. I observed him noting down even the peculiar little wild flowers and herbs that accidentally grew around and on the side of a bold crag near his intended cave of Guy Denzil, and could not help saying, that, as he was not to be on his oath in this work, daisies, violets and primroses, would be as poetic as any of the humble plants he was examining. I laughed, in short, at his scrupulousness; but I understood him when he replied that in nature herself no two scenes were exactly alike, and that whoever copied truly what was before his eyes, would possess the same variety in his descriptions, and exhibit, apparently, an imagination as boundless as the range of nature in the scenes which he describes; but whoever trusted to imagination, would soon find his own mind circumscribed and contracted to a few favorite images, and the repetition of these would soon produce that monotony and barrenness which have always haunted descriptive poetry in the hands of any but the *patient worshipper of truth.* 'Besides,' said he, 'local names and peculiarities make a fictitious story look so much better in the face.' In fact, he was but half satisfied with the most beautiful scenery which he could not *connect with some local legend.*"— Lockhart's Life of Scott, vol. 1, page 426.

Nor was Sir Walter Scott a close observer of nature merely in the forms of inanimate creation. His amazing power of delineating every variety of human character may be traced to the same source. When "The Pirate" appeared, every one wondered at the fertile fancy of the Great Unknown, and his power of conceiving so accurately the manners, and even the modes of conversation of the people of the Hebrides. Those, however, who had accompanied the author in his visit to these regions, recognized in many of the most striking passages of the novel an almost literal record of the events which had transpired under their own eyes. We thus perceive that the exhaustless richness of the imagination of the great novelist was derived from a remarkably exact observation of nature and mankind, aided by a memory from which nothing seems to have escaped that could minister to the success of his literary labors.

It is related of Stothard, an eminent English artist, that nothing could exceed the care with which he was in the habit of copying the minutest object in nature, in which he detected any special beauty. "He was beginning to paint the figure of a reclining sylph, when a difficulty arose in his mind how best to represent such a being of fancy. A friend present said, 'Give the sylph a butterfly-wing, and then you have it.' 'That I will,' said Stothard, 'and, to be correct, I will paint the wing from the butterfly itself.' He instantly sallied forth into the fields, caught one of these beautiful insects, and sketched it immediately. * * He became a hunter of butterflies. The more he caught, the greater beauty did he trace in their infinite variety, and he would often say that no one knew what he owed to these insects,—they had taught him the finest combinations in that difficult branch of art, coloring. * * Whenever he was in the fields, the sketch-book and the color-box were brought forth from his pocket, and many a wild plant, with its delicate formation of leaf and flower, was carefully copied on the spot. The springing of the tendrils from the stem, and every elegant bend and turn of the leaves, or the drooping of a bell, was observed and depicted with the utmost beauty." He who observes nature in this manner will never have occasion to complain of deficiency of materials for the use of the imagination.

2. It is evident, however, that the successful use of the imagination does not depend merely upon our power to form pictures. We must do more than this. To conceive of a mountain more vast than another mountain might be considered an exercise of the imagination. But this would excite no emotion either of novelty or sublimity. The theogony of Boodhism is replete with conceptions of this kind, but it awakens no other feeling than that of disgust. If we hope to cultivate this faculty, we must acquire the habit of associating the visible with the invisible, the material with the spiritual. Had Goldsmith, in his celebrated simile, compared the cliff to another cliff, or the village pastor to another village pastor, his conception would have been powerless, and would scarcely have escaped contempt. It is the unexpected coïncidence between a sublime object in nature and the moral elements of a noble character, that presents one of the finest images to be found in the English language. We must learn to associate these two classes of objects together, so that, whatever be the point of observation which the mind occupies, it shall habitually seek for appropriate analogies, and turn in the direction in which they will most readily be found. Thus, it was remarked above of Sir W. Scott, that "he was but half satisfied with the most beautiful scenery which he did not connect with some local legend." Thus, a poetic imagination instinctively sees all things double, blending, in beautiful harmony, thought, sentiment, subjective emotion, with whatever is most analogous to it in the objective world of nature or art.

We may cultivate the imagination by studying attentively works most distinguished for poetical combination

I say studying attentively, in distinction from the mere cursory perusal of classical authors. We must not only read, but meditate upon the beautiful and sublime in thought, until we feel the full force of every analogy; entering into the spirit of the writer himself if we would avail ourselves of the most successful efforts of human genius. We thus acquire the intellectual habits of the masters of human thought. In the language of poetry, we catch a portion of their inspiration, instead of servilely rendering their thoughts in our own language. It is by the diligent study of a few of the best writers, and not the hasty reading of many, that we derive the greatest benefit from the study of the classics of our own or any other country. The late Mrs. Grant, of Laggan, who had acquired uncommon power in the use of the English language, ascribed her success, more than to anything else, to the fact, that for several years in her youth, she was limited in her reading to the Bible, the Dictionary and Milton's Paradise Lost.

But, after all, the study of the classics is mainly beneficial as it enables us to study nature for ourselves, and to discover the fountains from which genius in all ages has been invigorated. When we have learned to associate the seen with the unseen, we have acquired a language which enables us to read with new eyes the inexhaustible volume of the works of God. The world of matter and the world of thought stand up before us in grand parallelism, each reflecting light upon the other. Thus, in the descriptions of Washington Irving, every flower, every animal, every bird, the hill-side, the waterfall, the field and the forest, all seem endowed with life, and almost with reason; they become our companions, and are ever suggesting to us some idea of playful humor or of affecting sentiment. Thus, the most common occurrences awakened in Burns those analogies with human life and manners, which gave occasion to some of his most exquisite odes.

But, lastly, this habit, like any other, can only be cultivated by practice. We must form the combinations of the imagination, if we would learn to form them. We must assiduously cultivate the practice of writing, if we would learn to write well. If we would write well, we must write earnestly, having an end in view, and being deeply interested in the effort to attain it. In this state of mind analogies the more readily suggest themselves. As they arise dimly and flit before us at a distance, we should summon them into our presence, and shape them if possible to our purpose. If they are intractable we must labor the more strenuously, viewing them from different points, and striving to seize upon their analogy with the idea which we wish them to illustrate. We may frequently fail, or at best succeed but imperfectly. This, however, should not discourage us. Nothing was ever exquisitely finished without unwearied and patient labor, and at the cost of repeated and mortifying failure. By untiring and well-directed effort, great things may in the end be accomplished. We must be patient with ourselves, and not expect to do without labor what other men have done in no other manner. Paradise Lost was the work of almost a lifetime. Cowper somewhere informs us that his poetry, which seems to flow without effort, cost him, on an average, half an hour for every line. If incessant toil was necessary to successful effort in minds so highly gifted, ordinary men surely need not to expect to succeed without it.

REFERENCES.

Imagination in general — Stewart, vol. i., chap. 7, sec. 1.
Steps in the process — Stewart, vol. i., chap. 7, sec. 1.

Difference between abstraction in reasoning and imagination — Stewart, vol. i., chap. 4, sec. 1.

Relation of imagination to character — Stewart, vol. i., chap. 7, secs. 4—6.

Manner in which imagination pleases us — Stewart, vol. i., chap. 5, Part 1, sec. 4.

Relation of imagination to fine arts — vol. i., ch. 7, sec. 2

SECTION IV. — PHILOSOPHICAL IMAGINATION.

There is another mode in which the imagination acts, of sufficient importance to deserve particular attention. It may be denominated Philosophical Imagination. With some remarks concerning it we shall conclude the present chapter.

In this form of imagination, as in the preceding, we combine the elements which previously existed in the mind. The elements, however, are in the two cases dissimilar. In poetic imagination, as I have said, we make use of parts of individual wholes, which we combine anew, forming an image at will. In philosophical imagination our elements are single general truths or separate laws of nature, or the various relations of these laws to each other. These we combine into a conception of a new and more complicated law or general philosophical truth.

The conceptions when formed by these separate acts of imagination are also exceedingly unlike. By poetical imagination we form an individual picture, which may be represented to the senses. By philosophical imagination we form not a picture, but an ideal conception of some general truth. By the one we form images, by the other we frame hypotheses. In the one case, the conception is addressed to the taste, and if the emotion of beauty or sublimity is awakened, our object is accomplished. In the other, the taste is wholly neglected, and our appeal is exclusively to the understanding. If the conception is analogous to truth, or if its truth or falsehood can be definitely determined, nothing more is required. The design of the one is to give us pleasure; of the other, to enlarge our knowledge.

The nature of the conceptions which we are considering may be understood by examples. Copernicus, having observed the various established facts respecting the motions of the heavenly bodies, sought to form a conception of their various relations which should account for every fact by bringing it under the control of some understood and acknowledged law. Ptolemy and Tycho Brahe had made the same attempt before, but they imagined laws nowhere existing, and left many of the facts wholly unaccounted for. Copernicus supposed the sun to be the centre of a single system, the stars being themselves centres of systems at infinite distances from it; the earth and planets to move around the sun in orbits nearly circular, and the moon to be a satellite of the earth, revolving around it, and thus with it revolving around the centre of the system. By this conception, all the facts thus far observed were accounted for. Dr. Black, reflecting upon the facts which he had observed respecting the freezing of water, the melting of ice, and the formation and condensation of vapor, sought to form a conception of some general law, which should account for all the phenomena. He was thus led to originate the doctrine of latent heat, and immediately saw that this would fulfil every requirement. Each of these is an instance of philosophical imagination. It is an original conception of some general law, or combination of laws, addressing itself to the understanding, and harmonizing facts otherwise apparently contradictory.

These illustrations appertain to science. But essentially the same exercise of the imagination must be employed in every original design. We can never either think or act efficiently, unless we think or act in conformity with a plan. There must always exist some ideal which we propose either to prove, or else to realize in action. This ideal must be the product of the imagination. The ideal of Paradise Lost was thoroughly thought out before a line of it was written. So the plan of every great enterprise must be matured, and its detail thoroughly arranged, before it can be commenced with any hope of success. We see, then, how important an element of individual or social progress is found in the exercise of this faculty.

It must be apparent that great diversities of character must necessarily arise from the different degrees in which this endowment is bestowed. Some men have no ideals. They form no plans beyond those demanded in the conduct of the ordinary affairs of life. In all things else they follow instinctively the beaten track, and yield with unquestioning submission to the opinions of those who have gone before them. They have no other rule of action than implicitly to follow their file-leader, fully convinced that nothing can be better than what has been, and that a course of action must of necessity be wise, provided it has been for a long while pursued. Others, again, are overburdened with imaginings. They do nothing but form plans, and originate projects which have no foundation in general principles, and must inevitably end in ludicrous failure. Such men, however, rarely attempt to realize their own schemes; they are satisfied with the attempt to force them upon others. They are the builders of castles in the air, ever striving after impossibilities, spending their lives in the fruitless labor of pursuing phantoms and grasping after unsubstantial shadows. That man is rarely endowed who is able to originate ideals resting on truth, and to work them out with that bold sagacity which ensures the possibility of realizing them in action. When such power is united with executive talent, and guided by enlarged benevolence, it designates a man who was created for the benefit of his race.

It is important to observe the relation which a philosophical imagination sustains to the reasoning power in our investigation of truth.

I have said that reasoning is the process by which we pass from the known to the unknown, and thus transform the unknown into the known. Suppose the philosopher to stand on the utmost limits of the known. His reason is prepared either to prove or disprove *any proposition that may be presented.* But there is no proposition presented. There is nothing within the cognizance of the understanding, but on the one side the known, and, on the other, absolute silence and darkness. Reason presents no proposition. Its sole province is either to prove or disprove what is placed before it. None of the other faculties which we have considered can present propositions to the reason, as the matter on which its powers shall be exerted. Hence the necessity of the imagination. Its office is to pass beyond the limits of the known, and form a conception which may be true of something in the unknown. This it presents in the shape of a proposition or a philosophical conception. As soon as this is done, an opportunity is offered for the exercise of the reasoning faculty. There is something now to be proved, and there may be something by which to prove it. We at once endeavor to discover some media of proof which may show a necessary connection between what is known, and this proposition which is, as yet, unknown. Until this connection can be shown, our proposition is a mere suggestion, a theory, an hypothesis. As soon as this connection has been established, what was before hypothesis becomes acknowledged truth, and by just so much is the dominion of science extended.

Or, to express the same idea in another form, experiment,

or the attempt to discover new truth, is nothing more than putting questions to nature. But a question supposes some definite object of inquiry. The answer of nature, if she answer at all, is always either yes or no. Philosophical imagination enables us to put the question in a form capable of a definite answer. It suggests a conception which may be true or false, but which must be either one or the other. By experiment or demonstration we put the question to nature, and receive her answer either affirmative or negative. If the answer be negative, we surrender our proposition as worthless, and the imagination suggests another, and another, until an affirmative answer is received. The work is then accomplished, and a new truth is added to the sum of human knowledge.

Thus the conceptions of Ptolemy and of Copernicus were both mere hypotheses of equal value, until one was proved to be true. The conception of Newton, that the motions of the bodies which compose the solar system are all subjected to the law of gravitation, was a mere hypothesis, a creation of the imagination, until it was scientifically established. He himself so considered it, and I believe never mentioned it until he had proved it. He considered it merely a question which he had put to nature, unworthy of attention until he had received an affirmative answer. At first, he supposed that the answer which he received was negative. Taking for one element of his calculations the length of a degree of the earth, as it had been measured by the French mathematicians, he found that his hypothesis could not be established, and he laid it aside for several years. A new and more accurate measurement was afterwards obtained, which brought to his recollection his almost forgotten computations. He commenced them anew, with more accurate data, and soon arrived at the result which added his name to the brief list of those who must always be remembered.

The same process must be performed in every case where a scientific truth is discovered. The proposition of the squares on the sides of a right-angled triangle was a mere hypothesis to Pythagoras until he had demonstrated its truth.

These illustrations have referred to science. The truth here suggested is, however, of wider application. Thus, the ingenious inventor has become acquainted with some natural law which he believes may be rendered available for the service of man. He must form in his own mind a conception of the manner in which this result may be accomplished. At first a rough draft is present before him. He perceives its imperfections, and labors to correct them. One and another plan suggests itself, until he has before him a whole system of arrangements by which the result may be attained. Months of anxious thought were consumed by Watt and Fulton before they perfected those conceptions, which, when realized in the form of inventions, have revolutionized the manufactures and commerce of the world. The same remark will apply to a military commander, who, before a sword is drawn, must form in his mind the whole plan of a campaign. Thus it is that an act of the imagination must precede every other, when an important truth is to be discovered, or great enterprise to be achieved. We must, first of all, form a conception of what we would do, or prove, and of the means by which it is to be accomplished. We may, it is true, fall short of our ideal; but, except by accident, we cannot go beyond it. Hence this creative power lies at the foundation of all great excellence. Other things being equal, he will certainly arrive at the most eminent success, who is able to take the largest, most comprehensive, and most truthful views of that which he desires to accomplish.

I shall close this chapter by a few suggestions on the mode of improving a philosophical imagination.

It is obvious that this power, to be of any practical value must derive its materials from essential truth. Fancies can never form the elements of a philosophical imagination. We desire to discover truth; but truth can only be discovered by means of truth. The more thoroughly, therefore, we are acquainted with the known, the more easily shall we discover the regions which may be reclaimed from the unknown. He will be more likely to extend the limits of human knowledge who has made himself acquainted with already discovered truth. Newton, at an early age, was familiar with all that was then known of the science of astronomy; and this knowledge pointed out to him the line in which discovery was to be made. Columbus was profoundly learned in the geography of his age. He was intimately acquainted with all that had been discovered of the figure of the earth, and the proportions in which its surface was covered with land and water. This knowledge first suggested to him the idea of a new continent. Had he known of nothing beyond the shores of the gulf of Genoa, his mind could never have formed this magnificent conception, and after-ages would never have heard of the "world-seeking Genoese."

2. I have before remarked the power of generalization to aid in the discovery of truth. We may here observe the mode in which it tends to this result. Every object in nature, every change, every law, is the type of a class more numerous than we are able to conceive. These types are repeated and diversified in infinite variety, but they are all characterized by the same essential elements, unseen, it may be, by the casual observer, but understood by the far-sighted interpreter of nature. He who is able to distinguish the essential elements of a type from its accidental circumstances, trace them out through their various manifestations, and expand them to their widest generalizations, will find his mind replete with conceptions of all possible truth. Gen-

eralization pointed out to Newton those conceptions which led to most of his discoveries, and also gave rise to many suggestions which were not proved to be discoveries until more than a century after his death. In his experiments on light, he observed that the refracting power of different bodies was in proportion to their combustibility, and that the diamond possessed the former power in an unusual degree. Applying this law to this particular case, he was led to conceive that the diamond itself might be combustible. Though a mineral, and the hardest of known substances, he disregarded these accidents, and, boldly generalizing his idea, predicted a discovery which only a few years since has been established.

3. In the works of a great artist, there is always to be observed a manner peculiar to himself, which a true connoisseur will readily detect. We call this peculiarity the style of an author or an artist. It is derived from the intellectual and moral character of the individual, and is that which renders his outward works the index of his inward and spiritual mind. It is natural to suppose that this peculiarity should be apparent in the works of the Creator. There is a speciality in his mode of treating subjects, a style which designates all the works of his hand. He who, by deep and profound reflection on the works of God, has become most familiar with the laws of that which we call nature, and with the relations which these laws sustain to each other, will be the most likely to penetrate into the unknown, and originate those conceptions which lead to the discovery of truth. The further he advances in his investigations, the richer will be the field of discovery that opens before him.

If I may be allowed, I will use an illustration which I once employed when treating on this subject. "Suppose I should present before you one of the paintings of Raphael, and, covering a part of it with a screen, ask you to proceed with the work, and designate where the next lines should be drawn. It is evident that none but a painter ever need make the attempt, and that, of painters, he would be the most likely to succeed who was best acquainted with the genius of Raphael, and had most thoroughly meditated on the manner in which that genius manifested itself in the work before him. So, of the system of the universe. We see but in part; all the rest is hidden from our view. He will, however, most readily discover where *the next lines are drawn* who is most thoroughly acquainted with the character of the author, and has observed with the greatest accuracy the manner in which that character is displayed in that portion of the system which he has revealed to us. It is evident, also, that just in proportion as the work advanced, and portion after portion of the screen was removed, just in that proportion would the difficulty of completing the whole be diminished."— Discourse on the Philosophy of Analogy.

If these remarks be true, they throw some light upon the subject of education. The power of forming conceptions which shall lead to discovery in science, or to the practicable in action, is clearly of vast importance. Can this power be cultivated? On this question there can be no doubt. It steadily increases with the progress of the human mind. We naturally inquire whether the cultivation of this element of intellectual character has been regarded with sufficient attention by those who form our courses of higher education. A large part of the studies which we pursue add very little to our power of forming conceptions of any character whatever. A larger infusion of the study of physical science, not merely as a collection of facts, but as a system of laws, with their relations and dependencies, would be of great value in this respect. We thus study the ideas and conceptions of the Creator. We become acquainted with his manner of accomplishing his purposes, and learn, in some measure, the style of the Author of all things. Surely, this habit of mind must be of unspeakable value to a philosopher in the discovery of truth, or to a man of affairs in devising his plans, since these can only succeed as they are in harmony with the designs of infinite wisdom and benevolence.

> "There 's a Divinity that shapes our ends,
> Rough-hew them as we will."

REFERENCES.

Nature of hypothesis — Reid, Essay 1, chap. 3.
Importance of ideals — Stewart, vol. i., chap. 7, sec. 6.
Certain style in nature's works — vol. ii., chap. 4, sec. 4.

CHAPTER VIII.

TASTE.

SECTION I.—THE NATURE OF TASTE.

We have now considered the most important of those powers of the human mind which may be strictly termed intellectual; that is, which are employed in the acquisition and increase of knowledge. By the use of these we might prosecute our inquiries in every direction, and extend the limits of science, as far as it has been permitted by our Creator. But were this all, we should be deprived of much of the innocent pleasure which accompanies the employment of our faculties, and thus lose an important inducement to mental cultivation. We find that many of the phenomena which we observe, are to us a source of happiness, frequently of an exquisite character. This happiness is bestowed upon us through means of another endowment, which we denominate taste. It is so intimately associated with the faculties purely intellectual, that our view of them would be imperfect did we not bestow upon it at least a brief examination.

Taste is that mental sensibility by which we cognize the beauties and deformities of nature and art,—enjoying pleasure from the one, and suffering pain from the other.

In this definition we speak of taste as a sensibility, rather than a faculty. A faculty is the power of doing something, of putting forth some act, or accomplishing some change. Such is not the nature of taste. It creates no change. It merely recognizes its appropriate object, and is the seat of the subjective emotion to which the object gives exercise. When an object is presented, taste recognizes its æsthetic quality; it is sensible of pleasure or pain, and here its office terminates.

Of the universality of this endowment there cannot be a question. The consciousness of every man bears testimony to its existence. When we look upon a rainbow, we are sensible of an emotion wholly different from that with which we look upon the dark cloud which it overspreads. The cause of the emotion we call the beauty of the rainbow, and the emotion itself we recognize as one of a peculiar character, unlike any other of which we are conscious. We observe that all men are affected by a multitude of objects in the same manner as ourselves. Young and old, cultivated and uncultivated, observe this quality in many of the same objects, and are affected by them in the same manner. It is not asserted, however, that all men recognize the quality of beauty in the same things, or that all men are conscious of the same intensity of æsthetic emotion. These may vary by association and culture. What is here affirmed, is, that all men, in various degrees, are conscious of the pleasure derived from the observation of objects which they term beautiful, and that there are objects, which all men of the same or a similar degree of culture, designate by this epithet. Hence, particular scenes have been, by all observers, denominated beautiful or sublime. Hence, descriptions of localities or events have been transmitted from age to age, from nation to nation, and from language to language, ever awakening the emotions to which they at first owed their celebrity. Anacreon's ode to Spring, Homer's description of a storm in the Ægean, Horace's Fountain of Brundusium and the pleasures of a country life, Milton's Garden of Eden, seem beautiful to all men; and every man, when he applies to them this designation, is certain that he uses language which is perfectly well understood by the men whom he addresses.

It may serve to render our notion of taste more definite if we distinguish it from some of the faculties with which it is liable to be confounded.

Taste is sometimes confounded with imagination. Thus figurative language and works of art in general are sometimes said to be addressed to the imagination. This is not strictly true. The conceptions of the fine arts are created by the imagination of one, and reproduced by the imagination of another. This is, however, only the means to an end. Our ultimate object is to present them to taste, for, unless the taste be gratified, no matter how strongly they may be imagined, the whole object for which they are created, fails.

Imagination is the faculty by which we combine; taste is the sensibility by which we feel. Imagination forms pictures; taste determines whether or not a certain quality exists in them after they are formed. By my imagination, I form a conception of a landscape; by my taste, I decide upon the beauty of the conception which I have created. Imagination creates; taste judges of the creation. Imagination itself is the seat neither of pleasure nor pain; all the pleasure which we enjoy, or the pain which we suffer, from the works of the imagination, is derived from taste.

These endowments may be conferred in very different degree upon the same person. A fertile imagination, as I have before remarked, is sometimes combined with a very imperfect taste. In such cases, an artist will form images in great profusion, but they fail to please, and sometimes disgust us. Such seems to have been the case with Fuseli, a painter of boundless imagination, but frequently combining in his conceptions the sublime and the ridiculous. This peculiar type of character is not uncommonly found in persons passing into insanity, or in that condition of the intellect, sometimes existing through life, in which the individual dwells habitually upon the narrow confine which separates sanity from madness. The late Edward Irving, a man of powerful imagination and withal of commanding eloquence, seems for many of the later years of his life to have exemplified this remark.

It is, however, more common to find men endowed with a correct taste, but deficient in imagination. Such persons, have no power of original creation, while they will decide correctly concerning the creations of others. They are good critics, but bad artists. For a man of so eminent endowments, I think that Addison may be considered much more remarkable for taste than imagination. I think it was the great Lord Chatham who remarked, that few men were endowed with the "*prophetic* eye of taste," that is, who could create for themselves a conception, and judge correctly concerning its beauty, before it had assumed a visible reality. His remark was made with reference to landscape gardening, but it is of general application. We know that almost every man can determine whether grounds are laid out beautifully, while very few men have the talent for so laying them out as to confer permanent pleasure on the beholder. Distinguished success in the fine arts can only be attained by those, in whom both of these endowments are in an eminent degree united. Homer, Milton, Shakspeare, M. Angelo, Raphael, were all thus preëminently gifted.

Taste and conscience have many points both of similarity and difference. Both of them belong to the class of original suggestions. Both take cognizance of a peculiar quality in an external object, and both derive either pleasure or pain from the cognizance of this quality. When I see an act done, I recognize in it the quality of right or wrong, and I am conscious also of a subjective emotion. So I perceive an external object. I observe in it the quality of beauty or deformity, and it awakens its corresponding æsthetic emotion, which is either the pleasure or pain of taste. In these respects they singularly coincide.

In many important particulars, however, they are widely dissimilar.

Conscience observes the peculiar quality which it detects, in nothing but the voluntary actions of responsible beings. Taste discovers the quality which it cognizes, in all objects material and spiritual, in all actions, and in all relations. The one is called into action by the quality of right or wrong; the other by beauty or deformity. The difference between these two qualities is manifest at once to our consciousness. Every one knows that the quality which he recognizes in a rose, and that which he recognizes in an act of noble self-sacrifice, are as different as any two objects within the range of his knowledge. The subjective emotion awakened by conscience is wholly unlike that awakened by taste. The emotion of conscience is complicated with a variety of other emotions, as, for instance, of moral approbation or disapprobation, the conviction of good or ill desert, the assurance of consequences which must result from moral action. The pleasure of taste is simple, terminating in itself, and wholly destitute of any moral emotion. No man can pay even a casual attention to the deliverances of consciousness, without being convinced of the wide difference both objective and subjective, of these two endowments.

The character of taste varies greatly with age. In youth, bright colors and strong contrasts please us. We are incapable of being affected by anything which does not impress us strongly. As we grow older, we derive more pleasure from form, proportion, symmetry and expression. Less dazzling colors, and more subdued contrasts become agreeable, and we behold with indifference what we once admired as beautiful. In this respect, savages resemble children. No color pleases them so much as scarlet, no matter in what form it may become a part of the dress. Their ornaments are such as force themselves upon the notice, without any regard to the relation which they sustain to the character of the wearer, or their harmony with the general impression which he supposes himself to produce. Ornaments, in a more advanced state of society, worn merely to attract attention, or for the display of wealth, manifest the same imperfection of taste which we observe in savages.

SECTION II. — TASTE CONSIDERED OBJECTIVELY. — MATERIAL QUALITIES AS OBJECTS OF TASTE.

THE objects adapted to awaken the emotion of taste are innumerable. The Creator, having bestowed upon us this sensibility, has made the universe around us to minister to its gratification. The heavens above, the earth beneath, all the changes of the seasons, all the products of animal and vegetable life, the gems of the mine and the pearls of the ocean, the ripple of the brook and the thunder of the cataract, the prancing of the war-horse and the bounding of the fawn, the wing of the butterfly and the plumage of the bird of Paradise, the carol of the lark and the wild scream of the eagle, with the ten thousand objects which meet us wherever we look abroad upon the works of God, are intended to awaken the emotions of beauty and sublimity, and fill us with humble adoration of Him who is the Giver of every good and perfect gift.

To attempt an enumeration of all the objects in which we discover beauty or sublimity would be useless. We shall merely indicate some of the classes of objects by which we are thus affected, principally for the sake of directing attention to the æsthetic elements existing in the world around us.

The qualities of external objects which address themselves to the taste are those which are perceived by the eye and the ear.

By the eye we perceive *color*, *form*, and *motion*.

Color as an object of beauty.

Colors may be divided into prismatic and plain.

The prismatic colors are violet, indigo, blue, green, yellow, orange and red. These all are beautiful separately, and, in an eminent degree, when combined. What can be more exquisitively beautiful in color, than the summer rainbow or the solar spectrum? No human being probably ever looked upon them without intense delight.

A distinction may, however, be discovered between the prismatic colors. The first three of the series, in the order in which I have mentioned them, may be denominated grave, the last three gay, while the remaining one, green, possesses a character intermediate between them. Hence, gay colors are most appropriate to festive occasions, while graver are adapted to occasions of solemnity. The dresses of men are generally either black or blue; those of women, of every variety of color, but more commonly gay. How strangely inappropriate would it seem if the dresses of a wedding party or a ball-room, and those of a court of justice were exchanged for each other! The colors of the garden and the field are commonly either white or some modification of red, orange, or yellow. The grave colors are here observed but rarely, and then in their lighter shades; or, by being mingled with the others, they increase their effect by contrast.

The color, however, which is most abundantly spread

over nature is green. It is universally agreeable; it admits of an infinite variety of shade, and, without producing any vivid emotion, harmonizes most happily with all. A grove is an appropriate place for a festive entertainment, and trees are the indispensable ornament of a cemetery, where everything reminds us of the sorrows of separation and the solemnities of eternity.

Color sometimes becomes an element of sublimity as well as of beauty. The sublimity of a thunder cloud is increased by its intense blackness. The deep blue of the heavens, in a clear night, adds greatly to the grandeur of the spectacle which they exhibit.

Many of the objects which we perceive are clothed with plain colors, as gray, brown, dusky, or wood color. These produce in us no emotion, either of pleasure or pain, but they relieve the eye when fatigued by the brilliancy of the prismatic colors. Thus, the earth when not covered with vegetation, the trunks and branches of trees, and most of our domestic animals, are clothed in plain colors.

Form. — We detect the quality of beauty in the simplest varieties of form. Thus, a straight is more beautiful than an irregular line. A curved, irrespective of utility, is more beautiful than a straight line. A spiral line, as of a vine entwined around a column, is more beautiful than either. The stems of flowers that bend gently downward, like the lily of the valley, are more beautiful than those which stand straight and inflexible, like the hollyhock. Every one has remarked the difference between the serpentine bending of a river, seeming to turn at will in any direction which it prefers, and the stiff rectilinearity of a canal, carried through hill and over valley, without a single graceful flexure to vary its monotony.

Angles seem capable of greater beauty than could have been anticipated. The obtuse angle of the roof of a Grecian temple is remarkably agreeable. The whole effect of the edifice would be destroyed by raising the roof to an acute angle. On the contrary, a pyramid standing on the ground, if its apex were obtuse, would appear squat and disgusting. Yet, an acute-angled roof is not always displeasing. To a Gothic edifice it is indispensable, and here an obtuse angle would be intolerable. That this difference exists must, I think, be admitted by all. The reason of it I am unable to discover.

Figure. — Irrespective of utility, figures bounded by curves are more beautiful than those bounded by straight lines. A sphere is more beautiful than a cube, a circle than a square, an ellipse than a parallelogram, a cylindrical than a rectangular column. The lines of beauty in the human countenance are all curves. What could be more shocking than a human face, formed by right lines? The petals of flowers, the outline of fruits, are almost universally bounded by curves.

Regular figures are always more beautiful than irregular. A square is more beautiful than a trapezoid. A room of which the opposite sides are not equal, or a window or door not exact parallelograms, affect us painfully. The roof of a house of which the sides slant unequally is everywhere disagreeable.

Simple forms are generally more beautiful than complex. Every one admires the simple majesty of a Grecian temple, the mere combination of a few right lines and circles. Yet this rule is, by no means, exclusive. The Gothic cathedral is remarkable for its extreme complexity, both of design and ornament, and yet it is preëminently beautiful.

Proportion. — Proportion is a relation existing between the parts of the same figure, as between the length and breadth of a parallelogram, the two diameters of an ellipse, the diameter and height of a column, or the base and elevation of a building. In some of these we discover beauty; in others deformity. A building with no other beauty than that of proportion is frequently decidedly agreeable. It requires the highest skill in an artist to determine beforehand the proportions that shall please all men in all ages. In this respect the taste of the Greeks was preëminent. The canons which they established for the proportions of the several parts of a temple have never been improved. It has been found that no material departure can be made from them without producing deformity.

Uniformity, or perfect similarity of corresponding parts, is another source of beauty. We admire a tree, of which the opposite branches are equal, and project at the same angle from the trunk. A building with equal wings on the opposite sides is frequently beautiful; but if the wings be of different magnitudes, or dissimilar construction, it is considered a deformity. The limbs on the opposite sides of the body, the features on the opposite sides of the face, are uniform; when it is otherwise, we are pained by what seems a monstrosity.

But, while uniformity is pleasing, it is necessary to observe that its opposite, *variety*, is equally pleasing. In objects designed to accomplish the same purpose we expect uniformity; but when the design is different, or even susceptible of modification, we are delighted with variety. We love to see the opposite branches of the same tree uniform; but we also love to see the different trees of a forest or a park marked by every possible variety. We are pleased when the windows of a house, in the same story, and in the same line, are uniform; but we are also pleased to see the windows of different stories dissimilar. If two rows of columns are placed one above the other, in the front of a building, it would be monstrous to see different orders of architecture occupying the same line; but we are pleased when the upper row is of a different order from the lower.

Magnitude has an important influence on all our æsthetic ideas. Vastness is a quality which addresses strongly the sensibility of taste. Every one has felt the emotion of sublimity when travelling through a mountainous country. Hence a region like Switzerland becomes a favorite resort for the lovers of nature from every part of the civilized world. The ocean is at all times a most impressive object, especially when lashed into tempest. Here vastness in magnitude combines with resistless force to create the strongest emotion of sublimity. On the other hand, smallness, if combined with regularity, may be eminently beautiful; but, without regularity, littleness awakens no emotion. An overhanging cliff is sublime; a fragment broken off from it is indifferent; but a delicately-formed crystal found in that fragment may be remarkably beautiful. The temple of Minerva, or Lincoln cathedral, impresses us with awe, and awakens the emotion of sublimity; but an accurate model of either, of a few inches in magnitude, would be exceedingly beautiful. A cascade in a brook is beautiful; but the cataract of Niagara is inexpressibly sublime.

Such are some of the facts relating to beauty of form. It is proper, however, to remark that they are only general, not universal; that is, we frequently observe beauty which seems at variance with the most commonly observed laws. We can never say that, because a particular form or proportion is beautiful, therefore, in different circumstances, a form directly the reverse must be disagreeable. Our notions on these subjects are frequently modified by association. But where no association exists, we observe contradictions which can be harmonized by no laws with which I am acquainted. A remarkable instance of this occurs in the wonderful beauty of the Grecian temple and the Gothic cathedral, of which the canons are precisely the reverse of each other. In deciding upon any form of beauty, our appeal must, therefore, be to the sensitiveness of our common nature. The taste of mankind is here ultimate, and seems frequently to set all our laws at defiance.

Motion as a source of beauty.

Motion is in itself pleasing. A ship under sail is vastly more beautiful than a ship lying at anchor or at the wharf.

But motion is of various kinds, each exhibiting some peculiar form of beauty.

Motion may be either quick or slow. Though both are agreeable objects to the taste, slow motion tends more to the beautiful, and swift to the sublime. The slow sailing of a hawk is beautiful; when pouncing upon his prey, the motion tends to the sublime. The gentle flow of a river is beautiful; when it falls over a precipice it is sublime.

In general, it may be remarked, that no motion is beautiful which betokens toil or violent effort. The nearer it approaches to utter unconsciousness of exertion, other things being equal, the more beautiful it becomes. Every one must have observed the æsthetic difference between the toilsome gait of a rhinoceros, or an elephant, and the elastic bounding of a deer. The motion of a vessel under sail, for this reason, is, I think, more beautiful than of one propelled by steam.

Motion in curves is more beautiful than that in straight lines, both because of the greater beauty of the curved line, and because curvilinear motion indicates less effort. For these reasons, the motion of a fish in the water has always seemed to me remarkably beautiful. The waving of a field of grain, presenting an endless succession of curved lines, advancing and receding with gentle motion, uniform in the midst of endless variety, has always seemed to me one of the most beautiful objects in nature. On the contrary jolting and angular motion always displeases us. How different is the effect produced by the motion of one man on crutches, and of another on skates!

Ascending motion is more graceful than descending, if it do not betoken effort. The ascent of a rocket is more beautiful than its descent, especially if it ascend in a curved line. For this reason a jet d'eau is vastly more beautiful than a waterfall of the same volume. Ascending motion in spiral lines is exceedingly beautiful, as for instance, the ascent of a hawk, as it moves slowly upward, in oft-repeated circles.

It is manifest that many objects derive their power to please us from a single one of these qualities. Thus, the evening cloud displays rarely any other beauty than that of color. Others combine several of them, conducing to the same result. Thus the rainbow unites beauty of color with beauty of form. The greater the number and the more intense the degree in which any object unites these several qualities, the more impressive does it become, and the more universally is it selected by poets and artists for æsthetic effect. Thus the human form, especially the countenance, combining beauty of color, form, motion, and expression, is always considered the most remarkable object in nature, and is selected by painters and sculptors, as the finest subject on which their art can be employed.

Objects of taste addressed to the ear, or beauty of sound.

That sound is a source of beauty, independently, and especially in combination with other objects, will be readily granted by every lover of nature. How greatly is the effect of a summer's landscape increased by the singing of birds!

Sounds differ in their degree of loudness.

Loudness awakens the emotion of sublimity, as in the instance of a peal of thunder or the roar of a cataract. Soothing sounds, as the singing of birds, the hum of bees, the rustling of the trees of a forest, add greatly to the effect of a summer's landscape. Low, continuous sound tends to repose, and harmonizes with all our ideas of the peace and quietness of a country life. These circumstances are beautifully combined by Virgil, in describing the peace of Italy, in contrast with the civil wars by which it had been so lately devastated :

"Sepes
Hyblæis apibus florem depasta salicti,
Sæpe levi somnum suadebit inire susurro
Hinc, alta sub rupe, canit frondator ad auras,
Nec tamen intereà, raucæ, tua cura, palumbes,
Nec gemere aeria cessabit turtur ab ulmo."

1 Bucolic.

So Shakspeare, alluding to the power of gentle sounds

"That strain again ; it had a dying fall.
O, it came o 'er my ear like the sweet south
That breathes upon a bank of violets,
Stealing and giving odor."

Twelfth Night, Act 1, Scene 1.

But, while loudness of sound awakens the emotion of sublimity, it must not be supposed that its opposite, absolute silence, is unimpressive. Deep silence is frequently eminently sublime, especially when it occurs in the intermission of the roar of the tempest, or in preparation for the awful catastrophe of a battle. Campbell, in his "Battle of the Baltic," illustrates this fact in these remarkable lines:

As they drifted on their path,
There was silence deep as death,
And the boldest held his breath
For a time.
'Hearts of oak !' our captain cried, and each gun,
From its adamantine lips,

Spread a death-shade round the ships,
Like the hurricane eclipse
Of the sun."

The late Dr. Jeffries, of Boston, in the narrative of his passage across the English Channel with Montgolfier, in a balloon, has the following striking remark:

"Amidst all the magnificent scenes around me and under me, nothing at the time more impressed me with its novelty than (if I may be allowed to use the expression) the awful stillness or silence in which we seemed to be enveloped, which produced a sensation that I am unable to describe, but which seemed at the time to be a certain kind of stillness (if I may so express it) that could be felt."— Narrative of Two Aerial Voyages, page 52.

Sound may be either lengthened or abrupt. Continuous sound is grave; abrupt sound is exciting. We all have observed the difference between the long, reëchoed bellowings of distant thunder, and the sudden rattling reverberation of thunder near at hand. Music with few or distant intervals harmonizes with a melancholy train of thought. Music with rapid and frequent intervals is cheering and animating. Every one knows the different effects of a dirge and a quick-step, or of the same air played in quick and in slow time.

The effect of music on our emotions is thus admirably described by Cowper:

" There is in souls a sympathy with sounds,
And as the mind is pitched, the ear is pleased
With melting airs or martial, brisk or grave.
Some chord in unison with what we hear
Is touched within us, and the heart replies.
How soft the music of yon village bells,
Rolling at intervals upon the ear
In cadence sweet! now dying all away,
Now pealing loud again, and louder still,

Clear and sonorous as the gale comes on
With easy force it opens all the cells
Where memory slept."
TASK, Book 6.

I have thus far spoken of sounds which produce an æsthetic effect upon us by themselves. It is, however, probable that sounds depend more upon association for their effect, than either color or form. The effect of music is greatly increased by uniting it with appropriate words. The most common air, if associated with the remembrance of home and country and friends, becomes deeply affecting. I have heard the Swiss herdsman's song, and it seemed to me dull and monotonous, without any power of appeal to the heart. Yet it is said to effect these mountaineers, when in a foreign land, even to weeping; so that the playing of it is forbidden in the armies with which they are in service.

It is on this account that common sounds, nay, sounds in themselves displeasing, become, under peculiar circumstances, delightful. There is nothing intrinsically pleasing in the lowing of cattle; when heard close at hand, it is disagreeable. Yet I have heard seamen speak with deep feeling of the delight with which they listened to these sounds, when, after a long voyage, they first heard them from their native shore. In a word, anything pleases us which recalls deeply-affecting reminiscences; and music possesses this power in a remarkable degree. Cowper expresses this truth with exquisite taste in the following passage:

" Nor rural sights alone, but rural sounds
Exhilarate the spirit, and restore
The tone of languid nature. Mighty winds,
That sweep the skirt of some far-spreading wood
Of ancient growth, make music not unlike
The dash of ocean on his winding shore.
Ten thousand warblers cheer the day, and one

The livelong night. Nor these alone, whose notes
Nice-fingered art must emulate in vain,
But cawing rooks, and kites, that soar sublime
In still repeated circles, screaming loud,
The jay, the pie, and e'en the boding owl,
That hails the rising morn, have charms for me.
Sounds inharmonious in themselves, and harsh,
Yet heard in scenes where peace forever reigns,
And only there, please highly, for her sake."

TASK, Book 1.

SECTION III — OBJECTS OF TASTE. IMMATERIAL QUALITIES.

THERE can be no doubt that we discover in the creation around us much that is beautiful which cannot be referred to any material quality. There are various attributes of human beings which do not discover themselves to the senses. There are various affections of our spiritual nature which we are able to contemplate distinctly by themselves. These affections are capable of producing in us the emotion of beauty and sublimity, or of deformity and meanness. A brief consideration of some of these is necessary to the completion of the plan which we have proposed.

The order in which these emotions arise is probably the following. We first become conscious of the emotion of beauty from the contemplation of material objects. Colors and sounds first delight us; then form and motion. But, as our minds assume a subjective tendency, we think of the actions, the motives, the governing principles, and characters of men. We find that some of these awaken in us an emotion exceedingly analogous to that of which we were conscious when we observed the beautiful and sublime in external nature. We give to both classes of emotion the same name, and designate the objects which awaken them by the same epithet. Thus, we speak of a beautiful flower, and of a beautiful sentiment, of a sublime scene and a sublime action, employing the same term to designate the æsthetic quality in the object, whether it be material or immaterial.

It may, however, be well to observe, in passing, that the emotion of taste, when we contemplate a moral action, is different from the moral emotion. In the latter case, we look upon it as right or wrong; as fulfilling or violating obligation; as a matter for moral approbation or disapprobation, and as involving consequences greater than we can adequately conceive. In this case, we merely contemplate its æsthetic quality, as something which excites within us the emotion of the beautiful or sublime, without any consideration of its merit or demerit, or any view of its consequences either here or hereafter. Hence it is that there are many more admirers of goodness than good men. A profane and impious poet may discourse eloquently on the character of a holy God, as Rousseau paid a striking tribute to the moral sublimity of the death of the Redeemer.

I proceed to mention a few examples of immaterial qualities which seem to possess remarkable æsthetic power.

Unusual power of intellect, successfully displayed, presents an object singularly pleasing to the taste. Newton, in his study, arriving at the result of his labors, and overwhelmed with the consciousness that he had revealed to mankind the mechanism of the universe; Milton, in poverty and blindness, working out his immortal epic; Gibbon, seated on the ruins of the Coliseum, resolving to develop the cause of the decline and fall of the Roman empire,—are illustrations of this form of sublimity.

High intelligence, leading to important and self-reliant action, presents a still more impressive object of the spiritually sublime. A general, on the eve of a great battle, prepared for a contest on which vast issues depend, as Napoleon at the battle of the Pyramids; Columbus meditating the discovery of America, and fully resolved to devote his life to the search for an unknown world; Clarkson resolving to lay aside every other object, and live thereafter only for the abolition of the African slave-trade,—may all be cited as instances of this kind.

The social and domestic affections, when conspicuously displayed, furnish many illustrations of beauty and sublimity. The affection of the parent for his prodigal son, in the inimitable parable of our Lord; the Roman daughter nourishing from her own breast her father who was condemned to die by starvation; the lament of David over Saul and Jonathan, and his bitter wailing over his son Absalom; the parting of Paul from the elders at Miletus,—are all illustrations of the power of affection to create the emotion of the beautiful, and they have been frequently used for this purpose by poets and artists.

Still more impressive are the exhibitions of high moral excellence.

The noble bearing of the three Hebrews, when threatened with instant death unless they would worship the golden image of the king of Babylon, is a fine illustration of the morally sublime. "O, Nebuchadnezzar, we are not careful to answer thee in this matter. If it be so, our God whom we serve is able to deliver us, and he will deliver us out of thy hand, O king! But if not, be it known unto thee, O, king, that we will not serve thy Gods, nor worship the golden image which thou hast set up."

The description by Horace of a man of steadfast purpose and incorruptible integrity, has for ages called forth the admiration of scholars:

> "Justum et tenacem propositi virum
> Non civium ardor prava jubentium,

Non vultus instantis tyranni,
Mente quatit solida, neque Auster,
Dux inquieti turbidus Hadriæ;
Nec fulminantis magna manus Jovis.
Si fractus illabatur orbis,
Impavidum ferient ruinæ."

Lib. 3. Carmen 3. 1–8.

An act of supposed patriotism is thus celebrated by Akenside:

"Look then abroad through nature, to the range
Of suns and stars and adamantine spheres,
Wheeling unshaken through the void immense,
And speak, O man! does this capacious scene
With half that kindred majesty dilate,
Thy strong conception, as when Brutus rose
Refulgent from the stroke of Cæsar's fate,
Amid the crowd of patriots, and his arm
Aloft extending, like Eternal Jove
When guilt brings down the thunder, called aloud
On Tully's name, and shook his crimson steel,
And bade the father of his country hail!
For lo! the tyrant prostrate in the dust,
And Rome is free again."

I adduce this passage without any sympathy with its ethical sentiments, and merely as an example of the power of supposed patriotism to awaken emotion. It is a conspicuous instance of the power of love of country to ennoble, for the moment, assassination itself. How different is the type of moral sublimity revealed to us in the New Testament! For example, I need only refer to the dying prayer of Jesus, "Father, forgive them, for they know not what they do!" The reply of our Lord to the soldier who smote him has always seemed to me eminently sublime: "If I have done evil, bear witness of the evil; but if well, why smitest thou me?"

The effect produced upon us either by material qualities or immaterial energies is greatly increased by contrast. A large object seems larger, and a small object smaller, when placed in juxtaposition. A beautiful form appears more beautiful by contrast with deformity. Lofty disinterestedness is more sublime when opposed to meanness, and bravery when contrasted with pusillanimity. Of this principle artists of every profession, wherever it is possible, avail themselves. We thus see youth and old age introduced into the same group, in an historical painting, wildness and cultivation into the same landscape. So, in romance and tragedy, characters of the most opposite elements are brought into contact, to deepen the impression produced by both. Thus, Brutus and Cassius, Othello and Iago, Duncan and Macbeth, add greatly to the impression of each other. Instances of the same kind may be given without number.

It is universally observed that the external indications of the benevolent affections, or of those which we recognize as beautiful, are themselves beautiful; while those which indicate the malevolent affections are displeasing. Hence, we frequently meet a person whose countenance, without a single beautiful feature, is remarkably agreeable, simply by reason of the expression. In other cases, when the features themselves are beautiful, they fail to impress us favorably, because they are disfigured by the indications of meanness. selfishness, passion, or treachery. Hence it is that moral and intellectual cultivation have so powerful an effect in improving the human countenance. It is only when the material and spiritual elements are united, that we observe the highest style of human beauty. We can thus readily distinguish the works of a first-rate artist. A sculptor or a painter may be able to delineate a form of faultless proportions, and yet only attain to mediocrity in his profession. He who to skill in delineation adds the power of expressing the indications of intellectual and moral character, is alone destined to the immortality which the arts of design can confer. It is one thing to copy a model, and is a very different thing to form a conception of character, and, then, to represent it in marble, or on canvas, so that we reproduce the same conception in the mind of every beholder.

Some of the innocent and painful emotions, as sorrow, grief, regret, disappointment, may be agreeable objects of taste, in their external manifestations. Here, however, a cautious line of discrimination must be observed. As soon as emotions become intense, they cease to be pleasant to the beholder. Thus, the external indication of sadness may render a beautiful countenance more attractive; but the distortion produced by convulsive grief is unpleasant. Hence, he who is overwhelmed by calamity, and is obliged to give utterance to his emotion in sobs and weeping, covers his face, or retires from the view of others. The same remark, in fact, applies to all the emotions. A smile may be pleasing in an historical picture, but a broad grin, or wide-mouthed laughter, would be intolerable. In reference to this subject, Dr. Moore, in his "View of Society and Manners in Italy," objects to the conception of the celebrated group of Laocoon. He affirms that the physical agony expressed in the contortion of the features and limbs of the parent and children, as they writhe within the folds of the serpents, is too intense to be contemplated without positive pain, and that, therefore, the effect of the group is distressing and, of course, unpleasant. The artist has exhibited his conception with admirable skill; the fault is in the conception itself.

SECTION IV.—THE EMOTION OF TASTE; OR TASTE CONSIDERED SUBJECTIVELY.

THE emotion of taste, or that state of mind of which we are conscious when we contemplate any object of unusual æsthetic power, is exceedingly simple. Every one knows what it is, yet it is impossible to analyze, and difficult to describe it. It is not connected by necessity with any result. Sometimes we may desire to possess the object, as, for instance, a picture that pleases us; but this desire is by no means universal. Who ever desired to own the falls of Niagara? Nor does the possession of a beautiful object increase the pleasure which it gives us. The traveller through a beautiful country enjoys the scenery around him just as much as if it were his own.

The emotion of gratified taste is eminently pleasing. To be assured of this, we need only observe the sacrifices which men undergo to obtain it. We travel hundreds of miles, at great personal inconvenience, and are satisfied if, at the end, we can look upon a magnificent cataract, or spend a few days amid scenes of picturesque beauty. What millions have been attracted to Italy to survey the creations of art which adorn the crumbling tomb of that "lone mother of dead empires!" And, if we look upon the world around us, we shall be surprised at the vastness of the expense incurred in the gratification of taste. We do not spend much on mere specimens of art, but when anything is demanded by utility, we are willing to treble the cost, if it also gratifies our love for the beautiful.

The emotion of taste, like the objects which excite it, is of a twofold character — that produced by the beautiful, and that by the sublime. The distinction easily unfolds itself to our consciousness. Every one knows that the emotion produced by a parterre of flowers, a jet d'eau, is unlike that produced by the sight of the ocean in a storm, a magnificent mountain, the Parthenon of Athens, or the pyramids of Egypt. Both are emotions of taste. Both are eminently sources of pleasure. The character of the one may, however, be readily distinguished from the other.

No sharp line of discrimination can, however, be drawn between the classes of objects which give rise to these different emotions. In many cases, they insensibly blend with each other. A river at its commencement, and for a portion of its course, is simply beautiful. When it pours itself into the ocean, like the Mississippi or Amazon, it becomes an object of sublimity. It may be, however, impossible to designate the point at which one quality ends, and the other begins. The same is true of immaterial qualities. An act of kindness, compassion, or gratitude, is generally beautiful, while a conspicuous act of justice is sublime. These, however, may be reversed. A trifling or graceful act of justice may be beautiful; an act of godlike compassion, as the death on the cross, is passing sublime.

We may observe a difference in the character of these emotions, and in the sentiments with which they harmonize. The emotion of beauty is calm, moderately exhilarating, attractive, and harmonizes with all the bland and social affections, whether grave or gay. The emotion of the sublime is exciting, engrossing, filling the mind with awe, sometimes with terror, and associating with grave resolves and momentous and soul-stirring action. Thus ornament may increase the hilarity of a ball-room, or it may add deeper impressiveness to the sadness of the tomb. The sublime may add intensity to the emotion which impels us to heroic achievement, or, overpowering all our faculties, may overwhelm us with sudden amazement.

The emotion of taste is commonly transient. Its object being to give us pleasure, the impression which it creates is easily effaced by collision with the sterner realities of life. It is, in its nature, evanescent. An object that pleases us to-day, will affect us less powerfully to-morrow, and, if it be continually in our presence, will soon cease to affect us at all. Persons living in the vicinity of he most magnificent scenery, view it without emotion. From this fact, the artist finds it necessary to employ every means in his power to deepen the impression which he designs to create. The manner in which this is done must depend upon the means at his disposal. The painter, in his representation, is limited to a single moment of time. In forming his conception, he must, therefore, arrange every circumstance of his picture, so that it shall on that instant conduce to the principal effect. In language, we are not thus limited, and may accomplish our result by means of repeated impressions. As, however, the mind affected by one object would be less affected by another precisely similar, it becomes necessary to arrange every circumstance climactically, so that the emotion first excited may be rendered at every step more intense. The effect of such an arrangement is beautifully illustrated by Shakspeare in the following passage:

> "Knew ye not Pompey? Many a time and oft
> Have ye climbed up to walls and battlements,
> To towers and windows, yea to window tops,
> Your infants in your arms, and there have sat
> The livelong day, in patient expectation,
> To see great Pompey pass the streets of Rome.
> And when you saw his chariot but appear,
> Have you not made an universal shout,
> That Tiber trembled underneath his banks,
> To hear the replication of your sounds
> Made in his concave shores?"
>
> JULIUS CÆSAR, Act 1, Scene 1.

For the same reason novelty adds greatly to the power of an æsthetic conception. The most beautiful object by repetition becomes incapable of moving us. Hence we are specially gratified with a new illustration, an unexpected resemblance or contrast, or any object, either of beauty or sublimity, which meets us for the first time. Hence the power of a mind that looks upon a subject by its own light, and discovers new relations that have escaped the observation of others. Such writers, even with many defects, will always please; while he who is content to be an imitator, may be faultlessly correct, and inimitably proper, but he comes to us with a thrice-told tale, and leaves us wholly unaffected.

Wit is generally mentioned as one of the objects by which the emotion of taste is excited. It seems to me but partially connected with the subject, and therefore cannot here claim any separate discussion. In the place of any analysis of its nature and effects, I shall merely quote the following passage from Dr. Barrow as the best description of wit and its modes of affecting us with which I am acquainted.

"Sometimes it lieth in pat allusion to a known story, or in seasonable application of a trivial saying, or in forging an apposite tale: sometimes it playeth in words and phrases, taking advantage from the ambiguity of their sense, or the affinity of their sound: sometimes it is lodged in a sly question, in a smart answer, in a quirkish reason, in a shrewd intimation, in cunningly diverting or cleverly retorting an objection: sometimes it is concealed in a bold scheme of speech, in a tart irony, in a lusty hyperbole, in a startling metaphor, in a plausible reconciling of contradictions, or in acute nonsense: sometimes a scenical representation of persons or things, a counterfeit speech, a mimical look or gesture passeth for it: sometimes an affected simplicity, sometimes a presumptuous bluntness, giveth it being: sometimes it riseth from a lucky hitting upon what is strange, sometimes from a crafty wresting obvious matter to the purpose: often it consisteth in one knows not what, and springeth up one knows not how. Its ways are unaccountable and inexplicable, being answerable to the rovings of fancy and the windings of language. It is, in short, a manner of speaking out of the plain way, which, by a pretty and surprising uncouthness in conceit or expression, doth affect and amuse the fancy, stirring in it some wonder, and breeding some delight thereto. It raiseth admiration, as signifying a nimble sagacity of apprehension, a special felicity of invention, a vivacity of spirit and reach of wit more than vulgar. It seemeth to argue a rare quickness of parts, that one can fetch in remote conceits applicable; a notable skill, that he can dexterously accommodate them to the purpose before him, together with a lively briskness of humor not apt to dash those sportful flashes of the imagination. It also procureth delight by gratifying curiosity with its rareness or semblance of difficulty (as monsters not for their beauty but their rarity; as juggling tricks, not for their use but their abstruseness, are beheld with pleasure), by diverting the mind from its road of serious thoughts, by instilling gayety and airiness of spirit in way of emulation or complaisance; and by seasoning matters, otherwise distasteful or insipid, with an unusual and thence grateful tang." — Sermon against Foolish Talking and Jesting.

A few remarks on the improvement of taste may be appropriate to the close of this chapter.

I have said above that taste is that sensibility by which we recognize the beauties and deformities of nature and art, deriving pleasure from the one, and suffering pain from the other. From this definition it is evident that the function of taste is two-fold; first, it discriminates between beauty and deformity, and, secondly, it is a source of pleasure and pain. Cultivation improves it in both these respects. It renders us better capable of distinguishing between beauty and deformity in their more delicate shades of difference; and, as this power of discrimination is improved, the pleasure which we derive from gratified taste becomes more exquisite and enduring, and the pain which we suffer from deformity is, in a corresponding degree, increased.

When we speak of the improvement of taste, the question

naturally arises, How may we know when our taste is improved? The taste of men varies greatly under different circumstances. The taste of childhood differs from that of youth, and that of youth from manhood. The taste of savages in all ages is unlike that of civilized man. And among nations that have made the greatest progress in civilization and refinement, we find that there have been great diversities in this respect. The taste of Egypt was exceedingly different from that of Greece. The taste of Greece and Rome were by no means identical. Neither of them bore any resemblance to the taste of India. Or, if we draw nearer to the present time, the taste of the Mahommedans was very dissimilar to that of the Catholics of the middle ages. And we perceive corresponding difference at the present day. The taste in architecture of France, Germany, Italy, and Great Britain, is by no means identical. The same remarks apply to poetry and the other fine arts.

Hence the question has frequently arisen, Is there any standard of taste? Are there any canons to which we may appeal when a difference of opinion exists, or by which we may be guided in our attempts at self-cultivation? It may be worth while briefly to examine this question.

If by a standard of taste be meant a system of arbitrary rules, established by reasonings or dictated by authority, to which all the works of art must conform, and by reference to which their merit must be decided, it is manifest that no such standard exists. Who ever established it? By what course of reasonings were its principles demonstrated? Who was ever competent to decide for all men, at all times; and to whose decisions have men ever yielded implicit submission? It is obvious that such a standard does not and cannot exist.

But, if, by a standard of taste, it be meant that on a great variety of questions in æsthetics there is a general agreement of mankind in all ages, and among all nations, of the same or of similar degrees of culture, and that this agreement having been observed, many general laws may be deduced from it by which the artist may be safely governed, and by which we may all test the accuracy of our individual decisions, then we must answer this question in the affirmative. No one will doubt that some forms, colors, and proportions, are more agreeable to mankind than others; that some positions are graceful, and others awkward; that some modes of thought and expression give us pleasure, and others give us pain. If mankind are made with similar faculties, such must be the result. Although nations may differ widely in their decisions at a particular time yet intercourse with each other and progress in civilization tend to unanimity of opinion even on questions upon which there existed at first great diversity. Thus, when Greece and Rome came into contact, Greece asserted her superiority over her conqueror, and every Roman artist and poet copied with even servile fidelity the models which were brought from the city of Pericles. It is the object of the artist to observe these general facts, not for the purpose of giving laws to nature, but of recording the laws which nature has herself established. Just so far as these laws have been discovered, they become the standard to which the artist must conform if he desires to succeed, that is, to please humanity.

It would seem, then, that in our inquiries on this subject we are merely determining a question of fact. We ask what æsthetical forms have been found universally to please mankind, or rather that portion of mankind whose circumstances have been favorable to a correct decision? When this question has been answered, we are to receive it as an ultimate fact. That which human nature pronounces to be beautiful is beautiful to man, and that which it pronounces deformed is deformed. We may, it is true, with advantage frequently analyze a complicated decision, in order to determine with more accuracy the particular elements on which it is founded, and thus arrive at a simpler and more general law. Thus, the voice of mankind has pronounced the epic of Homer to be beautiful. This decision cannot be questioned. We may, however, examine it, to determine the qualities on which this decision is founded. There is the general plot, the delineation of character, the description of events, the vivacity of dramatic action, the language and rhythmical power, the machinery or intervention of the gods, the quarrels of the chiefs, the catalogue of the ships, the lists of the slain, the slaughtering of animals, and the culinary arrangements of the chiefs. We may certainly analyze this complex variety of elements, and determine which is essential and which injurious to the general effect. In this manner we are enabled to ascertain what it is that pleases mankind, and thus form a more definite idea of the standard of poetic excellence.

Our labor here, however, consists mainly in analysis. We may examine separately the various elements of success or failure, but we cannot reason from them with any decided confidence. Because a particular form is beautiful in one position, we cannot determine that it will please under all circumstances. Because a particular combination of form is beautiful, we cannot determine what will be the effect of an entirely opposite combination. An artist of originality may repose a reasonable confidence in his own sensibilities, but he can never be sure that a conception will please, until he has submitted it to the judgment of mankind.

Writers on this subject, of distinguished ability, have contended that there is no established relation between the human sensibility and the external world, by which we are entitled to say that anything is in itself beautiful. They affirm that our idea of beauty is merely derived from association. In reply to this assertion, it may be remarked that our own consciousness testifies clearly to the character of the emotion of taste. It may clearly be distinguished from every other emotion, and also from every act of the imagination, the reason, or any of our other faculties. It differs from them all in its nature, its origin, and its results. If, then, it be an original and peculiar affection of the mind, its existence need not and cannot be accounted for by association. As Mr. Stewart very appositely remarks: "The theory which resolves the whole effect of the beautiful into association, must necessarily involve that species of paralogism to which logicians have given the name of reasoning in a circle. It is the province of association to impart to one thing the agreeable or disagreeable effect of another; but association can never account for the origin of a class of pleasures different in kind from all the others we know. If there was nothing originally pleasing or beautiful, the associating principle would have no material on which to operate."

As to the manner in which this faculty may be improved, but little can be said in addition to what was remarked when treating of the imagination. Both faculties are employed upon the same objects, and the mode of cultivation is in most respects the same. A few brief suggestions are all that I shall here offer.

It is universally admitted that all the forms of nature possess some portion of æsthetic power. As we become familiar with these, and hold communion with nature in all her aspects, whether grave or gay, beautiful or sublime, we cultivate our æsthetic sensibility, we more readily recognize the beautiful, and rejoice in it with more exquisite emotions.

We shall also derive great benefit from studying with care classical productions in the various departments of the fine arts. When an artist has been eminently successful, he has united in one conception all the elements of the beautiful within his power, excluding from it all that could distract the attention or diminish the effect. Hence, if we comprehend his design, understand his mode of developing it, and meditate upon his work, until we sympathize with his sentiments and share in his enthusiasm, our taste will become in some measure assimilated to his. He who has caught the inspiration of Raphael must possess already the spiritual element of a painter; and he who can feel the sentiments which inspired Milton and Shakspeare, must be endowed with some portion at least of poetic genius.

If, however, we desire to improve our taste, we must do it not by the indiscriminate study of models, but only by the contemplation of the most eminent. We must confine ourselves to the most faultless models if we would cultivate our love for the beautiful. If the student would form a classical style, and acquire a discriminating love for literary excellence, he must limit his reading to the works of those whom the suffrages of humanity have numbered among the masters of thought and expression. A vast amount of miscellaneous reading may enable us to abound in small knowledge and flippant criticism. It is only by communion with those whose works "the world will not willingly let die," that we learn to emulate their intellectual achievements, and become the instructors of our fellow-men.

In studying the works of others for our own improvement, one caution is however to be observed. They are the productions of fallible men like ourselves. We are, therefore, to bring to the examination of every work of art, the exercise of a calm, discriminating judgment, prepared to distinguish beauty from deformity wherever they exist. We must exercise our own taste, if we would cultivate our sensitive nature. When we study the works of others to awaken our own sensibilities, to correct our errors, and to arouse ourselves to emulation, we develop our own faculties. But, if we study only to bow before a master as we would worship our Creator, we become servile copyists and degraded idolaters. It is not impossible that our veneration for the ancients has in some degree produced this effect upon modern literature. I have always been struck with the remark of one of the Italian masters, who, when a work of an earlier artist was spoken of with servile adoration, turned away and said, "I too am a painter." To study the works of others that we may be able to equal them, cultivates the power of original creation. To study them only that we may learn how to do feebly, what they have done well, is fatal to all manly development, and must consign an individual or an age to the position of despairing and wondering mediocrity.

APPENDIX.

NOTE TO PAGES 101, 102.

It is stated in the text that, under certain abnormal circumstances, we become capable of perceptions, or cognitions, without the aid of the organs of sense. While I was lecturing on this subject, a few years since, one of my pupils informed me of some facts, of a very decided character, in possession of his brother, J. M. Brooke, Esq., of the United States Navy. At my request he wrote to his brother, stating my wish for information. Mr. Brooke soon after very kindly wrote to me as follows:

WASHINGTON, Oct. 27, 1851.

SIR: It affords me pleasure to comply with your request, made through my brother William, relative to some experiments performed on board of the U. S. steamer Princeton, in the latter part of the year 1847; she being then on a cruise in the Mediterranean. Nathaniel Bishop, the subject of the experiments, was a mulatto, about twenty-six years of age, in good health, but of an excitable disposition. The first experiment was of the magnetic or mesmeric sleep, which overpowered him in thirty minutes from the commencement of passes made in the ordinary way, accompanied with a steadfast gaze and effort of will that he should sleep.

In this state he was insensible to all voices but mine, unless I directed or willed him to hear others; he was also insensible to such amount of pain as one might inflict without injury, that is, what would have been pain to another. He would obey my directions to whistle, dance, or sing. When aroused from this sleep he had no recollection of what occurred while in it. That such an influence could be exerted I was already aware, having previously witnessed satisfactory experiments. Of clairvoyance I had never been convinced; indeed, considered it nothing more than a sort of dreaming produced by the will of the operator. I became aware of its truth rather through accident than design.

It happened one day that some one of my brother officers asked a question which the others could not answer. Bishop, who had been a few moments before in a mesmeric sleep, gave the desired information, speaking with confidence and apparent accuracy. As the information related to something which it seemed almost impossible to know without seeing, we were very much surprised. It struck me that he might be clairvoyant; and I at once asked him to tell me the time by a watch kept in the binnacle, on the spar or upper deck, we being on the berth or lower deck. He answered correctly, as I found upon looking at the watch, allowing eight or nine seconds for time occupied in getting on deck. I then asked him many questions with regard to objects at a distance, which he answered and, as far as I could ascertain, correctly.

For example, one evening, while at anchor in the port of Genoa, the captain was on shore. I asked Bishop, in the presence of several officers, where the captain then was. He replied, "At the opera with Mr. Lester, the consul." "What does he say?" I inquired. Bishop appeared to listen, and in a moment replied, "The captain tells Mr. Lester that he was much pleased with the port of Xavia; that the authorities treated him with much consideration."

Upon this, one of the officers laughed, and said that when the captain returned he would ask him. He did so; saying, "Captain, we have been listening to your conversation on shore." "Very well," remarked the captain. "What did I say?" expecting some jest. The officer then repeated what the captain had said of Xavia and its authorities. "Ah," said the captain, "who was at the opera? I did not see any of the officers there." The lieutenant then explained the matter. The captain confirmed its truth, and seemed very much surprised, as there had been no other communication with the shore during the evening. I may remark that we had touched at several ports between Xavia and Genoa.

On another occasion, an officer being on shore, I directed Bishop to examine his pockets; he made several motions with his hands, as if actually drawing something from the officer's pockets, saying, "Here is a handkerchief, and here a box — what a curious thing! — full of little white sticks with blue ends. What are they, Mr. Brooke?" I replied, "Perhaps they are matches." "So they are!" he exclaimed. My companions, expecting the officer mentioned, went on deck, and meeting him at the gangway, asked, "What have you in your pockets?" "Nothing," he replied. "But have you not a box of matches?" "O, yes!" said he. "How did you know it? I bought them just before I came on board." The matches were peculiar, made of white wax with blue ends.

The surgeons of the Princeton ridiculed these experiments, upon which I requested one of them (Farquharson), to test for himself, which he consented to do. With some care he placed Bishop and myself in one corner of the apartment, and then took a position some ten feet distant, concealing between his hands a watch, the long second-hand of which traversed the dial. He first asked for a description of the watch. To which Bishop replied, "'T is a funny watch, the second-hand jumps."

The doctor then asked him to tell the minute and second, which he did; directly afterwards exclaiming, "The second-hand has stopped!" which was the case, Dr. F. having stopped it. "Well," said the doctor, "to what second does it point, and to what hour; and what minute is it now?" Bishop answered correctly, adding, "'T is going again." He then told twice in succession the minute and second.

The doctor was convinced, saying that it was contrary to reason, but he must believe. I then proposed that the doctor should mark time; and directed Bishop to look in his mother's house in Lancaster, Pa. (where he had never been), for a clock; he said there was one there, and told the time by it; one of the officers calculated the difference in time for the longitudes of Lancaster and Genoa, and the clock was found to agree within five minutes of the watch time.

Several persons being still unconvinced, I proposed that the captain should select a letter from the files in his cabin and put it on the cabin table; and that Bishop should read it without leaving an apartment on the deck below the cabin, and some distance forward of it. Upon this the captain sent for me, and telling me that all the discipline in the service would be destroyed, ordered me to discontinue the practice. As Bishop retained his power of clairvoyance, I often amused myself in sending him to the United States, and, although I cannot assert that he always told the truth, I believe that in many instances he did so, as I have surprised persons when relating to them for confirmation such experiments in clairvoyance as concerned actions unknown, as they supposed, to any one but themselves.

As it was in my power to control Bishop in his wanderings, I usually limited his powers of observation, and meddled only so far in the affairs of my neighbors as might be honorable.

The power which I acquired by putting him to sleep remained after he woke, and was increased by its exercise. If not exerted for several days it decreased, sometimes rendering it necessary to repeat the passes and again put him to sleep. While awake and under my influence, I made many experiments, such as arresting his arm when raising food to his mouth, or fixing him motionless in the attitude of drinking. On one occasion I willed that he should continue pouring tea into a cup already full, which he did, notwithstanding the exclamations of those who were scalded in the operation. These influences were exerted without a word or change of position on my part. He remembered or forgot what he saw when clairvoyant, as I willed, of which I satisfied myself by experiment.

All his senses were under control, so completely, indeed, that had I willed him to stop breathing I believe that he would. You may wish to know something more with regard to my experience; if so, I shall be happy to inform you. I am, sir, respectfully,

Your obedient servant,

J. M. Brooke.

Dr. Wayland,

Providence, R. I.

Note to page 115.

When treating on the subject of consciousness, I have referred to the fact of double consciousness, and alluded to two or three cases which have been published. Within a few days, a case has been brought to my notice by my former pupil, S. P. Bates, Esq., of Meadville, Penn., which has seemed to me more remarkable than any that I have met with elsewhere. Mr. Bates, at my request, procured me a narrative, written by the patient herself. I give it in her own words, omitting only such passages as add nothing to the intrinsic value of the relation. The extracts are from a letter addressed to her nephew, Rev. John V. Reynolds:

My dear Nephew: I will now endeavor to give you a brief account of myself. When at the age of eighteen or twenty, I was occasionally afflicted with fits. In the spring of 1811, I had a very severe one. My frame was greatly convulsed, and I was extremely ill for several days. My sight and hearing were totally lost, and, during twelve weeks from the time of the fit mentioned, I continued in a very feeble state. But, at the end of five weeks, the senses of sight and hearing were again restored. But a more remarkable visitation of Providence awaited me. A little before the expiration of the twelve weeks, one morning, when I awoke, I had lost all recollection of everything. My understanding with an imperfect knowledge of speech remained; but my father, mother, brothers and sisters, and the neighbors, were altogether strangers to me. I had no disposition to converse either with my friends or with strangers. I had forgotten the use of written language, and did not know a single letter of the alphabet, nor how to discharge the duties of my domestic employment, more than a new-born babe. I presently, however, began to learn various kinds of knowledge.

I continued five weeks in this way, when I suddenly passed from this second state (as, for distinction, it may be called), into my first state. All consciousness of the five weeks just elapsed was totally gone, and my original consciousness was fully restored. My kindred and friends were at once recognized. Every kind of knowledge which I had ever acquired was as much at my command as at any former period of my life; but of the time, and of all events, which had transpired during my second state, I had not the most distant idea. For three weeks I continued in my first state. But in my sleep the transition was renewed, and I awoke in my second state. As before, so now, all knowledge acquired in my first state was forgotten, and of the circumstances of the three weeks' lucid interval, I had no conception. Of the small fund of knowledge I had gained in my former second state I was able to avail myself, and I continued from day to day to add to this little treasure.

From the spring of 1811, till within eight or ten years ago, I continued frequently changing from my first to second, and from my second to first state. More than three quarters of the time I was in the second state. There never was any periodical regularity as to the transitions. Sometimes I continued several months, and sometimes a few weeks, a few days, or only a few hours, in my second state; but in the lapse of five years I, in no one instance, continued more than twenty days in my first state.

Whatever knowledge I acquired at any time in my second state became familiar to me when in that state, and I made such proficiency, that I soon became as well acquainted with things, and was in general as intelligent in my second as in my first state. I went through the usual process of learning to write, and took as much satisfaction in the use of books as in my first state. Your father undertook to reteach me chirography. He gave me my name, which he had written, to copy. I took my pen, though in a very awkward manner, and actually began from the right to the left in the Hebrew mode. It was not long before I obtained tolerable skill in penmanship, and often amused myself in writing poetry. I acquired all kinds of knowledge in my second state, with much greater facility than a person who had never been instructed.

In my second state I was introduced to many persons whom I always recognized in that state (and no one enjoyed the society of friends better than I did), but if ever so well known to me, in my first state, I had no knowledge of them in the second, until an acquaintance had been again formed. In like manner all acquaintances formed in the second state, must be formed in the first in order to be known in that.

These transitions always took place in my sleep. In passing from my second to my first state, nothing was particularly noticeable in my sleep But in passing from my first to second state, my sleep was so profound that no one could awaken me, and it not unfrequently continued eighteen or twenty hours. [I] had generally some presentiment of the change for several days before the event.

My sufferings, in the near prospect of the transition from either the one or the other state, were extreme, particularly from the first to the second state When about to undergo the change I was harassed with fear lest I should never revert so as to know again in this world those who were dear to me My feelings in this respect were not unlike those of one who was about to be separated by death, though, in the second state, I did not anticipate the change with such distressing apprehensions as in the first. I was naturally cheerful, but more so in this than in my natural state. I believe I felt perfectly free from trouble when in my second state, and, for some time after I had been in that state, my feelings were such that, had all my friends been lying dead around me, I do not think it would have given me one moment's pain of mind. At that time my feelings were never moved with the manifestation of joy or sorrow. I had no idea of the past or the future. Nothing but the present occupied my mind. In the first stage of the disease, I had no idea of employing my time in anything that was useful. I did nothing but ramble about, and never tired walking about the fields. My mother, one day, thought she would try to rouse me a little. She told me that Paul says those who would not work, must not eat. I told her it made no matter of difference to me what Paul said, I was not going to work for Paul or any other person. I did not know who Paul was then. I had no knowledge of the Bible at that time.

As an evidence of my ignorance of any kind of danger in that early period, before I had attained any information of right or wrong, danger or safety, as I was, one afternoon, walking a short distance from the house, I discovered, as I thought, a beautiful creature. Insensible of danger, I ran to it, and, in attempting to take hold of it, it eluded my grasp by running under a pile of logs. It was a rattlesnake. I had my hand upon the rattle ; but fortunately my foot slipped and I fell back. I heard it rattle, and was still very unwilling to go home without it. I put my arm a considerable distance under the log where the snake had crept.

It may be remarked that whenever I changed into my natural state, I always felt very much debilitated. When in my second state I had no inclination for either food or sleep. My strength at such times was entirely artificial. I generally had a flush in one cheek, and continual thirst, which denoted inward fever.

When I was last down at home I was reading some letters which I had received from dear friends with whom I had corresponded previous to these changes, and who had been the companions of my younger days ; but their images are now entirely erased from my memory. It would be a source of gratification to me if I were in possession of my former recollection.

* * * * * *

In the early period of my disease I used to talk in my sleep, and tell my plans. Sometimes my friends would overhear me, which would cause them to watch my movements, and by that means I have been saved many unpleasant trips in my sleep. MARY REYNOLDS.

NOTE 1. Miss Reynolds could pronounce a word after any one, but could at first make no use of it herself.

NOTE 2. The hand-writing of Miss Reynolds in her second state was as different from her hand-writing in the first as that of two individuals

NOTE 3. At about forty years of age these changes ceased, and she lived on to the end of life in her second state. She would, of course, have no remembrance of her life previous to these changes. During the last part of her life Miss Reynolds taught school, and proved a very successful teacher.

In addition to the above Mr. Bates has obligingly procured for me the following memoranda from Rev. Mr. Reynolds:

Miss Reynolds was about forty years of age when these transitions ceased. Until the time of her death, at the age of sixty-nine, she continued in what she terms her second state. Hence, all the early part of her life was a complete blank. Her entire disregard of danger gradually disappeared, until there was, in this respect, nothing remarkable. Her two states were never in any measure blended.

One circumstance alluded to by Miss R. is thus stated more particularly by her nephew. "It was her habit, immediately after going to sleep, — and she usually dropped asleep very soon after retiring, — to begin to recount aloud the duties and incidents of the preceding day. She would go through all that she had done during the day, in the exact order in which it had occurred. She would frequently stop and comment upon things that had occurred, and would laugh heartily when she came to anything that pleased her.

"After going through with the duties and incidents of the preceding day, she would then lay her plans for the day to come. When the day came, she would begin and perform everything as she had planned. It seems that she was not aware of having formed any previous plan of action, as she frequently used to wonder how her friends could divine what she was going to do during the day, as she found that they evidently could do. This habit was of much service to her friends, as it enabled them to foresee and prevent her from doing many acts of mischief. This habit continued for more than a year."

Miss Reynolds, as I have mentioned, continued for nearly thirty years of her life in the second state. "She, however, ceased to manifest any of those symptoms bordering on insanity which she exhibited during its first periods. She taught school for several years, united with the church, was a consistent Christian, and performed all the duties of life in a way which exhibited nothing else than a perfectly rational state. No person would have discovered anything unusual in her manners and conversation. There was, perhaps, always rather an excessive measure of nervous excitability, that is, an excess above the average."

Elements of Anatomy, Physiology, and Hygiene. By Prof J. R. Loomis, President of Louisburgh University. Price $1 00.

This is a new work, beautifully illustrated with colored plates, and many original drawings.

From Rev. M. B. Anderson, D.D., President of Rochester University.

Rochester, June 30th, 1856.

"I have examined with some care the Physiology of President Loomis. It seems to me clear, concise, well arranged, and in all respects admirably adapted for the purposes of a text-book in schools and colleges. It has been used by the classes in this University with entire satisfaction."

Racine High School, March 1, 1858.

"We have used Loomis's Physiology in our school, and cheerfully recommend it as a work of real merit. Its arrangement is superior, and the author has anticipated the wants of the school-room. He has done much to draw the attention of teachers to the importance of the study, and the general adoption of his treatise, as a text-book in our schools, would be an advance in the work of Education.

"Jno. G. McMynn, Prin"

Prof. J. T. Champlin, of Waterville College, Maine, writes: —

"I am happy to commend to the public the work of Prof. Loomis on Physiology. Though not professionally engaged in physical studies, I have yet read the work attentively, and am satisfied that it is one of the very best treatises which has been produced on the subject. The known ability and experience of Prof. Loomis in this and kindred departments, are a sufficient guaranty for the excellence of the work."

From F. Douleavy Long, Principal of the Spring-Garden Academy, Philadelphia:

"I have examined 'Elements of Physiology' by Justin R. Loomis. Also Stoddard's 'Arithmetical Series.' I am much pleased with their appearance and adaptation to the wants of our Common and Academical schools.

"The work on Physiology is a work much needed upon a study which is by far too much neglected in all our schools. In forming new classes I shall introduce the work into my Academy."

From A. J. Prosser, Cambria Co., Penn.:

"I have carefully examined Loomis' Physiology, and consider it the best work which has yet been published for the use of schools. I shall commend it at the next meeting of the teachers of our district."

The Elements of Geology; adapted to Schools and Colleges. With numerous Illustrations. By J. R. Loomis, President of Lewisburg University, Pa. Cloth. 12mo. Price 75 cents.

It is surpassed by no work before the American public."—*M. B. Anderson, LL.D., President Rochester University.*

"This is just such a work as is needed for our schools. We see no reason why it should not take its place as a text-book in all the schools in the land."—*N. Y. Observer.*

"It gives a clear and scientific, yet simple analysis of the main features of the science."—*Congregationalist, Boston.*

A New Method of Learning the French Language. By JEAN GUSTAVE KEETELS, Professor of French and German in the Brooklyn Polytechnic Institute. 12mo. Price $1 50.

This is a later work than the Collegiate Course in French by the same author. It contains a clear and methodical exposé of the principles of the language, on a plan entirely new. The arrangement is admirable. The lessons are of a suitable length, and within the comprehension of all classes of students. The exercises are various, and well adapted to the purpose for which they are intended, of reading, writing and speaking the language. The Grammar part is complete, and accompanied by questions and exercises on every subject. The book possesses many attractions for the teacher and student, and is destined to become a popular school book. It has already been introduced into many of the principal schools in the country.

The following testimonials have been received during the past week

From Daniel Lynch, S. J., Director of Studies in Gonzaga College, Washington:—

"I have examined 'Keetels' New Method of learning the French Language,' and find it admirably adapted for conveying a thorough knowledge of the French language. It is an easy and sure method of both writing and speaking French with accuracy and elegance."

From M. M. Haliman, S. J., Prof. of French at St. Joseph's College, Philadelphia, Pa.:

"I have carefully examined 'Keetels' French Grammar,' and found it admirably well adapted to convey a knowledge of the French language. It will, I doubt not, supersede many of the grammars now used in our schools."

From Oswald Seidensticker, Principal of the Commercial and Classical Institute, Philadelphia:

"The 'New Method of Learning the French Language, by Professor Keetels,' appears to be exceedingly well adapted as an introduction into the study of French. It is emphatically a practical book, and bears the mark that it has resulted from the author's own experience in teaching. I shall take pleasure in soon giving it the test of a trial in my own Institute."

From S. A. Farrand, Trenton, N. J.:

"I have examined several works designed for pupils studying the French language, and among them 'Keetels' New Method of the French.' The last work I consider superior to any other which I have examined, and shall use it in my classes as the best text-book upon the subject."

From F. L. Barbier, Teacher of the French Language:

"I fully concur in the above testimony."

From Joseph McKie, Teacher of French, Newark, N. J.:

"I take great pleasure in adding my testimony to the value of 'Keetels' New Method of learning the French Language' as a school book. It will make its way, successfully among the multitude of similar books, as well by its typographic, as its scholastic merits I shall introduce it next term into my school."

From John Early, President Georgetown College:

"I have examined 'Keetels' New Method of learning the French Language,' and take pleasure in recommending it as a work admirably adapted for the purpose."

A Key to the New Method in French. By J. G. KEETELS 1 vol 12mo. Price 50 cents.

NORMAL MATHEMATICAL SERIES

COMPRISING

Stoddard's Juvenile Mental Arithmetic, by JOHN F. STODDARD, A.M., for Primary Schools. 72 pp. Price 20 cents.

Stoddard's American Intellectual Arithmetic, by the same. An extended work designed for Common Schools, Seminaries, and Academies. 164 pp. Price 30 cents.

Stoddard's Practical Arithmetic, by the same, embracing every variety of exercises appropriate to written Arithmetic. 299 pp. Price 60 cts.

Key to Stoddard's Intellectual and Practical Arithmetics, in one book. Price 60 cents.

Schuyler's Higher Arithmetic. A new and original work for Colleges, Seminaries, Academies, and High Schools, by A. SCHUYLER of Ohio 438 pages. 12mo. sheep. Price 90 cents.

Stoddard and Henkle's Elementary Algebra, for the use of Common Schools and Academies, by JOHN F. STODDARD, A.M., and Professor W. D. HENKLE, of Ohio South-Western Normal School. Price 90 cents.

Key to Stoddard and Henkle's Elementary Algebra. Price 90 cents.

Stoddard and Henkle's University Algebra, for High Schools, Academies, and Colleges, by JOHN F. STODDARD, A.M., and Professor W. D. HENKLE. 528 pp. Price $1.50.

Key to Stoddard and Henkle's University Algebra. $1 50.

Stoddard's Arithmetics are distinguished from all others by the originality of the questions, the brevity and perspicuity of the solutions and demonstrations, and the systematic classification of principles and arrangement of problems. Their use in the school-room has proved their admirable fitness for the quickening, strengthening, and harmonious growth of all the powers of thought, from the initiatory steps to the more advanced processes in mathematical reasoning.

The Elementary Algebra bears the relation to this science that Stoddard's Intellectual Arithmetic does to that of numbers. It is systematic in its arrangement, concise and clear in its solutions and demonstrations, and contains upward of *six hundred and thirty* examples and more than *three hundred practical questions*, mostly original, in which principles are so combined as to induce originality, continuity, and closeness of thought; it will, therefore, be found a desirable addition to the text-books on this subject now before the public.

The University Algebra contains *nineteen hundred* examples and more than *seven hundred and thirty* practical questions, and is the most extensive treatise on this subject ever published in America. It also contains much valuable information to be found in no other American work, and is remarkable for the comprehensiveness, conciseness, and completeness of its Rules, Solutions, and Demonstrations.

www.ingramcontent.com/pod-product-compliance
Lightning Source LLC
LaVergne TN
LVHW021146110826
845150LV00005B/1134

* 9 7 8 1 4 2 5 5 4 7 6 1 5 *